Ladies of the Veldt

Ladies of the Veldt
Two Accounts of Remarkable Women in South
Africa During the Boer War

South African Memories
Sarah Wilson

A Lady Trader in the Transvaal
Mrs. Heckford

LEONAUR

Ladies of the Veldt
Two Accounts of Remarkable Women in South Africa During the Boer War
South African Memories
by Sarah Wilson
and
A Lady Trader in the Transvaal
by Mrs. Heckford

First published under the titles
South African Memories
and
A Lady Trader in the Transvaal

FIRST EDITION

Leonaur is an imprint
of Oakpast Ltd

ISBN: 978-1-78282-192-2 (hardcover)
ISBN: 978-1-78282-193-9 (softcover)

http://www.leonaur.com

Contents

South African Memories

Sarah F. Wilson

Contents

Dedication
To the Memory of My
Beloved Sister,
Georgiana, Countess Howe,
To Whose Efforts and Unceasing
Labours in Connection With the Yeomanry Hospitals,
During the War in South Africa, the Early
Breakdown of Her Health, and
Subsequent Death, were
Undoubtedly Due,
This Book,
Containing Recollections of That
Great and Mysterious Land, the Grave
Of So Many Brave Englishmen, is Affectionately
Dedicated

Preface

Everything of interest that has happened to me in life chances to have been in connection with South Africa. In that land, where some of my happiest days have been spent, I have also experienced long periods of intense excitement and anxiety; there I have made acquaintance with all the charm of the *veldt*, in the vast country north of the great Zambesi River, hearing the roar of the lions at night, and following their "*spoor*" by day; and last, but not least, I have there made some very good friends. Only a few years ago, when peacefully spending a few weeks at Assouan in Egypt, I was nearly drowned by the capsizing of a boat in the Nile; again the spirit of the vast continent (on this occasion far away to the north) seemed to watch over me. For all these reasons I venture to claim the indulgence of the public and the kindness of my friends, for these recollections of days in South Africa, in which shade and sunshine have been strangely mingled, and which to me have never been dull. To sum up, I have always found that life is what you make it, and have often proved the truth of the saying, "*Adventures to the adventurous.*"

I am indebted to Colonel Vyvyan for statistics respecting the Mafeking Relief Fund; and to Miss A. Fielding, secretary to the late Countess Howe, for a *résumé* of the work of the Yeomanry Hospital during the Boer War.

S.I.W.

The Stud House,
Hampton Court.
September, 1909.

CHAPTER 1

First Voyage to South Africa—Cape Town

Oh that mine adversary had written a book!—Job xxxi. 35.

The above words, written by one of the greatest philosophers of olden time, have often impressed me, and I have frequently quoted them when asked why I did not write an account of the interesting travels and adventures I have had in my life. It has therefore required a great deal of courage to take up my pen and record a few recollections of South Africa. I felt that, were they ever to be written at all, it must be before the rapidly passing years diminish the interest in that land, which in the past has been the object of such engrossing attention; and that at the present time, when the impending Federation of South Africa has at length crowned the hopes of those patriots who have laboured patiently and hopefully to bring about this great result, it might be appropriate to recall those days when Englishmen, who had made South Africa their home, had much to contend with, even before the fierce struggle to keep "the flag flying" in the years of 1899-1902.

During that period, which commenced after the disaster at Majuba Hill, "equal rights" were a golden dream which only the most optimistic ever hoped to see realised. From then onwards, as old colonists have so often told me, the Boers brought up the younger generation in the belief that the "*roinek*"[1] was a coward, and in consequence their arrogance in the country districts became well-nigh intolerable, while at the Cape the Bond party grew so strong it bid fair to elbow out the English altogether. Now, while the country is still young, the fair pros-

---

1. Red neck or Englishman.

pect opens out of Briton and Boer living in amity and peace together, and mutually supplying, in the government of their vast inheritance, such elements as are wanting in the character of each.

My first visit to South Africa was a short one, and took place at the end of 1895. During the foregoing summer everyone's attention had been directed to the Transvaal, and more especially towards the Rand, by reason of the unprecedented and, as it turned out, totally unwarranted rise in the gold-mining shares of that district; in this boom, people both at home and in Johannesburg madly gambled, and large fortunes were quickly made by those who had foresight enough not to hold on too long. For already the political horizon was darkening, and the wrongs of the "*uitlanders*," real and apparent as they were, became a parrot-cry, which waxed and waned, but never died away, till the ultimatum of President Kruger, in October, 1899, brought matters to a climax.

We sailed from Southampton in December, 1895, in the *Tantallon Castle*, then one of the most modern and up-to-date of the Castle liners. The ship was crowded to its utmost capacity, and among the passengers, as I afterwards learned, were many deeply concerned in the plotting which was known to be going on at Johannesburg, either to extort concessions from President Kruger, or, failing this, to remove him altogether. I knew very little about all this then, but before I had been many days on board it was not difficult to discover that much mystery filled the air, and I was greatly excited at arriving in South Africa in such stirring times. There is no such place for getting to know people well as on a sea-voyage of eighteen days. Somehow the sea inspires confidence, and one knows that information imparted cannot, anyway, be posted off by the same day's mail. So those who were helping to pull the strings of this ill-fated rebellion talked pretty freely of their hopes and fears during the long, dark tropical evenings.

I became familiar with their grievances—their unfair taxation; no education for their children except in Dutch; no representation in Parliament—and this in a population in which, at that time, the English and Afrikanders at Johannesburg and in the surrounding districts outnumbered the Dutch in the proportion of about 6 to 1. They laid stress on the fact that neither the Boers nor their children were, or desired to become, miners, and, further, that for the enormous sums spent on developing and working the mines no proper security existed. I must admit it was the fiery-headed followers who talked the loudest—those who had nothing to lose and much to gain. The financiers, while directing and encouraging their zeal, seemed almost with the same hand to wish to put on the brake and damp their martial ardour. In any case, all were so eloquent that by the time our voyage was ended I felt as great a rebel against "Oom Paul" and his government as any one of them.

Before leaving the *Tantallon Castle*, however, I must pass in review some of those whose home it had been with ourselves for the best part of three weeks. First I remember the late Mr. Alfred Beit, interesting as the man who had made the most colossal fortune of all the South African magnates, and who was then already said to be the most generous of philanthropists and the kindest of friends; this reputation he fully sustained in the subsequent years of his life and in the generous disposition of his vast wealth. I have often been told that Mr. Cecil Rhodes owed the inspiration of some of his colossal ideas to his friend Mr. Beit, and when it came to financing the same, the latter was always ready to assist in carrying out projects to extend and consolidate the Empire. In these latter years, and since his comparatively early death, I have heard those who still bear the brunt of the battle lament his loss, and remark, when a railway was to be built or a new part of the country opened up, how much more expeditiously it would be done were Mr. Beit still alive.

Other names that occur to me are Mr. Abe Bailey, well known in racing circles today, and then reputed a millionaire, the foundation of whose fortune consisted in a ten-pound note borrowed from a friend. Mr. Wools Sampson,[2] who subsequently so greatly distinguished himself at Ladysmith, where he was dangerously wounded, had an individuality all his own; he had seen every side of life as a soldier of fortune, attached to different regiments, during all the fighting in South Africa of the preceding years. He was then a mining expert, associated with Mr. Bailey in Lydenburg, but his heart evidently lay in fighting and in pursuing the different kinds of wild animals that make their home on the African *veldt*. Dr. Rutherford Harris, then the Secretary of the Chartered Company; Mr. Henry Milner, an old friend; Mr. Geoffrey Glyn and Mr. F. Guest, are others whom I specially remember; besides many more, some of whom have joined the vast majority, and others whom I have altogether lost sight of, but who helped to make the voyage a very pleasant one.

We landed at Cape Town shortly before Christmas Day. As I have since learnt by the experience of many voyages, it is nearly always at

2. Later Sir A. Wools Sampsom.

dawn that a liner is brought alongside the quay at the conclusion of a long voyage; in consequence, sleep is almost out of the question the last night at sea, owing to the noisy manipulations of the mail-bags and luggage. However, one is always so glad to get on shore that it is of very little import, and on this occasion we were all anxious to glean the latest news after being cut off from the world for so many days. The papers contained gloomy accounts of the markets. "King Slump" still held his sway, and things abroad looked very unsettled; so most of our friends appeared, when we met later, with very long faces.

After breakfast, leaving our luggage to the tender mercies of some officious agent, who professed to see it "through the Customs," we took a hansom and drove to the Grand Hotel, *en route* to the hotel, in the suburb of Newlands, where we had taken rooms. My first impressions of Cape Town certainly were not prepossessing, and well I remember them, even after all these years. The dust was blowing in clouds, stirred up by the "south-easter" one hears so much about—an icy blast which appears to come straight from the South Pole, and which often makes its appearance in the height of summer, which season it then was. The hansom, of the oldest-fashioned type, shook and jolted beyond belief, and threatened every moment to fall to pieces. The streets from the docks to the town were unfinished, untidy, and vilely paved, and I remember comparing them very unfavourably with Melbourne or Sydney. However, I soon modified my somewhat hasty judgment.

We had seen the town's worst aspects, and later I noticed some attractive-looking shops; the imposing Houses of Parliament, in their enclosed grounds, standing out sharply defined against the hazy background of Table Mountain; and the Standard Bank and Railway-station, which would hold their own in any city. At the same time, as a place of residence in the summer months, I can well understand Cape Town being well-nigh deserted. Those who can boast of even the most moderate means have their residences in the attractive suburbs of Rondebosch, Newlands, or Wynberg, and innumerable are the pretty little villas and gardens one sees in these vicinities. There the country is beautifully wooded, thick arching avenues of oak extending for miles, interspersed with tracts of Scotch firs and pines, the latter exhaling a delicious perfume under the sun's powerful rays. Everywhere green foliage and abundant vegetation, which, combined with the setting of the bluest sky that can be imagined, make the drives round Cape Town some of the most beautiful in the world.

At Newlands, the governor's summer residence, a pretty but unpretentious abode, Sir Hercules and Lady Robinson then dispensed generous hospitality, only regretting their house was too small to accommodate visitors, besides their married daughters. We stayed at the Vineyard Hotel in the immediate neighbourhood—a funny old-fashioned hostelry, standing in its own grounds, and not in the least like an hotel as we understand the word. There whole families seemed to reside for months, and very comfortable it was, if somewhat primitive, appearing to keep itself far apart from the rush of modern improvements, and allowing the world to go by it unheeded. Only half a mile away, at Rondebosch, was situated then, as now, on the lower slopes of Table Mountain, the princely domain of the late Mr. Cecil Rhodes.

At the moment of which I write the house itself was only approaching completion, and I must now record a few particulars of our introduction to this great Englishman and his world-famed home. We drove to Groot Schuurr, or "Great Barn," one afternoon with Mr. Beit. The house is approached by a long avenue of enormously high Scotch firs, which almost meet aloft, and remind one of the nave of some mighty cathedral, such is the subdued effect produced by the sunlight even on the brightest summer day. A slight rise in the road, a serpentine sweep, and the house itself comes into view, white, low, and rambling, with many gables and a thatched roof. The right wing was then hidden by scaffolding, and workmen were also busy putting in a new front-door, of which more *anon*; for a tall, burly gentleman in a homely costume of flannels and a slouch hat emerged from the unfinished room, where he would seem to have been directing the workmen, and we were introduced to Cecil John Rhodes, the Prime Minister of Cape Colony.

I looked at the man, of whom I had heard so much, with a great deal of curiosity. Shy and diffident with strangers, his manner even somewhat abrupt, one could not fail to be impressed with the expression of power, resolution, and kindness, on the rugged countenance, and with the keen, piercing glance of the blue eyes, which seemed to read one through in an instant. He greeted us, as he did every newcomer, most warmly, and under his guidance we passed into the completed portion of the house, the rooms of which were not only most comfortable, but also perfect in every detail as regards the model he wished to copy—*viz.*, a Dutch house of 200 years ago, even down to the massive door aforementioned, which he had just purchased for £200 from a colonial family mansion, and which seemed to afford him immense pleasure.

As a first fleeting memory of the interior of Groot Schuurr, I call to mind Dutch armoires, all incontestably old and of lovely designs, Dutch chests, inlaid high-backed chairs, costly Oriental rugs, and everywhere teak panelling—the whole producing a vision of perfect taste and old-world repose. It was then Mr. Rhodes's intention to have no electric light, or even lamps, and burn nothing but tallow candles, so as to keep up the illusion of antiquity; but whether he would have adhered to this determination it is impossible to say, as the house we saw was burnt to the ground later on, and is now rebuilt on exactly the same lines, but with electric light, every modern comfort, and lovely old red tiles to replace the quaint thatched roof.

Passing through the rooms, we came to the wide verandah, or *stoep*, on the other or eastern side. This ran the whole length of the edifice, and was used as a delightful lounge, being provided with luxurious settees and armchairs. From here Mr. Rhodes pointed out the view he loved so well, and which comes vividly to my mind today. In front three terraces rise immediately beyond the gravel courtyard, which is enclosed on three sides by the *stoep*. These, bright with flowers, lead to a great grass plateau, on which some more splendid specimens of Scotch firs rear their lofty heads; while behind, covered with trees and vegetation, its brilliant green veiled by misty heat, Table Mountain forms a glorious background, in striking contrast to the cobalt of the heavens. To the right of the terraces is a glade, entirely covered with vivid blue hydrangeas in full bloom, giving the appearance of a tract of azure ground. Lower down the hillside, in little valleys, amidst oak and other English forest trees, a carpet is formed of cannas of many hues, interspersed with masses of gleaming white arum lilies, which grow here wild in very great profusion.

Our time was too short on this occasion to see any portion of Mr. Rhodes's estate or the animals—antelope of many kinds, wildebeests, elands, and zebras—which roamed through his woods. We lunched with him two days later on Christmas Eve, and then the weather was so hot that we only lazily enjoyed the shade and breezes on the *stoep*. Well do I remember on that occasion how preoccupied was our host, and how incessantly the talk turned to Johannesburg and the raging discontent there. In truth, Mr. Rhodes's position was then a very difficult one: he was Prime Minister of Cape Colony, and therefore officially neutral; but in his heart he remained the keen champion of the oppressed *uitlanders*, having nominated his brother, Frank Rhodes, to be one of the leaders of the Reform Committee at Johannesburg. No wonder he was graver than was his wont, with many complications overshadowing him, as one afterwards so fully realised. His kindness as a host, however, suffered no diminution, and I remember how warmly he pressed us to stay with him when we returned from the north, though he did add, "My plans are a little unsettled."

This suggested visit, however, was never paid; Mr. Rhodes a few weeks afterwards was starting for England, to, as he termed it, "*face the music.*" I shall have occasion to describe him in his home, and the life at Groot Schuurr, more fully later on, when I passed many happy and never-to-be-forgotten weeks beneath his hospitable roof. As years went on, his kindness to both friends and political foes grew almost proverbial, but even in 1895 Groot Schuurr, barely finished, was already known to be one of the pleasantest places near Cape Town—a meeting-place for all the men of the colony either on their way to and from England, or on the occasion of their flying visits to the capital.

CHAPTER 2

Kimberley and the Jameson Raid

Ex Africa semper aliquid novi.

In the last week of the old year we started on our journey to Kimberley, then a matter of thirty-six hours. The whole of one day we dawdled over the Great Karroo in pelting rain and mist, which reminded one of Scotland. This sandy desert was at that season covered with brown scrub, for it was yet too early for the rains to have made it green, and the only signs of life were a few ostriches, wild white goats, and, very rarely, a waggon piled with wood, drawn along the sandy road by ten or twelve donkeys. As to vegetation, there were huge clumps of mimosa-bushes, just shedding their yellow blossoms, through which the branches showed up with their long white thorns, giving them a weird and withered appearance. It must indeed have required great courage on behalf of the old *Voor-trekker* Boers, when they and their families left Cape Colony, at the time of the Great Trek, in long lines of white-tented waggons, to have penetrated through that dreary-waste in search of the promised land, of green *veldt* and running streams, which they had heard of, as lying away to the north, and eventually found in the Transvaal. I have been told that President Kruger was on this historical trek, a *voor-looper*, or little boy who guides the leading oxen.

Round Kimberley the country presented a very different appearance, and here we saw the real *veldt* covered with short grass, just beginning to get burnt up by the summer's heat. Our host, Mr. J. B. Currey, a name well known in Diamond-Field circles, met us at the station. This is a good old South African custom, and always seems to me to be the acme of welcoming hospitality, and the climax to the kindness of inviting people to stay, merely on the recommendation of friends—quite a common occurrence in the colonies, and one which, I think, is never sufficiently appreciated, the entertainers themselves thinking it so natural a proceeding.

Kimberley itself and the diamond industry have both been so often and so well described that I shall beware of saying much of either, and I will only note a few things I remarked about this town, once humming with speculation, business, and movement, but now the essence of a sleepy respectability and visible prosperity. For the uninitiated it is better to state that the cause of this change was the gradual amalgamation of the diamond-mines and conflicting interests, which was absolutely necessary to limit the output of diamonds. As a result the stranger soon perceives that the whole community revolves on one axis, and is centred, so to speak, in one authority. "De Beers" is the moving spirit, the generous employer, and the universal benefactor. At that time there were 7,000 men employed in the mines, white and black, the skilled mechanics receiving as much as £6 a week.

Evidence of the generosity of this company was seen in the model village built for the white workmen; in the orchard containing 7,000 fruit-trees, then one of Mr. Rhodes's favourite hobbies; and in the stud-farm for improving the breed of horses in South Africa. If I asked the profession of any of the smart young men who frequented the house where we were staying, for games of croquet, it amused me always to receive the same answer, "He is something in De Beers." The town itself boasts of many commodious public buildings, a great number of churches of all denominations, an excellent and well-known club; but whatever the edifice, the roofing is always corrugated iron, imported, I was told, from Wolverhampton.

This roofing, indeed, prevails over the whole of new South Africa; and although it appears a very unsuitable protection from the burning rays of the African sun, no doubt its comparative cheapness and the quickness of its erection are the reasons why this style was introduced, and has been adhered to. By dint of superhuman efforts, in spite of locust-plagues, drought, and heavy thunderstorms, the inhabitants have contrived to surround their little one-storied villas with gardens bright with flowers, many creepers of vivid hues covering all the trellis-work of the verandahs.

The interest of Kimberley, however, soon paled and waned as the all-engrossing events of the *uitlander* rebellion in Johannesburg rapidly succeeded each other. One sultry evening our host brought us news of tangible trouble on the Rand: some ladies who were about to leave for that locality had received wires to defer their departure. Instantly, I recollect, my thoughts flew back to the *Tantallon Castle* and the dark words we had heard whispered, so it was not as much of a surprise to me as to the residents at Kimberley; to them it came as a perfect bombshell, so well had the secret been kept. The next day the text of the Manifesto, issued by Mr. Leonard, a lawyer, in the name of the *uitlanders*, to protest against their grievances, appeared in all the morning papers, and its eloquent language aroused the greatest enthusiasm in the town. Thus was the gauntlet thrown down with a vengeance, and an ominous chord was struck by the statement, also in the papers, that Mr. Leonard had immediately left for Cape Town, "lest he should be arrested."

It must be remembered that any barrister, English or Afrikander, holding an official position in the Transvaal, had at that time to take the oath of allegiance to the Boer Government before being free to practise his calling. The explanation of the exceedingly acute feeling at Kimberley in those anxious days lay in the fact that nearly everyone had relations or friends in the Golden City. Our hosts themselves had two sons pursuing their professions there, and, of course, in the event of trouble with England, these young men would have been commandeered to fight for the Boer Government they served. One possibility, however, I noticed, was never entertained—*viz.*, that, if fighting occurred, the English community might get the worst of it. Such a contingency was literally laughed to scorn.

> The Boers were unprepared and lazy; they took weeks to mobilize; they had given up shooting game, hence their marksmen had deteriorated; and 200 men ought to be able to take possession of Johannesburg and Kruger into the bargain.

This was what one heard on all sides, and in view of more recent events it is rather significant; but I remember then the thought flashed across my mind that these possible foes were the sons of the men who had annihilated us at Majuba and Laing's Nek, and I wondered whether another black page were going to be added to the country's history.

The next day, December 29, Kruger was reported in the papers to be listening to reason; but this hopeful news was short-lived, for on Monday, the 30th—as usual, a fiercely hot day—we received the astounding intelligence that Dr. Jameson, administrator of Mashonaland and Matabeleland, had entered the Transvaal at the head of the Char-

Right Hon. L. S. Jameson, C.B.

tered Company's Police, 600 strong, with several Maxim and Gardner guns. No upheaval of Nature could have created greater amazement, combined with a good deal of admiration and some dismay, than this sensational news. The dismay, indeed, increased as the facts were more fully examined. Nearly all the officers of the corps held Imperial commissions, and one heard perfect strangers asking each other how these officers could justify their action of entering a friendly territory, armed to the teeth; while the fact of Dr. Jameson himself being at their head heightened the intense interest. I did not know that gentleman then, but I must say he occupied in the hearts of the people at Kimberley, and, indeed, of the whole country, quite a unique position.

It was in the diamond-fields he had worked as a young doctor, usurping gradually almost the entire medical practice by his great skill as well as by his charm of manner. Then, as Mr. Rhodes's nominee, he had dramatically abandoned medicine and surgery, and had gone to the great unknown Northern Territory almost at a moment's notice. He had obtained concessions from the black tyrant, Lobengula, when all other emissaries had failed; backwards and forwards many times across the vast stretch of country between Bulawayo and Kimberley he had carried on negotiations which had finally culminated, five years previously, in his leading a column of 500 hardy pioneers to the promising country of Mashonaland, which up to that time had lain in darkness under the cruel rule of the dusky monarch.

During three strenuous years Dr. Jameson, with no military or legal education, had laboured to establish the nucleus of a civilized government in that remote country; and during the first part of that period the nearest point of civilization, from whence they could derive their supplies, was Kimberley, a thousand miles away, across a practically trackless country. Added to this difficulty, the administrator found himself confronted with the wants and rights of the different mining communities into which the pioneers had gradually split themselves up, and which were being daily augmented by the arrival of "wasters" and others, who had begun to filter in as the country was written about, and its great mining and agricultural possibilities enlarged upon. Finally, goaded thereto and justified therein by Lobengula's continued cruelties, his raids on the defenceless Mashonas, and his threats to the English, Dr. Jameson had led another expedition against the king himself in his stronghold of Bulawayo.

On that occasion sharp fighting ensued, but he at length brought peace, and the dawning of a new era to a vast native population in the country, which, with Mashonaland, was to be known as Rhodesia. In fact, up to then his luck had been almost supernatural and his achievements simply colossal. Added to all this was his capacity for attaching people to himself, and his absolutely fearless disposition; so it is easy to understand that Kimberley hardly dared breathe during the next momentous days, when the fate of "the Doctor," as he was universally called, and of his men, who were nearly all locally known, was in suspense.

During many an evening of that eventful week we used to sit out after dinner under the rays of a glorious full moon, in the most perfect climatic conditions, and hear heated discussions of the pros and cons of this occurrence, which savoured more of medieval times than of our own. The moon all the while looked down so calmly, and the Southern Cross stood out clear and bright. One wondered what they might not have told us of scenes being enacted on the mysterious *veldt*, not 300 miles away. It was not till Saturday, January 4, that we knew what had happened, and any hopes we had entertained that the freebooters had either joined forces with their friends in Johannesburg, or else had made good their escape, were dashed to the ground as the fullness of the catastrophe became known.

For hours, however, the aghast Kimberleyites refused to believe that Dr. Jameson and his entire corps had been taken prisoners, having been hopelessly outnumbered and outmanoeuvred after several hours' fighting at Krugersdorp; and, when doubt was no longer possible, loud and deep were the execrations levelled at the Johannesburgers, who, it was strenuously reiterated, had invited the raiders to come to their succour, and who, when the pinch came, never even left the town to go to their assistance. If the real history of the raid is ever written, when the march of time renders such a thing possible, it will be interesting reading; but, as matters stand now, it is better to say as little as possible of such a deplorable fiasco, wherein the only points which stood out clearly appeared to be that Englishmen were as brave, and perhaps also as foolhardy, as ever; that President Kruger, while pretending to shut his eyes, had known exactly all that was going forward; that the Boers had lost nothing of their old skill in shooting and ambushing, while the rapid rising and massing of their despised forces was as remarkable in its way as Jameson's forced march.

It was said at the time that the proclamation issued by the government at home, repudiating the rebels, was the factor which prevented the Johannesburgers from joining forces with the raiders when they arrived at Krugersdorp, as no doubt had been arranged, and that this step of the Home Government had, curiously enough, not been foreseen by the organisers of this deeply-laid plot. There is no doubt that there were two forces at work in Johannesburg, as, indeed, I had surmised during our voyage out: the one comprising the financiers, which strove to attain its ends by manifesto and public meeting, with the hint of sterner measures to follow; and the other impatient of delay, and thus impelled to seek the help of those who undoubtedly became freebooters the moment they crossed the Transvaal border. Certainly Dr. Jameson's reported words seemed to echo with reproach and disappointment—the reproach of a man who has been deceived; but whatever his feelings were at that moment of despair, when his lucky star seemed at length to have deserted him with a vengeance, I happen to know he never bore any lasting grudge against his Johannesburg friends, and that he remained on terms of perfect friendship even with the five members of the Reform Committee, with whom all the negotiations had gone forward. These included Colonel Frank Rhodes,[1] always one of his favourite companions.

As an instance of how acute was the feeling suddenly roused respecting Englishmen, I remember that Mr. Harry Lawson, who was staying in the same house as ourselves, and had decided to leave for Johannesburg as special correspondent to his father's paper, the *Daily Telegraph*, was actually obliged to travel under a foreign name; and even then, if my memory serves me right, he did not succeed in reaching the Rand. In the meantime, as the daily papers received fuller details, harrowing accounts came to hand of the exodus from Johannesburg of men, women, and children travelling twenty in a compartment meant for eight, while others, not so fortunate, had to put up with cattle-trucks. The Boers were said to have shown themselves humane and magnanimous. Mr. Chamberlain, the papers wrote, was strengthening the hands of the president, to avert civil war, which must have been dangerously near; but the most important man of the moment in South Africa was grudgingly admitted to be "Oom Paul."

His personal influence alone, it was stated, had restrained his wild bands of armed *burghers*, with which the land was simply bristling, and he was then in close confabulation with Her Majesty's High Commissioner, Sir Hercules Robinson, whom he had summoned to Pretoria to deal with such refractory Englishmen. The journals also took advantage of the occasion to bid Kruger remember this was the op-

1. Died at Groot Svhuur in 1905.

portunity to show himself forgiving, and to strengthen his corrupt government, thereby earning the gratitude of those Afrikanders, for whom, indeed, he was not expected to have any affection, but to whom he was indebted for the present flourishing financial state of his republic, which, it was called to mind, was next door to bankrupt when England declared its independence in 1884.

If such articles were translated and read out to that wily old President, as he sipped his coffee on his *stoep*, with his bland and inscrutable smile, it must have added zest to his evening pipe. I read in Mr. Seymour Fort's *Life of Dr. Jameson* that the raid cost the Chartered Company £75,000 worth of material, most of which passed into the hands of the Boer Government, while the confiscated arms at Johannesburg amounted to several thousand rifles and a great deal of ammunition. Respecting the guns taken from Jameson's force, curiously enough, we surmised during the siege of Mafeking, four years later, that some of these were being used against us. Their shells fired into the town, many of which did not explode, and of which I possess a specimen, were the old seven-pound studded M.L. type, with the Woolwich mark on them.

CHAPTER 3

The Immediate Results of the Raid

The fly sat on the axle-tree of the chariot-wheel, and said, 'What a dust do I raise!'—Æsop.

Oom Paul was in the proud position of this fly in the weeks immediately following the Raid, as well as during many years to come. When we returned to Cape Town early in January, 1896, we found everything in a turmoil. Mr. Rhodes had resigned the premiership and had left for Kimberley, where he had met with a most enthusiastic reception, and Mr. Beit had been left in possession at Groot Schuurr. The latter gentleman appeared quite crushed at the turn events had taken—not so much on account of his own business affairs, which must have been in a critical state, as in regard to the fate of Mr. Lionel Philips, his partner; this gentleman, as well as the other four members of the Reform Committee,[1] and a few lesser lights besides, had all been arrested during the past week at Johannesburg, and charged with high treason.

Even at Cape Town, Captain Bettelheim and Mr. S. Joel, who had left the Transvaal, had one forenoon been requested to accompany some mysterious gentleman, and, very much to their surprise, had found themselves lodged in Her Majesty's gaol before lunch. This occurrence came as a bombshell to the Cape Town community, it having been assumed that there was no extradition for political offences. Johannesburg was known to be disarming almost unconditionally "in consequence of a personal appeal from the governor," and another telegram informed the world that the men in so doing were broken-hearted, but were making the sacrifice in order to save Dr. Jameson's life. Some unkind friends remarked that their grief must have been

---

1. Colonel Frank Rhodes, Mr. G. Farrar, Mr. Hammond, and Mr. C. Leonard.

tempered with relief, in ridding themselves of the weapons that they had talked so much about, and yet did not use when the time for action came. However, the ways of Providence are wonderful, and this inglorious finale was probably the means of averting a terrible civil war. Sir Hercules Robinson was still at Pretoria, conferring with the president, who, it was opined, was playing with him, as nothing either regarding the fate of Dr. Jameson and his officers, or of the political prisoners, had been settled.

It was even rumoured that there was a serious hitch in the negotiations, and that Lord Salisbury had presented an ultimatum to the effect that, unless the President ratified the Convention of 1884, and ceased intriguing with Germany, war with England would ensue. This story was never confirmed, and I think the wish was father to the thought. I remember, during those eventful days, attending with Mrs. Harry Lawson a garden-party at Newlands, given by Lady Robinson, who was quite a remarkable personality, and an old friend and admirer of the ex-prime minister's. The gardens showed to their greatest advantage in the brilliant sunshine, and an excellent band played charming tunes under the trees; but everyone was so preoccupied—and no one more than the hostess—that it was rather a depressing entertainment.

At last events began to shape themselves. We learnt that the governor had left Pretoria on January 15, and that the military prisoners, including most of the troopers, were to be sent home to England immediately, for the leaders to stand their trial. The same morning I heard privately that Mr. Rhodes meant to leave by that very evening's mail-steamer for England, to face the inquiry which would certainly ensue, and, if possible, to save the charter of that company with which he had so indissolubly connected himself, and which was, so to speak, his favourite child. I remember everyone thought then that this charter would surely be confiscated, on account of the illegal proceedings of its forces.

The fact of Mr. Rhodes's departure was kept a profound secret, as he wished to avoid any demonstration. The mail-steamer was the even then antiquated *Moor* of the Union Line, and she was lying a quarter of a mile away from the docks, awaiting her mail-bags and her important passengers. Besides Mrs. Harry Lawson and ourselves, Mr. Rhodes, Mr. Beit, and Dr. Rutherford Harris, the two latter of whom were also going to England, embarked quite unnoticed on a small launch, ostensibly to make a tour of the harbour, which as a matter of fact we did, whilst waiting for the belated mail. An object of interest was the chartered P. and O. transport *Victoria*, which had only the day before arrived from Bombay, with the Lancashire Regiment, 1,000 strong, on board, having been suddenly stopped here on her way home, pessimists at once declaring the reason to be possible trouble with Germany. A very noble appearance she presented that afternoon, with her lower decks and portholes simply swarming with red-coats, who appeared to take a deep interest in our movements. At last we boarded the mail-steamer, and then I had the chance of a few words with the travellers, and of judging how past events had affected them. Mr. Beit looked ill and worried; Mr. Rhodes, on the other hand, seemed to be in robust health, and as calm as the proverbial cucumber. I had an interesting talk to him before we left the ship; he said frankly that, for the first time in his life, during six nights of the late crisis he had not been able to sleep, and that he had been worried to death.

"Now," he added, "I have thought the whole matter out, I have decided what is best to be done, so I am all right again, and I do not consider at forty-three that my career is ended."

"I am quite sure it is not, Mr. Rhodes," was my reply; "and, what is more, I have a small bet with Mr. Lawson that in a year's time you will be in office again, or, if not absolutely in office, as great a factor in South African politics as you have been up to now."

He thought a minute, and then said:

"It will take ten years; better cancel your bet."[2] was careful not to ask him any questions which might be embarrassing for him to answer, but he volunteered that the objects of his visit to England were, first, to do the best he could for his friends at Johannesburg, including his brother Frank, who were now political prisoners, practically at the mercy of the Boers, unless the Imperial Government bestirred itself on their behalf; and, secondly, to save his charter, if by any means it could be saved. This doubt seemed to haunt him.

I remember he said:

My argument is they may take away the charter or leave it, but there is one fact that no man can alter—*viz.*, that a vast and valuable territory has been opened up by that company in about half the time, and at about a quarter the cost, which the Imperial Government would have required for a like task; so that whether, in consequence of one bad blunder, and partly in order to snub me, Cecil Rhodes, the Company is to cease, or

---

2. Mr. Rhodes died in the spring of 1902.

Right Hon. Cecil John Rhodes.

whether it is allowed to go on with its work, its achievements and their results must and will speak for themselves.

With reference to the political prisoners, I recollect he repeated more than once:

You see, I stand in so much stronger a position than they do, in that I am not encumbered with wife and children; so I am resolved to strain every nerve on their behalf.

About six o'clock the last bell rang, and, cutting short our conversation, I hurriedly wished him goodbye and good luck, and from the deck of our little steamer we watched the big ship pass out into the night.

We had now been a month in South Africa, and had seen very little of the country, and it appeared that we had chosen a very unfavourable moment for our visit. We were determined, however, not to return home without seeing the Transvaal, peaceful or the reverse. The question was, how to get there. By train one had to allow three days and four nights, and, since the rebellion, to put up with insults into the bargain at the frontier, where luggage and even wearing apparel were subjected to a minute search, involving sometimes a delay of five hours. Our projected departure by sea *via* Natal was postponed indefinitely, by the non-arrival of the incoming mail-steamer from England, the old *Roslin Castle*, which was living up to her reputation of breaking down, by being days overdue, so that it was impossible to say when she would be able to leave for Durban.

Under these circumstances Sir Hercules Robinson proved a friend in need; and, having admonished us to secrecy, he told us that the P. and O. *Victoria*, the troopship we had noticed in the harbour, was under orders to leave at once for Durban to pick up Dr. Jameson and the other Raiders at that port; and convey them to England; therefore, as we only wanted to go as far as Durban, he would manage, by permission of the admiral at Cape Town, to get us passages on board this ship. Of course we were delighted, and early next morning we embarked. It was the first time I had ever been on a troopship, and every moment was of interest.

As spick and span as a man-of-war, with her wide, roomy decks, it was difficult to imagine there were 2,000 souls on board the *Victoria*, and only in the morning, when the regiment paraded, appearing like ants from below, and stretching in unbroken lines all down both sides of the ship, did one realise how large was the floating population, and how strict must be the discipline necessary to keep so many men healthy, contented, and efficient. There were a few other civilians going home on leave, but we were the only so-called "indulgence passengers." The time passed all too quickly, the monotonous hours of all shipboard life, between the six-thirty dinner and bedtime, being whiled away by listening to an excellent military band.

We were told to be dressed and ready to disembark by 6 a.m. on the morning we were due at Durban, as the admiral had given stringent instructions not to delay there any longer than was necessary. I was therefore horrified, on awaking at five o'clock, to find the engines had already stopped, and, on looking out of the porthole, to see a large tender approaching from the shore, apparently full of people. I scrambled into my clothes, but long before I was dressed the tug was alongside, or as nearly alongside as the heavy swell and consequent deep rolls of our ship would allow. Durban boasts of no harbour for large ships. These have to lie outside the bar, and a smooth sea being the exception on this part of the coast, disembarking is in consequence almost always effected in a sort of basket cage, worked by a crane, and holding three or four people. When I got on deck, the prisoners were still on the tender, being mercilessly rolled about, and they must indeed have been glad when, at six o'clock, the signal to disembark was given.

I shall never forget that striking and melancholy scene. The dull grey morning, of which the dawn had scarcely broken; the huge rollers of the leaden sea, which were lifting our mighty ship as if she had been but a cockleshell; and the tiny steamer, at a safe distance, her deck crowded with sunburnt men, many of whose faces were familiar to us, and who were picturesquely attired, for the most part, in the very same clothes they had worn on their ill-fated march—flannel shirts, khaki breeches, high boots, and the large felt hats of the Bechuanaland Border Police, which they were wearing probably for the last time.

As soon as they came on board we were able to have a few hasty words with those we knew, and their faces seem to pass in front of me as I write: Sir John Willoughby and Captain C. Villiers, both in the Royal Horse Guards, apparently nonchalant and without a care in the world; Colonel Harry White—alas! dead—and his brother Bobby, who were as fit as possible and as cheery as ever, but inclined to be mutinous with their unwilling gaolers; Major Stracey,[3] Scots Guards, with his genial and courtly manners, apparently still dazed at finding

3. Later Colonel Stacey Clitheroe.

himself a prisoner and amongst rebels; Mr. Cyril Foley, one of the few civilians, and Mr. Harold Grenfell,[4] 1st Life Guards, like boys who expect a good scolding when they get home; and last, but not least, Dr. Jameson, to whom we were introduced. "What will they do with us?" was the universal question, and on this point we could give them no information; but it can be imagined they were enchanted to see some friendly faces after a fortnight's incarceration in a Boer prison, during the first part of which time they daily expected to be led out and shot.

I remember asking Dr. Jameson what I think must have been a very embarrassing question, although he did not seem to resent it. It was whether an express messenger from Johannesburg, telling him not to start, as the town was not unanimous and the movement not ripe, had reached him the day before he left Mafeking. He gave no direct answer, but remarked: "I received so many messages from day to day, now telling me to come, then to delay starting, that I thought it best to make up their minds for them, before the Boers had time to get together."

We were soon hurried on shore, as Mr. Beresford,[5] the 7th Hussars, who had brought the prisoners on board, had to return to the town to make some necessary purchases for them, in the way of clothes, for they possessed nothing but what they stood up in.

We left Durban immediately by train for Pietermaritzburg, where we were the guests of Sir Walter and Lady Hely Hutchinson, at Government House, a very small but picturesque residence where Lady Hely Hutchinson received us most kindly in the absence of her husband, who was in the Transvaal, superintending the departure of the remaining prisoners. Here we seemed to have left warlike conditions behind us, for the town was agog with the excitement of a cricket-match, between Lord Hawke's eleven and a Natal fifteen.

On the cricket-field we met again two of our *Tantallon Castle* fellow-passengers, Mr. Guest and Mr. H. Milner, who had come down from Johannesburg with the cricketers. We were interested to compare notes and to hear Mr. Milner's adventures, which really made us smile, though they could hardly have been a laughing matter to him at the time. He told us that, after twice visiting Captain C. Coventry, who was wounded in the raid, at the Krugersdorp Hospital without molestation, on the third occasion, when returning by train to Johan-

---

4. Later Colonel Grenfell, 3rd Dragoon Guards.
5. Later Major Beresford.

nesburg, he was roughly pulled out of his carriage at ten o'clock at night, and told that, since he had no passport, he was to be arrested on the charge of being a spy. In vain did he tell them that only at the last station his passport had been demanded in such peremptory terms that he had been forced to give it up. They either would not or could not understand him.

In consequence the poor man tasted the delights of a Boer gaol for a whole night, and, worst indignity of all, had for companions two criminals and a crowd of dirty *kaffirs*. The following morning, he said, his best friend would not have known him, so swollen and distorted was his face from the visitations of the inseparable little companions of the *kaffir* native. He was liberated on bail next day, and finally set free, with a scanty apology of mistaken identity. At any other time such an insult to an Englishman would have made some stir; as it was, everyone was so harassed that he was hardly pitied.

The governor returned two days before our departure, and we had a gay time, between entertainments for the cricketers and festivities given by the 7th Hussars. Feeling in Durban, with regard to the Raiders, was then running high, and for hours did a vast crowd wait at the station merely in order to give the troopers of the Chartered Forces some hearty cheers, albeit they passed at midnight in special trains without stopping. Very loyal, too, were these colonists, and no German would have had a pleasant time of it there just then, with the *Kaiser's* famous telegram to Kruger fresh in everyone's memory.

From Pietermaritzburg to Johannesburg the railway journey was a very interesting one. North of Newcastle we saw a station bearing the name of Ingogo; later on the train wound round the base of Majuba Hill, and when that was felt behind it plunged into a long rocky tunnel which pierces the grassy slope on which the tragedy of Laing's Nek was enacted—all names, alas! too well known in the annals of our disasters. After leaving the Majuba district, we came to the Transvaal frontier, where we had been told we might meet with scanty courtesy. However, we had no disagreeable experiences, and then the train emerged on the endless rolling green plains which extend right up to and beyond the mining district of the Rand.

Now and then one perceived a *trek* waggon and oxen with a Boer and his family, either preceded or followed by a herd of cattle, winding their slow way along the dusty red track they call road. At the stations wild-looking *kaffir* women, half naked and anything but attractive in appearance, came and stared at the train and its passengers. It is in this desolate country that Johannesburg, the Golden City, sprang up, as it were, like a fungus, almost in a night. Nine years previously the Rand—since the theatre of so much excitement and disappointment—the source of a great part of the wealth of London at the present day, was as innocent of buildings and as peaceful in appearance as those lonely plains over which we had travelled.

As we approached Johannesburg, little white landmarks like milestones made their appearance, and these, we were told, were new claims pegged out. The thought suggested itself that this part of South Africa is in some respects a wicked country, with, it would almost seem, a blight resting on it: sickness, to both man and beast, is always stalking round; drought is a constant scourge to agriculture; the locust plagues ruin those crops and fruit that hailstones and scarcity of water have spared; and all the while men vie with and tread upon one another in their rush and eagerness after the gold which the land keeps hidden. Small wonder this district has proved such a whirlpool of evil influences, where everyone is always striving for himself, and where disillusions and bitter experiences have caused each man to distrust his neighbour.

CHAPTER 4

Johannesburg and Pretoria in 1896

Little white mice of chance,
Coats of wool and corduroy pants,
Gold and wine, women and sin,
I'll give to you, if you let me in
To the glittering house of chance.
American Dice Incantation.

At Johannesburg we were the guests of Mr. Abe Bailey at Clewer Lodge. Our host, however, was unfortunately absent, "detained" in the precincts of the gaol at Pretoria, although allowed out on bail. In the same house he had entertained in 1891 my brother Randolph[1] and his friend Captain G. Williams, Royal Horse Guards, on their way to Mashonaland. One of my first visitors was another fellow-traveller of theirs, Mr. H.C. Perkins, the celebrated American mining expert. This gentleman was a great friend of Randolph's, and he spoke most touchingly of his great attachment to the latter, and of his grief at his death. For five years Mr. and Mrs. Perkins had lived in Johannesburg, where they both enjoyed universal respect, and their approaching departure, to settle once more in America, was deplored by all. Considered to be the highest mining expert of the day, Mr. Perkins had seen the rise of the Rand since its infancy, and he had been shrewd enough to keep out of the late agitation and its disturbances.

Under his guidance we saw the sights of the towns: the far-famed Rand Club; the Market Square, crammed, almost for the first time since the so-called "revolution," with *trek*-waggons and their Boer drivers; the much-talked-of "Gold-fields" offices, barred and barri-caded, which had been the headquarters of the Reform Commit-

---

1. Lord Randolph Churchill died in January, 1895.

tee; the Standard Bank, where the smuggled arms had been kept; and finally the Exchange and the street enclosed by iron chains, where the stock markets were principally carried on. We were also shown the interior of the Stock Exchange itself, though we were warned that it was scarcely worth a visit at that time of depression. We heard the "call of the shares," which operation only took twenty minutes, against nearly two hours during the time of the recent boom. Instead of the listless, bored-looking individuals below us, who only assumed a little excitement when the revolving, clock-like machine denoted any popular share, we were told that a few months ago every available space had been crowded by excited buyers and sellers—some without hats, others in their shirt-sleeves, almost knocking one another over in their desire to do business. Those must indeed have been palmy days, when the money so lightly made was correspondingly lightly spent; when champagne replaced the usual whisky-split at the Rand Club, and on all sides was to be heard the old and well-known formula, "Here's luck," as the successful speculator toasted an old friend or a newcomer.

However, to return to Johannesburg as we found it, after the 1895 boom. Even then it seemed to me that for the first time in South Africa I saw life. Cape Town, with its pathetic dullness and palpable efforts to keep up a show of business; Kimberley, with its deadly respectability—both paled in interest beside their younger sister, so light-hearted, reckless, and enterprising. Before long, in spite of gloomy reflections on the evils of gold-seeking, I fell under the fascination of what was then a wonderful town, especially wonderful from its youth. The ever-moving crowds which thronged the streets, every man of which appeared to be full of important business and in a desperate hurry, reminded one of the City in London. Smart carriages with well-dressed ladies drove rapidly past, the shops were cunningly arranged with tempting wares, and all this bustle and traffic was restored in little over a week.

A fortnight previously a revolution was impending and a siege was looming ahead. Business had been at a complete standstill, the shops and houses barred and barricaded, and many of the inhabitants were taking a hurried departure; while bitterness, discord, and racial feeling were rampant. Now, after a few days, that cosmopolitan and rapidly changing population appeared to have buried their differences, and the uninitiated would never have guessed the town had passed, and was, indeed, still passing, through troublous times. Mr. Perkins, however, was pessimistic, and told us appearances were misleading. He rightly foresaw many lean years for those interested in the immediate future of the Rand, though even he, perhaps, hardly realised how lean those would become. Since those days much water has flown under the bridge, and the trade of the town, not to speak of the mining industry, has gone from bad to worse.

Recently Federation, the dream of many a statesman connected with South Africa, has opened a new *vista* of political peace and prosperity to its chastened citizens. Many of these, in affluent circumstances in 1896, have since gone under financially; but some of the original inhabitants still remain to show in the future that they have learned wisdom from their past troubles, brought on principally by their mad haste to get rich too quickly.

During our stay at Johannesburg we made an expedition to Pretoria in order to see our host and other friends, who were still on bail there, awaiting their trial, and also to visit the seat of the Boer Government. By these remarkable State railways the short journey of thirty-two miles occupied three hours. We passed one very large Boer *laager*, or military camp, on the line, which looked imposing enough in the bright sunlight, with its shining array of white-tarpaulin-covered waggons; companies of mounted burghers, armed to the teeth, and sitting their ragged but well-bred ponies as if glued to the saddle, were to be seen galloping to and fro. Although the teeth of the enemy had been drawn for the present, the Boers were evidently determined to keep up a martial display. As Pretoria was approached the country became very pretty: low hills and many trees, including lovely weeping-willows, appeared on the landscape, and away towards the horizon was situated many a snug little farm; running streams caught the rays of the sun, and really rich herbage supplied the pasture for herds of fat cattle.

The town itself did not prove specially interesting. An imposing space called Church Square was pointed out to us with great pride by the Dutch gentleman who kindly did cicerone. There we saw the little primitive "*dopper*" church where the president always worshipped, overshadowed and dwarfed by the magnificent Houses of Parliament, built since the Transvaal acquired riches, and by the no less grand Government Offices. As we were standing before the latter, after the fashion of tourists, our guide suddenly became very excited, and told us we were really in good luck, for the president was just about to leave his office on his return home for his midday meal. In a few minutes the old gentleman emerged, guarded by four armed *burghers*, and passed rapidly into his carriage. We took a good look at this remarkable personage. Stout in figure, with a venerable white beard, in a somewhat worn frock-coat and a rusty old black silk hat, President Kruger did not look the stern dictator of his little kingdom which in truth he was.

Our Dutch friend told us Oom Paul was in the habit of commencing work at 5 a.m., and that he transacted business, either at his house or in the Government Offices, with short intermissions, until 5 p.m. Simply worshipped by his *burghers*, he was on a small scale, and in his ignorant fashion, a man of iron like Bismarck, notably in his strong will and in the way in which he imposed the same on his countrymen. The extent of his personal influence could be gauged when one considered that his mere orders had restrained his undisciplined soldier-*burghers*, who, irritated by being called away from their peaceful existences, maddened by the loss of some of their number who fell in the fighting, and elated by their easy victory, were thirsting to shoot down the leaders of the raid, as they stood, in the market-square at Krugersdorp.

The state of the Boer Government at that time added to the president's difficulties. He was hampered by the narrowest—minded *Volksraad* (Parliament) imaginable, who resented tooth and nail even the most necessary concessions to the *uitlanders*; he was surrounded by corrupt officials, most of whom were said to be implicated in the late rebellion; he was the head of a community which was known to be split up into several sections, owing to acute religious disputes; and yet he contrived, at seventy-one years of age, to outwit the 60,000 *uitlanders* at Johannesburg, and to present his rotten republic as a model of all that was excellent and high-minded to the world at large. At the same time he compelled his *burghers* to forget their own differences, as they hurled defiance at the common foe. It seems to be a truism that it requires a Boer to rule a Boer; and in some ways the mantle of President Kruger would appear to have descended in our days upon General Louis Botha. According to all accounts, his will is now law to the ignorant back *Veldt* Boers, although his guiding principles savour more of the big stick than of the spoon-feeding system. Undoubtedly loyal to England, he bids fair in the future to help found a nation, based upon the union of British and Boer, inheriting their traditions, cultivating their ideals, and pursuing their common ends.

But this Utopia seemed far away in 1896, and it was, alas! destined that many lives should be laid down, and much treasure expended, before its advent. For the moment lamentations were rife in Johannesburg, and at many a dinner-party unprofitable discussions raged as to what would have happened had Dr. Jameson entered the city. On this point no one could agree. Some people said the town could have been starved out in a few days, and the water-supply cut off immediately; others asserted that the Boers were in reality overawed by Dr. Jameson's name and prestige, and would have been glad to make terms. The practical spirits opined that the only thing which would have saved the inhabitants in any case was the tame ending which actually came about—namely, the high commissioner's intervention coupled with President Kruger's moderation and wisdom in allowing England to punish her own irregular soldiers.

The more one heard of the whole affair, the more it seemed to resemble a scene out of a comic opera. The only people at Johannesburg who had derived any advantage from the confusion were several hitherto unknown military commanders, who had proudly acquired the title of colonel, and had promptly named a body of horse after themselves. During the days before the final fiasco these leaders used to make short detours round the town in full regimentals, and finally fill up the time by being photographed in groups. Mercifully, as it turned out, they were not ready for active service when Dr. Jameson was reported at Krugersdorp.

We made an excursion to the so-called battlefield before leaving for the South. We started in a covered waggonette with no springs to speak of, drawn by six mules, and a pair of horses as leaders. Two *kaffirs* acted as charioteers, and kept up an incessant jabber in Dutch. The one who held the reins looked good-natured enough, but the other, whose duty it was to wield the enormously long whip, had a most diabolical cast of countenance, in which cruelty and doggedness were both clearly depicted. We found his face a true indication of his character before the end of the day. Bumping gaily along, we soon left the well-built houses behind, and after passing the Malay quarter of the town, remarkable by reason of the quaint houses these blacks make out of paraffin tins, flattened out and nailed together with wonderful neatness, we emerged on the open *veldt*.

Of course the road was of the roughest description, and sometimes we had to hold on with all our might to avoid the concussion of our heads with the wooden roof. In spite of this, as soon as the *kaffirs* saw an open space before them, the huge whip was cracked, and away went our team at full gallop, seemingly quite out of control, the driver leaning back in his seat with a contented grin, while his colleague manipulated the unwieldy whip. The tract ran parallel to the Rand for some distance, and we got a splendid view of Johannesburg and the row of chimney-shafts that so clearly define the reef.

On passing Langlaate village, we were stopped by a party of Boers, who had off-saddled by the side of the road. As they were fully armed and their appearance was not prepossessing, we expected to be ordered to alight while our conveyance was being searched. However, our fears were unfounded, and they were most polite. The driver muttered something in Dutch, whereupon the leader came to the door, and said in broken English: "Peeck neeck—I see all right." I am sorry to say one of the gentlemen of our party muttered "Brute" in an audible whisper; but, then, he had undergone a short, but a very unpleasant term of imprisonment, with no sort of excuse, at the instance of a Boer *veldtcornet*, so no wonder he had vowed eternal vengeance. Luckily, this officer did not hear, or else did not understand, the ejaculation, so after a civil interchange of good-days we drove on.

After about three hours we reached a shallow ford over a wide stream, and our driver informed us that this was our destination. Leaving the carriage, we walked up to some rocks overlooking the stream, which seemed an inviting place for luncheon; but we were quickly driven away, as thereon were lying seven or eight carcasses of dead horses and mules. Curiously enough, the vultures, or "*aas-vogels*," had left the skins on these poor beasts, for I remember noticing how their coats glistened in the sunshine. This sight was not very conducive to a good appetite, and a little farther on we saw another pathetic spectacle: a very deep trench, made in the past by some gold-prospector, had been filled in with rocky boulders, and was covered with withered ferns. Here lay those who had fallen of the Chartered Company's Forces.

No doubt by now the space is enclosed as a tiny part of God's acre, but at that time the rough stones in the deep grave, and the faded flowers, seemed to enhance the dreariness of the scene.[2] As to the locality of the final encounter and surrender of the raiders, there was not much to interest any but military men. Standing on the top of the eminence before alluded to, one could see the Boer position and the sore strait of their foes. Whether the column had come purposely

---

2. The soldiers' graves in South Africa have since been carefully tended by the Loyal Women's Guild.

towards this drift, as being the only possible ford for many miles, or whether they had been guided thereto by a treacherous guide, no one knew. One thing was certain: destruction or surrender must have stared them in the face. The *kopjes* on the farther side of the stream were bristling with Boers, and away on the *veldt* beyond was drawn up the Staats artillery.

And then one realised a most awful blunder of the Reform Committee, from their point of view. The Boer forces, arriving hereabouts in hot haste, from a rapid mobilisation, had been almost entirely without ammunition. We were told on good authority that each *burgher* had but six rounds, and that the field-guns were without any shells at all. During the night the necessary supply was brought by rail from Pretoria, actually right through Johannesburg. Either by accident or mature reflection on the part of the conspirators in that city, this train was allowed to pass to its destination unmolested. It proved to be one of those small happenings that completely alter the course of events. If the *burghers* had not stopped the raiders there, nothing could have prevented them from entering Johannesburg, for after another three miles the long-sought-for chimneys—the overhanging cloud of smoke—would have come into view.

The very stars in their courses seemed to have fought for the Boers, and justified President Kruger's belief that his people were specially under the protection of Providence.[3] Neither will anyone ever determine the number of Boers killed at Krugersdorp. One *veldtcornet* inserted in all the papers that he defied anyone to prove that more than four *burghers* were shot, and of these two were killed accidentally by their own rifles. Residents on the spot, however, averred that many more fell; but I think the point was not disputed in view of President Kruger's famous claim for "moral and intellectual damages," which was then already beginning to be mooted.

The lengthening shadows at last reminded us that we had to return to town for a dinner-party given in our honour. It usually takes some time to catch a team of six mules and two horses turned out to graze on the *veldt*; it is endless, however, when they are as frightened of their drivers as ours appeared to be. At length they were collected and we made a start, and then our adventures began. First the leader, a white horse, jibbed. Off jumped the *kaffir* coachman, and commenced hammering the poor brute unmercifully over head, ears, and body, with

---

3. The president's favourite psalm was said to be the 144th, which he always believed was aptly written to apply specially to the Boers.

what they called in Africa the *shambok*.[4] In consequence the team suddenly started off, but the long whip, left on the carriage roof, slipped down, and was broken in two by the wheel passing over it.

Anyone who has driven behind mules knows how absolutely powerless the Jehu is without a long whip; so here we were face to face with a real misfortune: increasing darkness, jibbing leaders, no whip, and fifteen sandy miles to traverse before dinner-time. With every sort of ejaculation and yell, and a perfect rain of blows with the *shambok* from the *kaffir* still on foot, we lurched forward at a gallop, escaping by a hair's-breadth another gold-prospector's trench. But the same leader jibbed again after another mile. I must admit he was a most irritating brute, whose obstinacy had been increased by the cruelty of the driver. It was now decided to put him in the "wheel," where he would be obliged to do his work. We crawled on again till our white friend literally threw himself down. I have related this incident to show how cruel *kaffirs* can be, for now the rage of the evil-looking driver burst forth. He not only hammered the prostrate horse to any extent, but then made the rest of the team pull on, so as to drag him along on his side.

Of course this could not be allowed, and Major —— jumped out and commanded him to desist, take out the useless horse, and tie him behind. At first the *kaffir* was very mutinous, and it was only when a stick was laid threateningly across his back that he sulkily complied, looking the while as if he would like to murder the man he was forced to obey. One hears so much nowadays of the black population having equal rights with the white inhabitants, that it is well to remember how ferociously their lack of civilization occasionally comes out. Doubtless there are cruel men both white and black, but for downright brutality the nigger is hard to beat, and it is also quite certain that whom the latter does not fear he will not love.

I have personally experienced great devotion and most attentive service on the part of natives, and they are deserving of the kindest and most considerate treatment; but it has often made me indignant to hear people, who have had little or no experience of living in the midst of a native population, prate of the rights of our "black brothers," and argue as if the latter thought, judged, amused themselves, or, in short, behaved, as the white men do, who have the advantage of hundreds of years of culture.

The day following our drive to Krugersdorp we left for Cape

4. Short whip.

Town and England. We made the voyage on the old *Roslin Castle*. Always a slow boat, she had on this occasion, in sporting parlance, a "wing down," having broken a piston-rod on her way out from England, when we had vainly awaited her at Cape Town, and I think it was nearly three weeks before we landed at Plymouth. Again Randolph's African journey was brought back to my recollection. The captain of the *Roslin Castle*, Travers by name, had commanded the *Scot*, which brought his party home from Mashonaland, and he had very agreeable recollections of many an interesting conversation and of quiet rubbers of whist.

Numerous and exciting events had been crowded into the past six weeks, and in spite of revolutions and strife we had found our South African visit a very pleasant one. A curious thing about that continent is: you may dislike it or fall under its charm, but in any case it nearly always calls you back. It certainly did in my case; and while recalling the people we had met and the information we had acquired it was impossible not to think a little of the Boers themselves, their characteristics and their failings. At Johannesburg I had been specially struck by men, who knew them from long experience, telling me how fully they appreciated the good points of the *burghers*—for instance, their bravery, their love of their country, and their simple, unquestioning, if unattractive faith, which savoured of that of the old Puritans. Against these attributes their pig-headedness, narrow-mindedness, laziness, and slovenliness had to be admitted. All these defects militated against their living in harmony with a large, increasing, and up-to-date community like the Johannesburg Uitlanders.

Still, one could not forget that the Transvaal was their country, ceded to them by the English nation. They left Cape Colony years ago, to escape our laws, which they considered unjust. It is certain we should never have followed them into the Transvaal but for the sudden discovery of the gold industry; it is equally true they had not the power or the wish to develop this for themselves, and yet without it they were a bankrupt nation. There is no doubt that the men who made the most mischief, and who for years embarrassed the president, were the "Hollanders," or officials sent out from the mother-country of the Dutch. They looked on the Transvaal only as a means for getting rich. Hence the fearful state of bribery and corruption among them, from the highest official downwards.

But this very bribery and corruption were sometimes exceedingly convenient, and I remember well, when I revisited Johannesburg in

1902, at the conclusion of the war, hearing people inveigh against the hard bargains driven by the English Government; they even went so far as to sigh again for the good old days of Kruger's rule. Now all is changed once more, after another turn of the kaleidoscope of time, and yet it is well to remember that such things have indeed been.

CHAPTER 5

Three Years After

There are many echoes in the world, but few voices.
—Goethe.

On May 6, 1899, we sailed from Southampton on the S.S. *Norman*. We purposed to spend a few months in Rhodesia, but such is the frailty of human plans that eventually we stayed in South Africa for one year and three months.

Dr. Jameson was our fellow-passenger to Cape Town, and with him we travelled up to Bulawayo, and passed five weeks there as the guests of Major Maurice Heaney.[1] Part of this time we spent on the *veldt*, far from civilization, sleeping in tents, and using riding ponies and mule waggons as transport. I can recommend this life as a splendid cure for any who are run down or overworked. The climate of Rhodesia in the month of June is perfection; rain is unknown, except as the accompaniment of occasional thunderstorms; and it is never too hot to be pleasant. Game was even then practically non-existent in Matabeleland, but our object was to inspect the mines of Major Heaney's various companies. The country was pretty and well wooded, and we crossed many river-beds, amongst them the wide Umzingwani. This stream is a mighty torrent during the rains, but, like many others in South Africa, it becomes perfectly dry during the winter season, a peculiarity of the continent, which caused a disappointed man to write that South Africa produced "*birds without song, flowers without smell, and rivers without water.*"

While camped on the banks of this vanished river, we used to hear lions roaring as evening fell, and could distinguish their soft pads in

---

1. Major Heaney is an American, and was one of the pioneers who accompanied Dr. Jameson to Mashonaland in 1891.

49

the dry sand next morning; but they were so shy that we never caught a glimpse of one, nor could they be tempted into any ambush.

During these weeks the abortive Bloemfontein Conference had been holding its useless sessions; the political world seemed so unsettled, and war appeared so exceedingly likely, that we decided to return to Cape Town, especially as Mr. Rhodes, who was expected out from England almost immediately, had cabled asking us to stay at Groot Schuurr, where we arrived early in July. A few days afterwards I had a ticket given me to witness the opening of the Legislative Council, or Upper House, by Sir Alfred Milner. It was an imposing ceremony, and carried out with great solemnity. The centre of the fine hall was filled with ladies—in fact, on first arriving, it gave one the idea of a ladies' parliament; but in a few minutes the members filed in, shortly before the state entry of His Excellency the Governor.

Then, for the first time, I saw the man of the hour; dignified without being stiff, and looking every inch his part, he went through his *rôle* to perfection. The speech was, as usual, utterly devoid of interest, and, contrary to the hope of excited partisans, Transvaal affairs were studiously avoided. A few days later we went to Government House to be introduced to Sir Alfred; he at once impressed a stranger as a man of intense strength of mind and purpose, underlying a somewhat delicate physique, which was at that time, perhaps, enhanced by a decidedly worn and worried expression of countenance. Later on I had many conversations with Mr. Rhodes about the governor. He used to say—and no one was better qualified to judge—that Sir Alfred Milner was one of the strongest men he had ever met.

"In the business I am constantly having to transact with him, connected with the Chartered Company," he remarked, "I find him, his mind once made up, unmovable—so much so that we tacitly agree to drop at once any subject that we do not agree on, for nothing could be gained by discussing it. I allow he makes his decisions slowly, but once made they are irrevocable."

Mr. Rhodes used also to say he admired beyond words Sir Alfred's behaviour and the line he adopted in that most difficult crisis before the war. "He assumes," said his appreciator, "an attitude of perfect frankness with all parties; he denies himself to no one who may give him any information or throw fresh light on the situation; to all he expresses his views, and repeats his unalterable opinions of what is required."

Other people told me how true these words were, and how ingeniously and yet ingenuously Sir Alfred Milner contrived to treat a unique position. Standing alone, the central isolated figure, surrounded by a young and inexperienced staff, his political advisers men for whom he could have but little sympathy, and whose opinions he knew to be in reality diametrically opposed to his and to the present policy at home, the governor steered clear of intrigue and personal quarrels by his intensely straightforward and able conduct. He was in the habit of almost daily seeing Mr. Rhodes, financiers from Johannesburg, military men thirsting for war, who were commencing to arrive from England, as well as his cabinet ministers. To these latter he probably volunteered information about the other interviews he had had, thereby disarming their criticisms.

From one great man I must pass to another. A few days after our arrival at Groot Schuurr, Mr. Rhodes and Sir Charles Metcalfe arrived from England. Incidentally I may mention the former's marvellous reception, and the fact that nearly five miles of road between Cape Town and Groot Schuurr were decorated with flags and triumphal arches, while the day was observed as a general holiday. This had happened to him in a minor degree so often before that it did not arouse much comment. The same evening we attended a monster meeting at the Drill Hall, where thousands of faces were turned simultaneously towards the platform to welcome back their distinguished citizen. The cheering went on for ten minutes, and was again and again renewed, till the enthusiasm brought a lump to many throats, and certainly deeply affected the central figure of the evening.

This meeting, at which no less than a hundred addresses were presented from every part of Africa—from the far-off Zambesi to the fruit-growing district of the Paarl, almost entirely populated by Dutch—even this great demonstration that one great man was capable of inspiring quickly faded from my memory in view of the insight which three weeks as his guest gave me of the many sides of his life, occupations, and character. The extraordinary strength of will and tenacity of purpose, points always insisted on in connection with him, seemed on nearer acquaintance to be merely but a small part of a marvellous whole.

It often used to occur to me, when with Mr. Rhodes, how desirable it would be to induce our sons and young men in general to imitate some of the characteristics which were the motive power of his life, and therefore of his success. I noticed especially the wonderful power of concentration of thought he possessed, and which he applied to any subject, no matter how trivial. The variety and scope of his many projects did not lessen his interest in any one of them. At that time he was building four railways in Rhodesia, which country was also pinning its faith to him for its development, its prosperity, and, indeed, its *modus vivendi*. Apart from this, Cape politics, although he then held no official position, were occupying a great deal of his time and thoughts in view of future Federation. It was, therefore, marvellous to see him putting his whole mind to such matters as his prize poultry and beasts at the home farm, to the disposing of the same in what he termed "my country," or to the arranging of his priceless collection of glass—even to the question of a domicile for the baby lioness lately presented to him.

Again, one moment he might be talking of De Beers business, involving huge sums of money, the next discussing the progress of his thirty fruit-farms in the Drakenstein district, where he had no fewer than 100,000 fruit-trees; another time his horse-breeding establishment at Kimberley was engaging his attention, or, nearer home, the road-making and improvements at Groot Schuurr, where he even knew the wages paid to the 200 Cape boys he was then employing. Mr. Rhodes was always in favour of doing things on a large scale, made easy, certainly, by his millionaire's purse. Sometimes a gardener or bailiff would ask for two or three dozen rose or fruit trees. "There is no use," he would exclaim impatiently, "in two dozen of anything. My good man, you should count in hundreds and thousands, not dozens. That is the only way to produce any effect or to make any profit." Another of his theories was that people who dwelt in or near towns never had sufficient fresh air.

During one of our morning rides I remember his stopping a telegraph-boy, and asking him where he lived. When the lad had told him, he said: "I suppose there are no windows in your cottage; you had better go to Rhodesia, where you will find space, and where you won't get cramped ideas." Then he rode on, leaving the boy staring at him with open eyes. An attractive attribute was his love of his early associations, his father especially being often the theme of his conversation. He used freely to express his admiration for the type the latter represented, now almost extinct, of the old-fashioned country clergyman-squire.

He held with tenacity to the traditions of his childhood in having always a cold supper on Sunday evenings, instead of the usual elaborate dinner, also in having the cloth removed for dessert, to display the mahogany, of which, alas! few of our tables are now made. With stupidity, or anything thereto approaching, he was apt to be impatient; neither could he stand young men who affected indifference to, or boredom with, the events and sights of the day. I often used to think, however, he frightened people, and that they did not show to their best advantage, nor was their intelligence at its brightest when talking with him. I now refer especially to those in his employ.

To his opponents in the political world he was generous when discussing them in private, however bitter and stinging his remarks were in public. I remember one evening, on Mr. Merriman's name being mentioned, how Mr. Rhodes dilated for some time on his charms as a friend and as a colleague; he told me I should certainly take an opportunity of making his acquaintance. "I am so fond of Merriman," he added; "he is one of the most cultivated of men and the most charming of companions that I know. We shall come together again some day." And this of the man who was supposed then to hate Cecil John Rhodes with such a deadly hatred that he, an Englishman born, was said to have been persuaded to Dutch sympathies by his vindictive feelings against one great fellow-countryman.

Before leaving the subject of Mr. Rhodes, I must note his intense kindness of heart and genuine hospitality. Groot Schuurr was a rendezvous for people of all classes, denominations, and politics; they were all welcome, and they certainly all came. From morn till eve they passed in and out, very often to proffer a request, or, again, simply to pay their respects and have the pleasure of a few minutes' chat. After his morning ride, Mr. Rhodes, if nothing called him to town, usually walked about his beautiful house, the doors and windows of which stood open to admit the brilliant sunshine and to enable him to enjoy glimpses of his beloved Table Mountain, or the brilliant colours of the salvia and plumbago planted in beds above the *stoep*. I often call to mind that tall figure, probably in the same costume in which he had ridden—white flannel trousers and tweed coat—his hair rather rough, from a habit he had of passing his hand through it when talking or thinking.

He would wander through the rooms, enjoying the pleasure of looking at his many beautiful pieces of furniture and curiosities of all sorts, nearly all of which had a history. Occasionally shifting a piece of rare old glass or blue Delft china, he would the while talk to anyone who chanced to come in, greeting heartily his old friends, and remembering every detail of their circumstances, opinions, and conduct. Concerning the latter, he did not fail to remind them of any failings he had taken note of. Those who were frauds, incompetent, or lazy, he never spared, and often such conversations were a source of much amusement to me. On the other hand, those who had been true to him, and had not veered round with the tide of public opinion after 1896, were ever remembered and rewarded. It was remarkable to note the various Dutch members of the Assembly who dropped in, sometimes stealthily in the early morning hours, or, like Nicodemus, by night.

One such gentleman came to breakfast one day, bringing as a gift two curious antique pipes and a pouch of Boer tobacco. The pipes were awarded a place in a glass cabinet, and the giver most heartily thanked; he finally departed, well pleased with himself. Now comes a curious trait in the man's character. Before leaving he whispered to a friend the request that the fact of his visit should not be mentioned in Cape Town circles. This request was naturally repeated at once to Mr. Rhodes, much to the latter's amusement. As ill-luck would have it, the cautious gentleman left his umbrella behind, with his name in full on the handle; this remained a prominent object on the hall table till, when evening fell, a trusted emissary came to recover it.

I often used to visit the House of Assembly or Lower House during that session, and it was instructive to note the faces of the Opposition when Rhodesia and its undoubted progress were subjects of discussion, and especially when Mr. Rhodes was on his feet, claiming the undivided attention of the House. It was not his eloquence that kept people so attentive, for no one could call him eloquent; it was the singularly expressive voice, the (at times) persuasive manner, and, above all, the interesting things his big ideas gave him to say, that preserved that complete silence. But, as I said before, the faces of his then antagonists—albeit quondam friends—hardly disguised their thoughts sufficiently. They were forced to consider the country of the man they feared—the country to which he had given his name—as a factor in their colony; they had to admit it to their financial calculations, and all the time they would fain have crushed the great pioneer under their feet. They had, indeed, hoped to see him humbled and abashed after his one fatal mistake, instead of which he had gone calmly on his way—a Colossus indeed—with the set purpose, as a guiding star ever before his eyes, to retrieve the error which they had fondly imagined would have delivered him into their hands. Truly an impressive and curious study was that House of Assembly in the session of 1899.

The number of people, more or less interesting, whom we met at Groot Schuurr, seemed to pass as actors on a stage, sometimes almost too rapidly to distinguish or individualize. But one or two stand out specially in my recollection. Among them, a type of a fine old gentleman, was Colonel Schermbrucker. A German by birth, and over seventy years of age, he had served originally in the Papal Guard, and had accompanied Pio Nono on the occasion of his famous flight from Rome. Somewhere in the fifties, at the time of the arrival of the German Legion, he had settled at the Cape, and had been a figure in politics ever since. His opinions were distinctly English and progressive, but it was more as an almost extinct type of the courtly old gentleman that he impressed me. His extreme activity for his years, his old-world manners, and his bright intelligence, were combinations one does not often meet, and would have made him an interesting figure in any assembly or country. Another day came Judge Coetzee, erstwhile Kruger's confidant and right hand, but then of a very different way of thinking to his old master. His remark on the warlike situation was as follows:

Kruger is only a white *kaffir* chief, and as such respects force, and force only. Send sufficient soldiers, and there will be no fighting.

This was also Mr. Rhodes's view, but, as it turned out, both were wrong. In the meantime the sands were running out, and the troops were almost on the water, and yet the old man remained obdurate.

Outside the hospitable haven of Groot Schuurr I one day met Mr. Merriman at lunch as the guest of Mr. and Mrs. Richard Solomon.[2] Considerably above the average height, with a slight stoop and grey hair, Mr. Merriman was a man whose appearance from the first claimed interest. It was a few days after his Budget speech, which, from various innovations, had aroused a storm of criticism, as Budgets are wont to do. Whatever his private feelings were about the English, to me the Finance Minister was very pleasant and friendly. We talked of fruit-farming, in which he takes a great interest, of England, and even of his Budget, and never did he show any excitement or irritation till someone happened to mention the word "Imperialist."

Then he burst out with, "That word and 'Empire' have been so done to death by every wretched little Jew stockbroker in this country that I am fairly sick of them." "But surely you are not a Little Englan-

2. Mr. Richard Soloman, the attorney-general, later Sir Richard Solomon.

der, Mr. Merriman," I said, "or a follower of Mr. Labouchere?" To this he gave an evasive reply, and the topic dropped. I must relate another incident of our sojourn at Cape Town. Introduced by Mr. Rhodes's architect, Mr. Baker, we went one day to see a Mrs. Koopman, then a well-known personage in Cape Town Dutch society, but who, I believe, is now dead. Her collection of Delft china was supposed to be very remarkable. She lived in a quaint old house with diamond-paned windows, in one of the back streets, the whole edifice looking as if it had not been touched for a hundred years.

Mrs. Koopman was an elderly lady, most suitably dressed in black, with a widow's cap, and she greeted us very kindly and showed us all her treasured possessions. I was disappointed in the contents of the rooms, which were certainly mixed, some very beautiful things rubbing shoulders with modern specimens of clumsy early Victorian furniture. A room at the back was given up to the Delft china, but even this was spoilt by ordinary yellow arabesque wall-paper, on which were hung the rare plates and dishes, and by some gaudy window curtains, evidently recently added. The collection itself, made by Mrs. Koopman at very moderate prices, before experts bought up all the Dutch relics, was then supposed to be of great value.

Our hostess conversed in good English with a foreign accent, and was evidently a person of much intelligence and culture. She had been, and still was, a factor in Cape politics, formerly as a great admirer of Mr. Rhodes, but after 1896 as one of his bitterest opponents, who used all her considerable influence—her house being a meeting-place for the Bond party—against him and his schemes. We had, in fact, been told she held a sort of political *salon*, though hardly in the same way we think of it in England as connected with Lady Palmerston, her guests being entirely confined to one party—*viz.*, the Dutch. This accounted for a blunder on my part. Having heard that Mrs. Koopman had been greatly perturbed by the young Queen of Holland's representations to President Kruger in favour of the *uitlanders*, and seeing many photographs of this charming-looking girl in the room, I thought I should be right in alluding to her as "your little Queen."

"She is not my Queen," was the indignant reply; "Queen Victoria is my Queen." And then, quickly turning to Mr. Baker, she continued: "What have you been telling Lady Sarah to make her think I am not loyal?" Of course I had to disclaim and apologize, but, in view of her well-known political opinions and sympathies, I could not help thinking her extreme indignation a little unnecessary.

CHAPTER 6

Preparations For War

War seldom enters, but where wealth allures.

—Dryden.

In August we left Cape Town, and I went to Bulawayo, where I spent two months. Gordon[1] had been appointed A.D.C. to Colonel Baden-Powell, and during this time was with his chief on the western borders. The latter was engaged in raising two regiments of irregular horse, which were later known as the Protectorate Regiments, and were recruited principally from the district between Mafeking and Bulawayo. At the latter town was also another English lady, Mrs. Godley, whose husband was second in command of one of these regiments. It can easily be imagined that there was little else discussed then but warlike subjects, and these were two dreary and anxious months. We had little reliable news; the local newspapers had no special cables, and only published rumours that were current in the town. Mr. Rochfort Maguire, who was then staying with Mr. Rhodes at Cape Town, used frequently to telegraph us news from there.

One day he would report President Kruger was climbing down; the next, that he had once more hardened his heart. And so this modern Pharaoh kept us all on tenterhooks. The drilling and exercising of the newly recruited troops were the excitements of the day. Soon Colonel Plumer[2] arrived, and assumed command of one of the regiments, which was encamped on the racecourse just outside the town; the other regiment had its headquarters at Mafeking. Colonel Baden-Powell and his staff used to dash up and down between the two towns.

---

1. Captain Gordon Wilson, Royal Horse Guards, later Lieutenant-Colonel Wilson, M.V.O.
2. Later Major-General Sir Hubert Plumer, K.C.B.

Nearly all the business men in Bulawayo enlisted, and amongst the officers were some experienced soldiers, who had seen all the Matabeleland fighting, and some of whom had even participated in the Raid. Others who used to drop in for a game of bridge were Lord Timmy Paulet,[3] Mr. Geoffrey Glyn, and Dr. Jameson. To while away the time, I took a course of ambulance lessons, learning how to bandage by experiments on the lanky arms and legs of a little black boy. We also made expeditions to the various mining districts. I was always struck with the hospitality shown us in these out-of-the-way localities, and with the cosiness of the houses belonging to the married mine-managers.

Only *kaffirs* were available as servants, but, in spite of this, an excellent repast was always produced, and the dwellings were full of their home treasures. Prints of the present king and queen abounded, and among the portraits of beautiful Englishwomen, either photographs or merely reproductions cut out of an illustrated newspaper, I found those of Lady de Grey,[4] Georgiana, Lady Dudley, and Mrs. Langtry,[5] most frequently adorning the walls of those lonely homes.

At last, at the end of September, a wire informed us that hostilities were expected to begin in Natal the following week, and I left for Mafeking, intending to proceed to Cape Town and home. On arrival at Mafeking everyone told us an attack on the town was imminent, and we found the inhabitants in a state of serious alarm. However, Baden-Powell's advent reassured them, and preparations for war proceeded apace; the townspeople flocked in to be enrolled in the town guard, spending the days in being drilled; the soldiers were busy throwing up such fortifications as were possible under the circumstances. On October 3 the armoured train arrived from the South, and took its first trip on the rails, which had been hastily flung down round the circumference of the town. This train proved afterwards to be absolutely useless when the Boers brought up their artillery. Night alarms occurred frequently; bells would ring, and the inhabitants, who mostly slept in their clothes, had to rush to their various stations. I must admit that these nocturnal incidents were somewhat unpleasant. Still war was not declared, and the large body of Boers, rumoured as awaiting the signal to advance on Mafeking, gave no sign of approaching any nearer.

3. Later Marquis of Winchester.
4. Later Marchioness of Ripon.
5. Later Lady de Bathe.

We were, indeed, as jolly as the proverbial sand-boys during those few days in Mafeking before the war commenced. If Colonel Baden-Powell had forebodings, he kept them to himself. Next to him in importance came Lord Edward Cecil, Grenadier Guards, C.S.O. I have often heard it said that if Lord Edward had been a member of any other family but that of the gifted Cecils he would have been marked as a genius, and that if he had not been a soldier he would surely have been a politician of note. Then there was Major Hanbury Tracy, Royal Horse Guards, who occupied the position of Director of Military Intelligence. This officer was always devising some amusing if wild-cat schemes, which were to annihilate or checkmate the Boers, and prove eventually the source of fame to himself.

Mr. Ronald Moncrieff,[6] an extra A.D.C., was, as usual, not blest with a superabundance of this world's goods, but had an unending supply of animal spirits, and he was looking forward to a siege as a means of economizing. Another of our circle was Major Hamilton Gould Adams,[7] Resident Commissioner of the Bechuanaland Protectorate, who commanded the town guard, representing the civil as opposed to the military interests. In contrast to the usual practice, these departments worked perfectly smoothly together at Mafeking.

Colonel Baden-Powell did not look on my presence with great favour, neither did he order me to leave, and I had a sort of presentiment that I might be useful, considering that there were but three trained nurses in the Victoria Hospital to minister to the needs of the whole garrison. Therefore, though I talked of going South every day by one of the overcrowded trains to Cape Town, in which the government was offering free tickets to any who wished to avail themselves of the opportunity, I secretly hoped to be allowed to remain. We had taken a tiny cottage in the town, and we had all our meals at Dixon's Hotel, where the food was weird, but where certainly no depression of spirits reigned. I even bought a white pony, called Dop,[8] from a Johannesburg polo-player, and this pony, one of the best I have ever ridden, had later on some curious experiences.

One day Dr. Jameson arrived on his way to Rhodesia, but he was hustled away with more haste than courtesy by General Baden-Powell, who bluntly told him that if he meant to stay in the town a battery of artillery would be required to defend it; and of field-guns, in spite

---

6. Died in Africa, 1909.

7. Later Sir Hamilton Gould Adams, Governor of the Orange River Colony.

8. Dutch for a peculiar kind of cheap brandy very popular with the Boers.

of urgent representations, not one had reached us from Cape Town. We used to ride morning and evening on the flat country which surrounds Mafeking, where no tree or hill obscures the view for miles; and one then realised what a tiny place the seat of government of the Bechuanaland Protectorate really was, a mere speck of corrugated iron roofs on the brown expanse of the burnt-up *veldt*, far away from everywhere. I think it was this very isolation that created the interest in the siege at home, and one of the reasons why the Boers were so anxious to reduce it was that this town was practically the jumping-off place for the Jameson Raid. So passed the days till October 13, and then the sword, which had been suspended by a hair, suddenly fell.

On that day Major Gould Adams received a wire from the high commissioner at Cape Town to the effect that the South African Republic had sent an ultimatum to Her Majesty's Government, in which it demanded the removal of all troops from the Transvaal borders, fixing five o'clock the following evening as a limit for their withdrawal. I had delayed my departure too long; it was extremely doubtful whether another train would be allowed to pass South, and, even when started, it would stand a great chance of being wrecked by the Boers tearing up the rails.

Under these circumstances I was allotted comparatively safe quarters at the house of Mr. Benjamin Weil, of the firm of the well-known South African merchants. His residence stood in the centre of the little town, adjacent to the railway-station. At that time bomb-proof underground shelters, with which Mafeking afterwards abounded, had not been thought of, or time had not sufficed for their construction. On all sides one heard reproaches levelled at the Cape Government, and especially at General Sir William Butler, until lately commanding the troops in Cape Colony, for having so long withheld the modest reinforcements which had been persistently asked for, and, above all, the very necessary artillery.

At that date the Mafeking garrison consisted of about seven or eight hundred trained troops. The artillery, under Major Panzera, comprised four old muzzle-loading seven-pounder guns with a short range, a one-pound Hotchkiss, one Nordenfeldt, and about seven ·303 Maxims—in fact, no large modern pieces whatever. The town guard, hastily enrolled, amounted to 441 defenders, among whom nationalities were curiously mixed, as the following table shows: [9]

---

9. This return was given me by Major Gould Adams.

British	378
Germans	4
Americans	4
Russians	6
Dutch	27
Norwegians	5
Swedes	2
Arabs and Indians	15
Total	441

This force did not appear sufficiently strong to resist the three or four thousand Boers, with field-guns, who were advancing to its attack under one of their best generals—namely Cronje—but everyone remained wonderfully calm, and the townspeople rose to the occasion in a most creditable manner.

Very late that same evening, just as I was going to bed, I received a message from Colonel Baden-Powell, through one of his staff, to say he had just been informed, on trustworthy authority, that no less than 8,000 *burghers* composed the force likely to arrive on the morrow, that it was probable they would rush the town, and that the garrison would be obliged to fight its way out. He concluded by begging me to leave at once by road for the nearest point of safety. Naturally I had to obey. I shall never forget that night: it was cold and gusty after a hot day, with frequent clouds obscuring the moon, as we walked round to Major Gould Adams's house to secure a Cape cart and some government mules, in order that I might depart at dawn. At first I was ordered to Kanya, a mission-station some seventy miles away, an oasis in the Kalahari Desert.

This plan gave rise to a paragraph which I afterwards saw in some of the daily papers, that I had left Mafeking under the escort of a missionary, and some cheery spirit made a sketch of my supposed departure as reproduced here. Later on, however, it was thought provisions might run short in that secluded spot, so I was told to proceed to Setlagoli, a tiny store, or hotel as we should call it, with a shop attached, thirty-five miles south in Bechuanaland, on the main road to Kimberley, from which quarter eventually succour was expected. My few preparations completed, I simply had to sit down and wait for daybreak, sleep being entirely out of the question. In the night the wind increased, and howled mournfully round the house. At four

The last coaches to leave Mafeking for the Transvaal before the war.

OFF TO THE KALAHARI DESERT

o'clock, when day was about to break, I was ready to start, and some farewells had to be said. These were calm, but not cheerful, for it was my firm belief that, in all human probability, I should never see the familiar faces again, knowing well they would sell their lives dearly.

It was reported amongst my friends at home that, in order to escape from Mafeking, my maid and myself had ridden 200 miles. One newspaper extract was sent me which said, concerning this fictitious ride, that it "was all very well for Lady Sarah, who doubtless was accustomed to violent exercise, but we commiserate her poor maid." Their pity was wasted, for the departure of my German maid Metelka and myself took place prosaically in that most vile of all vehicles, a Cape cart. Six fine mules were harnessed to our conveyance, and our two small portmanteaus were strapped on behind. The *jehu* was a Cape boy, and, to complete the cortege, my white pony Dop brought up the rear, ridden by a Zulu called Vellum. This boy, formerly Dr. Jameson's servant, remained my faithful attendant during the siege; beneath his dusky skin beat a heart of gold, and to him I could safely have confided uncounted treasures.

As the daylight increased so did the wind in violence; it was blowing a perfect gale, and the dust and sand were blinding. We outspanned for breakfast twelve miles out, at the farm of a presumably loyal Dutchman; then on again, the wind by now having become a hurricane, aggravated by the intensely hot rays of a scorching sun. I have never experienced such a miserable drive, and I almost began to understand the feelings of people who commit suicide. However, the long day wore to a close, and at length we reached Setlagoli store and hotel, kept by a nice old Scotch couple, Mr. and Mrs. Fraser. The latter was most kind, and showed us two nice clean rooms. Here, anyway, I trusted to find a haven of rest.

This hope was of short duration, for Sergeant Matthews, in charge of the Mounted Police *depôt*, soon came and told me natives reported several hundred Boers at Kraipann, only ten miles away. He said they were lying in wait for the second armoured train, which was expected to pass to Mafeking that very night, carrying the howitzers so badly needed there, and some lyddite shells. The sergeant opined the Boers would probably come on here if victorious, and loot the store, and he added that such marauding bands were more to be feared than the disciplined ones under Cronje. He even suggested my leaving by moonlight that very night. The driver, however, was unwilling to move, and we were all so exhausted that I decided to risk it and remain, the faithful sergeant promising to send scouts out and warn us should the enemy be approaching. I was fully determined that, having left Mafeking, where I might have been of use, I would run no risks of capture or impertinence from the *burghers*, who would also certainly commandeer our cart, pony, and mules.

Then followed another endless night; the moon set at 1 a.m., and occasionally I was roused by the loud and continuous barking of the farm dogs. At four o'clock Vellum's dusky countenance peered into the room, which opened on to the *stoep*, as do nearly all the apartments of these hotels, to ask if the mules should be inspanned, for these natives were all in wholesale dread of the Boers. Hearing all was quiet, I told him to wait till the sergeant appeared. About an hour later I opened my door to have a look at the weather: the wind had dropped completely, the sky was cloudless, and a faint tinge of pink on the distant horizon denoted where the east lay. I was about to shut it again and dress, when a dull booming noise arrested my attention, then almost froze the blood in my veins. There was no mistaking the firing of big guns at no very great distance.

We are accustomed to such a sound when salutes are fired or on a field-day, but I assure those who have not had a like experience, that to hear the same in actual warfare, and to know that each detonation is dealing death and destruction to human beings and property, sends a shiver down the back akin to that produced by icy cold water. I counted four or five; then there it was again and again and again, till altogether I reckoned twenty shots, followed by impressive silence once more, so intense in the quiet peace of the morning landscape. On the farm, however, there was stir and bustle enough: alarmed natives gathered in a group, weird figures with blankets round their shoulders—for the air was exceedingly cold—all looking with straining eyes in the direction of Kraipann, from where the firing evidently came.

I soon joined the people, white and back, in front of the store, and before long a mounted *kaffir* rode wildly up, and proceeded, with many gesticulations, to impart information in his own tongue. His story took some time, but at last a farmer turned round and told me the engagement had been with the armoured train, as we anticipated, and that the latter had "fallen down" (as the *kaffir* expressed it) owing to the rails being pulled up. What had been the fate of its occupants he did not know, as he had left in terror when the big gun opened fire. Curiously enough, as I afterwards learnt, these shots were the first fired during the war.

Remembering the sergeant's warning, I decided to start at once for Mosita, twenty-five miles farther away from the border, leaving Vellum to bring on any further intelligence when the sergeant, who had been away all night watching the Boers, returned. We now traversed a fine open grassy country, very desolate, with no human habitation. The only signs of life were various fine "*pows*"[10] stalking sedately along, or "*korans*," starting up with their curious chuckle rather like the note of a pheasant, or a covey of guinea-fowl scurrying across the road and losing themselves in the waving grass. Meanwhile the driver kept up an incessant conversation with the mules, and I found myself listening to his varying epithets with stupefied curiosity.

During that four hours' drive we only met two natives and one huge herd of cattle, which were being driven by mounted *kaffirs*, armed with rifles, to Mosita, our destination, where it was hoped they would be out of the way of marauding Boers. At last we reached the native *stadt* of Mosita, where our appearance created great excitement. Crowds of swarthy men and youths rushed out to question our driver as to news. The latter waxed eloquent in words and gestures, imitating even the noise of the big gun, which seemed to produce great enthusiasm among these simple folk.

Their ruling passion, I afterwards found, was hatred and fear of the Boers, and their dearest wish to possess guns and ammunition to join the English in driving them back and to defend their cattle. In the distance we could see the glimmering blue waters of a huge dam, beyond which was the farm and homestead of a loyal colonial farmer named Keeley, whose hospitality I had been told to seek. Close by were the barracks, with seven or eight occupants, the same sort of *depôt* as at Setlagoli. I asked to see Mrs. Keeley, and boldly announced we had come to beg for a few nights' lodging. We were most warmly received and made welcome. The kindness of the Keeleys is a bright spot in my recollections of those dark weeks. Mrs. Keeley herself was in a dreadful state of anxiety, as she had that very day received a letter from her husband in Mafeking, whither he had proceeded on business, to say he found he must remain and help defend the town; his assistance was urgently needed there in obtaining information respecting the Boers from the natives, whose language he talked like his own. She had five small children, and was shortly expecting an addition to her family, so at last I had found someone who was more to be pitied than myself. She, on the other hand, told me our arrival was a godsend to her, as it

10. African wild turkeys.

took her thoughts off her troubles.

Affairs in the neighbourhood seemed in a strange confusion. Mr. Keeley was actually the *veldtcornet* of the district, an office which in times of peace corresponded to that of a magistrate. In reality he was shut up in Mafeking, siding against the Dutch. The surrounding country was peopled entirely, if sparsely, by Dutch farmers and natives, the former of whom at first and before our reverses professed sympathy with the English; but no wonder the poor wife looked to the future with dread, fearful lest British disasters would be followed by Boer reprisals.

Towards sunset Vellum appeared with a note from Sergeant Matthews. It ran as follows:

> The armoured train captured; its fifteen occupants all killed.[11]
> Boers opened fire on the train with field artillery.

In our isolation these words sank into our souls like lead, and were intensified by the fact that we had that very morning been so near the scene of the tragedy—"reverse" I would not allow it to be called, for fifteen men had tried conclusions with 400 Boers, and had been merely hopelessly outnumbered. The latter had, however, scored an initial success, and the intelligence cast a gloom, even where all was blackest night. Vellum brought a few more verbal details, to the effect that Sergeant Matthews had actually succeeded in stopping the armoured train after pursuing it on horseback for some way, expecting every moment to be taken for a Boer and fired on. He asked to speak to the officer in charge, and a young man put his head over the truck. Matthews then told him that several hundred Boers were awaiting the train, strongly entrenched, and that the metals were up for about three-quarters of a mile. "Is that all?" was the answer; then, turning to the engine-driver, "Go straight ahead." Here was a conspicuous instance of English foolhardy pluck.

The evening was a lovely one. I took a walk along the road by which we had come in the morning, and was soothed by the peaceful serenity of the surrounding country.

It seemed to be impossible that men were killing each other only a few short miles away. The herd of cattle we had passed came into view, and caught sight of the water in the dam. It was curious to see the whole herd, some five or six hundred beasts, break into a clumsy can-

---

11. This was incorrect. The officer in charge and two others were severely wounded, the driver and stoker killed by the explosion of the boiler.

ter, and, with a bellowing noise, dash helter-skelter to the water—big oxen with huge branching horns, meek-eyed cows, young bullocks, and tiny calves, all joining in the rush for a welcome drink after a long hot day on the *veldt*.

The last news that came in that evening was that all the wires were cut north and south of Mafeking, and the telegraphists fled, as their lives had been threatened.

CHAPTER 7

In a Rebellious Colony

The days are so long, and there are so many of them.
—Du Maurier.

During the weeks I remained at Mosita, the only book I had to read was *Trilby*, which I perused many times, and the lament of the heroine in the line quoted above seemed to re-echo my sentiments. For days and days we were absolutely without news. It is impossible after a lapse of time to realise exactly what that short sentence really means. I must ask my readers to remember that we talked and thought of one topic only; we looked incessantly in the one direction by which messengers might come. Our nerves were so strained that, did we but see one of the natives running across the yard, or hear them conversing in louder tones than usual, we at once thought there must be news, and jumped up from any occupation with which we were trying to beguile the time, only to sink back on our chairs again disappointed.

As for knowing what was passing in the world, one might as well have been in another planet. We saw no papers, and there was not much prospect of obtaining any. Before the war we had all talked lightly of wires being cut and railway-lines pulled up, but, in truth, I do not think anyone realised what these two calamities really meant. My only comfort was the reflection that, no matter how hard they were fighting in Mafeking, they could not be suffering the terrible boredom that we were enduring. To such an extent in this monotony did I lose the count of time, that I had to look in the *almanac* to be able to say, in Biblical language, "The evening and the morning were the sixth day."

At length one evening, when we were sitting on the *stoep* after supper, we descried a rider approaching on a very tired horse. Rushing to the gate, we were handed letters from Mafeking. It can be imagined how we devoured them. They told of three determined attacks on the town on the third day after I had left, all successfully repulsed, and of a bombardment on the following Monday. The latter had been somewhat of a farce, and had done no damage, except to one or two buildings which, by an irony of fate, included the Dutch church and hotel and the convent. The shells were of such poor quality that they were incapable of any explosive force whatever.[1] After nine hours' bombardment, although some narrow escapes were recorded, the only casualties were one chicken killed and one dog wounded. An emissary from Commandant Snyman had then come solemnly into the town under a flag of truce, to demand an unconditional surrender "to avoid further bloodshed."

Colonel Baden-Powell politely replied that, as far as he was concerned, operations had not begun. The messenger was given refreshment at Dixon's Hotel, where lunch was laid out as usual. This had astonished him considerably, as presumably he had expected to find but few survivors. He was then sent about his business. Gordon, who imagined me at Setlagoli, concluded his letter by saying the colonel had informed General Cronje of my presence at Mrs. Fraser's, and begged him to leave me unmolested. This news, which had come by a *Daily Mail* correspondent, on his way south to send off cables, was satisfactory as far as it went, and we at once despatched a trusty old nigger called Boaz with a tiny note, folded microscopically in an old cartridge-case, to give the garrison news of the surrounding country. This old man proved a reliable and successful messenger. On many occasions he penetrated the cordon into the beleaguered town, and during the first two months he was practically the sole means they had of receiving news. His task was of course a risky one, and we used to pay him £3 each way, but he never failed us.

Now commenced a fresh period of anxious waiting, and during this time I had leisure and opportunity to study the characteristics of these Boer farmers and their wives, and to learn what a curious race they are. Mrs. Keeley told me a great deal of their ideas, habits, and ways, in which low cunning is combined with extreme curiosity and naïve simplicity. Many of the fathers and sons in the neighbourhood had slunk off to fight across the border, sending meanwhile their wives and daughters to call on Mrs. Keeley and condole with her in what

---

1. The Boers used better ammunition later.

they termed "her trouble," and to ascertain at the same time all the circumstances of the farm and domestic circle.

A curious thing happened one day. Directly after breakfast an old *shandrydan* drove up with a typical Dutch family as occupants. Mrs. Keeley, busy with household matters, pulled a long face, knowing what was before her. No questions as to being at home, disengaged, or follies of that sort, were asked; the horses were solemnly outspanned and allowed to roam; the family party had come to spend the day. Seated gravely in the dining-room, they were refreshed by coffee and cold meat. Mrs. Keeley remarked to me privately that the best thing to do was to put quantities of food before them and then leave them; and, beyond a few passing words as she went in and out of the room, I did not make out that they went in for entertaining each other. So they sat for hours, saying nothing, doing nothing.

When Mrs. Keeley wanted me to have lunch, she asked them to remove to the *stoep*, and in this request they seemed to find nothing strange. Finally, about five o'clock they went away, much to the relief of their hostess; not, however, before the latter had shrewdly guessed the real object of their visit, which was to find out about myself. Report had reached them that Mafeking was in the hands of the Dutch, that the only survivor of the garrison had escaped in woman's clothes, had been wandering on the *veldt* for days, and had finally been taken in here.

"*Ach!*" said the old *vrow*, "I would be afraid to meet him. Is he really here?" This remark she made to Mrs. Keeley's brother, who could hardly conceal his amusement, but, to reassure her, displayed the cart and mules by which I had come. If in England we had heard of the arrival of a "unicorn" in an aeroplane, we should not have shown more anxiety or taken more trouble to hear about the strange creature than did they concerning myself. Their curiosity did not end here. What was Mr. Keeley doing in Mafeking? Was he fighting for the English? How many head of cattle had they on the farm? And so on *ad libitum*. Mrs. Keeley, however, knew her friends well, and was quite capable of dealing with them, so they probably spent an unprofitable day.

On another occasion an English farmer named Leipner looked in, and gave us some information about Vryburg. This town was absolutely undefended, and was occupied by the Boers without a shot being fired. The ceremony of the hoisting of the *Vierkleur*[2] had been attended by the whole countryside, and had taken place with much

---

2. Boer national flag.

psalm-singing and praying, interlarded with bragging and boasting. He told me also that some of the rumours current in the town, and firmly credited, reported that Oom Paul had annexed Bechuanaland, that he was then about to take Cape Colony, after which he would allow no troops to land, and the "*roineks*" would have been pushed into the sea. His next step would be to take England. Mr. Leipner assured me the more ignorant Boers had not an idea where England was situated, nor did they know that a great ocean rolled between it and this continent. In fact, they gloried in their want of knowledge, and were insulted if they received a letter in any tongue but their own. He related one tale to illustrate their ignorance: An old *burgher* and his *vrow* were sitting at home one Sunday afternoon. Seeing the "*predicant*"[3] coming, the old man hastily opened his Bible and began to read at random.

The clergyman came in, and, looking over his shoulder, said: "Ah! I see you are reading in the Holy Book—the death of Christ."

"*Alle machter!*" said the old lady. "Is He dead indeed? You see, Jan" (to her husband) "you never will buy a newspaper, so we never know what goes on in the world."

Mr. Leipner said this story loses in being told in English instead of in the original Dutch. He reiterated they did not wish for education for themselves or for their children. If the young people can read and write, they are considered very good scholars. This gentleman also expressed great satisfaction at Sir Alfred Milner and Mr. Chamberlain being at the head of affairs, which he said was the only thing that gave the colonials confidence. Even now, so many feared England would give way again in the end. I assured him of this there was no possibility, and then he said: "The Transvaal has been a bad place for Englishmen to live these many years; but if Great Britain fails us again, we must be off, for then it will be impossible." I was given to understand that the Boers exhibited great curiosity as to who Mr. Chamberlain was, and that they firmly believed he had made money in Rand mining shares and gold companies; others fancied he was identical with the maker of Chamberlain's Cough Syrup, which is advertised everywhere in the colony.

Early in November we had a great surprise. Mr. Keeley himself turned up from Mafeking, having been given leave from the town guard to look after his wife and farm. He had to ride for his life to escape the Boers, who were drawing much closer to the town, and the news he brought was not altogether reassuring. True, he stated that

3. Cleryman.

the garrison were in splendid spirits, and that they no longer troubled themselves about the daily bombardments, as dug-out shelters had been constructed. The young men, he said, vied with each other in begging for permission to join scouting-parties at night, to pepper the Boers, often, as a result, having a brush with the enemy and several casualties. All the same, they would return at a gallop, laughing and joking.

There had been, however, several very severe fights, notably one on Canon Kopje, where two very able officers and many men had been killed. In such a small garrison this loss was a serious one, and the death-roll was growing apace, for, besides the frequent attacks, the rifle fire in the streets was becoming very unpleasant. Intelligence was also to hand of the Boers bringing up one of the Pretoria siege guns, capable of firing a 94-pound shell. This was to be dragged across the Transvaal at a snail's pace by a team of twenty oxen, so secure were they against any interruption from the South. Against these depressing items, he gave intelligence of an incident that had greatly alarmed the Boers. It seemed that, to get rid of two trucks of dynamite standing in the railway-station, which were considered a danger, the same had been sent off to a siding some eight miles north. The engine-driver unhitched them and made good his escape.

The Boers, thinking the trucks full of soldiers, immediately commenced bombarding them, till they exploded with terrific force. This chance affair gave the Boers the idea that Mafeking was full of dynamite, and later, when I was in the *laager*, they told me one of the reasons why they had never pressed an attack home was that they knew the whole town was mined. Mr. Keeley also told us of a tragedy that had greatly disturbed the little circle of defenders. The very evening that the victims of the Canon Kopje fight were laid to rest, Lieutenant Murchison,[4] of the Protectorate Regiment, had, in consequence of a dispute, shot dead with his revolver at Dixon's Hotel the war-correspondent of the London *Daily Chronicle*, a Mr. Parslow.

I afterwards learnt that the court-martial which sat on the former had fourteen sessions in consequence of its only being able to delib-

---

4. Mr. Murchison was shut up in the gaol awaiting Lord Roberts's confirmation of his sentence. When Eloff succeeded in entering Mafeking many months later, the former was liberated with the other prisoners, and given a rifle to fire on the Boers, which he did with much effect. I believe he was afterwards taken to a gaol in the Isle of Wight, but I do not know if his life-sentence is still in force, (as at time of first publication).

erate for half an hour at a time in the evening, when the firing was practically over. The prisoner was ably defended by a Dutch lawyer named De Koch, and, owing to his having done good service during the siege, was strongly recommended to mercy, although sentenced to be shot. The most satisfactory points we gleaned were the splendid behaviour of the townspeople, and the fine stand made by the natives when the Boers attacked their *stadt*, adjacent to the town. The number of Boer field-guns Mr. Keeley stated to be nine, of the newest type, besides the monster expected from Pretoria. He also said more expert gunners and better ammunition had arrived. As to his own position, Mr. Keeley was by no means sure that either his life or his property were safe, but he relied on his influence with his neighbours, which was considerable, and he thought he would be able to keep them quiet and on their farms.

One night, just as my maid was going to bed, she suddenly saw, in the bright moonlight, a tall figure step out of the shadow of the fir-trees. For an instant a marauding Boer—a daily bugbear for weeks—flashed across her mind, but the next moment she recognized Sergeant Matthews from Setlagoli. He had ridden over post-haste to tell us the Boers were swarming there, and that he and his men had evacuated the barracks. He also warned us the same commando was coming here on the morrow, and advised that all the cattle on the farm should be driven to a place of safety. This information did not conduce to a peaceful night, but, anyway, it gave one something to think of besides Mafeking. I buried a small jewel-case and my despatch-box in the garden, and then we went calmly to bed to await these unwelcome visitors. Mr. Keeley had fortunately left the day before on a business visit to a neighbouring farmer, for his presence would rather have contributed to our danger than to our safety.

When we awoke all was peaceful, and there was every indication of a piping hot day. Mrs. Keeley was very calm and sensible, and did not anticipate any rudeness. We decided to receive the *burghers* civilly and offer them coffee, trusting that the exodus of all the cattle would not rouse their ire. Our elaborate preparations were wasted, for the Boers did not come. The weary hours dragged on, the sun crawled across the steely blue heavens, and finally sank, almost grudgingly, it seemed, into the west, leaving the coast clear for the glorious full moon; the stars came out one by one; the goats and kids came wandering back to the homestead with loud bleatings; and presently everything seemed to sleep—everything except our strained nerves and aching eyes, which

LADY SARAH WILSON

had looked all day for Boers, and above all for news, and had looked in vain.

We still continued to have alarms. One day we saw a horseman wrapped in a long cloak up to his chin, surmounted by a huge slouch hat, ride into the yard. Mrs. Keeley exclaimed it was certainly a Boer, and that he had no doubt come to arrest Mr. Keeley. I was positive the unknown was an Englishman, but she was so shrewd that I really believed her, and kept out of sight as she directed, while she sent her brother to question him. It turned out that the rider was the same *Daily Mail* correspondent who had cut his way out of Mafeking in order to send his cables, and that he was now on his way back to the besieged town. The growth of a two weeks' beard had given him such an unkempt appearance as to make even sharp Mrs. Keeley mistake him for a Boer. He had had an interesting if risky ride, which he appeared to have accomplished with energy and dash, if perhaps with some imprudence.[5]

It was the continued dearth of news, not only concerning Mafeking, but also of what was going on in the rest of South Africa, that made me at length endeavour to get news from Vryburg. As a first step I lent Dop to a young Dutchman named Brevel, who was anxious to go to that township to sell some fat cattle. This youth, who belonged to a respectable Boer family—of course heart and soul against the English—was overwhelmed with gratitude for the loan of the horse, and in consequence I stood high in their good graces. They little knew it was for my sake, not theirs, that they had my pony. By this messenger we sent letters for the English mail, and a note to the magistrate, begging him to forward us newspapers and any reliable intelligence. I also enclosed a cheque to be cashed, for I was running short of English gold wherewith to pay our nigger letter-carriers. I must confess I hardly expected to find anyone confiding enough to part with bullion, but Mr. Brevel duly returned in a few days with the money, and said they were very pleased to get rid of gold in exchange for a cheque on a London bank.

He also, however, brought back our letters, which had been refused at the post-office, as they would take no letters except with Transvaal stamps, and for ours, of course, we had used those of Cape Colony.

---

5. This gentleman on a later occasion again attempted to leave Mafeking on horseback, and was taken prisoner by the Boers and sent to Pretoria, leaving the *Daily Mail* without a correspondent in Mafeking. At the request of that paper I then undertook to send them cables about the siege.

The magistrate wrote me a miserable letter, saying his office had been seized by the Boers, who held a daily Kriegsraad there, and that he had received a safe-conduct to depart. The striking part of the communication was that a line had been put through "On H.M. Service" on the top of the official envelope. I was really glad to find the young man had done no good with his own business, having failed to dispose of any of his cattle. He, a Dutchman, had returned with the feeling that no property was safe for the moment, and much alarmed by the irresponsible talk of those *burghers* who had nothing to lose and everything to gain by this period of confusion and upheaval. He also greatly disturbed Mr. Keeley by saying they meant to wreak vengeance on any who had fought for the English, and by warning him that a commando would surely pass his way.

Further news which this young man proceeded to relate in his awful jargon was that Oom Paul and all his grandchildren and nephews had gone to Bulawayo; from there he meant to commence a triumphal march southward; that Kimberley had capitulated; and that Joubert and his army had taken possession of Ladysmith. To all this Mrs. Keeley had to listen with polite attention. Luckily, I did not understand the import of what he said till he had taken himself off, with an unusually deep bow of thanks to myself. The only comfort we derived was the reflection that these lies were too audacious to be aught but inventions made up to clinch the wavering and timid spirits.

No matter how miserable people in England were then, they will never realise fully what it meant to pass those black months in the midst of a Dutch population; one felt oneself indeed alone amongst foes. Smarting under irritation and annoyance, I decided to go myself to Vryburg—Dutch town though it had become—and see if I could not ascertain the truth of these various reports, which I feared might filter into Mafeking and depress the garrison. Mr. Keeley did not disapprove of my trip, as he was as anxious as myself to know how the land lay, and he arranged that Mrs. Keeley's brother, Mr. Coleman, should drive me there in a trap and pair of ponies.

For the benefit of the gossips, I stated as an ostensible reason for my visit that I had toothache. I was much excited at the prospect of visiting the Boer headquarters in that part of the country, and seeing with my own eyes the Transvaal flag flying in the town of a British colony. Therefore I thought nothing of undertaking a sixty miles' drive in broiling heat and along a villainous road. The drive itself was utterly uneventful. We passed several Dutch farmhouses, many of them untenanted, owing to the so-called loyal colonial owners having flocked to the Transvaal flag at Vryburg. All these houses, distinguished by their slovenly and miserable appearance, were built of rough brick or mud, with tiny windows apparently added as an afterthought, in any position, regardless of symmetry. Towards sundown we arrived at a roadside store, where we were kindly entertained for the night by the proprietors, a respectable Jewish couple.

About five miles from Vryburg a party of thirty horsemen appeared on the brow of the hill; these were the first Boers I had seen mounted, in fighting array, and I made sure they would ride up and ask our business; but apparently we were not interesting enough in appearance, for they circled away in another direction. The road now descended into a sort of basin or hollow, wherein lay the snug little town of Vryburg, with its neat houses and waving trees, and beyond it we could see the white tents of the Boer *laager*. A young Dutchman had recently described Vryburg to me as a town which looked as if it had gone for a walk and got lost, and as we drove up to it I remembered his words, and saw that his simile was rather an apt one.

There seemed no reason, beyond its site in a sheltered basin, why Vryburg should have been chosen for the capital of British Bechuanaland. The railway was at least a mile away on the east, and so hidden was the town that, till you were close on it, you could barely see the roofs of the houses. Then suddenly the carriage drove into the main street, which boasted of some quite respectable shops. The first thing that attracted our notice was the Court House, almost hidden in trees, through which glimmered the folds of the gaudy Dutch standard. Before the court were armed Boers, apparently sentries, whilst others were passing in and out or lounging outside. Another group were busy poring over a notice affixed on a tree, which we were told was the latest war news:

War News
Latest Reports
Price 3d.
Vryburg, Oct. 31, 1899
Mafeking Speechless With Terror
Kimberley Trembles
40 English Soldiers Desert to Join Our Ranks

It appears by telegram received this morning that the *burghers* started firing on Mafeking with the big cannon. The town is on fire and is full of smoke.

The British troops in Natal met the *burghers* at Elandslaagte. The battlefield was kept by the *burghers* under General Prinsloo. Two were killed, four wounded.

We drove down the street, and pulled up at the Central Hotel, where I got capital rooms and was most civilly received by the manager, an Englishman. The latter, however, could hardly conceal his surprise at my visit at this moment. He at once advised me not to mention my name, or show myself too much, as that very day a new *Landrost* had arrived to take charge of the town, and strict regulations respecting the coming and going of the inhabitants and visitors were being made. He then gave me some splendid news of the Natal border, the first intelligence of the victories of Dundee, Elandslaagte, and Glencoe. To hear of those alone was worth the long drive, and he also showed me the Dutch reports of these same engagements, which really made one smile. On every occasion victory had remained with the *burghers*, while the English dead and prisoners varied in numbers from 500 to 1,300, according to the mood of the composer of the despatch.

The greatest losses the *burghers* had sustained up to then in any one engagement were two killed and three wounded. The spoils of war taken by the Dutch were of extraordinary value, and apparently they had but to show themselves for every camp to be evacuated. They were kind enough to translate these wonderful despatches into a sort of primitive English, of which printed slips could be bought for threepence. The hotel manager said if they did not invent these lies and cook the real account the *burghers* would desert *en masse*. So afraid were their leaders of news filtering in from English sources that all messengers were closely watched and searched. In the afternoon I drove up to the little hospital to see three of the occupants of the ill-fated armoured train. They were all convalescent, and said they were being very kindly treated in every way, but that the Boer doctoring was of the roughest description, the surgeon's only assistant being a chemist-boy, and trained nurses were replaced by a few well-meaning but clumsy Dutch girls, while chloroform or sedatives were quite unknown.

It was grievous to hear of all the government military provisions, police and private properties, being carted off by the "powers that be," and not a little annoying for the inhabitants to have to put all their stores at the disposal of the *burghers*, who had been literally clothed from head to foot since their arrival. The owners only received a "brief" or note of credit on the Transvaal Government at Pretoria, to be paid after the war. For fear of exciting curiosity, I did not walk about much, but observed from the windows of my sitting-room the mounted *burghers* patrolling the town, sometimes at a foot's pace, more often at a smart canter. I felt I never wished to see another Boer. I admitted to myself they sat their horses well and that their rifle seemed a familiar friend, but when you have seen one you have seen them all. I never could have imagined so many men absolutely alike: all had long straggling beards, old felt hats, shabby clothes, and some evil-looking countenances. Most of those I saw were men of from forty to fifty years of age, but there were also a few sickly-looking youths, who certainly did not look bold warriors. These had not arrived at the dignity of a beard, but, instead, cultivated feeble whiskers.

After I had seen and heard all I could, came the question of getting away. The manager told me the *Landrost* had now forbidden any of the residents to leave the town, and that he did not think I could get a pass. However, my Dutch friend was equal to the occasion; he applied for leave to return to his farm with his sister, having only come in for provisions. After a long hesitation it was given him, and we decided to set out at daybreak, fearful lest the permission might be retracted, as it certainly would have been had my identity and his deception been discovered, and we should both have been ignominiously lodged in a Boer gaol. As the sun was rising we left Vryburg. On the outskirts of the town we were made to halt by eight or ten Boers whose duty it was to examine the passes of travellers. It can be imagined how my heart beat as I was made to descend from the cart. I was wearing a shabby old ulster which had been lent me at the hotel for this purpose; round a battered sailor hat I had wound a woollen shawl, which with the help of a veil almost completely concealed my identity. It had been arranged that Mr. Coleman should tell them I was suffering from toothache and swollen face. The ordeal of questioning my supposed brother and examining our passports took some minutes—the longest I have ever experienced. He contrived to satisfy these inquisitors, and with a feeling of relief we bundled into the cart again and started on our long drive to Mosita. On that occasion we accomplished the sixty miles in one day, so afraid were we of being pursued.

On my return to Mosita I at once despatched old Boaz to Mafeking, giving them the intelligence of the victories in Natal. This proved to be the first news that reached them from the more important theatre of the war. Our life now became uneventful once more. One day an old Irish lady, wife of a neighbouring farmer, dropped in for a chat. She was a nice old woman, as true as steel, and terribly worried by these dreadful times. She had a married daughter in the Transvaal, and a brother also, whose sons, as well as daughters' husbands, would, she sorely feared, be commandeered to fight, in which case they might unknowingly be shooting their own relations over the border. It was the same tale of misery, anxiety, and wretchedness, everywhere, and the war was but a few weeks old.

The population in that colony, whether Dutch or English, were so closely mixed together—their real interests so parallel—that it resolved itself locally into a veritable civil war. It was all the more dreadful that these poor farmers, after having lost all their cattle by *rinderpest*, had just succeeded in getting together fresh herds, and were hoping for renewed prosperity. Then came the almost certain chance of their beasts being raided, of their stores being looted, and of their women and children having to seek shelter to avoid rough treatment and incivility. Often during the long evenings, especially when I was suffering from depression of spirits, I used to argue with Mr. Keeley about the war and whether it was necessary. It seemed to me then we were not justified in letting loose such a millstream of wretchedness and of destruction, and that the alleged wrongs of a large white population—who, in spite of everything, seemed to prosper and grow rich apace—scarcely justified the sufferings of thousands of innocent individuals.

Mr. Keeley was a typical old colonist, one who knew the Boers and their character well, and I merely quote what he said, as no doubt it was, and is, the opinion of many other such men. He opined that this struggle was bound to come, declaring that all the thinking men of the country had foreseen it. The intolerance of the Boers, their arrogance, their ignorance, on which they prided themselves, all proclaimed them as unfit to rule over white or black people. Of late years had crept in an element of treachery and disloyalty, emanating from their jealousy of the English, which by degrees was bound to permeate the whole country, spreading southward to Cape Colony itself, till the idea of "Africa for the Dutch, and the English in the sea," would have been a war-cry that might have dazzled hundreds of today's so-called loyal colonists. He even asserted that those at the head of affairs in England had shown great perspicacity and a clear insight into the future.

If at the Bloemfontein Conference, or after, Kruger had given the five years' franchise, and the dispute had been patched up for the moment, it would have been the greatest misfortune that could have happened. The intriguing in the colony, the reckless expenditure of the Transvaal Secret Service money, the bribery and corruption of the most corrupt Government of modern times, would have gone on as before, and things would soon have been as bad as ever. Mr. Keeley was positive that it was jealousy that had engendered this race hatred one heard so much about; even the well-to-do Dutch knew the English were superior to them in knowledge and enterprise.

At the same time any English invention was looked upon with awe and interest; they were wont to copy us in many respects, and if a Dutch girl had the chance of marrying an Englishman, old or young, poor or rich, she did not wait to be asked a second time. There is no doubt the women were a powerful factor in Boerland. Even a British-er married to a Dutchwoman seemed at once to consider her people as his people, and the Transvaal as his fatherland. These women were certainly the most bitter against the English; they urged their husbands in the district to go and join the commandoes, and their language was cruel and bloodthirsty.

★★★★★★

Towards the middle of November I decided that I could not remain in my present quarters much longer. My presence was attracting unwelcome attention to my kind host and hostess, albeit they would not admit it. From the report that I was a man dressed as a woman, the rumour had now changed to the effect that I was a granddaughter of Queen Victoria, sent specially out by Her Majesty to inform her of the proceedings of her rebellious subjects. Another person had heard I was the wife of the general who was giving the Boers so much trouble at Mafeking. I determined, therefore, to return to Mrs. Fraser's hotel, which was always a stage nearer Mafeking, whither I was anxious to return eventually. As a matter of fact, there was no alternative resting-place. It was impossible to pass south to Kimberley, to the west lay the Kalahari Desert, and to the east the Transvaal.

With many grateful thanks to the Keeleys, I rode off one morning, with Vellum in attendance, to Setlagoli, which I had left a month before. We thought it prudent to make sure there were no Boers about before bringing the government mules and cart. Therefore I arranged for my maid to follow in this vehicle if she heard nothing to the contrary within twenty-four hours. Mrs. Fraser was delighted to see me, and reported the Boers all departed after a temporary occupation, so there I settled down for another period of weary waiting.

CHAPTER 8

Betrayed by a Pigeon

For a bird of the air shall carry the voice, and that which has wings shall tell the matter.
　　　　　—Eccles. x. 20.

The day after my arrival at Setlagoli some natives came in with apparently well-authenticated news of an English victory near Vryburg. They also asserted that the line was already being relaid to Maribogo, and that the railway servants had returned to that station. I drove over at once to prove the truth of their statements; of course, I found they were all false, except the fact of the station-master having returned to the barricaded and desolate station. I discovered him sitting disconsolately at the door of his ruined house, gloomily perusing *Nicholas Nickleby*. On returning home, I was delighted to find interesting letters from Mr. and Mrs. Rochfort Maguire, who were shut up in Kimberley, as was also Mr. Rhodes. The latter had despatched them by a boy, ordered to continue his journey to Mafeking with other missives and also with some colonial newspapers.

These latter, only about a fortnight old, we fairly spelled through before sending them on. They were already so mutilated by constant unfolding that in parts they were scarcely decipherable, but none the less very precious. Two days later arrived a representative of Reuter's Agency, whom I shall call Mr. P. He had come by rail and horseback straight from Cape Town and he was also under orders to proceed to Mafeking; but his horses were so done up that he decided to give them a few days' rest. I took advantage of his escort to carry out a long-cherished desire to see the wreck of the armoured train at Kraipann. Accompanied by a boy to show us the way, we started after an early lunch

As it was a Sunday, there was not much fear of our meeting any Boers, as the latter were always engaged that day in psalm-singing and devotions. We cantered gaily along, passing many *kaffir* huts, outside of which were grouped wondering natives, in their Sunday best. These kept up a lively conversation with our guide as long as we remained within earshot. I was always impressed with the freemasonry that existed in that country among the blacks. Everywhere they found acquaintances, and very often relations. They used to tell me that such and such a man was their wife's cousin or their aunt's brother. Moreover, as long as you were accompanied by a native, you were always sure of certain information concerning the whereabouts of the Boers; but to these latter they would lie with stupid, solemn faces. When we neared Kraipann, we came to a region of rocks and *kopjes*, truly a Godforsaken country. Leaving our horses in the native *stadt*, we proceeded on foot to the scene of the disaster. There was not much to see, after all—merely a pilot armoured engine, firmly embedded its whole length in the gravel.

Next to this, an ordinary locomotive, still on the rails, riddled on one side with bullets, and on the other displaying a gaping aperture into the boiler, which told its own tale. Then came an armoured truck—H.M.'s *Mosquito*—that I had seen leaving Mafeking so trim and smart, but now battered with shot; and lastly another truck, which had been carrying the guns. This had been pushed back into a culvert, and presented a dilapidated appearance, with its front wheels in the air. The whole spectacle was forlorn and eerie. All the time I gave cursory glances right and left, to make sure no Boers were prowling about, and I should not have been surprised to have seen an unkempt head bob up and ask us our business. But all remained as silent as the grave. Swarms of locusts were alone in possession, and under the engine and carriages the earth was a dark brown moving mass, with the stream of these jumping, creeping things. I had soon gratified my curiosity, and persuaded my companion, who was busy photographing, also to leave this desolate spot.

The Boers continued to ride roughshod over the land, commandeering oxen and cattle, putting up to public auction such government properties as they had seized at the different railway-stations, and employing hundreds of *kaffirs* to tear up the railway-line. Our enemies were perfectly secure in the knowledge that no help could come for months, and the greater number believed it would never come at all, and that the "*roineks*" were being cut to pieces in the South. They openly stated there would be no more railway traffic, but that in future trade and transit would be carried on by transport riding—*i.e.*, by ox-waggon, their favourite amusement and occupation. In the meantime the cry of the loyal colonists went up from all sides: "How much longer can it last?"

After a few days Mr. P. duly returned from Mafeking, having had a risky but successful trip in and out of the town. He reported it all well, and that the inhabitants were leading a mole existence, owing to the constant shelling. The Boers evidently preferred dropping in shells at a safe distance to risking their lives by a storming attack. With great pride Mr. P. showed me a basket of carrier pigeons, by which he assured me I could now communicate swiftly and safely with the garrison. He was even kind enough to send off one at once on a trial trip, with a short note signed with his name, informing Colonel Baden-Powell that I was at Setlagoli, and that I would be able to forward any letters or information they might wish to send. I had never had any experience of such birds, and was delighted to think how much quicker they would travel than old Boaz.

When the pigeon was released, however, I must confess it was rather disturbing to note that it did not seem at all sure of the direction it should take, circling round at least twenty times in the air. However, Mr. P. assured me this was their usual habit, and that this particular bird knew its business, having taken several prizes; so, as it eventually disappeared, I thought no more about it. The next day Mr. P. left for Cape Town, and passed out of our ken, but we were soon to be reminded of him in an unpleasant fashion.

On going into the dining-room to lunch one day, I saw little Mr.———, a kinsman of Mrs. Fraser's, and particularly short of stature, with an axe in hand, in the act of taking up the boards in a corner of the room, revealing as he did so a sort of shallow cellar, with no light or ventilation. Watching the operation was another man, an Englishman, the dispossessed manager of a local store, who had sought a temporary lodging at the hotel, and was a big, strong individual, over 6 feet in height. I inquired in amazement, of this strangely assorted pair, what they were trying to do. "We are going to hide, Lady Sarah," chirped the former. "The Boers are on the premises." So saying, he was about to descend into the cavity, and evidently expected the companionship of his tall friend.

When I pointed out to them that they would probably suffocate in this modern Black Hole of Calcutta, the little man proceeded to dance round the room, still shouldering his axe, jibbering the while: "I will not go to fight; I am an American. I will not be put in the front rank to be shot by the English, or made to dig trenches." The whole scene was so comic that I sat down and laughed, and the climax was reached when the cock-sparrow, who had always talked so big of what he was going to do and to say to the Boers, crawled under the old grand piano in the farther corner of the big room. I was forced to tell him that no American or Englishman could be found in such an igno-minious position, should the house be searched, and I even assured the little gentleman that I did not think it was the least likely his services would be wanted.

The other man, whose position was more risky, I advised to lie down on the sofa and feign illness; and I really believe anxiety and worry had so preyed on him that he was as ill as he looked. When calm had been restored, I sat down to lunch, Mrs. Fraser coming in at intervals to report what our visitors were doing at the store. They had demanded coffee and many tins of salmon and sardines. Of these delicacies they seemed particularly fond, eating the latter with their fingers, after which they drank the oil, mixed for choice with golden syrup. After their repast they fitted themselves out in clothes and luxu-ries, such as silver watches and chains, white silk pocket-handkerchiefs, cigarettes, saddles, and even harness, taking altogether goods to the amount of about £50.

This amusement finished, they proceeded to practise shooting, set-ting up bottles at a distance of about 50 yards. We followed all their doings from behind the green Venetian blinds, kept down on account of the heat. Up to this time none of them had come up to the house, for which we had reason to be grateful, as the "*dop*" they had found, and quickly finished, was beginning to affect their demeanour and spirits, particularly of the one named Dietrich, who appeared to be the boss of the party. At last the immediate reason for their visit fil-tered out. This slightly intoxicated gentleman inquired of Mr. Fraser where they could find a man named Mr. P. and the English lady of whom he had written. The old gentleman, who could be more than common deaf when he chose, affected utter vacancy at the mention of these individuals, merely stating that he knew a man of the name of P. fifteen years ago.

Then the whole story was told. They had captured our pigeon, with its tell-tale note. This confiding bird had flown straight to the *laager*, had perched on the general's house, where it had been shot by this same Dietrich, and we owed the present visit to the information supplied therein by Mr. P., Dietrich informing us he attributed this occurrence to the Almighty working for the Boers. They stated they were now awaiting the arrival of the *veldtcornet* and of Mr. Lamb, a neighbouring farmer, whom they had sent for, and they proceeded to make their preparations to spend the night. After supper we were relieved to hear Mr. Lamb's cheerful voice, as he rode up in the dark with the jovial Dietrich, who had ridden out to meet him, and who, it appeared, was an old friend of his. I must say the pleasure of meeting was more on the Dutchman's side than on the Englishman's.

By this time the former was quite intoxicated, and Mr. Lamb cleverly managed to get him to his room, and after having, as he thought, disposed of him, he came and joined us on the *stoep*. There we freely discussed our visitors, and were having a cheery conversation, when I suddenly looked up, and round the corner of the verandah saw the unsteady form of a typical Boer—slouch hat, *bandolier*, and rifle, complete—staggering towards us, truly a weird apparition. The rising moon shining on the rifle-barrel made it glitter like silver. I confess I disappeared round the corner to my room with more haste than dignity. To Boers by daytime, when sober, I had by now become accustomed, but at night, after liberal doses of "*dop*," armed with a loaded rifle, I preferred their room to their company.

Luckily, Mr. Lamb was equal to the occasion, and persuaded Dietrich to return to his quarters, in spite of his assurance that he (Dietrich) "was the man who watched, and who did not sleep." With the morning arrived nine or ten more, including the newly-appointed *veldtcornet*, by name De Koker, who had been lately convicted of sheep-stealing. After a long idle morning and more refreshments, they all adjourned to the living-room, where, with much difficulty, one of them stumbled through the reading of a printed proclamation, which enacted that:

This country now being part of the Transvaal, the residents must within seven days leave their homes or enrol themselves as *burghers*.

Nothing was mentioned about fighting, so all there complied with what was required—namely, to sign their names on a blank sheet of paper. By evening all had left for Mosita, as Mr. P. had also mentioned Mr. Keeley's name in his unlucky note. Three, however, remained to keep a watch on myself, and one of these, I regretted to observe, was the jovially-inclined Dietrich. It can be imagined that our irritation with Mr. P. was great for having so foolishly mentioned names and places, and still more with the idiotic bird, the real origin of a very unpleasant two days. I reflected that, if these were the tricks carrier-pigeons were wont to play, I greatly preferred the old nigger as a letter-carrier in wartime.

We were not to wait long for more developments. Next day at dusk arrived a large cavalcade, which included Mr. Keeley, a prisoner. He went on with his escort at daybreak, leaving us full of sympathy for his poor wife. I sent by his bodyguard, under the command of another Dietrich, brother to the drunkard, who seemed a decent sort of man, a letter to General Snyman, begging for a pass into Mafeking to rejoin my husband. Mr. Keeley told me their Intelligence Department was very perfect, as they had been aware of every one of my movements since I left Mafeking, and even of my rides during the last fortnight. He also told me General Cronje and a great number of Boers had left Mafeking and trekked South. This encouraged me in my belief that it would be better for me to be in that beleaguered town than to submit to the possible insults of Boer sentinels at Setlagoli.

The next day was Sunday, and in the morning returned the energetic *Veldtcornet* De Koker. He had heard of my letter to Snyman, and, wishing to be important, had come to offer me a pass to the *laager* for a personal interview with the general, assuring me the latter was always very polite to ladies. He even wished to escort me there that very day. However, I had no mind to act hastily, so I made an excuse of the mules being away—also that I did not like to travel on a Sunday. This latter reason he fully appreciated, and arranged with me to come to his house the following day, for which purpose he left me a permit, vilely scrawled in Dutch. I mentally reserved to myself the decision as to keeping the rendezvous.

We sat down to breakfast together, although, as he could speak no English and I could speak no Dutch, the conversation was nil. He was pleased with the cigarette I offered him, and observed me with some curiosity, probably never having seen anything approaching an English lady previously. Before he left, I complained, through an interpreter, of the insobriety of my self-constituted sentinel Dietrich, remarking it was quite impossible I could stand such a man dogging my footsteps much longer. He promised to report the matter, and insisted on shaking hands with great cordiality.

It was fortunate I had not accompanied De Koker, for that very evening back came Mr. Keeley, who had luckily succeeded in satisfying the suspicions of General Snyman, and who had received a permit to reside on his farm during the war. He brought me a letter in Dutch from the same authority, refusing, "owing to the disturbed state of the country," to give me a pass to Mafeking, and requesting me to remain where I was, under the "surveillance of his *burghers*."

It was exactly the surveillance of one of his said *burghers* I wished to avoid; but there seemed no possibility of getting rid of Dietrich, who evidently preferred his comfortable quarters at the hotel to roughing it in the *laager*. I was exceedingly disappointed, and also somewhat indignant with Mr. Keeley, who firmly believed, and was much cast down by, some telegrams he had read out in the *laager*, relating the utter defeat of 15,000 English at the Modder River;[1] 1,500 Boers, he stated, had surrounded this force, of which they had killed 2,000. I stoutly refused to credit it till I had seen it in an English despatch. But all this was enough to subdue the bravest spirit; we had received practically nothing but Dutch information during the last six weeks, telling of their successes and English disasters; we had seen nobody but our enemies.

Even if one did not allow oneself to believe their tales, there was always a sort of uncomfortable feeling that these must contain some element of truth. Fortunately, however, I was reading an account of the Franco-German War in 1870, and there I found that the same system of inventing successes was carried on by the French press right up to, and even after, the emperor's capitulation at Sedan. So it was comforting to think that, if it had been necessary to keep up the spirits of paid and regular soldiers, it must be a thousand times more essential for the Transvaal authorities to do so, as regards their unpaid mixed army, who had no encouragement to fight but knowledge of successes and hopes of future loot. All the same, it was a great trial of patience.

---

1. This news must have been a garbled account of the fighting with Lord Methuen's column.

CHAPTER 9

How I was Made a Prisoner

Ah, there, Piet! be'ind 'is stony kop,
With'is Boer bread an' biltong, an' 'is flask of awful dop;
'Is mauser for amusement an' 'is pony for retreat,
I've known a lot o' fellers shoot a dam' sight worse than Piet.
                                                        —Kipling.

Provisions at Setlagoli and in the surrounding districts were now fast running out, and Mrs. Fraser announced to me one morning she had only full allowance of meal for another week. In that colony no meal meant no bread, and it was, in fact, the most important factor in the housewife's mind when thinking of supplies. While on this subject, I must remark what very excellent bread is that made by the Dutch; no matter how poor or dilapidated the farmhouses, large loaves of beautiful, slightly browned bread are always in evidence, baked by the mother or daughters. The non-existence of the railway was beginning to cause much distress, Dutch and English suffering alike. In fact, if it had not been for the locusts, unusually numerous that year, and always a favourite food with the natives, these latter would also have been starving.

As every mouth to feed was a consideration, I determined to see if I could personally induce the Boer general to pass me into Mafeking. Under Mrs. Fraser's charge I left my maid, as I did not wish to expose her to any hardships in the laager; and to her I gave the custody of my pony Dop, to whom I had become much attached. After detaining me a prisoner, the Boers returned to Setlagoli specially to secure this animal; they had heard the natives speak of her in terms of high appreciation, and describe her as "not a horse, but lightning." Metelka, with much spirit, declared the pony to be her property, having been given her, she said, in lieu of wages. She further stated she was a German subject, and that if her horse were not returned in three days she should write to the *Kaiser*. All this was repeated to General Snyman by the awestruck *veldtcornet*. After a week spent with the Boers, Dop arrived back at Setlagoli, carefully led, as if she were a sacred beast, and bringing a humble letter of apology from the commandant.

But I am anticipating, and must return to my solitary drive to the *laager*, accompanied only by Vellum and another black boy. I took the precaution of despatching a nigger with a note to Mafeking, telling Colonel Baden-Powell of my plan, and that, having heard a Dutch woman called Mrs. Delpoort, in Mafeking, wished to join her friends in the Transvaal, I intended asking General Snyman to exchange me for her. The distance we had to drive was forty-five miles, along villainous sandy roads and under a burning African sun. We outspanned for the second time at the house of De Koker, who had been the first to advise me to visit the *laager*. His dwelling was situated close to the railway-line, or, rather, to where the railway-line had been. Here there was a great stir and bustle; men were hurrying in and out, nearly all armed; horses were tethered before the door; and, on hearing my cart drive up, the *veldtcornet* himself came out to meet me, and gravely invited me to descend.

I now saw the interior of a typical Dutch house, with the family at home. The *vrow* came forward with hand outstretched in the awkward Boer fashion. The Dutch do not shake hands; they simply extend a wooden member, which you clasp, and the greeting is over. I had to go through this performance in perfect silence with about seven or eight children of various ages, a grown-up daughter, and eight or ten men, most of whom followed us into the poky little room which appeared to serve as a living-room for the whole family. Although past ten o'clock, the remains of breakfast were still on the table, and were not appetizing to look at. We sat down on chairs placed in a circle, the whole party commencing to chatter volubly, and scarcely a word being intelligible to me. Presently the *vrow* brought me a cup of coffee in a cracked cup and saucer.

Not wishing to give offence, I tried to swallow it; the coffee was not bad, if one could only have dissociated it from that dreadful breakfast-table. I then produced some cigarettes, and offered them to the male element. They were enchanted, laid aside their pipes, and conversed with more animation than ever; but it was only occasionally that I caught a word I could understand; the sentence "twee tozen

Engelman dood"[1] recurred with distressing frequency, and enabled me to grasp their conversation was entirely about the war. I meanwhile studied the room and its furniture, which was of the poorest description; the chairs mostly lacked legs or backs, and the floor was of mud, which perhaps was just as well, as they all spat on it in the intervals of talk, and emptied on to it the remains of whatever they were drinking.

After a short time a black girl came in with a basin of water, with which she proceeded to plentifully sprinkle the floor, utterly disregarding our dresses and feet. Seeing all the women tuck their feet under their knees, I followed their example, until this improvised water-cart had finished its work. The grown-up daughter had a baby in her arms, as uncared for as the other children, all of whom looked as if soap and water never came their way. The men were fine, strong-looking individuals, and all were very affable to me, or meant to be so, if I could but have understood them. Finally four or five more women came into this tiny overcrowded room, evidently visitors. This was the finishing stroke, and I decided that, rested or not, the mules must be inspanned, that I might leave this depressing house. One of the young *burghers* brought me the pass to General Snyman, the calligraphy of which he was evidently very proud of; and having taken leave of all the ladies and men in the same peculiar stiff manner as that in which I had greeted them, I drove off, devoutly thankful to be so far on my journey.

About four in the afternoon we came to a rise, and, looking over it, saw the white roofs of Mafeking lying about five miles away in the glaring sunlight. Then we arrived at the spot where General Cronje's *laager* had been before he trekked South, marked by the grass being worn away for nearly a square mile, by broken-down waggons, and by sundry *aas-vogels* (the scavengers of South Africa) hovering over carcasses of horses or cattle. Mafeking was now only three miles distant, and, seeing not a solitary soul on the flat grass plains, I felt very much tempted to drive in to the native *stadt*; but the black boys resolutely declined to attempt it, as they feared being shot, and they assured me that many Boer sharpshooters lay hidden in the scrub. Thinking discretion the better part of valour, I regretfully turned away from Mafeking by the road leading up an incline to the *laager*, still several miles distant.

The cart was suddenly brought to a standstill by almost driving into a Boer outpost, crouched under a ruined wall, from which point of vantage they were firing with their rifles at the advance trenches

---

1. Two thousand Englishmen dead.

92

of the town. The officer in charge of this party told me I must stay here till sundown, when he and his men would accompany me to headquarters, as he averred the road I was now pursuing was not safe from the Mafeking gun-range. I therefore waited their good pleasure for an hour, during which time the firing from all round the town went on in a desultory sort of way, occasionally followed by a boom from a large Boer gun, and the short, sharp, hammering noise from the enemy's one-pounder Maxim.

The sun was almost down when the *burgher* in charge gave the signal to bring up their horses, and in a few minutes we were under way. This time I was attended by a bodyguard of about eighteen or twenty *burghers*, and we went along, much to my annoyance, at a funereal pace. On our way we met the relieving guard coming out to take the place just evacuated by my escort. When seen riding thus more or less in ranks, a Boer squadron, composed of picked men for outpost duty, presented really a formidable appearance. The men were mostly of middle age, all with the inevitable grizzly beard, and their rifles, gripped familiarly, were resting on the saddle-bow; nearly all had two *bandoliers* apiece, which gave them the appearance of being armed to the teeth—a more determined-looking band cannot be imagined. The horses of these *burghers* were well bred and in good condition, and, although their clothes were threadbare, they seemed cheerful enough, smoking their pipes and cracking their jokes.

When we at last drew up at headquarters, I was fairly startled to find what an excitement my appearance created, about two or three hundred Boers swarming up from all over the *laager*, and surrounding the cart. The general was then accommodated in a deserted farmhouse, and from this building at last issued his secretary, a gentleman who spoke English perfectly, and to whom I handed my letter requesting an interview. After an interminable wait among the gaping crowd, the aforementioned gentleman returned, and informed me I could see the general at once. He literally had to make a way for me from the cart to the house, but I must admit the *burghers* were very civil, nearly all of them taking off their hats as I passed through them.

Once inside the house, I found myself in a low, dark room, and in the farthest corner, seated on a bench, were two old gentlemen, with extra long beards, who were introduced to me as General Snyman and Commandant Botha.[2] I was at once struck by the anything but affable expression of their countenances. They motioned to me

2. Not to be confounded with General Louis Botha.

General Snyman and Commandant Botha

to take a chair; someone handed me a bowl with a brown mixture—presumably coffee—which I found very embarrassing to hold during our conversation. This was carried on through the secretary, and the general got more and more out of temper as he discovered what my request was. I informed him I had come at the suggestion of his *veldt-cornet*; that all my relations were in England, except my husband, who was in Mafeking; that there was no meal in the colony where I had been living; and that I was prepared to ask Colonel Baden-Powell to exchange me for a Dutch lady whom I heard wished to leave, if he (General Snyman) would accept the exchange. He promptly and with much decision refused.

Then it occurred to me this old gentleman meant to keep me as a prisoner of war, and my heart sank into my shoes. The only concession I could obtain was that he would consider my case, and in the meantime he ordered that I should be accommodated in the field hospital. Accompanied by the secretary, and leaving the staring crowd behind, I drove off to a little house, about half a mile away, where we found our destination. I was shown into a tiny room, smelling strongly of disinfectants, which from the large centre-table I at once recognized as the operating-room, and here I was told I could sleep. I was too tired to care much. There was no bed, only a broken-down sofa, and in the corner a dilapidated washstand; the walls and windows were riddled with bullets, denoting where the young *burghers* had been amusing themselves with rifle practice. The secretary then informed me that they had to search my luggage, which operation lasted fully half an hour, although I had but one small portmanteau and a dressing-case.

The latter two Dutch nurses were told off to look through, which, I am bound to say, they did most unwillingly, remarking to me they had not contemplated searching people's luggage as part of their already onerous duties. I had even to undress, in order that they might reassure the officials I had no documents on my person. Meanwhile the men examined my correspondence and papers almost microscopically. Needless to say, they found nothing. They had barely finished their researches, when a messenger came from the General to say, if Colonel Baden-Powell would exchange me for a Dutchman imprisoned in Mafeking, a certain Petrus Viljoen, he would consent to my going in. I found, on inquiry, that this man had been imprisoned for theft several months before the war, and I told them plainly it was manifestly unfair to exchange a man and a criminal for a woman; further, that I could not even ask Colonel Baden-Powell officially to do such a thing, and could only mention it, as an impossible condition, in a letter to my husband, if they chose to send it in. To this they agreed, so I indited the following letter, couched in terms which the secretary might peruse:

December 2, 1899.

My Dear Gordon,

I am at the *laager*. General Snyman will not give me a pass unless Colonel Baden-Powell will exchange me for a Mr. Petrus Vil-joen. I am sure this is impossible, so I do not ask him formally. I am in a great fix, as they have very little meal left at Setlagoli or the surrounding places. I am very kindly looked after here.

I then went to sleep in my strange surroundings, with small hope of any success from my application to Mafeking. The next day, Sunday, was observed by both parties as a day of rest. About seven one of the nurses brought me a cup of coffee, and then I proceeded to dress as best I might. So clearly did that horrid little room imprint itself on my memory that I seem to see it as I write. The dusty bare boards, cracked and loose in places, had no pretence to any acquaintance with a scrubbing-brush, and very little with a broom. A rickety old chest of drawers stood in one corner, presumably filled with hospital necessaries, from the very strong smell of drugs emanating from it, and from the fact that the nurses would bustle in and rummage for some desired article, giving glimpses of the confusion inside.

On the top of the drawers were arranged a multitude of medicine-bottles, half full and half empty, cracked and whole. The broken old washstand had been of valuable service during the night, as with it I barricaded the door, innocent of any lock or key. When I was dressed, I walked out on to the tiny *stoep*, surrounded by a high paling. My attention was at once attracted to a woman in a flood of tears, and presently the cause of her weeping was explained, as an elderly man came round the corner of the house with both his hands roughly tied up with bandages covered with blood—a sight which caused the young woman to sob with renewed vigour.

After a little talk with the man, who, in spite of his injuries, seemed perfectly well, the latter went away, and I entered into conversation with the weeping female, whom I found to speak good English, and to be the daughter of the wounded warrior, Hoffman by name and German by birth. They were Transvaal subjects, and her father had been among the first of the *burghers* to turn out when hostilities threatened.

She then proceeded to tell me that she and her mother and a numerous collection of young brothers and sisters had trekked in from their home in the Transvaal to spend the Sunday in the *laager* with their father.

On their arrival early that morning, they learnt, to their horror, that he had been wounded, or, rather, injured, late the night before, as the mutilated state of his hands arose from a shell exploding in the high-velocity Krupp gun just as he was loading it. She told me her father was one of the most valued artillerymen on the Boer side, and that he was also an adept in the art of making fireworks, his last triumph in this line having been at Mafeking on the occasion of the celebration of Queen Victoria's Diamond Jubilee. Fully appreciating the value of his services, the Transvaal authorities had from the commencement given him the most arduous tasks, and always, she indignantly added, in the forefront of the battle. As regarded the present accident, she said her father had repeatedly told the authorities these particular shells were not safe to handle. Apparently the safety-bolt was missing from all of them, making them when loaded as brittle as an eggshell.

This young lady and her mother were certainly very anti-Boer in their sympathies, though terribly afraid of allowing their feelings to be known. All that day and the next they spent in the *laager*, looking after the injured *père de famille*, whom, by the way, I got quite friendly with, but who, I think, was rather relieved to see his family depart. I rather regretted them, as Miss Hoffman used to bring me a lot of gossip overheard in the *laager*, where she assured me public opinion was running very strongly against me, and that all were of opinion the general should certainly not allow me to join my friends in Mafeking.

The morning dragged on. It was a hot, gusty day, and I found the shelter of my poky little room the most comfortable resting-place, although instead of a chair I had but a wooden case to sit on. About eleven I saw a clerical gentleman arriving, who I rightly concluded was the parson coming to conduct the service. Presently the strangest of noises I have ever heard arose from the back-premises of the tiny house. It is difficult to conceive anything so grotesque as some Dutch singing is. Imagine a doleful wail of many voices, shrill treble and deep bass, all on one note, now swelling in volume, now almost dying away, sung with a certain metre, and presumably with soul-stirring words, but with no attempt to keep together or any pretensions to an air of any kind, and you will have an idea of a Dutch chant or hymn.

This noise—for it cannot be called a harmony—might equally

well be produced by a howling party of dogs and cats. Then followed long prayers—for only the parson's voice could be heard—then more dirges, after which it was over, and all trooped away, apparently much edified. One of the nurses brought me some lunch and spread it on the rickety table, with a dirty napkin as a tablecloth. As regards the food, which these young ladies told me they took it in turn to cook, it was very fair; only one day we got no meat and no meal; the other days they gave me eggs, very good beef, splendid potatoes, and bread in any quantity. Besides this, I was able to buy delicious fruit, both figs and apricots. As beverages there were tea and coffee, the latter, of course, being the Transvaal national drink—that is to say, when "*dop*" cannot be had. Beer is almost unknown, except the imported kinds of Bass and Schlitz, for what is known as "*Kaffir* beer" is a filthy decoction. About midday I received a formal reply from Gordon, as follows:

> Mafeking,
> December 3, 1899.

My Dear Sarah,
I am delighted to hear you are being well treated, but very sorry to have to tell you that Colonel Baden-Powell finds it impossible to hand over Petrus Viljoen in exchange for you, as he was convicted of horse-stealing before the war. I fail to see in what way it can benefit your captors to keep you a prisoner. Luckily for them, it is not the custom of the English to make prisoners of war of women.

> Gordon Wilson.

Of course I was grievously disappointed, but at the same time I had really expected no other answer, as I informed Mr. Brink (the general's second secretary), who had brought me the letter. He was gravely apologetic, and informed me the general and commandant were holding a Kriegsraad early on the following morning, when my case would receive their full consideration. In the afternoon we had the excitement of seeing the Pretoria coach drive up to the *laager* with much horn-blowing and whip-cracking. Later some newspapers were brought across, and I was able actually to peruse a Transvaal paper only two days old. The general's other secretary, who presented them to me, made some astounding statements, which he said had just come up on official wires—namely, that England and Russia would be at war before that very week was out, in what locality he did not know; and that Germany had suddenly increased her fleet by many ships, spending thereon £10,000,000.

To this I ventured to remark that the building of those ships would take four or five years, which would make it almost too late to assist the Transvaal in the present war. I also reminded him casually that Germany's emperor and empress were, according to their own papers, then paying a visit to Queen Victoria, which did not look as if that country was exactly unfriendly to England. To this he had nothing to reply, and I saw that this imperial visit was a sore subject with my entertainers. For this reason I made a point of referring to it on every possible occasion. As I was eating my solitary supper, Mr. Brink appeared with a letter from Colonel Baden-Powell as follows:

December 5, 1899.

Dear Lady Sarah,

I am so distressed about you. You must have been having an awful time of it, and I can't help feeling very much to blame; but I had hoped to save you the unpleasantness of the siege.

However, I trust now that your troubles are nearly over at last, and that General Snyman will pass you in here.

We are all very well, and really rather enjoying it all.

I wrote last night asking for you to be exchanged for Mrs. Delpoort, but had no answer, so have written again today, and sincerely hope it will be all right.

Hope you are well, in spite of your troubles.

Yours sincerely,

R. Baden-Powell.

I then learnt from another letter that Mrs. Delpoort, who had originally expressed the wish to leave Mafeking, where she was residing with many other friends in the women's *laager*, had changed her mind, or her relatives did not encourage her to leave the shelter of the town; for the staff had experienced some difficulty in persuading her to agree to the exchange, even if General Snyman allowed the same. I asked if an answer had been returned to the colonel's letter, and Mr. Brink replied in the negative. Very indignant, I said that I did not mean to be kept in my present wretched quarters indefinitely, and that, if no exchange could be effected, I would request a pass to return to Setlagoli, and risk the scarcity of food. He looked rather confused, and said somewhat timidly that no doubt the general would allow me to go to Pretoria, where I should find "pleasant ladies' society."

Seeing my look of angry surprise, he hastily added that he only wished he had a house of his own to place at my disposal. I saw it was no use venting my annoyance on this young man, who was civility itself, so I merely remarked I had no intention of visiting their capital, and that the present was certainly not a time for an English lady to travel alone in the Transvaal. To this he gushingly agreed, but added that, of course, the general would give me a proper escort. These words were quite enough to denote which way the wind was blowing. I would not for an instant admit they had a right to detain me or to send me to any place against my will, having come there voluntarily, merely to ask the general a favour.

I was therefore conveniently blind and deaf, and, begging my amiable young friend to submit Colonel Baden-Powell's suggestion to the Kriegsraad on the following morning, and to apprise me of the result, I wished him goodnight, and went to bed once more on the wretched sofa, in anything but a hopeful frame of mind. However, as is so often the case, my spirits revived in the morning, and, on considering the situation, I could not see what object the Transvaal authorities could have in detaining me a prisoner. I was certainly very much in the way of the hospital arrangements, and I fully made up my mind to refuse absolutely to go to Pretoria, unless they took me by force. I also determined to leave them no peace at the headquarters till they gave me a definite reply. The day dragged on; the flies simply swarmed in my poky little room. Never have I seen anything like the plague of these insects, but the nurses assured me that at the *laager* itself they were far worse, attracted, doubtless, by the cattle, horses, and food-stuffs.

At length I received a letter in an enormous official envelope, saying General Snyman had wired to Pretoria about me, and expected an answer every minute, which reply should be immediately communicated to me. By my own free will I had put myself completely in their power. This did not prevent me, however, from speaking my mind freely on what I termed "the extraordinary treatment I was receiving," to both of the secretaries, to the nurses, and to the patients. The latter, being men, were very sympathizing; the nurses, though kind and attentive, were not quite so friendly, and seemed somewhat suspicious of my business. Neither of these, I ascertained, had gone through any previous training, but had volunteered their services, as they thought it "would be a lark."

Whether their expectations were realised was doubtful, as they told me they were worked off their legs; that they had to cook, wash their clothes, and clean out the wretched little rooms, besides looking after the patients. In addition to these two girls there was a "lady doctor," the first of her species I had ever come across, and with whom I was not favourably impressed. Very untidy in her appearance, her head covered with curls, her costume composed of the remnants of showy finery, this lady had been a handsome woman, but her personality, combined with a very discontented expression of countenance, did not exactly form one's idea of a substitute for the skilful, kind, and cheerful hospital doctor that we know at home. In fact, she looked singularly out of place, which I remarked to several people, partly from the irritation I felt on hearing her addressed as "Doctor." No doubt these remarks were repeated to her, and this accounted for her black looks.

I must not omit a few words about the patients and visitors of the hospital, with all of whom I was most friendly. One and all were exceedingly civil, and I never encountered any rudeness whatever. Even the *burghers* of no importance, poorly clad, out at elbow, and of starved appearance, who came to the hospital for advice and medicines, all alike made me a rough salutation, evidently the best they were acquainted with. Those of more standing nearly always commenced to chat in very good English; in fact, I think a great many came up with the purpose of observing the captured *rara avis*, an Englishwoman. We did not actually discuss the progress of the war and what led to it, sticking more to generalities.

One hope was universally expressed, that it would soon be over, and this I heartily re-echoed. I told one of them I thought they had been foolish to destroy all the railway-line, as it had left their own people so terribly short of food; to this he replied that such minor matters could not be helped, that they must all suffer alike and help each other; also that they were well aware that they were taking on a very great power, and that every nerve must be strained if they could hope for success. So another day and night passed. I continued to send down letters without end to headquarters; but it was always the same answer: they were waiting for the reply from Pretoria.

One afternoon we had a very heavy thunderstorm and deluges of rain, the heaviest I had seen in South Africa; the water trickled into my room, and dripped drearily on the floor for hours; outside, the stream between the hospital and *laager* became a roaring torrent. No one came near us that afternoon, and I really think communication was not possible. Later it cleared and the flood abated; a lively bombardment was then commenced, on the assumption, probably, that the Mafeking trenches were filled with water and uninhabitable.

It was trying to the nerves to sit and listen to the six or seven guns all belching forth their missiles of death on the gallant little town, which was so plainly seen from my windows, and which seemed to lie so unprotected on the *veldt*. Just as I had barricaded my door and gone to rest on my sofa about nine o'clock, the big siege gun suddenly boomed out its tremendous discharge, causing the whole house to shake and everything in the room to jingle. It seemed a cruel proceeding, to fire on a partially sleeping town, but I did not know then how accustomed the inhabitants were to this evening gun, and how they took their precautions accordingly.

I must say I disliked the nights at the hospital exceedingly. It was insufferably hot and stuffy in the little room, and the window, only about 2 feet above the ground, had to be left open. The sentries, about six in number—doubled, as I understood, on my account—lay and lounged on the *stoep* outside. Instead of feeling them anything of a protection, I should have been much happier without them. It must be recollected that these *burghers* were very undisciplined and independent of authority, only a semblance of which appeared to be exercised over them. They included some of a very low type, and it appeared to be left to themselves to choose which post they would patronize. It was remarked to me they preferred the hospital, as it was sheltered, and that the same men had latterly come there every night. Their behaviour during their watch was very unconventional.

They came on duty about 6 p.m., and made themselves thoroughly comfortable on the *stoep* with mackintoshes and blankets. Their rifles were propped up in one corner, and the *bandoliers* thrown on the ground. There were a couple of hammocks for the patients' use, and in these two of them passed the night. Before retiring to rest, they produced their pipes and foul-smelling Boer tobacco, proceeding to light up just under my windows, meanwhile talking their unmusical language with great volubility. At length, about ten, they appeared to slumber, and a chorus of snoring arose, which generally sent me to sleep, to be awakened two or three hours later by renewed conversations, which now and then died away into hoarse whispers. I always imagined they were discussing myself, and devising some scheme to step over the low sill into my room on the chance of finding any loot.

I complained one day to the nurses of the fact that their extreme loquacity really prevented my sleeping, and, as she told me that the patients suffered in the same way, I advised her to speak to the sentinels and ask them to be more quiet. She told me afterwards she had done so, and that they said they had been insulted, and would probably not come again. We both laughed, and agreed it would not matter much if this calamity occurred.

The next day I was still put off, when I requested to know what had been decided about my fate. I was getting desperate, and had serious thoughts of taking "French leave," risking Boer sentries and outposts, and walking into Mafeking at night; but it was the fear of being fired on from our own trenches that deterred me. Fortunately, however, assistance was at hand. On the afternoon of the fifth day that I had spent at the *laager*, a fine-looking *burgher* rode up to the hospital, and I heard him conversing in very good English. Presently, after staring at me for some time, he came up and said he had known Randolph Churchill, who, he heard, was my brother, and that he should so like to have a little talk. He then informed me his name was Spencer Drake, to which I said: "Your name and your conversation would make me think you are an Englishman, Mr. Drake."

"So I am," was his reply. "I was born in Norfolk. My father and grandfather before me were in Her Majesty's Navy, and we are descended from the old commander of Queen Elizabeth's time."

To this I observed that I was sorry to see him in the Boer camp amongst the queen's enemies. He looked rather sheepish, but replied: "Our family settled in Natal many years ago, and I have ever since been a Transvaal *burgher*. I owe everything I possess to the South African Republic, and of course I fight for its cause; besides which, we colonials were very badly treated and thrown over by the English Government in 1881, and since then I have ceased to think of England as my country."

As he seemed well disposed toward me, I did not annoy him by continuing the discussion, and he went on to inform me that he was the general's adjutant, and had been away on business, therefore had only just heard that I was in the *laager*, and he had come at once to see if he could be of any service. I took the opportunity of telling him what I thought of the way in which they were treating me, pointing out the wretched accommodation I had, and the fact that they had not even supplied me with a bed. He was very sympathetic, and expressed much sorrow at my discomforts, promising to speak to the General immediately, though without holding out much hope of success, as he told me the latter was sometimes very difficult to manage.

After a little more talk, during which I made friends with his horse, described by him as a wonderful beast, he rode off, and I was full of renewed hope. A little later the young secretary came up again to see me. To supplement my messages through Mr. Drake, I requested this young man to tell the general that I could see they were taking a cowardly advantage of me because I was a woman, and that they would never have detained a man under similar circumstances. In fact, I was on every occasion so importunate that I am quite sure the general's staff only prayed for the moment that I should depart. That afternoon I had a long talk to two old German soldiers, then *burghers*, who were both characters in their way. Hoffman, before alluded to, had been a gunner in the Franco-German War, and was full of information about the artillery of that day and this; while the other had been through the Crimea, and had taken part in the charge of the Light Brigade, then going on to India to assist in repressing the Mutiny.

He had evidently never liked the service into which he had been decoyed by the press-gang, and had probably been somewhat of a *mauvais sujet*, for he told me the authorities were glad enough to give him his discharge when the regiment returned to England. He had married and settled in the Transvaal, making a moderate fortune, only to be ruined by a lawsuit being given against him, entirely, he naively admitted, because the judge was a friend of the other side. In spite of this he remained a most warm partisan of the corrupt Boer Government, and at sixty-seven he had gladly turned out to fight the country whose uniform he had once worn. Whenever I found we were approaching dangerous ground, I used quickly to change the conversation, which perhaps was wise, as I was but one in a mighty host.

Chapter 10

Exchanged For a Horse-Thief

Hail, fellow! well met!—Swift.

Next morning I was awakened at 6 a.m. by Mr. Drake knocking at my door, and telling me I was to be ready in half an hour, as Colonel Baden-Powell had consented to exchange me for Petrus Viljoen. This exchange had placed our commanding officer in an awkward position. The prisoner was, as I stated before, a criminal, and under the jurisdiction of the civil authorities, who would not take upon themselves the responsibility of giving him up. Under these circumstances Lord Edward Cecil had come forward and represented to Colonel Baden-Powell that it was unseemly for an Englishwoman to be left in the hands of the Boers, and transported to Pretoria by the rough coach, exposed to possible insults and to certain discomforts.

He even declared himself prepared to take any consequent blame on his shoulders, and, being the prime minister's son, his words had great weight. As a matter of fact, Petrus Viljoen was anything but a fighting man, and could be of very little service to our enemies. The *burghers* had told me his presence was so persistently desired from the fact of the republic having private scores to settle with him. In any case, he was very reluctant to leave Mafeking and the safety of the prison, which fact had influenced Colonel Baden-Powell in finally agreeing to the exchange.

As may be imagined, I could hardly believe my good fortune, and I lost no time in scrambling into my clothes while the cart was being inspanned. A vexatious delay occurred from the intractability of the mules, which persistently refused to allow themselves to be caught. The exchange of prisoners had to be effected before 8 a.m., when the truce would be over, and I shall never forget how I execrated those

MAJOR HANBURY-TRACY

COLONEL LORD EDWARD CAPTAIN
BADEN-POWELL CECIL GORDON WILSON
COLONEL BADEN-POWELL AND STAFF AT MAFEKING

stubborn animals, as the precious minutes slipped by, fearful lest my captors would change their minds and impose fresh conditions. However, at length all was ready, and, escorted by some artillery officers, I drove to headquarters, where I was requested to descend in order to have another interview with the general. Again an inquisitive crowd watched my movements, but civilly made way for me to pass into the little room where General Snyman was holding a sort of levee. The latter asked me a few purposeless questions. I gravely expressed a hope that his eyes were better (he had been suffering from inflamed sight); then he rose and held out his hand, which I could not ignore, and without further delay we were off.

About 2,000 yards from Mafeking I noticed the enemy's advanced trenches, with some surprise at their proximity to the town; and here we met the other party with a white flag escorting Mr. Viljoen, who looked foolish, dejected, and anything but pleased to see his friends. He was forthwith given over to their care, the mules were whipped up, and at a gallop we rattled into the main street. From the first redoubt Colonel Baden-Powell and Lord Edward Cecil ran out to greet me, and the men in the trench gave three ringing English cheers, which were good to hear; but no time had to be lost in getting under cover, and I drove straight to Mr. Wiel's house, and had hardly reached it when "*Creechy*" (a Dutch pet-name which had been given to the big siege gun) sent a parting salute, and her shell whizzed defiantly over our heads.

Then commenced a more or less underground existence, which continued for five and a half months; but, surrounded by friends, it was to me a perfect heaven after so many weeks passed amidst foes. I had much to hear, and it took some time to realise all the changes in the little town since I had left. First and foremost, the town guard were coming splendidly out of their long-protracted ordeal. Divided into three watches, they passed the night at the different redoubts, behind each of which was a bomb-proof shelter. Those of the second watch were ready to reinforce the men on duty, while the third were only to turn out if summoned by the alarm-bell. All the defences had, indeed, been brought to a wonderful pitch of perfection by the C.O. First there was a network of rifle-pits, which gave the Boers no peace day or night, and from which on one side or the other an almost incessant sniping went on. These were supplemented by dynamite mines, the fame of which had frightened the Boers more than anything else, all connected with Headquarter Staff Office by electric wires.

In addition there was barbed-wire fencing round the larger earth-works, and massive barricades of waggons and sandbags across the principal streets. All this looked very simple once erected and in working order, but it was the outcome of infinite thought and ever-working vigilance. Then there was a complete system of telephones, connecting all the redoubts and the hospital with the Staff Office, thereby saving the lives of galloping orderlies, besides gaining their services as defenders in a garrison so small that each unit was an im-portant factor. Last, but certainly not least, were the bomb-proof shel-ters, which black labour had constructed under clever supervision all over the town, till at that time, in case of heavy shelling, nearly every inhabitant could be out of harm's way. What struck me most forcibly was that, in carrying out these achievements, Colonel Baden-Powell had been lucky enough to find instruments, in the way of experienced men, ready to his hand.

One officer was proficient in bomb-proofs, the postmaster thor-oughly understood telephones, while another official had proved himself an expert in laying mines. The area to be defended had a pe-rimeter of six miles; but, in view of the smallness of the garrison and the overwhelming number of the Boers, it was fortunate the authori-ties had been bold and adventurous enough to extend the trenches over this wide space, instead of following the old South African idea of going into *laager* in the market-square, which had been the first suggestion. The town was probably saved by being able to present so wide a target for the Boer artillery, and although we were then, and for the next few weeks, cut off from all communication with the outer world, even by nigger letter-carriers, and in spite of bullets rattling and whizzing through the market-square and down the side-streets, the Boer outposts were gradually being pushed away by our riflemen in their invisible pits.

While on this subject, I must mention that a day spent in those trenches was anything but an agreeable one. Parties of six men and an officer occupied them daily before dawn, and remained there eighteen hours, as any attempt to leave would have meant a hail of bullets from the enemy, distant only about 600 yards. They were dug deep enough to require very little earthwork for protection; hence they were more or less invisible by the enemy in their larger trenches. These latter were constantly subjected to the annoyance of bullets coming, apparently, from the ground, and, though other foes might have acted differently in like circumstances, the Boers did not care for the job of advancing

COLONEL BADEN-POWELL AT THE SUNDAY SPORTS

INTERIOR OF LADY SARAH WILSON'S BOMB-PROOF

across the open to dislodge the hidden enemy.

In a very few days a new bomb-proof shelter had been constructed for me, and to inaugurate it I gave an underground dinner with six guests. This bomb-proof was indeed a triumph in its line, and I must describe it. About 18 by 15 feet, and 8 feet high, it was reached by a flight of twelve wooden steps, at the top of which was a door that gave it the privacy of a room. It was lighted besides by three horizontal apertures, which resembled the very large portholes of a sailing-ship, and this illusion was increased by the wooden flaps that could be closed at will. The roof was composed of two lots of steel rails placed one above the other, and on these were sheets of corrugated iron and a huge tarpaulin to keep out the rain.

Above, again, were 9 feet of solid earth, while rows upon rows of sandbags were piled outside the entrance to guard against splinters and stray bullets. The weighty roof was supported, as an additional precaution, on the inside by three stout wooden posts, which, together with the rather dim light, most apparent when descending from the brilliant sunshine outside, gave the bomb-proof the appearance of a ship's cabin; in fact, one of my visitors remarked it much reminded him of the well-known print of the *Victory's* cockpit when Nelson lay a-dying. The interior panelling was painted white. One wall was entirely covered with an enormous Union Jack, and the other was decorated with native weapons, crowned by a trophy of that very war—namely, the only Mauser carbine then taken from the Boers. To complete the up-to-date nature of this protected dwelling, a telephone was installed, through the medium of which I could in a second communicate with the Staff Headquarters, and have due notice given me of "*Creechy's*" movements. In this shelter it was certainly no hardship to spend those hot days, and it was known to be the coolest place in town at that hot season of the year.

On Sundays we were able, thanks to the religious proclivities of the Boers, to end our mole existence for twenty-four hours, and walk and live like Christians. To almost the end of the siege this truce was scrupulously observed on both sides, and from early dawn to late at night the whole population thoroughly enjoyed themselves. The relieved expression on the faces of all could not fail to be apparent to even a casual observer. Pale women and children emerged from their *laager*, put on their finery, sunned themselves, and did their shopping. The black ladies went in a body to the *veldt* to collect firewood with all their natural gaiety and light-heartedness, which not even shell-fire and numerous casualties amongst themselves seemed seriously to disturb. Those of us who had horses and carriages at our disposal rode and drove anywhere within our lines in perfect safety. The first Sunday I was in Mafeking I was up and on my pony by 6 a.m., unwilling to lose a moment of the precious day.

We rode all round our defences, and inspected Canon Kopje, the scene of the most determined attack the Boers had made, the repulse of which, at the beginning of the siege, undoubtedly saved the town. From there we looked through the telescope at "*Creechy*," whose every movement could be watched from this point of vantage, and whose wickedly shining barrel was on the "day of rest" modestly pointed to the ground. Returning, we rode through the native *stadt*, quite the most picturesque part of Mafeking, where the trim, thatched, beaver-shaped huts, surrounded by mud walls, enclosing the little gardens and some really good-sized trees, appeared to have suffered but little damage from the bombardment, in spite of the Boers having specially directed their fire against the inhabitants (the Baralongs), who were old opponents of theirs. These natives were only armed by the authorities when the invaders specially selected them for their artillery fire and made raids on their cattle. The variety and sizes of these arms were really laughable. Some niggers had old-fashioned Sniders, others elephant guns, and the remainder weapons with enormously long barrels, which looked as if they dated back to Waterloo. To their owners, however, the maker or the epoch of the weapon mattered little. They were proud men, and stalked gravely along the streets with their precious rifles, evidently feeling such a sense of security as they had never experienced before.

On the Sunday I alluded to, after our ride we attended morning service, held as usual in the neat little church, which, with the exception of a few gashes in the ceiling rafters, caused by fragments of shell, had up to date escaped serious injury. The Dutch Church, on the other hand, curiously enough, was almost demolished by shell-fire at the beginning of the siege. We then drove up to the hospital, where Miss Hill, the plucky and youthful-looking matron, received us and showed us round. This girl—for she was little more—had been the life and prop of the place for the past two months, during which time the resources of the little hospital had been taxed almost past belief. Where twenty was the usual number of patients, there were actually sixty-four on the occasion of my first visit

The staff was composed of only a matron and three trained nurses.

In addition to their anxieties for the patients, who were being so frequently brought in with the most terrible injuries, these nurses underwent considerable risks from the bombardment, which, no doubt from accident, had been all along directed to the vicinity of the hospital and convent, which lay close together. The latter had temporarily been abandoned by the nuns, who were living in an adjacent bombproof, and the former had not escaped without having a shell through one of the wards, at the very time a serious operation was taking place. By a miraculous dispensation no patient was injured, but a woman, who had been previously wounded by a Mauser bullet while in the *laager*, died of fright.

The afternoon was taken up by a sort of gymkhana, when a happy holiday crowd assembled to see the tilting at the ring, the lemon-cutting, and the tug-of-war. At this entertainment Colonel Baden-Powell was thoroughly in his element, chatting to everyone and dispensing tea from a travelling waggon. In the evening I dined at Dixon's with our old party, and, really, the two months that had elapsed since I was at that same table had effected but little change in the surroundings and in the fare, which at that early stage of the siege was as plentiful as ever, even the stock of Schweppes' soda-water appearing inexhaustible. Besides this luxury, we had beautiful fresh tomatoes and young cabbages. The meat had resolved itself into beef, and beef only, but eggs helped out the menu, and the only non-existent delicacy was "fresh butter." This commodity existed in tins, but I must confess the sultry weather had anticipated the kitchen, in that it usually appeared in a melted state.

The most formidable weapon of the Boers was, naturally, the big siege Creusot gun. The very first day I arrived in Mafeking "*Creechy*" discharged a shell that killed a trooper of the Protectorate Regiment, who happened to be standing up in the stables singing a song, whilst four or five others were seated on the ground. The latter were uninjured, but the dead man was absolutely blown to bits, and one of his legs was found in the roof. A few days after two more shells landed in the market-square, one going through the right window of the chemist's shop, the other demolishing the left-hand one. Some of the staff were actually in the shop when the second shell came through the window, and were covered with dust, broken bits of glass, and shattered wood, but all providentially escaped unhurt.

Others were not so fortunate, for a nigger in the market-square was literally cut in half, and a white man 100 yards away had his leg torn off. Again, in Mr. Wiel's store a shell burst while the building was full of people, without injuring anyone; but one of the splinters carried an account-book from the counter and deposited it in the roof on its outward passage. Indeed, not a day passed but one heard of marvellously narrow escapes.

As the heat increased, the shelling grew certainly slacker, and, after an hour or two spent in exchanging greetings in the early morning, both besieged and besiegers seemed to slumber during the sultry noonday hours. About four they appeared to rouse themselves, and often my telephone would then ring up with the message: "The gun is loaded, and pointed at the town." Almost simultaneously a panting little bell, not much louder than a London muffin-bell, but heard distinctly all over the town in the clear atmosphere, would give tongue, and luckless folk who were promenading the streets had about three seconds to seek shelter, the alarm being sounded as the flash was seen by the look-out. One afternoon they gave us three shots in six minutes, but, of course, this rapid firing was much safer for the inhabitants than a stray shot after a long interval, as people remained below-ground expecting a repetition of that never-to-be-forgotten crashing explosion, followed by the sickening noise of the splinters tearing through the air, sometimes just over one's head, like the crack of a very long whip, manipulated by a master-hand. The smallest piece of one of these fragments was sufficient to kill a man, and scarcely anyone wounded with a shell ever seemed to survive, the wounds being nearly always terribly severe, and their poison occasioning gangrene to set in.

There were many comic as well as tragic incidents connected with the shells of the big gun. A monkey belonging to the post-office, who generally spent the day on the top of a pole to which he was chained, would, on hearing the alarm-bell, rapidly descend from his perch, and, in imitation of the human beings whom he saw taking shelter, quickly pop under a large empty biscuit-tin. Dogs also played a great part in the siege. One, belonging to the base-commandant, was wounded no less than three times; a rough Irish terrier accompanied the Protectorate Regiment in all its engagements; and a third amused itself by running after the small Maxim shells, barking loudly, and trying to retrieve pieces. On the other hand, the resident commissioner's dog was a prudent animal, and whenever she heard the alarm-bell, she would leave even her dinner half eaten, and bolt down her master's bomb-proof.

On one occasion I remember being amused at seeing a nigger,

working on the opposite side of the road, hold up a spade over his head like an umbrella as the missile came flashing by, while a fellow-workman crawled under a large tarpaulin that was stretched on the ground. These natives always displayed the most astonishing *sang-froid*. One day we saw a funny scene on the occasion of a *kaffir* wedding, when the bridegroom was most correctly attired in morning-dress and an old top-hat. Over his frock-coat he wore his *bandolier*, and carried a rifle on his shoulder; the bride, swathed in a long white veil from head to foot, walked by his side, and was followed by two young ladies in festive array, while the procession was brought up by more niggers, armed, like the bridegroom, to the teeth. The party solemnly paraded the streets for fully half an hour, in no wise disconcerted by a pretty lively shelling and the ring of the Mausers on the corrugated iron roofs.

Quite as disagreeable as "*Creechy*," although less noisy, was the enemy's 1-pound Maxim. A very loud hammering, quickly repeated, and almost simultaneously a whirring in the air, followed by four quick explosions, and then we knew this poisonous devil was at work. The shells were little gems in their way, and when they did not burst, which was often the case, were tremendously in request as souvenirs. Not much larger than an ordinary pepper-caster, when polished up and varnished they made really charming ornaments, and the natives were quick to learn that they commanded a good price, for after a shower had fallen there was a helter-skelter amongst the black boys for any unexploded specimens. One evening we had a consignment into the road just outside my bomb-proof, attracted by a herd of mules going to water. Immediately the small *piccaninny* driving these animals scampered off, returning in triumph with one of these prizes, which he brought me still so hot that I could not hold it.

It used often to strike me how comic these scenes at Mafeking would have been to any aeronaut hovering over the town of an evening, especially when the shelling had been heavy. Towards sundown the occupants of the various bomb-proofs used to emerge and sit on the steps or the sandbags of their shelters, conversing with their neighbours and discussing the day's damage. All of a sudden the bell would tinkle, and down would go all the heads, just as one has often seen rabbits on a summer evening disappear into their holes at the report of a gun. In a few minutes, when the explosion was over, they would bob up again, to see if any harm had been done by the last missile. Then night would gradually fall on the scene, sometimes made almost as light as day by a glorious African moon, concerning which I shall always maintain that in no other country is that orb of such brightness, size, and splendour.

The half-hour between sundown and moonrise, or twilight and inky blackness, as the case happened to be, according to the season or the weather, was about the pleasantest time in the whole day. As a rule it was a peaceful interval as regards shelling. Herds of mules were driven along the dusty streets to be watered; cattle and goats returned from the *veldt*, where they had been grazing in close proximity to the town, as far as possible out of sight; foot-passengers, amongst them many women, scurried along the side-walks closely skirting the houses. Then, when daylight had completely faded, all took shelter, to wait for the really vicious night-gun, which was usually fired between eight and nine with varying regularity, as our enemies, no doubt, wished to torment the inhabitants by not allowing them to know when it was safe for them to seek their homes and their beds. There was a general feeling of relief when "*Creechy*" had boomed her bloodthirsty "Good-night." Only once during the whole siege was she fired in the small hours of the morning, and that was on Dingaan's Day (December 16), when she terrified the sleeping town by beginning her day's work at 2.30 a.m., followed by a regular bombardment from all the other guns in chorus, to celebrate the anniversary of the great Boer victory over the Zulus many years ago.

Frequent, however, were the volleys from the trenches that suddenly broke the tranquillity of the early night, and startling were they in their apparent nearness till one got accustomed to them. At first I thought the enemy must be firing in the streets, so loud were the reports, owing to the atmosphere and the wind setting in a particular direction. The cause of these volleys was more difficult to discover, and, as our men never replied, it seemed somewhat of a waste of ammunition. Their original cause was a sortie early in the siege, when Captain Fitzclarence made a night attack with the bayonet on their trenches. Ever afterwards an animal moving on the *veldt*, a tree or bush stirred by the wind, an unusual light in the town, was sufficient for volley after volley to be poured at imaginary foes. By nine o'clock these excitements were usually over, and half an hour afterwards nearly every soul not on duty was asleep, secure in the feeling that for every one who reposed two were on watch; while, as regards Colonel Baden-Powell, he was always prowling about, and the natives revived his old Matabele nickname of "the man that walks by night."

CHAPTER 11

Life in a Besieged Town

There is a reaper whose name is Death.—Longfellow.

We celebrated Christmas Day, 1899, by a festive luncheon-party to which Colonel Baden-Powell and all his staff were invited. By a strange and fortunate coincidence, a turkey had been overlooked by Mr. Weil when the government commandeered all live-stock and food-stuffs at the commencement of the siege, and, in spite of the grilling heat, we completed our Christmas dinner by a real English plum-pudding. In the afternoon a tea and Christmas-tree for the Dutch and English children had been organised by some officers of the Protectorate Regiment. Amongst those who contributed to the amusement of these poor little white-faced things, on whom the close quarters they were obliged to keep was beginning to tell, none worked harder than Captain Ronald Vernon. I remember returning to my quarters, after the festivity, with this officer, and his telling me, in strict confidence, with eager anticipation, of a sortie that was to be made on the morrow, with the object of obtaining possession of the Boer gun at Game Tree Fort, the fire from which had lately been very disastrous to life and property in the town.

He was fated in this very action to meet his death, and afterwards I vividly recalled our conversation, and reflected how bitterly disappointed he would have been had anything occurred to prevent his taking part in it. The next day, Boxing Day, I shall ever remember as being, figuratively speaking, as black and dismal as night. I was roused at 4.30 a.m. by loud cannonading. Remembering Captain Vernon's words, I telephoned to Headquarters to ask if the Colonel and Staff were there. They had all left at 2.30 a.m., so I knew the projected action was in progress. At five o'clock the firing was continuous, and the

A BOER FORT BEFORE MAFEKING.

boom of our wretched little guns was mingled with the rattle of Boer musketry. Every moment it grew lighter—a beautiful morning, cool and bright, with a gentle breeze.

In Mr. Wiel's service was a waiter named Mitchell, a Cockney to the backbone, and a great character in his way. What had brought him to South Africa, or how he came to be in Mafeking, I never discovered; but he was a cheerful individual, absolutely fearless of shells and bullets. That morning I began to get very anxious, and Mitchell was also pessimistic. He mounted to the roof to watch the progress of the fight, and ran down from time to time with anything but reassuring pieces of intelligence, asking me at intervals, when the firing was specially fierce: "Are you scared, lady?" At length he reported that our men were falling back, and that the ambulances could now be seen at work. With marvellous courage and coolness, the soldiers had advanced absolutely to under the walls of the Boer fort, and had found the latter 8 feet high, with three tiers of loopholes. There it was that three officers—Captains Vernon, Paton, and Sandford—were shot down, Captain Fitzclarence having been previously wounded in the leg, and left on the *veldt* calling to his men not to mind him, but to go on, which order they carried out, nothing daunted by the hail of bullets and the loss of their officers.

Thanks to the marvellous information the Boers constantly received during the siege, no doubt from the numerous Dutch spies which were known to be in the town, Game Tree Fort had been mysteriously strengthened in the night; and, what was still more significant, the gun had not only been removed, but General Snyman and Commandment Botha were both on the scene with reinforcements shortly after our attack commenced, although the Boer Headquarter camp was fully three miles away. Without scaling-ladders, it was impossible to mount the walls of the fort. Our soldiers sullenly turned and walked slowly away, the idea of running or getting under shelter never even occurring to them. Had the Boers then had the determination required to come out of their fort and pursue the retiring men, it is possible very few would have returned alive; but, marvellous to relate, and most providentially as we were concerned, no sooner did they observe our men falling back than they ceased firing, as if relief at their departure was coupled with the fear of aggravating the foes and causing a fresh attack.

The Boers were exceedingly kind in picking up our dead and wounded, which were immediately brought in by the armoured train, and which, alas! mounted up to a disastrous total in the tiny community which formed our garrison. No less than twenty-five men were killed, including three officers; and some twenty or thirty were wounded, most of them severely. The Boers told the ambulance officers they were staggered at our men's pluck, and the commandant especially appreciated the gallantry required for such an attack, knowing full well how difficult it would have been to induce the *burghers* to make a similar attempt.

About 10 a.m. a rush of people to the station denoted the arrival of the armoured train and its sad burden, and then a melancholy procession of stretchers commenced from the railway, which was just opposite my bomb-proof, to the hospital. The rest of the day seemed to pass like a sad dream, and I could hardly realise in particular the death of Captain Vernon, who had been but a few short hours before so full of health, spirits, and confidence.

Recognising what a press of work there would be at the hospital, I walked up there in the afternoon, and asked to be made useful. No doubt out of good feeling, the Boers did not shell at all that day till late evening, but at the hospital all was sad perturbation. There had only been time to attend to the worst cases, and the poor nurses were just sitting down to snatch a hasty meal. The matron asked me if I would undertake the management of a convalescent home that had to be organised to make more room for the new patients. Of course I consented, and by evening we were busy installing sixteen patients in the railway servants' institute, near the station. To look after the inmates were myself, four other ladies, and one partly professional nurse. We arranged that the latter should attend every day, and the four ladies each take a day in turn, while I undertook to be there constantly to order eatables and superintend the housekeeping.

On the first evening, when beds, crockery, kitchen utensils, and food, all arrived in a medley from the universal provider, Wiel, great confusion reigned; and when it was at its height, just as the hospital waggon was driving up with the patients, "*Creechy*" sent off one of her projectiles, which burst with a deafening explosion about a hundred yards beyond the improvised hospital, having absolutely whizzed over the approaching ambulance vehicles. The patients took it most calmly, and were in no way disconcerted. By Herculean efforts the four ladies and myself got the place shipshape, and all was finished when the daylight failed. As I ran back to my quarters, the bugle-call of the "*Last Post*," several times repeated, sounded clear in the still atmosphere of a calm and beautiful evening, and I knew the last farewells were being said to the brave men who had gone to their long rest.

Of course Mafeking's losses on that black Boxing Day were infinitesimal compared to those attending the terrible struggles going on in other parts of the country; but, then, it must be remembered that not only was our garrison a very small one, but also that, when people are shut up together for months in a beleaguered town—a handful of English men and women surrounded by enemies, with even spies in their midst—the feeling of comradeship and friendship is tremendously strengthened. Every individual was universally known, and therefore all the town felt they had lost their own friends, and mourned them as such.

From that date for three weeks I went daily to the convalescent home. The short journey there was not totally without risk, as the enemy, having heard of the foundry where primitive shells were being manufactured, and which was situated immediately on the road I had to take, persistently sent their missiles in this direction, and I had some exciting walks to and fro, very often alone, but sometimes accompanied by any chance visitor. One morning Major Tracy and I had just got across the railway-line, when we heard the loading bell, and immediately there was a *sauve qui pent* among all the niggers round us, who had been but a moment before lolling, sleeping, and joking, in their usual fashion. Without losing our dignity by joining in the stampede, we put our best foot forward, and scurried along the line till we came to some large coal-sheds, where my companion made me crawl under a very low arch, he mounting guard outside. In this strange position I remained while the shell came crashing over us, a bad shot, and continued its course away into the *veldt*.

Another evening the same officer was escorting me to the institute, and, as all had been very quiet that afternoon, we had not taken the precaution of keeping behind the railway buildings, as was my usual custom. We were in the middle of an open space, when suddenly an outburst of volleys from the Boer trenches came as an unpleasant surprise, and the next moment bullets were falling behind us and even in front of us, their sharp ring echoing on the tin roofs. On this occasion, as the volleys continued with unabated vigour, I took to my heels with a view to seeking shelter; but Major Tracy could not be moved out of a walk, calling out to me I should probably run into a bullet whilst trying to avoid it. My one idea being to get through the zone of fire, I paid no attention to his remonstrances, and soon reached a safe place. The Boers only learnt these detestable volleys from our troops, and carried them out indifferently well; but the possibility of their occurrence, in addition to the projectiles from "*Creechy*," added greatly to the excitement of an evening stroll, and we had many such episodes when walking abroad after the heat of the day.

In January, Gordon was laid up by a very sharp attack of peritonitis, and was in bed for over a week in my bomb-proof, no other place being safe for an invalid, and the hospital full to overflowing. When he began to mend, I unfortunately caught a chill, and a very bad quinsy sore throat supervened. I managed, however, to go about as usual, but one afternoon, when I was feeling wretchedly ill, our hospital attendant came rushing in to say that a shell had almost demolished the convalescent home, and that, in fact, only the walls were standing. The patients mercifully had escaped, owing to their all being in the bomb-proof, but they had to be moved in a great hurry, and were accommodated in the convent. For weeks past this building had not been shot at, and it was therefore considered a safe place for them, as it was hoped the Boer gunners had learned to respect the hospital, its near neighbour.

Owing to the rains having then begun, and being occasionally very heavy, the bomb-proofs were becoming unhealthy. My throat was daily getting worse, and the doctor decided that Gordon and myself had better also be removed to the convent, hoping that being above-ground might help recovery in both our cases. There was heavy shelling going on that afternoon, and the drive to our new quarters, on the most exposed and extreme edge of the town, was attended with some excitement. I could scarcely swallow, and Gordon was so weak he could hardly walk even the short distance we had to compass on foot. However, we arrived in safety, and were soon made comfortable in this strange haven of rest.

As I have before written, the convent in Mafeking was from the commencement of the bombardment picked out by the enemy as a target, and during the first week it was hit by certainly ten or twelve projectiles, and reduced more or less to a ruined state. At no time can the building have laid claims to the picturesque or the beautiful, but it had one peculiarity—namely, that of being the only two-storied building in Mafeking, and of standing out, a gaunt red structure, in front of the hospital, and absolutely the last building on the north-east side of the town. It was certainly a landmark for miles, and, but for its sacred origin and the charitable calling of its occupants, would have

CORRIDOR IN THE CONVENT WHERE THE SHELL EXPLODED.

been a fair mark for the enemy's cannon. Very melancholy was the appearance it presented, with large gaping apertures in its walls, with its shattered doors and broken windows; whilst surrounding it was what had been a promising garden, but had then become a mere jungle of weeds and thorns.

The back of the edifice comprised below several large living-rooms, over them a row of tiny cubicles, and was practically undamaged. The eighteen convalescent patients had been comfortably installed on the ground-floor, and we had two tiny rooms above. This accommodation was considered to be practically safe from shells, in spite of the big gun having been shifted a few days previously, and it being almost in a line with the convent. On the upper floor of the eastern side a large room, absolutely riddled with shot and shell, was formerly occupied as a dormitory by the children of the convent school. It was now put to a novel use as a temporary barracks, a watch being always on duty there, and a telescope installed at the window. Since the nuns left to take up their abode in a bomb-proof shelter, a Maxim had been placed at one of the windows, which commanded all the surrounding country; but it was discreetly covered over, and the window-blind kept closely drawn to avert suspicion, as it was only to be used in case of real emergency.

To reach our cubicles there was but a single staircase, which led past this room allotted to the soldiers—a fact which left an unsatisfactory impression on my mind, for it was apparent that, were the convent aimed at, to reach *terra-firma* we should have to go straight in the direction of shells or bullets. However, the authorities opined it was all right; so, feeling very ill, I was only too glad to crawl to bed. Just as the sun was setting, the soldiers on watch came tearing down the wooden passage, making an awful clatter, and calling out: "The gun is pointed on the convent!" As they spoke, the shell went off, clean over our heads, burying itself in a cloud of dust close to a herd of cattle half a mile distant. This did not reassure me, but we hoped it was a chance shot, which might not occur again, and that it had been provoked by the cattle grazing so temptingly within range. I must say there was something very weird and eerie in those long nights spent at the convent.

At first my throat was too painful to enable me to sleep, and endless did those dreary hours seem. We had supper usually before seven, in order to take advantage of the fading daylight, for lights were on no account to be shown at any of the windows, being almost certain to attract rifle-fire. By eight we were in total darkness, except for the dim little paraffin hand-lamp the Sisters kindly lent me, which, for precaution's sake, had to be placed on the floor. Extraordinary noises emanated from those long uncarpeted passages, echoing backwards and forwards, in the ceiling, till they seemed to pertain to the world of spirits. The snoring of the men on the relief guard was like the groans of a dying man, the tread of those on duty like the march of a mighty army. Then would come intense stillness, suddenly broken by a volley from the enemy sounding appallingly near—in reality about a mile off—and provoked, doubtless, by some very innocent cause. Many of these volleys were often fired during the night, sometimes for ten minutes together, at other times singly, at intervals; *anon* the boom of a cannon would vary the entertainment.

Occasionally, when unable to sleep, I would creep down the pitch-dark corridor to a room overlooking the sleeping town and the *veldt*, the latter so still and mysterious in the moonlight, and, peeping through a large jagged hole in the wall caused by a shell, I marvelled to think of the proximity of our foes in this peaceful landscape. At length would come the impatiently-longed-for dawn about 4 a.m.; then the garrison would appear, as it were, to wake up, although the greater part had probably spent the night faithfully watching. Long lines of sentries in their drab khaki would pass the convent on their homeward journey, walking single file in the deep trench connecting the town with the outposts, and which formed a practically safe passage from shell and rifle fire. Very quickly did the day burst on the scene, and a very short time we had to enjoy those cool, still morning hours or the more delightful twilight; the sun seemed impatient to get under way and burn up everything.

Of course we had wet mornings and wet days, but, perhaps fortunately, the rains that year were fairly moderate, though plentiful enough to have turned the yellow *veldt* of the previous autumn into really beautiful long green grass, on which the half-starved cattle were then thriving and waxing fat. The view from our tiny bedrooms was very pretty, and the coming and going of every sort of person in connection with the convalescent hospital downstairs made the days lively enough, and compensated for the dreariness of the nights. The splendid air blowing straight from the free north and from the Kalahari Desert on the west worked wonders in the way of restoring us to health, and I began to talk of moving back to my old quarters. I must confess I was never quite comfortable about the shells, which seemed so constantly to narrowly miss the building, although the look-out men always maintained they were aiming at some other object.

One morning I was still in bed, when a stampede of many feet down the passage warned me our sentinels had had a warning. Quickly opening my door, I could not help laughing at seeing the foremost man running down the corridor towards our rooms with the precious Maxim gun, enveloped in its coat of canvas, in his arms as if it were a baby. "They're on us this time," he called out; then came a terrific explosion and a crash of some projectile against the outer walls and doors. The shell had fallen about 40 feet short of the convent, on the edge of the deserted garden. Many explanations were given to account for this shot, none of which seemed to me to be very lucid, and I secretly determined to clear out as soon as the doctor would permit. The very next day we had the narrowest escape of our lives that it is possible to imagine. There had been very little shelling, and I had taken my first outing in the shape of a rickshaw drive during the afternoon.

The sun was setting, and our little supper-table was already laid at the end of the corridor into which our rooms opened, close to the window beside which we used to sit. Major Gould Adams had just dropped in, as he often did, to pay a little visit before going off to his night duties as commandant of the Town Guard, and our repast was in consequence delayed—a circumstance which certainly helped to save our lives. We were chatting peacefully, when suddenly I recollect hearing the big gun's well-known report, and was just going to remark, "How near that sounds!" when a terrifying din immediately above our heads stopped all power of conversation, or even of thought, and the next instant I was aware that masses of falling brick and masonry were pushing me out of my chair, and that heavy substances were falling on my head; then all was darkness and suffocating dust. I remember distinctly putting my hands clasped above my head to shelter it, and then my feeling of relief when, in another instant or two, the bricks ceased to fall. The intense stillness of my companions next dawned upon me, and a sickening dread supervened, that one of them must surely be killed.

Major Gould Adams was the first to call out that he was all right; the other had been so suffocated by gravel and brick-dust that it was several moments before he could speak. In a few minutes dusty forms and terrified faces appeared through the gloom, as dense as the thickest London yellow fog, expecting to find three mutilated corpses. Imagine their amazement at seeing three human beings, in colour more like Red Indians than any other species, emerge from the ruins and try to shake themselves free from the all-pervading dust. The great thing was to get out of the place, as another shell might follow, the enemy having seen, from the falling masonry, how efficacious the last had been. So, feeling somewhat dazed, but really not alarmed, as the whole thing had been too quick for fear, I groped my way downstairs.

Outside we were surrounded by more frightened people, whom we quickly reassured. The woman cook, who had been sitting in her bomb-proof, was quite sure *she* had been struck, and was calling loudly for brandy; while the rest of us got some soda-water to wash out our throats—a necessary precaution as far as I was concerned, as mine had only the day previously been lanced for quinsy. By degrees the cloud of dust subsided, and then in the fading light we saw what an extraordinary escape we had had. The shell had entered the front wall of the convent, travelled between the iron roof and the ceiling of the rooms, till it reached a wall about 4 feet from where we were sitting. Against this it had exploded, making a huge hole in the outside wall and in the other which separated our passage from a little private chapel. In this chapel it had also demolished all the sacred images. It was not, however, till next day, when we returned to examine the scene of the explosion, that we realised how narrowly we had escaped death or terrible injuries.

Three people had been occupying an area of not more than 5 feet square; between us was a tiny card-table laid with our supper, and on this the principal quantity of the masonry had fallen—certainly 2 tons of red brick and mortar—shattering it to atoms. If our chairs had been drawn up to the table, we should probably have been buried beneath this mass. But our most sensational discovery was the fact that two enormous pieces of shell, weighing certainly 15 pounds each, were found touching the legs of my chair, and the smallest tap from one of these would have prevented our ever seeing another sunrise. Needless to say, we left our ruined quarters that evening, and I reposed more peacefully in my bomb-proof than I had done for many nights past. The air at the convent had accomplished its healing work. We were both practically recovered, and we had had a hairbreadth escape; but I was firmly convinced that an underground chamber is preferable to a two-storied mansion when a 6-inch 100-pound shell gun, at a distance of two miles, is bombarding the town you happen to be residing in.

Many Happier Returns of the Anniversary of 1st Jany 1900 at Mafeking (81st day of Siege.)

From R.S.S.B.P.

SKETCH BY COLONEL BADEN-POWELL

CHAPTER 12

Life in a Besieged Town (continued)

And so we sat tight.—Despatch from Mafeking to War Office.

February came and went without producing very much change in our circumstances, and yet, somehow, there was a difference observable as the weeks passed. People looked graver; a tired expression was to be noted on many hitherto jovial countenances; the children were paler and more pinched. Apart from the constant dangers of shells and stray bullets, and the knowledge that, when we were taking leave of any friend for a few hours, it might be the last farewell on earth—apart from these facts, which constituted a constant wear and tear of mind, the impossibility of making any adequate reply to our enemy's bombardment gradually preyed on the garrison. By degrees, also, our extreme isolation seemed to come home to us, and not a few opined that relief would probably never come, and that Mafeking would needs have to be sacrificed for the greater cause of England's final triumph.

Since Christmas black "runners" had contrived to pass out of the town with cables, bringing us on their return scrappy news and very ancient newspapers. For instance, I notice in my diary that at the end of March we were enchanted to read a *Weekly Times* of January 5. On another occasion the Boers vacated some trenches, which were immediately occupied by our troops, who there found some Transvaal papers of a fairly recent date, and actually a copy of the *Sketch*. I shall never forget how delighted we were with the latter, and the amusement derived therefrom compensated us a little for the accounts in the Boer papers of General Buller's reverses on the Tugela. About the middle of February I was enchanted to receive a letter from Mr. Rhodes, in Kimberley, which I reproduce.

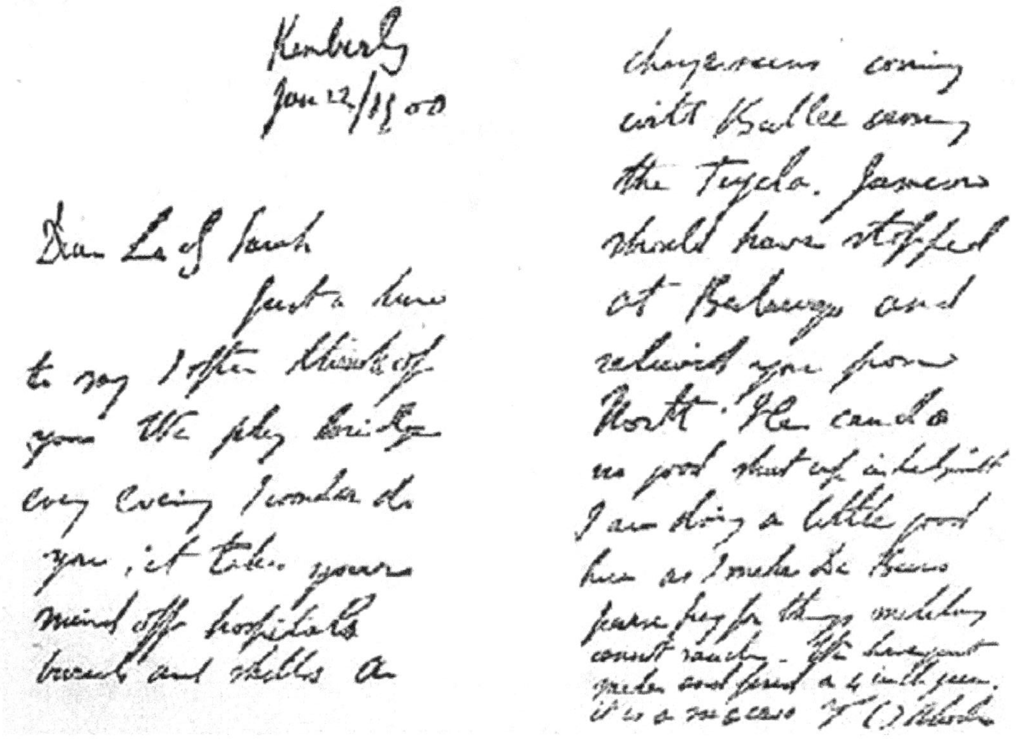

FACSIMILE OF LETTER FROM MR. CECIL RHODES

TRANSCRIPTION OF LETTER:

Kimberly

Jan 12 / 1900

Dear Lady Sarah,

Just a line to say I often think of you. I wonder do you play bridge, it takes your mind off hospitals, burials and shells. A change seems coming with Buller crossing the Tulega. Jameson should have stopped at Bulawayo and relieved you from North. He can do no good shut up in Ladysmith. I am doing a little good here as I make De Beers purse pay for things military cannot sanction. We have just made and fired a 4 inch gun, it is a success.

Yrs..Rhodes

This characteristic epistle seemed a link with the outer world, and to denote we were not forgotten, even by those in a somewhat similar plight to ourselves.

The natives and their splendid loyalty were always a source of interest. Formed into a "cattle guard," under a white man named Mackenzie, the young bloods did excellent service, and were a great annoyance to the Boers by making daring sorties in order to secure some of the latter's fat cattle. This particular force proudly styled itself "Mackenzie's Black Watch." There were many different natives in Mafeking. Besides the Baralongs before alluded to, we had also the Fingos, a very superior race, and 500 natives belonging to different tribes, who hailed from Johannesburg, and who had been forcibly driven into the town by Cronje before the siege commenced. These latter were the ones to suffer most from hunger, in spite of government relief and the fact that they had plenty of money; for they had done most of the trench-work, and had been well paid. The reason was that they were strangers to the other natives, who had their own gardens to supplement their food allowance, and blacks are strangely unkind and hard to each other, and remain quite unmoved if a (to them) unknown man dies of starvation, although he be of their own colour.

The native *stadt* covered altogether an area of at least a square mile, and was full of surprises in the shape of pretty peeps and rural scenery. Little naked children used to play on the grass, pausing to stare open-eyed at the passer-by, and men and women sat contentedly gossiping in front of their huts. The whole gave an impression of prosperity, of waving trees, green herbage, and running water, and was totally different to the usual African landscape. To ride or drive through it on a Sunday was quite a rest, when there was no risk of one's illusions being dispelled by abominable shells, whose many visible traces on the sward, in the shape of deep pear-shaped pits, were all the same in evidence.

Standing in a commanding position among the thatched houses of the picturesque native *stadt* was the Mission Church, of quaint shape, and built of red brick, the foundation of which had been laid by Sir Charles Warren in 1884. One Sunday afternoon we attended service in this edifice, and were immensely struck with the devotion of the enormous congregation of men and women, who all followed the service attentively in their books. The singing was most fervent, but the sermon a little tedious, as the clergyman preached in English, and his discourse had to be divided into short sentences, with a long pause between each, to enable the black interpreter at his side to translate what he said to his listeners, who simply hung on his words.

All the natives objected most strongly to partaking of horse soup, supplied by the kitchens, started by the C.O., as they declared it gave them the same sickness from which the horses in Africa suffered, and also that it caused their heads to swell. The authorities were therefore compelled to devise some new food, and the resourceful genius of a Scotchman introduced a porridge called "*sowens*" to the colonel's no-tice. This nutriment, said to be well known in the North of Scotland, was composed of the meal which still remained in the oat-husks after they had been ground for bread and discarded as useless. It was slightly sour, but very wholesome, and enormously popular with the white and the black population, especially with the latter, who preferred it to any other food.

I must now mention the important item of supplies and how they were eked out. The provisions sent to Mafeking by the Cape Government before the war were only sufficient to feed 400 men for a little over a fortnight. At that time a statement was made, to reassure the inhabitants, that the Cape Ministry held themselves personally responsible for the security of the railway in the colony. Providentially, the firm of Weil and Company had sent vast stores to their *depôt* in the town on their own initiative. This firm certainly did not lose fi-nancially by their foresight, but it is a fact that Mafeking without this supply could have made no resistance whatever. There were 9,000 human beings to feed, of which 7,000 were natives and 2,000 white people. It can therefore be imagined that the task of the D.A.A.G. was not a light one.

Up to April the town consumed 4,099 tons of food-stuffs; 12,256 tons of oats, fodder, meal, and flour; and 930 tons of fuel; making a total of 17,285 tons. Of matches, the supply of which was soon exhausted, 35,400 boxes were used, and to take their place tiny paraffin lamps were supplied to all, which burnt night and day. Fortunately, the supply of liquid fuel was very large, and it would have taken the place of coal if the siege had been indefinitely prolonged. Among miscellaneous articles which were luckily to be obtained at Weil's stores were 2 tons of gunpowder and other ammunition, 132 rifles, insulated fuses, and electric dynamos for discharging mines, etc.

About a month after the siege started, the C.O. placed an embargo on all food-stuffs, and the distribution of rations commenced. From then onward special days were allowed for the sale of luxuries, but always in strictly limited quantities. At first the rations consisted of 1¼ pounds of meat and 1¼ pounds of bread, besides tea, coffee, sugar, and rice. As time went on these were reduced, and towards the end of March we only had 6 ounces of what was called bread and 1 pound of fresh meat, when any was killed; otherwise we had to be content with bully beef. As to the "staff of life," it became by degrees abominable and full of foreign substances, which were apt to bring on fits of choking. In spite of this drawback, there was never a crumb left, and it was remarkable how little the 6 ounces seemed to represent, especially to a hungry man in that keen atmosphere.

One day it was discovered there was little, if any, gold left of the £8,000 in specie that was lodged at the Standard Bank at the beginning of the siege. This sum the Boers had at one time considered was as good as in their pockets. It was believed the greater portion had since been absorbed by the natives, who were in the habit of burying the money they received as wages. In this quandary, Colonel Baden-Powell designed a paper one-pound note, which was photographed on to thick paper of a bluish tint, and made such an attractive picture that the government must have scored by many of them never being redeemed.

It was not till Ash Wednesday, which fell that year on the last day of February, that we got our first good news from a London cable, dated ten days earlier. It told us Kimberley was relieved, that Colesberg was in our hands, and many other satisfactory items besides. What was even of greater importance was a message from Her Majesty Queen Victoria to Colonel Baden-Powell and his garrison, applauding what they had done, and bidding them to hope on and wait patiently for relief, which would surely come. This message gave especial pleasure from its being couched in the first person, when, as was universally remarked, the task of sending such congratulations might so easily have been relegated to one of Her Majesty's Ministers.

I really think that no one except a shipwrecked mariner, cast away on a desert island, and suddenly perceiving a friendly sail, could have followed our feelings of delight on that occasion. We walked about thinking we must be dreaming, and finding it difficult to believe that we were in such close contact with home and friends. In less than ten minutes posters were out, and eager groups were busy at the street-corners, discussing the news, scrappy indeed, and terribly deficient in all details, but how welcome, after all the vague native rumours we had had to distract us during the past weeks! We were content then to wait any length of time, and our lives varied very little as the weeks slipped by.

The bombardment was resumed with vigour, and the old monster gun cruised right round the town and boomed destruction at us from no less than five different points of vantage. When the shelling was very heavy, we used to say to ourselves, "What a good thing they are using up their ammunition!" when again for a few days it was slack, we were convinced our foes had had bad news. What matter if our next information was that the Boers had been seen throwing up their hats and giving vent to other visible expressions of delight: we had passed a few peaceful hours.

Many casualties continued to take place; some were fatal and tragic, but many and providential were the escapes recorded. Among the former, one poor man was blown to bits while sitting eating his breakfast; but the same day, when a shell landed in or near a house adjacent to my bomb-proof, it merely took a cage containing a canary with it through the window, while another fragment went into a dwelling across the street, and made mince-meat of a sewing-machine and a new dress on which a young lady had been busily engaged. She had risen from her pleasant occupation but three minutes before. The coolness of the inhabitants, of both sexes, was a source of constant surprise and admiration to me, and women must always be proud to think that the wives and daughters of the garrison were just as conspicuous by their pluck as the defenders themselves.

Often of a hot afternoon, when I was sitting in my bomb-proof, from inclination as well as from prudence—for it was a far cooler resort than the stuffy iron-roofed houses—while women and children were walking about quite unconcernedly outside, I used to hear the warning bell ring, followed by so much scuffling, screaming, and giggling, in which were mingled jokes and loud laughter from the men, that it made me smile as I listened; then, after the explosion, they would emerge from any improvised shelter and go gaily on their way, and the clang of the blacksmith's anvil, close at hand, would be resumed almost before the noise had ceased and the dust had subsided.

One day a lady was wheeling her two babies in a mail-cart up and down the wide road, while the Boers were busily shelling a distant part of the defences. The children clapped their hands when they heard the peculiar siren and whistle of the quick-firing Krupp shells, followed by dull thuds, as they buried themselves in the ground. On my suggesting to her that it was not a very favourable time to air the children, she agreed, and said that her husband had just told her to go home, which she proceeded leisurely to do. Another morning the cattle near the convent were being energetically shelled, and later I happened to see the Mother Superior, and commiserated with her in having been in such a hot corner. "Ah, shure!" said the plucky Irish lady, "the shells were dhroppin' all round here; but they were only nine-pounders, and we don't take any notice of them at all."

No words can describe the cheerful, patient behaviour of those devoted Sisters through the siege. They bore uncomplainingly all the hardships and discomforts of a flooded bomb-proof shelter, finally returning to their ruined home with any temporary makeshifts to keep out the rain; and whereas, from overwork and depression of spirits, some folks were at times a little difficult to please, not a word of complaint during all those months ever came from the ladies of the convent. They certainly gave an example of practical religion, pluck, charity, and devotion.

And so the moons waxed and waned, and Mafeking patiently waited, and, luckily, had every confidence in the resource and ability of Colonel Baden-Powell. An old cannon had been discovered, half buried in the native *stadt*, which was polished up and named "The Lord Nelson," from the fact of its antiquity. For this gun solid cannon-balls were manufactured, and finally fired off at the nearest Boer trenches; and the first of these to go bounding along the ground certainly surprised and startled our foes, which was proved by their quickly moving a part of their laager. In addition a rough gun, called "The Wolf," was actually constructed in Mafeking, which fired an 18-pound shell

4,000 yards. To this feat our men were incited by hearing of the magnificent weapon which had been cast by the talented workmen of Kimberley in the De Beers workshops. In spite of there being nothing but the roughest materials to work with, shells were also made, and some Boer projectiles which arrived in the town without exploding were collected, melted down, and hurled once more at our enemy. Truly, there is no such schoolmaster as necessity.

On Sundays we continued to put away from us the cares and worries of the week, and the Church services of the various denominations were crowded, after an hour devoted to very necessary shopping. During the whole siege the Sunday afternoon sports on the parade-ground were a most popular institution; when it was wet, amusing concerts were given instead at the Masonic Hall. On these occasions Colonel Baden-Powell was the leading spirit, as well as one of the principal artistes, anon appearing in an *impromptu* sketch as "Signor Paderewski," or, again, as a *coster*, and holding the hall entranced or convulsed with laughter. He was able to assume very various *rôles* with "Fregoli-like" rapidity; for one evening, soon after the audience had dispersed, suddenly there was an alarm of a night attack.

Firing commenced all round the town, which was a most unusual occurrence for a Sunday night. In an instant the man who had been masquerading as a buffoon was again the commanding officer, stern and alert. The tramp of many feet was heard in the streets, which proved to be the reserve squadron of the Protectorate Regiment, summoned in haste to headquarters. A Maxim arrived, as by magic, from somewhere else, the town guard were ordered to their places, and an A.D.C. was sent to the hall, where a little dance for the poor overworked hospital nurses was in full swing, abruptly to break up this pleasant gathering. It only remained for our defenders to wish the Boers would come on, instead of which the attack ended in smoke, after two hours' furious volleying, and by midnight all was quiet again.

During the latter part of this tedious time Colonel Plumer and his gallant men were but thirty miles away, having encompassed a vast stretch of dreary desert from distant Bulawayo. This force had been "under the stars" since the previous August, and had braved hardships of heat, fever districts, and flooded rivers, added to many a brush with the enemy. These trusty friends were only too anxious to come to our assistance, but a river rolled between—a river composed of deep fortified trenches, of modern artillery, and of first-rate marksmen with many Mausers.

One day Colonel Plumer sent in an intrepid scout to consult with Colonel Baden-Powell. This gentleman had a supreme contempt for bullets, and certainly did not know the meaning of the word "fear," but the bursting shells produced a disagreeable impression on him. "Does it always go on like that?" he asked, when he heard the vicious hammer of the enemy's Maxim. "Yes," somebody gloomily answered, "it always goes on like that, till at length we pretend to like it, and that we should feel dull if it were silent."

Although the soldiers in Mafeking were disposed to grumble at the small part they seemed to be playing in the great tussle in which England was engaged, the authorities were satisfied that for so small a town to have kept occupied during the first critical month of the war 10,000—and at later stages never less than 2,000—Boers, was in itself no small achievement. We women always had lots to do. When the hospital work was slack there were many Union Jacks to be made—a most intricate and tiresome occupation—and these were distributed among the various forts. We even had a competition in trimming hats, and a prize was given to the best specimen as selected by a competent committee. In the evenings we never failed to receive the Mafeking evening paper, and were able to puzzle our heads over its excellent acrostics, besides frequently indulging in a pleasant game of cards.

In the meantime food was certainly becoming very short, and on April 3 I cabled to my sister in London as follows: "Breakfast to-day, horse sausages; lunch, minced mule, curried locusts. All well." Occasionally I used to be allowed a tiny white roll for breakfast, but it had to last for dinner too. Mr. Weil bought the last remaining turkey for £5, with the intention of giving a feast on Her Majesty's birthday, and the precious bird had to be kept under a Chubb's lock and key till it was killed. No dogs or cats were safe, as the Basutos stole them all for food. But all the while we were well aware our situation might have been far worse. The rains were over, the climate was glorious, fever was fast diminishing, and, in spite of experiencing extreme boredom, we knew that the end of the long lane was surely coming.

CHAPTER 13

Eloff's Determined Attack on Mafeking, and the Relief of the Town

War, war is still the cry—war even to the knife!—Byron.

"The Boers are in the *stadt!*" Such was the ominous message that was quickly passed round from mouth to mouth on Saturday morning, May 12, 1900, as day was breaking. One had to be well acquainted with the labyrinth of rocks, trees, huts, and cover generally, of the locality aforementioned, all within a stone's-throw of our dwelling, to realise the dread import of these words.

All the previous week things had been much as usual: inferior food, and very little of it; divine weather; "bridge" in the afternoons; and one day exactly like another. Since the departure of the big gun during the previous month, we had left our bomb-proofs and lived above-ground. In the early hours of the morning alluded to came the real event we had been expecting ever since the beginning of the siege—namely, a Boer attack under cover of darkness. The moon had just set, and it was pitch-dark. A fierce fusillade first began from the east, and when I opened the door on to the *stoep* the din was terrific, while swish, swish, came the bullets just beyond the canvas blinds, nailed to the edge of the verandah to keep off the sun. Now and then the boom of a small gun varied the noise, but the rifles never ceased for an instant.

To this awe-inspiring tune I dressed, by the light of a carefully shaded candle, to avoid giving any mark for our foes. The firing never abated, and I had a sort of idea that any moment a Dutchman would look in at the door, for one could not tell from what side the real attack might be. In various stages of *deshabille* people were running round the house seeking for rifles, fowling-pieces, and even sticks, as weapons of defence. Meanwhile the gloom was still unbroken, but for the starlight, and it was very cold. The Cockney waiter, who was such a fund of amusement to me, had dashed off with his rifle to his redoubt, taking the keys of the house in his pocket, so no one could get into the dining-room to have coffee, except through the kitchen window. The two hours of darkness that had to elapse were the longest I have ever spent. Hurried footsteps passed to and fro, dark lanterns flashed for an instant, intensifying the blackness, and all of a sudden the sound I had been waiting for added to the weird horror of the situation, an alarm bugle, winding out its tale, clear and true to the farthest byways and the most remote shanties, followed by our tocsin, the deep-toned Roman Catholic Church bell, which was the signal that a general attack was in progress.

We caught dim glimpses of the town guard going to their appointed places in the most orderly manner, and I remember thinking that where there was no panic there could be but little danger. An officer of this guard came down the road and told us all his men had turned out without exception, including an old fellow of seventy, and stone-deaf, who had been roused by the rifle-fire, and one minus several fingers recently blown off by a shell. I went out to the front of the house facing the *stadt*, and therefore sheltered from the hail of bullets coming from the east; and just as we were noticing that objects could be discerned on the road, that before were invisible, forked tongues of lurid light shot up into the sky in the direction where, snug and low by the Malopo River, lay the natives' habitations. Even then one did not realise what was burning, and someone said: "What a big grass fire! It must have commenced yesterday."

At the same moment faint cries, unmistakable for *kaffir* ejaculations, were borne to us by the breeze, along with the smell of burning thatch and wood, and the dread sentence with which I commenced this chapter seemed to grow in volume, till to one's excited fancy it became a sort of chant, to which the yells of the blacks, the unceasing rattle of musketry, formed an unholy accompaniment. "Hark, what is that?" was a universal exclamation from the few folk, mostly women, standing in front of Mr. Weil's house, as a curious hoarse cheer arose— not in the *stadt*, half a mile away, but nearer, close by, only the other side of the station, where was situated the B.S.A.P. fort, the headquarters of the officer commanding the Protectorate Regiment. This so-called fort was in reality an obsolete old work of the time of Sir

Charles Warren's 1884 expedition, and was but slightly fortified.

The Boers, after setting fire to the *stadt*, had rushed it, surprising the occupants; and the horrible noise of their cheering arose again and again. Then a terrific fusillade broke out from this new direction, rendering the roadway a place of the greatest danger. My quarters were evidently getting too hot, and I knew that Weil's house and store would be the first objective of the Boers. I bethought me even novices might be useful in the hospital, so I decided to proceed there in one way or another. Although the rifle-fire was slackening towards the east, from the fort, on the west it was continuing unabated; and the way to the hospital lay through the most open part of the town.

Calling to our soldier servant of the Royal Horse Guards to accompany me, I snatched up a few things of value and started off. "You will be shot, to a certainty," said Mr. Weil. But it was no use waiting, as one could not tell what would happen next. The bullets were fortunately flying high; all the same, we had twice to stop under a wall and wait for a lull before proceeding. Then I saw a native boy fall in front of me, and at the same moment I stumbled and fell heavily, the servant thinking I was hit; and all the while we could hear frightened cries continuing to emanate from the flaming *stadt*.

The day had fully broken, and never had the roads appeared so white and wide, the sheltering houses so few and far between. At length we reached the hospital trench, and the last 500 yards of the journey were accomplished in perfect safety. My dangerous experiences ended for the rest of that dreadful day, which I spent in the haven of those walls, sheltering so much suffering, and that were, alas! by evening crammed to their fullest capacity. It was a gruesome sight seeing the wounded brought in, and the blood-stained stretchers carried away empty, when the occupants had been deposited in the operating-room. Sometimes an ambulance waggon would arrive with four or five inmates; at others we descried a stretcher-party moving cautiously across the recreation-ground towards us with a melancholy load. It is easy to imagine our feelings of dread and anxiety as we scanned the features of the new arrivals, never knowing who might be the next.

During the morning three wounded Boers were brought in—the first prisoners Mafeking could claim; then a native with his arm shattered to the shoulder. All were skilfully and carefully attended to by the army surgeon and his staff in a marvellously short space of time, and comfortably installed in bed. But the Boers begged not to have sheets, as they had never seen such things before. Among the English casualties, one case was a very sad one. A young man, named Hazelrigg, of an old Leicestershire family, was badly shot in the region of the heart when taking a message to the B.S.A.P. fort, not knowing the Boers were in possession. Smart and good-looking, he had only just been promoted to the post of orderly from being a private in the Cape Police, into which corps he had previously enlisted, having failed in his army examination. When brought to the hospital, Hazelrigg had nearly bled to death, and was dreadfully weak, his case being evidently hopeless. I sat with him several hours, putting *eau-de-Cologne* on his head and brushing away the flies. In the evening, just before he passed into unconsciousness, he repeated more than once: "Tell the colonel, Lady Sarah, I did my best to give the message, but they got me first." He died at dawn.

All through the weary hours of that perfect summer's day the rifles never ceased firing. Sometimes a regular fusillade for ten minutes or so; then, as if tired out, sinking down to a few single shots, while the siren-like whistle and sharp explosion of the shells from the high-velocity gun continued intermittently, and added to the dangers of the streets. So the hours dragged on. All the time the wildest rumours pervaded the air. Now the Boers had possession of the whole *stadt*; again, as soon as night fell, large reinforcements were to force their way in. Of course we knew the colonel was all the while maturing his plans to rid the town of the unbidden guests, but what these were no one could tell. About 8 p.m., when we were in the depth of despair, we got an official message to say that the Boers in the *stadt* had been surrounded and taken prisoners, and also that the fort had surrendered to Colonel Hore, who, with some of his officers, had been all day in the curious position of captives in their own barracks.

Of course our delight and thankfulness knew no bounds. In spite of the dead and dying patients, those who were slightly wounded or convalescent gave a feeble cheer, which was a pathetic sound. We further heard that the prisoners, in number about a hundred, including Commandant Eloff, their leader, were then being marched through the town to the Masonic Hall, followed by a large crowd of jeering and delighted natives. Two of the nurses and myself ran over to look at them, and I never saw a more motley crew. In the dim light of a few oil-lamps they represented many nationalities, the greater part laughing, joking, and even singing, the *burghers* holding themselves somewhat aloof, but the whole community giving one the idea of a body of men who knew they had got out of a tight place, and were devoutly thankful still to have whole skins. Eloff and three principal officers were accommodated at Mr. Weil's house, having previously dined with the colonel and staff.

At 6 a.m. Sunday morning we were awakened by three shells bursting close by, one after the other. I believe no one was more frightened than Eloff; but he told us that it was a preconcerted signal, and that, if they had been in possession of the town, they were to have answered by rifle-fire, when the Boers would have marched in. These proved to be the last shells that were fired into Mafeking.

The same morning at breakfast I sat opposite to Commandant Eloff, who was the President's grandson, and had on my right a most polite French officer, who could not speak a word of English, Dutch, or German, so it was difficult to understand how he made himself understood by his then companions-in-arms. In strong contrast to this affable and courteous gentleman was Eloff, of whom we had heard so much as a promising Transvaal general. A typical Boer of the modern school, with curiously unkempt hair literally standing on end, light sandy whiskers, and a small moustache, he was wearing a sullen and dejected expression on his by no means stupid, but discontented and unprepossessing, face. This scion of the Kruger family did not scruple to air his grievances or disclose his plans with regard to the struggle of the previous day.

That he was brilliantly assisted by the French and German freelances was as surely demonstrated as the fact of his having been left more or less in the lurch by his countrymen when they saw that to get into Mafeking was one thing, but to stay there or get out of it again was quite a different matter. In a few words he told us, in fairly good English, how it had been posted up in the *laager*, "We leave for Mafeking tonight: we will breakfast at Dixon's Hotel tomorrow morning"; how he had sent back to instruct Reuter's agent to cable the news that Mafeking had been taken as soon as the fort was in their hands; how he had left his camp with 400 volunteers, and how, when he had counted them by the light of the blazing *stadt*, only 240 remained; moreover, that the 500 additional men who were to push in when the fort was taken absolutely failed him.[1]

---

1. Later on, when I was at Zeerust, I met a telegraph clerk who had then been in the employ of the Boers, and he told me how indignant all were with General Snyman for deserting Eloff on that occasion. When one of the *veldtcornets* went and begged his permission to collect volunteers as reinforcements, all the general did was to scratch his head and murmur in Dutch, "*Morro is nocher dag*" (Tomorrow is another day).

He was also betrayed in that the arranged forward movement all round the town, which was to have taken place simultaneously with his attack, was never made. The burghers instead contented themselves by merely firing senseless volleys from their trenches, which constituted all the assistance he actually received. This, and much more, he told us with bitter emphasis, while the French officer conversed unconcernedly in the intervals of his discourse about the African climate, the weather, and the Paris Exhibition; finally observing with heartfelt emphasis that he wished himself back once more in "La Belle France," which he had only left two short months ago. The Dutchman, not understanding what he was saying, kept on the thread of his story, interrupting him without any compunction. It was one of the most curious meals at which I have ever assisted. That afternoon these officers were removed to safer quarters in gaol while a house was being prepared for their reception.

As after-events proved, Eloff's attack was the Boers' last card, which they had played when they heard of the approaching relief column under Colonel Mahon,[2] and of his intention to join hands with Colonel Plumer, coming from the North. After lunch, two days later, we saw clouds of dust to the south, and, from information to hand, we knew it must be our relievers. The whole of Mafeking spent hours on the roofs of the houses. In the meantime the Boers were very uneasy, with many horsemen coming and going, but the *laagers* were not being shifted. In the late afternoon a desultory action commenced, which to us was desperately exciting. We could see little but shells bursting and columns of dust. One thing was certain: the Boers were not running away, although the Colonel declared that our troops had gained possession of the position the Boers had held, the latter having fallen a little farther back.

As the sun set came a helio-message:

Diamond Fields Horse.—All well. Goodnight.

We went to dinner at seven, and just as we were sitting down I heard some feeble cheers. Thinking something must have happened, I ran to the market-square, and, seeing a dusty khaki-clad figure whose appearance was unfamiliar to me, I touched him on the shoulder, and said: "Has anyone come in?" "We have come in," he answered— "Major Karri-Davis and eight men of the Imperial Light Horse." Then I saw that officer himself, and he told us that, profiting by an

---

2. Later Major-General Mahon.

hour's dusk, they had ridden straight in before the moon rose, and that they were now sending back two troopers to tell the column the way was clear. Their having thus pushed on at once was a lucky inspiration, for, had they waited for daylight, they would probably have had a hard fight, even if they had got in at all. This plucky column of 1,100 men had marched nearly 300 miles in twelve days, absolutely confounding the Boers by their rapidity.

We heard weeks afterwards how that same day of the relief of Mafeking was celebrated in London with jubilation past belief, everyone going mad with delight. The original event in the town itself was a very tame if impressive affair—merely a score or so of people, singing "Rule, Britannia," surrounding eight or nine dust-begrimed figures, each holding a tired and jaded horse, and a few women on the outskirts of the circle with tears of joy in their eyes. Needless to say, no one thought of sleep that night. At 3.30 a.m. someone came and fetched me in a pony-cart, and we drove out to the polo-ground, where, by brilliant moonlight, we saw the column come into camp. Strings and strings of waggons were soon drawn up; next to them black masses, which were the guns; and beyond these, men, lying down anywhere, dead-tired, beside their horses. The rest of the night I spent at the hospital, where they were bringing in those wounded in the action of the previous afternoon.

At eight o'clock we were having breakfast with Colonel Mahon, Prince Alexander of Teck, Sir John Willoughby, and Colonel Frank Rhodes, as additional guests. We had not seen a strange face for eight months, and could do nothing but stare at them, and I think each one of us felt as if he or she were in a dream. Our friends told of their wonderful march, and how they had encamped one night at Setlagoli, where they had been taken care of by Mrs. Fraser and Metelka, who had spent the night in cooking for the officers, which fact had specially delighted Colonel Rhodes, who told me my maid was a "charming creature." But this pleasant conversation was interrupted by a message, saying that, as the Boer *laagers* were as intact as yesterday, the artillery were going to bombard them at once. Those of us who had leisure repaired at once to the convent, and from there the sight that followed was worth waiting all these many months to see.

First came the splendid batteries of the Royal Horse Artillery trotting into action, all the gunners bronzed and bearded. They were followed by the Canadian Artillery, who had joined Colonel Plumer's force, and who were that day horsed with mules out of the Bulawayo coach. These were galloping, and, considering the distance all had come, both horses and mules looked wonderfully fit and well. Most of the former, with the appearance of short-tailed English hunters, were stepping gaily out. The Imperial Light Horse and the Diamond Fields Horse, the latter distinguished by feathers in their felt hats, brought up the procession. Everybody cheered, and not a few were deeply affected. Personally, ever since, when I see galloping artillery, that momentous morning is brought back to my mind, and I feel a choking sensation in my throat.

About a quarter of a mile from town the guns unlimbered, and we could not help feeling satisfaction at watching the shells exploding in the *laager*—that *laager* we had watched for so many months, and had never been able to touch. The Boers had evidently never expected the column to be in the town, or they would have cleared off. We had a last glimpse of the tarpaulined waggons, and then the dust hid further developments from sight. After about thirty minutes the artillery ceased firing, and as the atmosphere cleared we saw the *laager* was a desert. Waggons, horses, and cattle, all had vanished.

After their exertions of the past fortnight, Colonel Mahon did not consider it wise to pursue the retreating Boers; but later in the afternoon I went out with others in a cart to where the *laager* had been— the first time since December that I had driven beyond our lines. I had the new experience of seeing a "loot" in progress. First we met two soldiers driving a cow; then some more with bulged-out pockets full of live fowls; natives were staggering under huge loads of food-stuffs, and eating even as they walked. I was also interested in going into the very room where General Snyman had treated me so scurvily, and where everything was in terrible confusion: the floor was littered with rifles, ammunition, food-stuffs of all sorts, clothes, and letters.

Among the latter some interesting telegrams were found, including one from the president, of a date three days previously, informing Snyman that things were most critical, and that the enemy had occupied Kroonstadt. We were just going on to the hospital, where I had spent those weary days of imprisonment, when an officer galloped up and begged me to return to Mafeking, as some skirmishing was going to commence. It turned out that 500 Boers had stopped just over the ridge to cover their retreating waggons, but they made no stand, and by evening were miles away.

On Friday, May 18, the whole garrison turned out to attend a thanksgiving service in an open space close to the cemetery. They

The Artillery that defended Mafeking.

were drawn up in a three-sided square, which looked pathetically small. After the service Colonel Baden-Powell walked round and said a few words to each corps; then three volleys were fired over the graves of fallen comrades, and the "Last Post" was played by the buglers, followed by the National Anthem, in which all joined. It was a simple ceremony, but a very touching one. The same afternoon Colonel Plumer's force was inspected by the colonel, prior to their departure for the North to repair the railway-line from Bulawayo. They were striking-looking men in their campaigning kit, having been in the field since last August. Some wore shabby khaki jackets and trousers, others flannel shirts and long boots or *putties*. However attired, they were eager once more for the fray, and, moreover, looked fit for any emergency.

The next few days were a period of intense excitement, and we were constantly stumbling against friends who had formed part of the relief column, but of whose presence we were totally unaware. Letters began to arrive in bulky batches, and one morning I received no less than 100, some of which bore the date of September of the year before. My time was divided between eagerly devouring these missives from home, sending and answering cables (a telegraph-line to the nearest telephone-office had been installed), and helping to organise a new hospital in the school-house, to accommodate the sick and wounded belonging to Colonel Mahon's force. All the while my thoughts were occupied by my return to England and by the question of the surest route to Cape Town. The railway to the South could not be relaid for weeks, and, as an alternative, my eyes turned longingly towards the Transvaal and Pretoria.

It must be remembered that we shared the general opinion that, once Lord Roberts had reached the latter town, the war would be practically over. How wrong we all were after-events were to prove, but at the end of May, 1900, it appeared to many that to drive the 200 miles to Pretoria would be very little longer, and much more interesting, than to trek to Kimberley, with Cape Town as the destination. Mrs. Godley (to whom I have before alluded) had arrived at Mafeking from Bulawayo, and we agreed to make the attempt, especially as the Boers in the intervening country were reported to be giving up their arms and returning to their farms. In the meantime it had been decided that Colonel Plumer should occupy Zeerust in the Transvaal, twenty-eight miles from the border, while Colonel Baden-Powell and his force pushed on to Rustenburg.

On May 28 Colonel Mahon and the relief column all departed to rejoin General Hunter in or near Lichtenburg, and Mafeking was left with a small garrison to look after the sick and wounded. This town, so long a theatre of excitement to itself and of interest to the world at large, then resumed by degrees the sleepy, even tenor of its ways, which had been so rudely disturbed eight months before.

CHAPTER 14

Across the Transvaal to Pretoria
During the War

There never was a good war or a bad peace.—Benjamin Franklin.

On Sunday morning, June 4, we packed into a Cape cart, with four siege horses in fair condition, and started to drive to Zeerust. It was a glorious day of blue skies and bright sun, with just enough breeze to prevent the noonday from being too hot. As we left Mafeking and its outworks behind, I had a curious feeling of regret and of gratitude to the gallant little town and its stout citizens: to the former for having been a haven in the midst of fierce storms during all these months; to the latter for their stout arms and their brave hearts, which had warded off the outbursts of the same tempests, whose clouds had hung dark and lowering on our horizon since the previous October. We also experienced a wonderful feeling of relief and freedom at being able to drive at will over the very roads which we had seen covered by Boer waggons, *burghers*, and guns, and, needless to say, we marked with interest the lines of their forts, so terribly near our little town.

We noted the farmhouse lately the headquarters of General Snyman, standing naked and alone. Formerly surrounded by a flourishing orchard and a carefully tended garden, it was now the picture of desolation. The ground was trampled by many feet of men and horses; straw, forage, packing-cases, and rubbish of all kinds, were strewn about, and absolutely hid the soil from view. Away on the hill beyond I spied the tiny house and hospital where I had spent six weary nights and days; and between these two buildings a patch of bare ground nearly half a mile square, indescribably filthy, had been the site of the white-hooded waggons and ragged tents of the laager itself. The road was of no interest, merely rolling *veldt* with a very few scattered farmhouses, apparently deserted; but one noticed that rough attempts had been made in the way of irrigation, and that, as one approached the Transvaal, pools of water were frequently to be seen.

A shallow ditch was pointed out to us by the driver, as the boundary between Her Majesty's colony and the South African Republic, and after another eight or ten miles we saw a few white roofs and trees, which proved to be Otto's Hoep, in the Malmani Gold District, from which locality great things had been hoped in bygone days, before the Rand was ever thought of. At the tiny hotel we found several officers and men of the Imperial Light Horse, who, warned by a telephone message from Mafeking, had ordered us an excellent hot lunch. The proprietor, of German origin, could do nothing but stare at us while we were eating the meal, apparently amazed at finding his house reopened after so many months of inactivity, and that people were actually prepared to pay for what they had. We soon pushed on again, and just after leaving the hotel a sharp turn brought us to a really wide river, close to where the Imperial Light Horse were encamped.

Our driver turned the horses' heads towards it, and without any misgivings we plunged in. The water grew deeper and deeper, and our thoughts flew to our portmanteaus, tied on behind, which were practically submerged. Just then the leaders took it into their heads they preferred not to go any farther, and forthwith turned round and faced us. The black coachman, however, did not lose his head, but pulled the wheelers round also, and we soon found ourselves again on the same bank from which we had started. Had it not been for a kind trooper of the Imperial Light Horse, our chances of getting across would have been nil. This friend in need mounted a loose horse, and succeeded in coaxing and dragging our recalcitrant leaders, and forcing them to face the rushing stream.

Once again our portmanteaus had a cold bath, but this time we made a successful crossing, and went gaily on our way. The road was now much improved and the country exceedingly pretty. Many snug little houses, sheltered by rows of cypress, tall eucalyptus and huge orange-trees laden with yellow fruit, their gardens intersected by running brooks, appeared on all sides; while in the distance rose a range of blue hills, at the foot of which we could perceive the roofs of Zeerust.

As the sun was almost sinking, clouds of dust arose on the road in front, denoting a large body of men or waggons moving. A few weeks—nay, days—ago these would have been a *burgher* commando; now we knew they were our friends, and presently we met Major Weston Jarvis and his dust-begrimed squadron of the Rhodesian Regiment, followed by a large number of transport waggons, driven cattle, and donkeys. This living testimony that war was still present in the land only disturbed the peaceful evening landscape till the long line of dust had disappeared; then all was stillness and beauty once more. The young moon came out, the stars twinkled in the dark blue heavens, and suddenly, below the dim range of hills, shone first one light and then another; while away to the left, on higher ground, camp-fires, softened by a halo of white smoke, came into view. The scene was very picturesque. No cloud obscured the star-bespangled sky or the crescent of the Queen of the Night. Still far away, the lights of the little town were a beacon to guide us. The noise and cries of the camp were carried to us on the gentlest of night breezes, and, to complete the calm beauty of the surroundings, the deep, slow chime of a church-bell struck our ears.

We had reached our destination, and were in a few minutes driving through the quiet little street, pulling up in front of the Central Hotel, kept by a colonial Englishman and his wife. The former had been commandeered twice during the war, but he hastened to assure us that, though he had been at the *laager*, and even in the trenches before Mafeking, he had never let off his rifle, and had given it up with great pleasure to the English only the day before. This old-fashioned hostelry was very comfortable and commodious, with excellent cooking, but it was not till the next day that we realised how pretty was the town of Zeerust, and how charmingly situated. The houses, standing back from the wide road, were surrounded by neat little gardens and rows of cypresses. Looking down the main street, in either direction, were purple, tree-covered hills. A stream wound its way across one end of the highway, and teams of sleepy fat oxen with bells completed the illusion that we had suddenly been transported into a town of Northern Italy or of the Lower Engadine.

However, other circumstances contributed to give it an air of depression and sadness. On the stoeps of the houses were gathered groups of Dutch women and girls, many of them in deep mourning, and all looking very miserable, gazing at us with unfriendly eyes. Fine-looking but shabbily-clad men were to be met carrying their rifles and *bandoliers* to the *Landrost's* late office, now occupied by Colonel Plumer and his Staff. Sometimes they were leading a rough-coated, ill-fed pony, in many cases their one ewe lamb, which might or might not be required for Her Majesty's troops. They walked slowly and dejectedly, though some took off their hats and gave one a rough "Good-day." Most of them had their eyes on the ground and a look of mute despair.

Others, again, looked quite jolly and friendly, calling out a cheery greeting, for all at that time thought the war was really over. I was told that what caused them surprise and despair was the fact of their animals being required by the English: "requisitioned" was the term used when the owner was on his farm, which meant that he would receive payment for the property, and was given a receipt to that effect; "confiscated," when the *burgher* was found absent, which signified he was still on commando. Even in the former case he gave up his property sadly and reluctantly, amid the tears and groans of his wife and children, for, judging by the ways of his own government, they never expected the paper receipt would produce any recognition. Many of the cases of these poor *burghers* seemed indeed very hard, for it must be remembered that during the past months of the war all their things had been used by their own government for the patriotic cause, and what still remained to them was then being appropriated by the English.

All along they had been misled and misinformed, for none of their leaders ever hinted there could be but one end to the war—namely, the decisive success of the Transvaal Republic. It made it easy to realise the enormous difficulties that were connected with what was airily talked of as the "pacification of the country," and that those English officers who laboured then, and for many months afterwards, at this task had just as colossal and arduous an undertaking as the soldiers under Lord Roberts, who had gloriously cut their way to Johannesburg and Pretoria. Someone said to me in Zeerust: "When the English have reached Pretoria their difficulties will only begin." In the heyday of our Relief, and with news of English victories constantly coming to hand, I thought this gentleman a pessimist; but the subsequent history of the war, and the many weary months following the conclusion of peace, proved there was much truth in the above statement.

Two days later we heard that Lord Roberts had made his formal entry into Pretoria on June 5, but our journey thither did not proceed as smoothly as we had hoped. We chartered a Cape cart and an excellent pair of grey horses, and made our first attempt to reach Pretoria *via* the lead-mines, the same route taken by Dr. Jameson and the Raiders. Here we received a check in the shape of a letter from General Baden-Powell requesting us not to proceed, as he had received information that Lord Roberts's line of communication had been temporarily interrupted. The weather had turned exceedingly wet and cold, like an English March or late autumn, and after two days of inactivity in a damp and gloomy Dutch farmhouse we were perforce obliged to return to our original starting-point, Zeerust. A few days later we heard that Colonel Baden-Powell had occupied Rustenburg, and that the country between there and Pretoria was clear; so we decided to make a fresh start, and this time to take the northern and more mountainous route.

We drove through a very pretty country, with many trees and groves of splendid oranges, and we crossed highly cultivated valleys, with numerous farms dotted about. All those we met described themselves as delighted at what they termed the close of the war, and gave us a rough salutation as we went on our way, after a friendly chat. Presently we passed an open trolley with a huge red-cross flag flying, but which appeared to contain nothing but private luggage, and was followed by a man, evidently a doctor, driving a one-horse buggy, and wearing an enormous red-cross badge on his hat. At midday we outspanned to rest the horses and eat our lunch, and in the afternoon we crossed the great Marico River, where was situated a deserted and ruined hotel and store. The road then became so bad that the pace of our horses scarcely reached five miles an hour, and to obtain shelter we had to reach Eland's River before it became quite dark. A very steep hill had to be climbed, which took us over the shoulder of the chain of hills, and rumbling slowly down the other side, with groaning brake and stumbling steeds, we met a typical Dutch family, evidently trekking back from the *laager* in a heavy ox waggon.

The sad-looking mother, with three or four children in ragged clothes, was sitting inside; the father and the eldest boy were walking beside the oxen. Their apparent misery was depressing, added to which the day, which all along had been cold and dismal, now began to close in, and, what was worse, rain began to fall, which soon grew to be a regular downpour. At last we could hardly see our grey horses, and every moment I expected we should drive into one of the many pitfalls in the shape of big black holes with which the roads in this part of the Transvaal abounded, and a near acquaintance with any one of these would certainly have upset the cart.

At last we saw twinkling lights, but we first had to plunge down another river-bed and ascend a precipitous incline up the opposite bank. Our horses were by now very tired, and for one moment it seemed to hang in the balance whether we should roll back into the water or gain the top. The good animals, however, responded to the whip, plunged forward, and finally pulled up at a house dimly outlined in the gloom. In response to our call, a dripping sentry peered out, and told us it was, as we hoped, Wolhuter's store, and that he would call the proprietor. Many minutes elapsed, during which intense stillness prevailed, seeming to emphasize how desolate a spot we had reached, and broken only by the splash of the heavy rain. Then the door opened, and a man appeared to be coming at last, only to disappear again in order to fetch coat and umbrella.

Eventually it turned out the owner of the house was a miller, by birth a German, and this gentleman very kindly gave us a night's hospitality. He certainly had not expected visitors, and it took some time to allay his suspicions as to who we were and what was our business. Accustomed to the universal hospitality in South Africa, I was somewhat surprised at the hesitation he showed in asking us into his house, and when we were admitted he claimed indulgence for any shortcomings by saying his children were ill. We assured him we should give no trouble, and we were so wet and cold that any roof and shelter were a godsend. Just as I was going to bed, my maid came and told me that, from a conversation she had had with the *kaffir* girl, who seemed to be the only domestic, she gathered that two children were suffering from an infectious disease, which, in the absence of any medical man, they had diagnosed as smallpox. To proceed on our journey was out of the question, but it may be imagined that we left next morning at the very earliest hour possible.

This very district round Eland's River was later the scene of much fighting, and it was there a few months afterwards that De la Rey surrounded an English force, who were only rescued in the nick of time by the arrival of Lord Kitchener. At the date of our visit, however, all was peaceful, and, but for a few *burghers* riding in haste to surrender their arms, not a trace of the enemy was to be seen.

The next day we reached Rustenburg, where we stayed the night, and learnt that General Baden-Powell and his Staff had left there for Pretoria, to confer with Lord Roberts. Our gallant grey horses were standing the strain well, and the worst roads as well as the most mountainous country were then behind us; so, without delay, we continued on the morrow, spending the third night at a storekeeper's house at Sterkstrom. Towards the evening of the fourth day after leaving Zeerust, we entered a long wide valley, and by degrees overtook vehicles of many lands, wearied pedestrians, and horsemen—in fact, the inevitable stragglers denoting the vicinity of a vast army. The valley was enclosed by moderately high hills, and from their summits we watched helio messages passing to and fro during all that beautiful afternoon, while we slowly accomplished the last, but seemingly endless, miles of our tedious drive.

At 5 p.m. we crawled into the suburbs of the Boer capital, having driven 135 miles with the same horses. The description of Pretoria under British occupation, and the friends we met there, I must leave to another chapter.

CHAPTER 15

Pretoria and Johannesburg Under Lord Roberts and Military Law

With malice to none … with firmness in the right, as
God gives us to see the right, let us finish the work we are in.
—Abraham Lincoln.

At Pretoria Mrs. Godley and I found accommodation, not without some difficulty, at the Grand Hotel. Turned for the moment into a sort of huge barrack, this was crowded to its utmost capacity. The polite manager, in his endeavour to find us suitable rooms, conducted us all over the spacious building, and at last, struck by a bright thought, threw open the door of an apartment which he said would be free in a few hours, as the gentleman occupying it was packing up his belongings preparatory to his departure. Great was my surprise at discovering in the khaki-clad figure, thus unceremoniously disturbed in the occupation of stowing away papers, clothes, and campaigning kit generally, no less a personage than my nephew, Winston Churchill, who had experienced such thrilling adventures during the war, the accounts of which had reached us even in far-away Mafeking. The proprietor was equally amazed to see me warmly greet the owner of the rooms he proposed to allot us, and, although Winston postponed his departure for another twenty-four hours, he gladly gave up part of his suite for our use, and everything was satisfactorily arranged.

Good-looking figures in khaki swarmed all over the hotel, and friends turned up every minute—bearded *pards*, at whom one had to look twice before recognizing old acquaintances. No less than a hundred officers were dining that night in the large restaurant. Between the newly liberated prisoners and those who had taken part

155

THE ENGLISH TROOPS TAKING POSSESSION OF KRUGER'S HOUSE AT PRETORIA, JUNE 5, 1900

in the victorious march of Lord Roberts's army one heard surprised greetings such as these: "Hallo, old chap! where were you caught?" or a late-comer would arrive with the remark: "There has been firing along the outposts all day. I suppose the beggars have come back." (I was relieved to hear the outposts were twelve miles out.) The whole scene was like an act in a Drury Lane drama, and we strangers seemed to be the appreciative audience. Accustomed as we were to a very limited circle, it appeared to us as if all the inhabitants of England had been transported to Pretoria.

Early next day we drove out to see the departure of General Baden-Powell[1] and his staff, who had been most warmly received by Lord Roberts, and who, after receiving his orders, were leaving to rejoin their men at Rustenburg. As an additional mark of favour, the commander-in-chief and his retinue gave the defender of Mafeking a special send-off, riding with him and his officers some distance out of the town. This procession was quite an imposing sight, and was preceded by a company of turbaned Indians. Presently, riding alongside of General Baden-Powell, on a small, well-bred Arab, came the hero of a thousand fights, the man who at an advanced age, and already crowned with so many laurels, had, in spite of a crushing bereavement, stepped forward to help his country in the hour of need.

We were delighted when this man of the moment stopped to speak to us. He certainly seemed surprised at the apparition of two ladies, and observed that we were very daring, and the first of our sex to come in. I shall, however, never forget how kindly he spoke nor the inexpressible sadness of his face. I told him how quiet everything appeared to be along the road we had taken, and how civil were all the Boers we had met. At this he turned to the guest whose departure he was speeding, and said, with a grave smile, "That is thanks to you, general." And then the cortege rode on. On reflection, I decided, rather from what Lord Roberts had left unsaid than from his actual words, that if we had asked leave to travel home *via* Pretoria, it would have been refused.

The rest of that day and the next we spent in seeing the town under its new auspices, and it certainly presented far more to interest a visitor than on the occasion of my last visit in 1896. In a suburb known as Sunny Side was situated Lord Roberts's headquarters, at a house known as the Residency. Close by was a charming villa inhabited for the nonce by General Brabazon, Lord Dudley, Mr. John Ward, and Captain W. Ba-

1. ColonelBaden-Powell had been promoted to the rank of major-general.

got. The surroundings of these dwellings were exceedingly pretty, with shady trees, many streams, and a background of high hills crowned by forts, which latter were just visible to the naked eye. From Sunny Side we were conducted over some of these fortifications: there was Schantz's Kop Fort, of very recent construction, and looking to the uninitiated of tremendous strength, with roomy bomb-proof shelters. Here a corner of one of the massive entrance pillars had been sharply severed off by a British lyddite shell. Later we inspected Kapper Kop Fort, the highest of all, where two British howitzer guns, firing a 280-pound shell, had found a resting-place. Surrounded by a moat with a drawbridge, the view from this fort was magnificent. The Boers were in the act of making a double-wire entanglement round it, and had evidently meant to offer there a stubborn resistance, when more prudent counsels prevailed, and they had left their work half finished, and decamped, carrying off all their ammunition. In the town itself General French and his staff had established themselves at the Netherlands Club, from which resort the members had been politely ejected.

To outward appearances, civil as well as military business was being transacted in Pretoria with perfect smoothness, in spite of the proximity of the enemy. The yeomanry were acting as police both there and in Johannesburg. The gaol, of which we had a glimpse, was crowded with 240 prisoners, but was under the competent direction of the usual English under-official, who had been in the service of the Transvaal, and who had quietly stepped into the shoes of his chief, a Dutchman, when the latter bolted with Kruger. This prison was where the Raiders and the Reformers had been in durance vile, and the gallows were pointed out to us with the remark that, during the last ten years, they had only been once used, their victim being an Englishman. A Dutchman, who had been condemned to death during the same period for killing his wife, had been reprieved.

In the same way the Natal Bank and the Transvaal National Bank were being supervised by their permanent officials, men who had been at their posts during the war, and who, although under some suspicions, had not been removed. At the latter bank the manager told us how President Kruger had sent his Attorney-General to fetch the gold in coins and bar just before he left for Delagoa Bay, and how it was taken away on a trolley. The astute president actually cheated his people of this bullion, as he had already forced them to accept paper tokens for the gold, which he then acquired and removed. We also saw the Raad Saals—especially interesting from being exactly as they were left after the last session on May 7—Kruger's private room, and the Council Chamber. These latter were fine apartments, recently upholstered by Maple, and littered with papers, showing every evidence of the hurried departure of their occupants. Finally, specially conducted by Winston, we inspected the so-called "Bird-cage," where all the English officers had been imprisoned, and the "Staat Model" School, from where our cicerone had made his escape. These quarters must have been a particularly disagreeable and inadequate residence.

After a day in Pretoria we realised that, in spite of the shops being open and the hotels doing a roaring trade, notwithstanding the marvellous organisation visible on all sides, events were not altogether satisfactory; and one noted that the faces of those behind the scenes were grave and serious. Louis Botha, it was evident, was anything but a defeated foe. This gentleman had actually been in the capital when the English entered, and he was then only sixteen miles away. During the previous week a severe action had been fought with him at Diamond Hill, where the English casualties had been very heavy.

The accounts of this engagement, as then related, had a touch of originality. The commander-in-chief and staff went out in a special train, sending their horses by road, which reminded one forcibly of a day's hunting; cab-drivers in the town asked pedestrians if they would like to drive out and see the fight. The real affair, however, was grim earnest, and many were the gallant men who lost their lives on that occasion. All the while De Wet was enjoying himself to the south by constantly interrupting the traffic on the railway. No wonder the generals were careworn, and it was a relief to meet Lord Stanley,[2] A.D.C. to Lord Roberts, with a smiling face, who, with his unfailing spirits, must have been an invaluable companion to his chief during those trying weeks. One specially sad feature was the enormous number of sick in addition to wounded soldiers.

Of the former, at that time, there were over 1,500, and the recollection of the large numbers buried at Bloemfontein was still green in everyone's memory. The origin of all the sickness, principally enteric, was undoubtedly due to the Paardeberg water in the first instance, and then to that used at Bloemfontein; for Pretoria was perfectly healthy—the climate cool, if rainy, and the water-supply everything that could be desired. As additional accommodation for these patients, the magnificent and recently finished Law Courts had been arranged to hold seven or eight hundred beds. Superintended by Sir William Thomp-

2. Later Earl of Derby.

son, this improvised establishment was attended to by the personnel of the Irish hospital, and Mr. Guinness was there himself, organising their work and doing excellent service.

One evening we were most hospitably entertained to dinner by Lord Stanley, Captain Fortescue, the Duke of Westminster, and Winston. As it may be imagined, we heard many interesting details of the past stages of the war. Winston, even at that early stage of his career, and although he had been but a short time, comparatively, with Lord Roberts's force, had contrived therein to acquire influence and authority. The "bosses," doubtless, disapproved of his free utterances, but he was nevertheless most amusing to listen to, and a general favourite. The next day we saw him and the Duke of Westminster off on their way South, and having fixed my own departure for the following Monday, and seen most of the sights, I determined to avail myself of an invitation Captain Laycock, A.D.C. to General French, had given me, and go to the Netherlands Club in order to peruse the goodly supply of newspapers and periodicals of which they were the proud possessors. It was a cold, windy afternoon, and, finding the front-door locked and no bell visible, I went to one of the long French windows at the side of the house, through which I could see a cosy fire glimmering.

Perceiving a gentleman sitting in front of the inviting blaze, I knocked sharply to gain admittance. On nearer inspection this gentleman proved to be asleep, and it was some minutes before he got up and revealed himself as a middle-aged man, strongly built, with slightly grey hair. For some unknown reason I imagined him to be a major in a cavalry regiment, no doubt attached to the staff, and when, after rubbing his eyes, he at length opened the window, I apologized perfunctorily for having disturbed him, adding that I was acting on Captain Laycock's suggestion in coming there. In my heart I hoped he would leave me to the undisturbed perusal of the literature which I saw on a large centre table. He showed, however, no signs of taking his departure, and made himself so agreeable that I was perforce obliged to continue the conversation he commenced. I told him of the Mafeking siege, giving him my opinion of the Boers as opponents and of their peculiarities as we had experienced them; also of how, in the west and north, the enemy seemed to have practically disappeared.

Presently, by way of politeness, I asked him in what part of the country, and under which general, he had been fighting. He answered evasively that he had been knocking about, under several commanders, pretty well all over the place, which reply left me more mystified than ever. Soon Captain Laycock came in, and after a little more talk, during which I could see that he and my new acquaintance were on the best of terms, the latter went out, expressing a hope I should stay to tea, which I thought exceedingly kind of him, but scarcely necessary, as I was Captain Laycock's guest.

When he had gone, I questioned the latter as to the identity of his friend, and was horrified to learn that it was General French himself whom I had so unceremoniously disturbed, and to whom I had volunteered information. When the general returned with some more of his staff, including Lord Brooke, Colonel Douglas Haig,[3] Mr. Brinsley Fitzgerald, and Mr. Brinton, 2nd Life Guards,[4] I was profuse in my apologies, which he promptly cut short by asking me to make the tea, and we had a most cheery meal, interspersed with a good deal of chaff, one of his friends remarking to me that it was probably the only occasion during the last six months in South Africa that General French had been caught asleep.

The following day, Sunday, we attended a very impressive military service, at which Lord Roberts and his Staff, in full uniform, were present, and at the conclusion the whole congregation sang the National Anthem with the organ accompaniment. The volume of sound, together with the well-loved tune, was one not soon to be forgotten.

In the evening I had a visit from a stranger, who announced himself to be Mr. Barnes, correspondent to the *Daily Mail*. This gentleman handed me a letter from my sister, Lady Georgiana Curzon, dated Christmas Day of the previous year, which had at last reached me under peculiar circumstances. It appeared that, when my resourceful sister heard I had been taken prisoner by the Boers, she decided the best way of communicating with me would be through the President of the South African Republic, *via* Delagoa Bay. She had therefore written him a letter as follows:

Christmas Day, 1899.
Lady Georgiana Curzon presents her compliments to His Honour President Kruger, and would be very much obliged if he would give orders that the enclosed letter should be forwarded to her sister, Lady Sarah Wilson, who, according to the latest reports, has been taken prisoner by General Snyman.

In this letter was enclosed the one now handed to me by Mr. Barnes.

---

3. Later Major-General Haig.
4. Later Major Brinton.

The president, in the novel experience of receiving a letter from an English lady, had sent for the American Consul, and had handed him both epistles without a remark of any kind, beyond asking him to deal with them. Thus the missive finally reached its destination. This visitor had hardly departed when another was announced in the person of a Dr. Scholtz, whom, with his wife, I had met at Groot Schuurr as Mr. Rhodes's friends. This gentleman, who is since dead, had always seemed to me somewhat of an enigmatical personage. German by origin, he combined strong sympathies with the Boers and fervent Imperialism, and I was therefore always a little doubtful as to his real sentiments. He came very kindly on this occasion to pay a friendly call, but also to inform me that he was playing a prominent part in the abortive peace negotiations which at that stage of the war were being freely talked about.

Whether he had acted on his own initiative, or whether he had actually been employed by the authorities, he did not state; but he seemed to be full of importance, and proud of the fact that he had spent two hours only a few days before on a *kopje* in conference with Louis Botha, while the same kopje was being energetically shelled by the English. He gave me, indeed, to understand that the successful issue of the interview had depended entirely on the amount the English Government was prepared to pay, and that another £2,000,000 would have ended the war then and there. He probably did not enjoy the full confidence of either side, and I never verified the truth of his statements, which were as strange and mysterious as the man himself, whom, as events turned out, I never saw again.

It had been difficult to reach Pretoria, but the departure therefrom was attended by many formalities, and I had to provide myself, amongst other permits, with a railway pass, which ran as follows:

RAILWAY PASSES.

The bearer, Lady Sarah.Wilson (and maid) is permitted to travel at her own expense from Pretoria to Cape Town *via* the Vaal River.

O.S. NUGENT,
Major, Provost Marshal
(For Major-General, Military
Governor of Pretoria).

To R.S.O.
Pretoria, June 25, 1900.

Everything being then pronounced in order, I said goodbye to Mrs. Godley, who was returning by road to Zeerust and Mafeking, and, accompanied by Captain Seymour Fortescue, who had a few days' leave, and by Major Bobby White, I left on June 25 for Johannesburg. The train was painfully slow, and rarely attained a speed of more than five or six miles an hour. At Elandsfontein the engine gave out entirely, and a long delay ensued while another was being procured. At all the stations were small camps and pickets of bronzed and bearded soldiers, and on the platforms could be seen many officers newly arrived from England, distinguished by their brand-new uniforms, nearly all carrying the inevitable Kodak. At length we arrived at Johannesburg as the daylight was fading, and found excellent accommodation at Heath's Hotel. In the "Golden City," as at Pretoria, the shops were open, and seemed wonderfully well supplied, butter and cigarettes being the only items that were lacking.

I remember lunching the next day at a grill-room, called Frascati's, underground, where the *cuisine* was first-rate, and which was crowded with civilians of many nationalities, soldiers not being in such prominence as at Pretoria. The afternoon we devoted to seeing some of the principal mines, including the Ferreira Deep, which had been worked by the Transvaal Government for the last eight months. For this purpose they had engaged capable managers from France and Germany, and therefore the machinery was in no way damaged. At a dinner-party the same evening, given by Mr. A. Goldmann, we met a German gentleman who gave an amusing account of the way in which some of the city financiers had dashed off to the small banks a few days before Lord Roberts's entry, when the report was rife that Kruger was going to seize all the gold at Johannesburg as well as that at Pretoria. They were soon seen emerging with bags of sovereigns on their backs, which they first carried to the National Bank, but which, on second thoughts, they reclaimed again, finally confiding their treasure to the *Banque de la France.*

CHAPTER 16

My Return to Civilization Once More

Let us admit it fairly,
As business people should,
We have had no end of a lesson:
It will do us no end of good.
                    —Kipling.

On June 27 I left Johannesburg under the escort of Major Bobby White, who had kindly promised to see me safely as far as Cape Town. We travelled in a shabby third-class carriage, the only one on the train, which was merely composed of open trucks. Our first long delay was at Elandsfontein, practically still in the Rand District. There the officer in charge came up with the pleasing intelligence that the train we were to join had broken down, and would certainly be four hours late; so we had to get through a very weary wait at this most unattractive little township, whose only interesting features were the distant chimneys and unsightly shafts of the Simmer and Jack and the Rose Deep Mines, and far away, on the horizon, the little white house, amid a grove of trees, which had been Lord Roberts's headquarters barely a month ago, and from which he had sent the summons to Johannesburg to surrender.

All around, indeed, was the scene of recent fighting, and various polite transport officers tried to while away the tedium of our enforced delay by pointing out various faint ridges, and explaining that *there* the Gordons had made their splendid charge, or, again, that farther back General French had encountered such a stubborn resistance, and so on, *ad libitum*. In response I gazed with enthusiastic interest, but the flat, hideous country, which guards its deeply buried treasure so closely, seemed so alike in every direction, and the operations of the victorious army covered so wide an area, that it was difficult to make a brain picture of that rapid succession of feats of arms. At the station itself the "Tommys" buzzed about like bees, and the officers were having tea or dinner, or both combined, in the refreshment-room. One overheard scraps of conversation, from a subaltern to his superior officer: "A capital bag today, sir. Forty Mausers and ten thousand rounds of ammunition."

Then someone else remarked that a railway-train from the South passed yesterday, riddled with bullets, and recounted the marvellous escape its occupants had had, which was not encouraging in view of our intended journey over the same route. A young man in uniform presently entered with a limp, and, in answer to inquiries, said his wounded leg was doing famously, adding that the bullet had taken exactly the same course as the one did not six weeks ago—only then it had affected the other knee; "so I knew how to treat it, and I am off to the Yeomanry Hospital, if they will have me. I only left there a fortnight ago, and, by Jove! it was like leaving Paradise!" Another arrival came along saying the Boers had received a proper punishing for their last depredations on the railway, when De Wet had brought off his crowning *coup* by destroying the mail-bags. But this gentleman had hardly finished his tale when a decided stir was observable, and we heard a wire was to hand saying the same De Wet was again on the move, and that a strong force of men and guns were to leave for the scene of action by our train tonight.

At this juncture, seeing there was no prospect of any immediate departure, I installed myself comfortably with a book in the waiting-room, and was so absorbed that I did not even notice the arrival of a train from Heidelberg, till the door opened, and my nephew, the Duke of Marlborough, looked in, and we exchanged a surprised greeting, being totally unaware of each other's whereabouts. Except for meeting Winston in Pretoria, I had not seen the face of one of my relations for more than a year, but so many surprising things happen in wartime that we did not evince any great astonishment at this strange and unexpected meeting. In answer to my inquiries as to what brought him there, he told me he was returning to Pretoria with his temporarily incapacitated chief, General Ian Hamilton, who was suffering from a broken collar-bone, incurred by a fall from his horse.

Expecting to find the general in a smart ambulance carriage, it was somewhat of a shock to be guided to a very dilapidated old cattle-truck, with open sides and a floor covered with hay. I peeped in, and extended on a rough couch in the farther corner, I perceived the successful general, whose name was in everybody's mouth. In spite of his unlucky accident, he was full of life and spirits, and we had quite a long conversation. I have since often told him how interesting was his appearance, and he, in reply, has assured me how much he was impressed by a blue bird's-eye cotton dress I was wearing, the like of which he had not seen since he left England, many months before. His train soon rumbled on, and then we had a snug little dinner in the ladies' waiting-room that the station-commandant, a gallant and hospitable major, had made gay with trophies, photographs, and coloured pictures out of various journals. From a deep recess under his bed he produced an excellent bottle of claret, and the rest of the dinner was supplied from the restaurant.

The short African winter's day had faded into a blue and luminous night, resplendent with stars, and still our belated train tarried. However, the situation was improved, for later advices stated that the Boers had cleared off from the vicinity of the railway-line, and that we should surely leave before midnight. All these rumours certainly added to the excitement of a railway-journey, and it occurred to me how tame in comparison would be the ordinary departure of the "Flying Scotsman," or any other of the same tribe that nightly leave the great London termini.

At length, with many a puff and agonized groan from the poor little undersized engine, we departed into the dim, mysterious night, which hourly became more chill, and which promised a sharp frost before morning. As we crawled out of the station, our kind military friends saluted, and wished us, a little ironically, a pleasant journey. When I was about to seek repose, Major White looked in, and said: "Sleep with your head away from the window, in case of a stray shot"; and then I turned down the light, and was soon in the land of dreams.

The much-dreaded night passed quite quietly, and in the morning the carriage windows were thickly coated with several degrees of frost. The engines of the Netherlands Railway, always small and weak, were at that time so dirty from neglect and overpressure during the war, that their pace was but a slow crawl, and uphill they almost died away to nothing. However, fortunately, going south meant going downhill, and we made good progress over the flat uninteresting country, which, in view of recent events, proved worthy of careful attention. Already melancholy landmarks of the march of the great army lay on each side of the line in the shape of carcasses of horses, mules, and oxen. Wolvehoek was the first stop.

Here blue-nosed soldiers descended from the railway-carriages in varied and weird costumes, making a rush with their billies[1] for hot water, wherewith to cook their morning coffee, cheerily laughing and cracking their jokes, while shivering natives in blankets and tattered overcoats waited hungrily about for a job or scraps of food. After leaving Wolvehoek, we entered on Commandant De Wet's hunting-ground and the scene of his recent exploits. There, at almost every culvert, at every ganger's house, were pickets of soldiers, all gathered round a crackling fire at that chill morning hour; and at every one of these posts freshly constructed works of sandbags and deep trenches were in evidence to denote that their sentry work was no play, but grim earnest.

We next crossed the Rhenoster Spruit, and passed the then famous Rhenoster position, so formidable even to the unskilled eye, and where my military friends told me the Boers would have given much trouble, had it not been for the two outspread wings of the commander-in-chief's army. A little farther on, the deviation line and the railway-bridge were pointed out as one of the many triumphs of engineering skill to be seen and marvelled at on that recently restored line. The achievements of these lion-hearted engineers could not fail to impress themselves even on a civilian. Many amongst them were volunteers, who had previously occupied brilliant positions in the great mining community in Johannesburg, and whose brains were the pride of a circle where intellectual achievements and persevering resource commanded at once the greatest respect and the highest remuneration.

Some of these latter had family ties besides their considerable positions, but they gladly hastened to place their valuable services at the disposal of their queen, and, in conjunction with the regular Royal Engineers, were destined to find glory, and in many cases death, at their perilous work. The task of the engineers is probably scarcely realised by people who have not seen actual warfare. We do not read so frequently of their doings as of those of their gallant colleagues on foot or on horse; but soldiers know that neither the genius of the generals nor the intrepidity of the men could avail without them; and as the scouts are called the eyes, so might the engineers, both regular

1. Small kettles.

and volunteer, be termed the hands and feet, of an advancing force. The host sweeps on, and the workers are left with pickaxe and shovel, rifles close at hand, to work at their laborious task loyally and patiently, while deeds of courage and daring are being done and applauded not many miles away from them.

This particular Rhenoster bridge was destroyed and rebuilt no less than three times up to the date of which I write, and the third time was only ten days previously, when Christian De Wet had also worked havoc among the mail-bags, the only cruel thing attributed to that commander, respected both by friends and foes. The sad, dumb testimony of this lamented misfortune was to be seen in the shape of thousands of mutilated envelopes and torn letters which covered the rails and the ground beyond—letters which would have brought joy to many a lonely heart at the front. It was really heartbreaking to behold this melancholy remnant of 1,500 mail-bags, and, a little farther on, to see three skeleton trucks charred by fire, which told how the warm clothing destined for the troops perished when De Wet and his *burghers* had taken all they needed.

Many yarns were related to me about the chivalry of this farmer-general, especially respecting the mail-bags, and how he said that his *burghers* should not make fun of the English officers' letters, and therefore that he burnt them with his own hands. Another anecdote was remarkable—namely, that of an officer searching sadly among the heap of debris for some eagerly expected letter, and who came across an uninjured envelope directed to himself, containing his bankbook from Messrs. Cox and Sons, absolutely intact and untouched. It can only be conjectured whether he would as soon have known it in ashes.

On arriving in the vicinity of Kroonstadt, the most risky part of the journey was over, and then a wonderfully novel scene unfolded itself as we crawled over a rise from the desolate, barren country we had been traversing, and a tented city lay in front of us. Anyway, such was its appearance at a first glance, for white tents stretched far away east and west, and appeared to swamp into insignificance the unpretentious houses, and even a fairly imposing church-spire which lay in the background. I had never seen anything like this vast army *depôt*, and examined everything with the greatest attention and interest. Huge mountains of forage covered by tarpaulin sheets were the first things to catch my eye; then piles upon piles of wooden cases were pointed out as "rations"—that mysterious term which implies so much and may mean so little; again, there was a hillock of wicker-covered bottles with handles which puzzled me, and which were explained as "cordials" of some kind.

Powerful traction-engines, at rest and in motion, next came into sight, and weird objects that looked like lifeboats mounted on trucks, but which proved to be pontoons—strange articles to perceive at a railway-station. Then we passed a vast concourse of red-cross tents of every description, proclaiming a hospital. As far as outward appearances went, it looked most beautifully arranged in symmetrically laid-out streets, while many of the marquees had their sides thrown back, and showed the patients within, either in bed or sitting about and enjoying the breeze and the rays of a sun never too hot at that time of year. "How happy and comfortable they look!" was my remark as we left them behind.

Someone who knew Kroonstadt said: "Yes, they are all right; but the Scotch Hospital is the one to see if you are staying long enough—spring-beds, writing-tables, and every luxury." I was sorry time admitted of no visit to this establishment or to the magnificent Yeomanry Hospital at Deelfontein, farther south, to which I shall have occasion to allude in a later chapter. This last establishment was, even at that early stage of the war, a household word among the soldiers at the front, a dearly longed-for Mecca amongst the sick and wounded.

Our train had come to an abrupt standstill, and, on looking out, the line appeared so hopelessly blocked that the only way of reaching the station and lunch appeared to be on foot. We walked, therefore, upwards of half a mile, undergoing many perils from shunting engines, trains undecided whether to go on or to go back, and general confusion. It certainly did not look as if our train could be extricated for hours, but it proved there was method in this apparent muddle, and we suffered no delay worth speaking of. The station was densely packed with staff officers and soldiers.

Presently someone elbowed a way through the crowd to make way for the general, just arrived from Bloemfontein. A momentary interest was roused as an elderly, soldierly gentleman, with white hair and a slight figure, passed out of sight into one of the officials' rooms, and then we joined the throng trying to get food in the overtaxed refreshment-room. We had some interesting conversation with the officer in command of the station, and learnt how the Kroonstadt garrison were even then living in the midst of daily alarms from De Wet or his followers; added to these excitements, there was a colossal amount of work to be got through in the way of supplying Pretoria with food, by a line liable to be interrupted, and in coping with the task of receiving and unloading remounts, which were arriving from the South in large numbers. I saw some of these poor animals packed nine in a truck, marvellously quiet, and unmindful of strange sights and sounds, and of being hurled against each other when the locomotive jerked on or came to a stop. They were in good condition, but their eyes were sad and their tails were woefully rubbed. After seeing Kroonstadt Railway-station, I realised that the work of a Staff officer on the lines of communication was no sinecure.

Marvellous to relate, in the early afternoon we found our train in the station, and, climbing into our carriage once more, we proceeded on our road without delay, congratulating ourselves on our good fortune in not being held up at Kroonstadt, as had been the fate of many travellers going south. Immediately south of Kroonstadt we crossed the Vaal River, with its fine high-level bridge reduced to atoms by dynamite. This had given the engineers another opportunity to display their skill by a clever deviation of a couple of miles in length, winding down almost to the water-level, and then serenely effecting the crossing by a little wooden bridge, from which its ruined predecessor was visible about a quarter of a mile up the stream.

Darkness and approaching night then hid the landscape. That evening we were told we need have no fears, for we were practically out of the dangerous zone. We dined comfortably in our compartment, and I heard many more reminiscences of the advance from two travelling companions who had taken part in it. Suddenly in the next compartment a party of Canadian officers commenced singing part-songs with real musical talent. We relapsed into silence as we heard the "Swanee River" sung more effectively than I have ever heard it before or since, and it reminded me that we, too, were going home. Presently we found ourselves joining in the chorus of that most touching melody, "Going back to Dixie," greatly to the delight of our sociable and talented neighbours. Daylight next morning brought us to Bloemfontein and civilization, and what impressed me most was the fact of daily newspapers being sold at a bookstall, which sight I had not seen for many months.

On arriving at Cape Town, I was most hospitably entertained at Groot Schuurr by Colonel Frank Rhodes, in the absence of his brother. This mansion had been a convalescent home for many officers ever since the war began. There I passed a busy ten days in seeing heaps of friends, and I had several interviews with Sir Alfred Milner, to whom events of the siege and relief of Mafeking were of specially deep interest. I gave him as a memento a small Mauser bullet mounted as a scarf-pin, and before leaving for England I received from him the following letter:

> Government House,
> Cape Town,
> November 7, 1900.

Dear Lady Sarah,

How very kind of you to think of giving me that interesting relic of Mafeking! It will indeed revive memories of anxiety, as well as of the intensest feeling of relief and thankfulness that I have ever experienced.

Hoping we shall meet again when 'distress and strain are over,'

> I am,

> Yours very sincerely,

> Alfred Milner.

Much of my time was also occupied in corresponding with Mafeking about the distribution of the fund which was being energetically collected in London by my sister, Lady Georgiana Curzon. Many weeks before we were relieved I had written to Lady Georgiana, then hard at work with the organisation of the Yeomanry Hospital, suggesting to her to start a relief fund for the inhabitants of Mafeking. It had all along seemed to me that these latter deserved some substantial recognition and compensation beyond what they could expect from the government, for damage done to their homes and their shops, and for the utter stagnation of the trade in the town during the siege. The nurses, the nuns and their convent, were also worthy objects for charity. This latter residence, but lately built, and including a nicely decorated chapel with many sacred images, had been, as I have said, practically destroyed; and the Sisters had borne their part most nobly, in nursing the sick and wounded, while many were suffering in health from the privations they had undergone. In response to my appeal, Lady Georgiana inserted the following letter in the *Times* just before the news of the Relief reached England:

> 20, Curzon Street, W.,
> May 11.

Sir,

I venture to address an appeal to the people of the United Kingdom, through the columns of your paper, on behalf of the inhabitants of Mafeking. Nothing but absolute knowledge of their sufferings prompts me to thus inaugurate another fund, and one which must come in addition to the numerous subscriptions already started in connection with the South African War. I admit the generous philanthropy of our country has been evinced to a degree that is almost inconceivable, and I hesitate even now in making this fresh appeal, but can only plead as an excuse the heartrending accounts of the sufferings of Mafeking that I have received from my sister, Lady Sarah Wilson.

The last mail from South Africa brought me a letter from her, dated March 3. In it she implores me to take active measures to bring before the generous British public the destitute condition of the nuns, refugees, and civilians generally, in Mafeking. She writes with authority, having witnessed their sufferings herself, and, indeed, having shared equally with them the anxieties and privations of this prolonged siege. Her letter describes the absolute ruin of all the small trades-people, whose homes are in many cases demolished. The compensation they will receive for damaged goods will be totally inadequate to cover their loss. Years must pass ere their trade can be restored to the proportions of a livelihood.

Meanwhile starvation in the immediate future lies before them. The unfortunate Sisters in the convent have for weeks hardly had a roof over their heads, the Boer shells having more or less destroyed their home. In consequence, their belongings left intact by shot or shell have been ruined by rain. The destruction of their small and humble properties, in addition to their discomfort, has added to their misery; and yet no complaining word has passed their lips, but they have throughout cheerfully and willingly assisted the hospital nurses in their duties, always having smiles and encouraging words for the sick and wounded.

Sitting at home in our comfortable houses, it is hard to realise the actual sufferings of these besieged inhabitants of Mafeking. My letter tells me that for months they have not slept in their beds, and although no opposition to the Boer forces in the first instance would have saved their town, their properties, and in many cases their lives, yet they one and all bravely and nobly 'buckled to,' and stood by that gallant commander, Baden-Powell. Loyalty was their cry, and freedom and justice their household gods. Have not their courage and endurance thrilled the whole world? I feel I need not ask forgiveness for issuing yet this one more appeal. It comes last, but is it least? A handful of soldiers, nearly all colonials, under a man who must now rank as a great and tried commander, have for six months repelled the Boer attacks.

Could this small force have for one moment been a match for the well-equipped besiegers if the inhabitants had not fought for and with the garrison? Some worked and fought in actual trenches; others demonstrated by patient endurance their cool and courageous determination never to give in. Would it not be a graceful recognition of their courage if, on that glorious day, which we hope may not be far distant, when the relief of Mafeking is flashed across thousands of miles to the 'heart of the Empire,' we could cable back our congratulations on their freedom, and inform Mafeking that a large sum of money is ready to be placed by this country for the relief of distress amongst the Sisters, refugees, and suffering civilians of the town?

I feel I shall not ask in vain, but that our congratulations to Mafeking will take most material form by generous admirers in the United Kingdom.

Subscriptions will be received by Messrs. Hoare and Co., bankers, Fleet Street, E.C.

  I remain,

    Your obedient servant,

        Georgiana Curzon.

The fund had reached unhoped-for proportions. In our most optimistic moments we did not expect to collect more than two or three thousand pounds, but subscriptions had poured in from the very commencement, and the grand amount of £29,267 was finally the total contributed. This sum was ably administered by Colonel Vyvyan of the Buffs, who had been Base-Commandant of Mafeking during the siege. He was assisted by a committee, and the principal items allocated by these gentlemen were as follows:

	£
Widows and orphans	6,536
Refugees	4,630
Town relief	3,741
Seaside fund	2,900
Churches, convent, schools, etc.	2,900

Wounded men	2,245
Small tradesmen	1,765
Hospital staff, nuns, etc.	1,115
Colonel Plumer's Rhodesian column, etc.	1,000

Lady Georgiana Curzon's eloquent appeal proved to be the salvation of many a family in Mafeking.

The popularity of the fund was enormously helped by the interest of the then Prince and Princess of Wales, later our king and queen, in the town and in the assistance of the same. This interest was evinced by the following letters, given to me later by my sister:

> Treasurer's House,
> York
> June 20, 1900.

My Dear Lady Georgie.

The princess and I thank you very much for sending your sister's letters for us to read. They are most interesting, and admirably written. She has certainly gone through experiences which ought to last her a lifetime! If the papers are correct in stating that you start on Saturday for Madeira to meet her, let me wish you *bon voyage*.

> Ever yours very sincerely,
> (Signed) Albert Edward.

The Princess of Wales had already written as follows:

My Dear Georgie,

I saw in yesterday's *Times* your touching appeal for poor, unfortunate, forsaken Mafeking, in which I have taken the liveliest interest during all these months of patient and brave endurance. I have therefore great pleasure in enclosing £100 for the benefit of the poor nuns and other inhabitants. I hope very soon, however, they will be relieved, and I trust poor sister Sarah will be none the worse for all she has gone through during her forced captivity. Many thanks for sending me that beautifully drawn-up report of your Yeomanry Hospital. How well you have explained everything! Hoping to meet soon,

> Yours affectionately,
> (Signed) Alexandra.[2]

---

2. I am allowed to reproduce the foregoing letters by the gracious permission of Their Majesties the King and Queen.

Some fourteen months after my return home a *Gazette* appeared with the awards gained during the early part of the war, and great was my delight to find I had been selected for the coveted distinction of the Royal Red Cross. The king had previously nominated Lady Georgiana Curzon and myself to be Ladies of Grace of the Order of St. John of Jerusalem, which entitles its members to wear a very effective enamel locket on a black bow; but, next to the Red Cross, the medal which I prize most highly is the same which the soldiers received for service in South Africa, with the well-known blue and orange striped ribbon. This medal was given to the professional nurses who were in South Africa, but I think I was, with one other exception, the only amateur to receive it, and very unworthy I felt myself when I went to St. James's Palace with all the gallant and skilful sisterhood of army nurses to share with them the great honour of receiving the same from His Majesty in person.

CHAPTER 17

The Work of Lady Georgiana Curzon, Lady Chesham, and the Yeomanry Hospital, During the War

Fight the good fight.

On the pages of history is recorded in golden letters the name and deeds of Florence Nightingale, who, as the pioneer of scientific hospital nursing, did so much to mitigate the horrors of war. Her example was nobly followed half a century later by two other English ladies, who, although they had not to encounter the desperate odds connected with ignorance and old-fashioned ideas which Miss Nightingale successfully combated, did marvellous service by displaying what private enterprise can do in a national emergency—an emergency with which, in its suddenness, gravity, and scope, no government could have hoped to deal successfully. I must go back to the winter of 1899 to call their great work to mind.

War had already been waging some weeks in South Africa when the government's proclamation was issued calling for volunteers from the yeomanry for active service at the front, and the lightning response that came to this appeal from all quarters and from all grades was the silver lining shining brightly through the black clouds that hovered over the British Empire during that dread winter. Thus the loyalty of the men of Britain was proven, and among the women who yearned to be up and doing were Lady Georgiana Curzon and Lady Chesham. Not theirs was the sentiment that "men must work and women must weep"; to them it seemed but right that they should take their share of the nation's burden, and, as they could not fight, they could, and did, work.

Filled with pity for all who were so gallantly fighting at the seat of war, it was the yeomen—called suddenly from peaceful pursuits to serve their country in her day of distress—who claimed their deepest sympathies, and, with the object of establishing a hospital for this force at the front, Lady Georgiana Curzon and Lady Chesham, on December 29, 1899, appealed to the British public for subscriptions. The result far exceeded their expectations, and every post brought generous donations in cash and in kind. Even the children contributed eagerly to the Yeomen's Fund, and one poor woman gave a shilling towards the cost of providing a bed in the hospital, "in case her son might have to lie on it."

The Queen—then Princess of Wales—allowed herself to be nominated President; the present Princess of Wales and the Duchess of Connaught gave their names as Vice-Presidents of the Imperial Yeomanry Hospitals. The working committee was composed of the following: Adeline, Duchess of Bedford, the Duchess of Marlborough, the Countesses of Essex and Dudley, the Ladies Chesham and Tweedmouth, Mesdames S. Neumann, A.G. Lucas, Blencowe Cookson, Julius Wernher (now Lady Wernher), and Madame von Andre. Amongst the gentlemen who gave valuable assistance, the most prominent were: Viscount Curzon, M.P. (now Lord Howe), Hon. Secretary; Mr. Ludwig Neumann, Hon. Treasurer; General Eaton (now Lord Cheylesmore); and Mr. Oliver Williams.

Lady Georgiana Curzon was a born leader, and it was but natural that the capable ladies aforementioned appointed her as their chairman. Passionately devoted to sport though she was, she willingly forsook her beloved hunting-field, leaving a stable full of hunters idle at Melton Mowbray, for the committee-room and the writing-table. The scheme was one fraught with difficulties great and numerous, and not the least amongst them was the "red tape" that had to be cut; but Lady Georgiana Curzon took up the good cause with enthusiasm and ability, and she and her colleagues worked to such purpose that, on March 17, 1900, a base hospital containing over 500 beds (which number was subsequently increased to 1,000), fully equipped, left our shores.

So useful did these institutions prove themselves, that as time went on, and the evils of war spread to other parts of South Africa, the committee were asked to inaugurate other hospitals, and, the funds at their disposal allowing of acquiescence, they established branches at Mackenzie's Farm, Maitland Camp, Eastwood, Elandsfontein, and

Lady Georgiana Curzon

Pretoria, besides a small convalescent home for officers at Johannesburg. Thus in a few months a field-hospital and bearer company (the first ever formed by civilians), several base hospitals, and a convalescent home, were organised by the Imperial Yeomanry Hospitals Committee, who frequently met, with Lady Georgiana Curzon presiding, to discuss ways and means of satisfactorily working those establishments so many thousands of miles away.

The Hospital Commissioners who visited Deelfontein in November, 1900, said it was one of the best-managed hospitals in Africa. A similar opinion was expressed by Colonel A.G. Lucas, M.V.O., when he visited it in the autumn, and this gentleman also reported most favourably on the section at Mackenzie's Farm. Through Colonel Kilkelly, Lord Kitchener sent a message to the committee early in 1901, expressing his admiration of the Pretoria Hospital. In this branch Lady Roberts showed much interest, and, with her customary kindness, rendered it every assistance in her power. At a time when military hospitals were being weighed in the balance, and in some instances found wanting, the praise bestowed on the Yeomanry Institutions was worthy of note.

From first to last the various staffs numbered over 1,400 persons, and more than 20,000 patients were treated in the Yeomanry Hospitals whilst they were under the management of Lady Georgiana Curzon and her committee. Although sick and wounded from every force under the British flag in South Africa were taken in, and many Boers as well, a sufficient number of beds was always available for the immediate admittance of patients from the force for which the hospitals were originally created. The subscriptions received for this great national work totalled over £145,300, in addition to a subsidy of £3,000 from the government for prolonging the maintenance of the field-hospital and bearer company from January 1 to March 31, 1901. The interest on deposits alone amounted to over £1,635, and when, with the cessation of hostilities, there was, happily, no further need for these institutions, the buildings, etc., were sold for £24,051. The balance which the committee ultimately had in hand from this splendid total of over £174,000 was devoted to the maintenance of a school which had since been established at Perivale Alperton, for the benefit of the daughters of yeomen who were killed or disabled during the war.

There has been ample testimony of the excellent way in which this admirable scheme was created and carried out. Numerous letters, touching in their expressions of gratitude, were received from men of all ranks whose sufferings were alleviated in the Yeomanry Hospitals; newspapers commented upon it at the time, but it is only those who were behind the scenes that can tell what arduous work it entailed, and of how unflinchingly it was faced by the chairman of the committee. Constant interviews with War Office officials, with doctors, with nurses; the hundreds of letters that had to be written daily; the questions, necessary and unnecessary, that had to be answered; the estimates that had to be examined, would have proved a nightmare to anyone not possessed of the keenest intellect combined with the strongest will. It involved close and unremitting attention from morning till night, and this not for one week, but for many months; and yet no detail was ever momentarily shirked by one who loved an outdoor life. Lady Georgiana realised to the full the responsibilities of having this vast sum of money entrusted to her by the British public, and not wisely, but too well, did she devote herself to discharging it.

Her services to the country were as zealous as they were invaluable. By her quick grasp of the details of administration, by the marvellous tact and skill she exercised, and by the energy she threw into her undertaking, every difficulty was mastered. At this present time many hundreds of men, who were ten years ago facing a desperate foe, can reflect gratefully, if sadly, that they owe their lives to the generous and unselfish efforts of a brave woman who is no longer with us; for, after all, Lady Georgiana Curzon was human, and had to pay the price of all she did. Her great exertions seriously told upon her health, as was only to be expected, and long before the conclusion of her strenuous labours she felt their effects, although she ignored them. Lady Chesham was no less energetic a worker, and had as an additional anxiety the fact of her husband and son[1] being both at the front.

It was imperative that one of these two ladies, who were responsible for starting the fund, should personally superintend the erection and the opening of the large base hospital at Deelfontein, and as Lady Georgiana Curzon had made herself almost indispensable in London by her adroitness in managing already sorely harassed War Office officials, and in keeping her committee unanimous and contented, it was decided that Lady Chesham should proceed to the scene of the war. My sister gladly gave up this stirring role for the more prosaic, but equally important, work in London, and when I returned home,

1. Lieutenant the Hon. C.W.H. Cavendish, 17th Lancers, was killed at Diamond Hill, June 11, 1900.

in July, 1900, I found her still completely absorbed by her self-imposed task. Already her health was failing, and overtaxed nature was having its revenge. During the next two years, in spite of repeated warnings and advice, she gave herself no rest, but all the while she cherished the wish to pay a visit to that continent which had been the theatre of her great enterprise.

At length, in August, 1902, in the week following the coronation of Their Majesties, we sailed together for Cape Town, a sea-voyage having been recommended to her in view of her refusal to try any of the foreign health-resorts, which might have effected a cure. By the death of her father-in-law, my sister was then Lady Howe, but it will be with her old name of Lady Georgiana Curzon or "Lady Georgie"—as she was known to her intimates—that the task she achieved will ever be associated.

More than seven years had elapsed since my first visit, and nearly twenty-six months from the time I had left South Africa in the July following the termination of the Mafeking siege, when I found myself back in the old familiar haunts. Groot Schuurr had never looked more lovely than on the sunny September morning when we arrived there from the mail-steamer, after a tedious and annoying delay in disembarking of several hours, connected with permits under martial law. This delay was rendered more aggravating by the fact that, on the very day of our arrival,[2] the same law ceased to exist, and that our ship was the last to have to submit to the ordeal. Many and sad were the changes that had come to pass in the two years, and nowhere did they seem more evident than when one crossed the threshold of Mr. Rhodes's home. The central figure, so often referred to in the foregoing pages, was no more, and one soon perceived that the void left by that giant spirit, so inseparably connected with vast enterprises, could never be filled. This was not merely apparent in the silent, echoing house, on the slopes of the mountain he loved so well, in the circle of devoted friends and adherents, who seemed left like sheep without a shepherd, but also in the political arena, in the future prospects of that extensive Northern Territory which he had practically discovered and opened up. It seemed as if Providence had been very hard in allowing one individual to acquire such vast influence, and to be possessed of so much genius, and then not to permit the half-done task to be accomplished.

That this must also have been Mr. Rhodes's reflection was proved

2. Peace had been declared in the previous June.

by the pathetic words he so often repeated during his last illness: "*So little done, so much to do.*"

Groot Schuurr was outwardly the same as in the old days, and kept up in the way one knew that the great man would have wished. We went for the same rides he used to take. The view was as glorious as ever, the animals were flourishing and increasing in numbers, the old lions gazed placidly down from their roomy cage on a ledge of Table Mountain, the peacocks screamed and plumed themselves, and the herd of zebras grazed in picturesque glades. Nothing was changed there to outward appearances, and one had to go farther afield to see evidences of the dismay caused by the pillar being abruptly broken off. Cape Town itself, I soon noted, was altered by the war almost beyond recognition. From the dull and uninteresting seaport town I remembered it when we came there in 1895, it seemed, seven years later, one of the busiest cities imaginable, with the most enormous street traffic. The pavements were thronged, the shops were crowded, and numerous were the smart, khaki-clad figures, bronzed and bearded, that were to be seen on all sides. The Mount Nelson Hotel, which had been opened just before the war, was crowded with them—some very youthful, who had early acquired manhood and self-reliance in a foreign land; others grey-headed, with rows of medal ribbons, dimmed in colour from exposure to all weathers, whose names were strangely familiar as recording heroic achievements.

At that time Sir Gordon Sprigg, of the Progressive Party, was in power and prime minister; but he was only kept in office by the Bond, who made the Ministers more or less ridiculous in the eyes of the country by causing them to dance like puppets at their bidding. It was in the House of Assembly—where he was a whale amongst minnows—that the void was so acutely felt surrounding the vacant seat so long occupied by Mr. Rhodes, and it was not an encouraging sight, for those of his supporters who tried to carry on his traditions, to gaze on the sparsely filled ranks of the Progressive Party, and then at the crowded seats of the Bond on the other side.

We were told, by people who had met the Boer generals on their recent visit to the colony, that these latter were not in the least cast down by the result of the war; that they simply meant to bide their time and win in the Council Chamber what they had lost on the battle-field; that the oft-reiterated sentence, "South Africa for the Dutch," was by no means an extinct volcano or a parrot-cry of the past. It was evident that political feeling was, in any case, running very high; it almost stopped social intercourse, it divided families. To be a member of the Loyal Women's League was sufficient to be ostracized in any Dutch village, the Boers pretending that the name outraged their feelings, and that distinctions between loyal and disloyal were invidious. Federation—Mr. Rhodes's great ideal—which has since come rapidly and triumphantly to be an accomplished fact, was then temporarily relegated to the background; the Bond, apparently, had not made up their minds to declare for it, but they were hard at work in their old shrewd way, obtaining influence by getting their own men appointed to vacancies at the post-office and in the railway departments, while the Loyalists appeared to be having almost as bad a time as in the old days before the war.

At the present moment, in spite of all the goodwill borne to the new Union of South Africa by great and small in all lands where the British flag flies, it is well to remember, without harbouring any grudge, certain incidents of the past. A thorough knowledge of the people which are to be assimilated with British colonists is absolutely necessary, that all may in the end respect, as well as like, each other.

From Cape Town, where my sister transacted a great deal of business connected with the winding-up of the Yeomanry Hospital, we went to Bloemfontein, and were the guests at Government House of my old Mafeking friend, Sir Hamilton Gould Adams, promoted to the important post of Governor of the Orange River Colony. From that town we drove across to Kimberley, taking two days to accomplish this somewhat tedious journey. We stayed one night with a German farmer, who had surrendered to the English when Bloemfontein was occupied by Lord Roberts, and his case was typical of many similar awkward predicaments which occurred frequently during the ups and downs of the war. When Lord Roberts's army swept on from Bloemfontein, the Boers in a measure swept back, and our host was for months persecuted by his own people, finally made a prisoner, and was within an ace of being shot; in fact, it was only the peace that saved his life.

Next day we made our noonday halt at Poplar Grove, the scene of one of Lord Roberts's fights, and farther on we passed Koodoos Rand Drift, where General French had cut off Cronje and forced him back on Paardeberg. All along these roads it was very melancholy to see the ruined farms, some with the impoverished owner in possession, others still standing empty. A Boer farmhouse is not at any time the counterpart of the snug dwelling we know in England, but it was heartbreaking to see these homes as they were at the conclusion of the war, when, in nearly every instance, the roof, window-frames, and doors, were things of the past. When a waggon could be espied standing near the door, and a few lean oxen grazing at hand, it was a sign that the owner had returned home, and, on closer inspection, a whole family of children would probably be discovered sheltered by a tin lean-to fixed to the side of the house, or huddled in a tent pitched close by. They all seemed wonderfully patient, but looked despairing and miserable. At one of these houses we spoke to the daughter of such a family who was able to converse in English. She told us her father had died during the war, that two of her brothers had fought for the English, and had returned with khaki uniforms and nothing else, but that the third had thrown in his lot with the Boers, and had come back the proud possessor of four horses.

At Kimberley we had motors placed at our disposal by Mr. Gardner Williams, manager of the De Beers Company, and were amused to hear how excited the *kaffirs* had been at the first automobile to appear in the Diamond City, and how they had thrown themselves down to peer underneath in order to discover the horse. These motors, however, were not of much use on the *veldt*, and we soon found Kimberley very dull, and decided to make a flying tour through Rhodesia to Beira, taking a steamer at that port for Delagoa Bay, on our road to Johannesburg. Our first halting-place was at Mafeking, where we arrived one bitterly cold, blowy morning at 6 a.m. I do not think I ever realised, during all those months of the siege, what a glaring little spot it was. When I returned there two years later: the dust was flying in clouds, the sun was blinding, and accentuated the absence of any shade.

Six hours spent there were more than sufficient, and it was astounding to think of the many months that it had been our home. It has often been said, I reflected, that it is the people you consort with, not the place you live at, that constitute an agreeable existence; and of the former all I could find to say was, "Where are they gone, the old familiar faces?" Beyond the mayor of the town, who called to reiterate warm thanks for the Mafeking Fund, and a nigger coachman who used to take me out for Sunday drives, I failed to perceive one face I knew in the town during the siege; but at the convent we received the warmest welcome from the Mother Superior and the nuns. This community appeared to be in quite affluent circumstances: the building was restored, the chapel rebuilt and plentifully decorated

CEMETERY AT MAFEKING, 1902

with new images; there was a full complement of day-boarders, who were energetically practising on several pianos, and many new Sisters had made their appearance; upstairs, the room where was located the Maxim gun was filled by thirty snow-white beds.

It was quite refreshing to find one circle who had recovered from their hardships, and who, if anything, were rather more prosperous than before the war. We paid a flying visit to the little cemetery, which was beautifully kept, and where many fairly recent graves were in evidence, chiefly due to enteric fever after the siege. There we particularly noted a very fine marble cross, erected to the memory of Captain Ronald Vernon; and as we were admiring this monument we met an old Kimberley acquaintance in the person of Mrs. Currey, who had been our hostess at the time of the Jameson Raid. Her husband had since died, and this lady was travelling round that part of Africa representing the Loyal Women's League, who did such splendid work in marking out and tending the soldiers' graves.

At Mafeking we picked up the Rhodesian *train de luxe*, and travelled in the greatest comfort to Bulawayo, and on to Salisbury. At that town we met a party, comprising, amongst others, Dr. Jameson and the late Mr. Alfred Beit, who were making a tour of inspection connected with satisfying the many wants of the Rhodesian settlers. These pioneers were beginning to feel the loss of the great man to whom they had turned for everything. His faithful lieutenants were doing their best to replace him, and the *rôle* of the first-named, apparently, was to make the necessary speeches, that of the latter to write the equally important cheques.

With these gentlemen we continued our journey to Beira, stopping at a few places of interest on the way. The country between Salisbury and Beira is flat and marshy, and was, till the advent of the railway, a veritable Zoological Garden as regards game of all sorts. The climate is deadly for man and beast, and mortality was high during the construction of the Beira Railway, which connected Rhodesia with an eastern outlet on the sea. Among uninteresting towns, I think Beira should be placed high on the list; the streets are so deep in sand that carriages are out of the question, and the only means of transport is by small trucks on narrow rails. As may be imagined, we did not linger there, but went at once on board the German steamer, which duly landed us at Lorenzo Marques forty-eight hours later, after an exceedingly rough voyage.

The following day was Sunday, and having been told there was a service at the English Church at 9.30 a.m., we duly went there at that hour, only to find the church apparently deserted, and not a movement or sound emanating therefrom. However, on peeping in at one of the windows, we discovered a clergyman most gorgeously apparelled in green and gold, preparing to discourse to a congregation of two persons! Evidently the residents found the climate too oppressively hot for church that Sunday morning.

In the afternoon we were able to see some portions of that wonderful harbour, of worldwide reputation. Literally translated, the local name for the same means the "English River," and it is virtually an arm of the sea, stretching inland like a deep bay, in which three separate good-sized streams find an outlet. Some few miles up these rivers, we were told, grand shooting was still to be had, the game including hippopotami, rhinoceroses, and buffalo, which roam through fever-stricken swamps of tropical vegetation. The glories of the vast harbour of Delagoa Bay can better be imagined than described. In the words of a resident, "It would hold the navies of the world," and some years back it might have been purchased for £12,000. With the war just over, people were beginning to realise how trade and development would be facilitated if this great seaport belonged to the British Empire.

A "United Africa" was already looming in the distance, and it required but little imagination on the part of the traveller, calling to mind the short rail journey connecting it with the mining centres of the Transvaal, to determine what a thriving, busy place Lorenzo Marques would then become. During the day the temperature was tropical, but by evening the atmosphere freshened, and was almost invigorating as the fierce sun sank to rest and its place was taken by a full moon. From our hotel, standing high on the cliff above the bay, the view was then like fairyland: an ugly old coal-hulk, a somewhat antiquated Portuguese gunboat, and even the diminutive and unpleasant German steamer which had brought us from Beira, all were tinged with silver and enveloped in romance, to which they could certainly lay no claim in reality.

Early in the morning of the next day we left for Johannesburg. The line proved most interesting, especially after passing the almost historical British frontier town, Koomati Poort. It winds like a serpent round the mountains, skirting precipices, and giving one occasional peeps of lovely fertile valleys. During a greater part of the way the Crocodile River follows its sinuous course in close proximity to the railway, while above tower rocky boulders. To describe their height and character, I can only say that the steepest Scotch mountains we are familiar with fade into insignificance beside those barren, awe-inspiring ranges, and one was forced to wonder how the English soldiers—not to speak of heavy artillery—could have safely negotiated those narrow and precipitous passes. For the best part of twelve hours our train slowly traversed this wild and magnificent scenery, and evening brought us to Waterfall Onder, where, at the station restaurant, kept by a Frenchman, we had a most excellent dinner, with a cup of coffee that had a flavour of the Paris *boulevards*. This stopping-place was adjacent to Noitgedacht, whose name recalled the unpleasant association of having been the home, for many weary weeks, of English prisoners, and traces of high wire palings which had been their enclosure were still to be seen.

From Waterfall Onder the train puffed up a stupendous hill, the gradient being one foot in twenty, and to assist its progress a cogwheel engine was attached behind. In this fashion a two-thousand-feet rise was negotiated, the bright moonlight enhancing the beauty of the sudden and rocky ascent by increasing the mystery of the vast depths below. We then found ourselves at Waterfall Boven, in a perfectly cool atmosphere, and also, as regards the landscape, in a completely different country, which latter fact we only fully appreciated with the morning light, as we drew near to Pretoria. The stranger landing at Delagoa Bay, and travelling through those bleak and barren mountains, might well ask himself the reason of the late prolonged and costly war; but as he approaches the Rand, and suddenly sees the rows and rows of mining shafts and chimneys, which are the visible signs of the hidden wealth, the veil is lifted and the recent events of history are explained. At that time, owing to the war, there were no signs of agriculture, and in many districts there appeared to be absolute desolation.

At Johannesburg we stayed at Sunnyside, as the guests of Lord Milner. This residence is small and unpretentious, but exceedingly comfortable, and has the advantage of commanding wide views over the surrounding country. Our host was then engrossed in his difficult task of satisfying the wants and desires of many communities and nationalities, whose countless differences of opinion seemed well-nigh irreconcilable. During our stay the visit of the Right Hon. J. Chamberlain was announced as likely to take place during the next few months, and the advent of this distinguished Colonial Minister was a subject of great satisfaction to the harassed High Commissioner. As at Cape

Viscount Milner, 1902

Town, his staff was composed of charming men, but all young and with no administrative experience. Among its members were included Colonel W. Lambton, who was Military Secretary; Captain Henley and Lord Brooke, A.D.C.'s; and Mr. Walrond.

The Golden City itself was, to all outward appearances, as thriving as ever, with its busy population, its crowded and excellent shops, and its general evidences of opulence, which appeared to overbalance— or, in any case, wish to conceal—any existing poverty or distress. Among many friends we met was a French lady, formerly the Marquise d'Hervé, but who had married, as her second husband, Comte Jacque de Waru. This enterprising couple were busy developing some mining claims which had been acquired on their behalf by some relatives during the war. In spite of having been deserted at Cape Town by all the servants they had brought from Paris, this clever lady, nothing daunted, had replaced them by blacks, and one night she and her husband offered us, at the small tin-roofed house where they were residing, a sumptuous dinner which was worthy of the best traditions of Parisian hospitality.

Notwithstanding the fact of her having no maid, and that she had herself superintended most of the cooking of the dinner, our hostess was charmingly attired in the latest Paris fashion, with elaborately dressed hair, and the pleasant company she had collected, combined with an excellent cuisine, helped to make the entertainment quite one of the pleasantest we enjoyed during our stay. Among the guests was General "Bully" Oliphant, who had just been recalled to England to take up an important appointment, much to the regret of his Johannesburg friends, with whom he had made himself exceedingly popular; and the witty conversation of this gentleman kept the whole dinner-table convulsed with laughing, to such an extent that his colleague-in-arms, our quondam Mafeking commander, General Baden-Powell, who was also of the party, was reduced to mere silent appreciation. This impromptu feast, given under difficulties which almost amounted to siege conditions, was again an evidence of the versatility and inherent hospitality of the French nation, and the memory of that pleasant evening lingers vividly in my recollections.

The duration of our two months' holiday was rapidly approaching its close. My sister was recalled to England by social and other duties, and was so much better in health that we were deluded into thinking the wonderful air and bracing climate had effected a complete cure. After a short but very interesting visit to the Natal battlefields, whither we were escorted by General Burn-Murdoch and Captain Henry Guest, we journeyed to Cape Town, and, regretfully turning our backs on warmth and sunshine, we landed once more in England on a dreary December day.

CHAPTER 18

Fourth Voyage to the Cape

We propose now to go on and cross the Zambesi just below the Victoria Falls. I should like to have the spray of the water over the carriages.—Letter from the Right Hon. C.J. Rhodes to E.S. Grogan, Esq., September 7, 1900.[1]

—Introduction to Mr. Grogan's work,
From the Cape to Cairo

These words came to my mind as I sat under the verandah of one of the newly thatched huts which formed the camp of the Native Commissioner at Livingstone, Victoria Falls, on a glorious morning early in July, 1903, gazing at one of the fairest landscapes to be seen on God's earth. I was ostensibly occupied with my mail home, but the paper lay in all its virgin whiteness before me, while my eyes feasted on the marvellous panorama stretching away to the south, east, and west. My heart sank as I realised how difficult—nay, impossible—it would be for anyone with only a very limited vocabulary and very moderate powers of description to convey to those far away even a limited idea of this glorious vision—of these vivid colourings intensified by the lonely grandeur of the whole scene and the absence of human habitations.

"Constitution Hill," as the aforesaid camp had been christened, was situated on high ground, four miles to the north of the then drift of the Zambesi River, which, again, was several miles above the actual falls themselves. With the advent of the railway and of the magnificent bridge now spanning the mighty river, that drift has actually fallen into disuse, but at the time of our visit it was the scene of much activity, and quite a nest of stores, houses, and huts, had sprung up near the rough landing-stage on the north side. As transport, not only for individuals and for every ounce of food required by the vast country stretching away to the north, but also for the huge and valuable machinery, boilers, boats in sections, etc., destined for the various mining companies, the only means of maintaining communication with the struggling but promising new colony were one very rickety steam-launch and one large rowing-boat, beside a few canoes and native dugouts.

A fine steam-barge, which would greatly have facilitated the passage of all kinds of merchandise, had most disastrously slipped its moorings during one stormy night of last wet season, and had not since been seen, the presumption being that the relentless stream had carried it to the mighty cataract, which, like a huge ogre, had engulfed it for all time. But this disaster had not caused anything like consternation among the small community to whom it meant so much, and the thought occurred to one how remarkable are the qualities of dogged perseverance, calm disregard of drawbacks and of any difficult task before them, which makes Englishmen so marvellously successful as pioneers or colonists. The precious barge for which they had waited many weary months had disappeared, and there was nothing more to be said. Such means as remained were made the most of.

Owing to this calamity, however, the stores on the north bank were well-nigh run out of their usual stock, but I was amazed to find such luxuries of life as eau de Cologne, scented soaps, ladies' boots and shoes, and brightly coloured skirts. Leaving the small river township— the embryo Livingstone—we followed a very sandy road uphill till we reached the summit of Constitution Hill, already mentioned. There our buggy and two small, well-bred ponies swept into a smartly-kept compound surrounded by a palisade, the feature of the square being a flagstaff from which the Union Jack was proudly fluttering. As a site for a residence Constitution Hill could not well be surpassed, and many a millionaire would cheerfully have given his thousands to obtain such a view as that which met our eyes from the humble huts, and held me enthralled during the whole of my stay.

It must be remembered we had been travelling, since leaving the rail-head, eighty miles north of Bulawayo, through a thickly wooded and mountainous country where any extensive views were rare. Even when nearing the Zambesi, with the roar of the Falls in one's ears, so little opening-up had hitherto been done that only an occasional peep of coming glories was vouchsafed us; hence the first glimpse of a vast stretch of country was all the more striking. I must ask my readers to imagine the bluest of blue skies; an expanse of waving grass of a golden hue, resembling an English cornfield towards the harvest time, stretching away till it is lost in far-distant tropical vegetation of intense green, which green clearly marks the course of the winding Zambesi; again, amid this emerald verdure, patches of turquoise water, wide, smooth, unruffled, matching the heavens in its hue, are to be seen—no touch of man's hand in the shape of houses or chimneys to mar the effect of Nature and Nature's colouring.

If you follow with your eyes this calm, reposeful river, now hiding itself beneath its protecting banks with their wealth of branching trees, tall cocoanut palms, and luxuriant undergrowth, now emerging like a huge blue serpent encrusted with diamonds, so brightly does the clear water sparkle in the sun, you note that it finally loses itself in a heavy, impenetrable mass of green forest. And now for a few moments the newcomer is puzzled to account for a dense white cloud, arisen apparently from nowhere, which is resting where the forest is thickest and most verdant, now larger, then smaller, anon denser or more filmy, but never changing its place, never disappearing, while the distant thunder, to which you had almost got accustomed, strikes upon your ear and gives the explanation you are seeking.

Yes, that white cloud has been there for centuries, and will be there while the world lasts, in spite of trains, bridges, etc. It marks the Victoria Falls, and is a landmark for many miles round. How amazed must the great Livingstone and his intrepid followers have been to see this first sign of their grand discovery after their weary march through a country of dense forests and sandy wastes, the natural features of which could not in the least have suggested such marvels as exist in the stupendous river and the water-power to which it gives birth!

When mentioning that great explorer—whose name in this district, after a lapse of nearly fifty years, remains a household word among the natives, handed down from father to son—it is a curious fact, and one that should prove a lesson to many travellers from the old world as well as from the new, that only on one tree is he believed to have cut his initials in Africa, and that tree stands on the island in the centre of the Zambesi, the island that bears his name, and that absolutely over-hangs and stems the centre of the awe-inspiring cataract.

I must now try in a few words to give a short account of what we saw at the Victoria Falls in July, 1903, when the breath of civilization had scarcely touched them. Today they are easy of access, and the changes that have been wrought have come so swiftly that, no doubt, recent visitors will scarcely recognize the localities of which I write. I must first ask such to be lenient with me, and to follow me down the sandy road leading from the Constitution Hill Compound to the Controller's Camp on the bank of the river, about two miles nearer the Falls. There were to be seen a collection of huts and offices, where the controller conducted his important business of food-purveyor to the community, and a Government inspector of cattle had equally arduous duties to perform.

I must mention that, owing to disease in the south, cattle were then not allowed to cross the Zambesi, and horses and dogs had to be disinfected before they were permitted to leave the south bank. Their troubles were not even then over, as they had to be swum across the river, and, owing to its enormous width, the poor horses were apt to become exhausted halfway over, and had to be towed the rest of the way, their heads being kept out of the water—an operation attended with a certain amount of risk. It followed that very few horses were crossed over at all, and that these animals in North-Western Rhodesia were at a premium.

From the Controller's Camp I had another opportunity to admire the river itself, just as wonderful in its way as the Falls, and I remember thinking of the delights that might be derived from boating, sailing, or steaming, on its vast surface. Since that day the enterprising inhabitants have actually held regattas on the mighty stream, in which some of the best-known men in the annals of rowing in England have taken part. But seven years ago our river trip was attended with mild excitements; the small skiff, carrying our party of six, was an excessively leaky canoe, which had to be incessantly baled out to keep it afloat, and wherein, notwithstanding our efforts, a deep pool of water accumulated, necessitating our sitting with feet tucked under us in Oriental fashion. Hence I cannot say we realised to the full the enjoyments of boating as we know it at home in far less beautiful surroundings, or as others know it there at the present time.

The principal features that struck me were, first, the colossal width of the river. As we gazed across the translucent surface, reflecting as in a looking-glass the fringe of trees along the edge, the first impression was that your eyes actually perceived the opposite bank; but we were undeceived by one of the residents, who observed that was only an island, and that there were several such between us and the north side. Secondly, we marvelled at the clearness of the water, reflecting the blueness above; and, thirdly, at the rich vegetation and the intense green of the overhanging foliage, where the graceful and so rarely seen palms of the Borassus tribe were growing to an immense height. All was enhanced by the most intense solitude, which seemed to accentuate the fact that this scene of Nature was indeed as God left it. These reflections were made as we floated on in our rickety canoe to a creek, where we landed to walk to the actual Falls.

A new path had just been cut in the wooded part of the north bank, and we were almost the first visitors to profit by it. Formerly the enterprising sight-seers had to push their way through the scrubby undergrowth, but we followed a smooth track for two miles, the roar of the cataract getting louder and louder, with only occasional peeps of the river, which was fast losing its calm repose and degenerating into restless rapids hurrying on to their bourne. Now and then a buck would dance across our path, pause affrighted for an instant at the unusual sight of man, and bound away again into the thickness beyond; and once three fine wart-hogs almost stumbled into our party, only to gallop away again like greyhounds, before the rifles, which were carried by the black boys behind, could be made use of.

At last we emerged suddenly, without any warning, on the northern extremity of the cataract, which at this point measures over a mile from bank to bank, but of which only about a quarter of that distance is visible, owing to the blinding spray. It is wellnigh impossible to describe a scene of such wonder, such wildness. It is awe-inspiring, almost terrible in its force and majesty, and the accompanying din prevents speech from being heard. Standing on a point flush with the river before it makes its headlong leap, we gazed first on the swirling water losing itself in snowy spray, which beat relentlessly on face and clothes, while the great volume was nosily disappearing to unknown and terrifying depths. The sight-seer tries to look across, to strain his eyes and to see beyond that white mist which obscures everything; but it is an impossible task, and he can but guess the width of the Falls, slightly horseshoe in shape, from the green trees which seem so far away on the opposite bank, and are only caught sight of now and then as the wind causes the spray to lift.

At the same time his attention is fixed by a new wonder, the much-talked-of rainbow. Never varying, never changing, that perfect-shaped arc is surely more typical of eternity there than anywhere else. Its perfection of colours seems to be reflected again and yet again in the roaring torrent, and to be also an emblem of peace where all is turmoil. We were hurried away to remove our wet rainproof coats and to dry our hats and faces in the brilliant sunshine. It seemed as if the Falls guard their beauties jealously, and do not allow the spectator to gaze on them without paying the price of being saturated by their spray. For the next two hours we were taken from one point of vantage to the other, and yet felt we had not seen half of even what is known as the north side. We were shown the barely commenced path leading right away down to the edge of the foaming, boiling gorge, which is to be known as "The Lovers' Walk," and from its steepness it occurred to me that these same lovers will require to possess some amount of endurance.

We examined from afar the precipitous Neck jutting right out opposite the main cataract, its sides running sheer down to unfathomable depths of water, which has caused this rocky formation to be called "The Knife's Edge," and along which, up to the date of our visit, only two men had ventured. We saw the actual site for the existing railway-bridge, which site had only been finally selected a few days before by two of the party who were with us.[1] The travellers over this great work now see all we saw on that long morning, and a great deal more besides, while the carriage windows are soused by the all-pervading spray, thus carrying out one of Mr. Rhodes's cherished sentiments.

Finally—musing at the marvellous and confusing twists and turns of the river, changing in character and appearance so as to be well-nigh unrecognisable—we walked on a hundred yards, and came upon a deep, deep gorge, rocky, barren, and repelling, at the bottom of which, sluggish and dirty in colour, a grey stream was winding its way, not a hundred yards wide, but of unfathomable depths; and this represented the Zambesi *after* it has taken its great leap, when, bereft of all life and beauty, it verily looks tired out. This gorge continues for forty miles, and so desolate is the surrounding country, that not only is it uninhabited by man, but even game cannot live there. The shadows were lengthening and the day was approaching its close. Early on the morrow we were to leave for the northern hunting grounds. We regained our canoe, and paddled away to our temporary camp.

Again we were delighted with the calm beauty of that river scene, and found it difficult to decide when it was most beautiful—whether the morning light best gilded its glories or whether the evening lent additional calm. We passed island after island in bewildering succession. Away towards the drift three huge black masses were splashing in

1. Sir Charles Metcalfe, Bart. Consulting engineer of the Chartered Company, and Mr. G. Pauling, contractor for the same company.

the water, which we easily made out to be hippopotami taking their evening bath, and as we glided along a sleepy crocodile slipped back into the water from a muddy eminence where it had been basking in the sun. Then our canoe ran into a creek where leaves and ferns grew in delightful confusion, and we landed in soft marshy ground just as the sun was sinking like a red ball into the river, and giving way to the sovereignty of a glorious full moon, which soon tinged everything with a silver light, making glades of palms look delightfully romantic.

Civilization has since found its way to Livingstone. Engines are whistling and trains are rumbling where then the only tracks were made by the huge hippos and the shy buck, but they can never efface the grandeur of the river in its size and calmness; the incomparable magnificence of the cataract itself; the rainbow, which one cannot see without retaining a lasting impression of its beauty; and, lastly, that cloud of white spray, seemingly a sentinel to watch over the strength and might of the huge river, for so many ages undiscovered.

Many who knew the Falls in their pristine solitude have gladly welcomed there the advent of twentieth-century developments, of sign-posts, of advertisements, of seats, of daily posts and papers; but others, some of the older pioneers, still, perchance, give a passing sigh for the days when they paddled about the river in a leaky canoe, and letters and telegrams were not events of everyday occurrence.

In spite of the railway constructed since our visit, few people, comparatively, have been to North-Western Rhodesia, and yet it is a country of over 400,000 square miles. It was in October, 1897, that the then administrator of the country,[2] with five policemen, crossed the Zambesi and declared the territory to be under the protection of Her Late Gracious Majesty, Queen Victoria. For many years previously the natives, who are not of a particularly warlike disposition, had been decimated, and the country laid waste, by the fierce Matabele, who were in the habit of making periodical raids into this fair land, and of killing the old men and the young warriors, who made but a slight resistance; of annexing the attractive ladies as wives and the fat cattle as prized booty, and then of retreating again south of the mighty river without fear of reprisals.

For this reason there was, in 1903, a very meagre population for many hundreds of miles north of the Zambesi in this direction; and of cattle, for which there is pasture in abundance, there was hardly one to be seen. One has to travel much farther north and west to find the

2. R. T. Coryndon, Esq.

densely populated valleys, whose inhabitants own Lewanika, Chief of the Barotse, as their ruler, who look to the great white British king as their protector, and to the Chartered Company as the immediate purveyor of their wants.

Of these natives the chief tribes are, first, the Barotse themselves, who are the most numerous, and who inhabit the low-lying country along the Zambesi Valley north of Sesheke, and up to Lia-Lui, their capital.

The second in importance are the Mushukulumbwe, which, translated literally, means "naked people." This designation was given them as a reproach by their friends, as the male element wear no clothes; and should they possess a blanket, they would only throw it round their shoulders whilst standing still or sitting down. When remonstrated with by the well-meaning missionaries on the absence of any attire, they are wont to reply: "Are we women or children, that we should fear the cold? Our fathers needed no clothes, nor do we." They are keen hunters and trackers, essentially a warlike people, tall and good-looking, while the women also are of more than average height, and gracefully made. What the men lack in clothes they make up for in their head-dress, which has been so often illustrated, and which is sometimes 5 feet in height.

It is the result of much care and trouble, and the cause of great pride to the wearer. Ruled over by a number of small chiefs, they mostly own Lewanika as their paramount chief, and to him they pay tribute. They are withal a curious, wild kind of people, but are now becoming less afraid of, and in consequence less hostile to, the white man, the first of whose race they saw in 1888, when Mr. Selous[3] penetrated into their country, and very nearly lost his life at their hands. Now they are well-disposed, and it is safe to travel through their land with a comparatively small escort.

Thirdly, the Batokas. These are, and always have been, a servile race. They are lazy in disposition, for the most part of unprepossessing appearance, and their country has the Kafue River on the east, and the Zambesi on the south, as natural boundaries. As carriers they do fairly well, and, while also owning Lewanika's authority, they are well aware of the fact that this chief only rules in virtue of the support of the "Great King" in a far-off land, whom they often hear of, but can never hope to see.

In consequence of having lived for so many generations in terror

3. *Life and Adventures in South-East Africa*, by F.C. Selous.

of being raided by their more bellicose neighbours, all these tribes acclaimed with joy the advent of their English protectors, and their demeanour is strikingly expressive of gratitude and respect. This is evinced by their native greeting, which consists of sitting down and clapping their hands together in a slow rhythm whenever a white man passes. Sometimes a traveller hears this clapping proceeding out of the immensely high and thick grass which encloses the road, and he is by this sound alone made aware of the presence of a human being. Their food consists entirely of grain, which they greatly prefer to meat, even when this is offered to them. They boil this grain, which resembles millet or canary seed, into a sort of porridge, which they eat with the greatest gusto, and one meal a day seems to suffice them.

And now to describe the fatherland of these natives, just emerging as it is from darkness and strife to prosperity, peace, and, quite possibly, riches beyond the dreams of avarice, but in any case riches, sufficiently proved to enable it to take its place ere long among the treasure-producing territories of God's earth. Once north of the Zambesi, and with the thunder of those magnificent Falls still ringing in one's ears, two things were evident even to the most casual traveller—viz., the changed aspect of the country and of its inhabitants. Of the latter and of their quaint greeting I have already spoken. And as regards the road itself and the surrounding landscape there is a still greater change. Instead of a track of deep sand blocked with huge stones or by veritable chasms of soft, crumbling earth, one finds there good roads, while numerous streams of clear running water constantly intersect the highway.

In England it is difficult to realise the inestimable boon this plentiful supply of water is to the traveller and his beasts, who are thereby saved the very serious necessity of frequently having to push on, weary and thirsty, another stretch of eight or ten miles, simply because of the oft-heard cry, "No water." The scenery itself is fair and restful to the eye; there are no huge mountains, no precipitous dongas, yet an ever-changing kaleidoscope which prevents any monotony. Now the road winds for several miles through woods and some small trees; again, these are left behind, and the traveller emerges on plains of yellow waving grass (so high as to hide both horse and rider), resembling from afar an English barley-field, and broken up by clumps of symmetrically arranged trees.

In these clumps the tropical euphorbia sends up its long and graceful shoots, reminding one of Gargantuan candelabra, and the huge "*baobab*," of unwieldy bulk, seems to stand as the sentinel stretching out its bare arms to protect those who shelter beneath. These trees are the great feature of the country, owing to the enormous size they attain, and to the fact that, being the slowest-growing trees known, their ages can only be reckoned by thousands of years. Except these kings of the forest, the trees indigenous to the land are somewhat dwarfed, but cacti of all kinds flourish, clinging to and hanging from the branches of the mahogany and of the "*m'pani*" trees, looking now and then for all the world like long green snakes.

The "*m'hoba-hoba*" bush, with its enormous leaves, much loved by the elephant, forms patches of vivid green summer and winter. This shrub is supposed to have been introduced by the Phoenicians, when these wonderful people were occupied with their mineral workings in this land, the remains of which are to be seen in many places. In the grass itself, and round the edge of these groups so artistically assorted by the hand of Nature, lies slyly hidden the "wait-a-bit" bush,[3] according to the literal translation from the Dutch, whose thorny entanglements no one can gauge unless fairly caught.

During July and August, which is mid-winter, the grass plains are set on fire, in parts purposely, but sometimes accidentally. They are usually left intact near the road, for transport oxen find plenty of pasture in the coarse high grass which no other animal will touch; but the seeker after game will burn miles and miles of this grass when it is sufficiently dry at the roots. It has acted as a sheltering mantle for its four-footed population for many months, and now the "hunters' moon" is fairly risen and the buck must beware. Therefore, if one leaves the road for two or three miles to the right or left, vast black plains are discovered, on which only about a fortnight after burning a very vivid green, and, it is said, a very sweet, grass springs up, which game of all sorts greatly love. Here they graze in herds morning and evening, and here probably they meet their death—but of this more *anon*. It took our party ten days to reach Kalomo,[4] then the capital of North-Western Rhodesia. This included a six days' halt in quest of game on a rocky kopje eight miles off the road—a veritable Spion Kop, rising from a flat country and commanding views for miles round.

As regards travelling, I can only say it was very comfortable as we did it. Riding ourselves, our baggage (divided into loads each weighing about 30 pounds) was carried by natives, who generally preceded

---

3. *Wacht-een-bietze.*
4. The seat of government was later transferred to Livingstone, on the Zambesi.

us out of camp. The day's journey was divided as follows: Up before the sun, and dressing by the uncertain light of a candle lantern. It was cold enough to render no dawdling possible, and one hurried one's toilet in order to get to the already brightly burning fire and steaming hot coffee. The sun would just then be showing its red head in the far east, and already the camp was in commotion; tents were being struck, bedding rolled up, while a certain amount of scrambling would be going on amongst the cunning blacks, each wishing to possess himself of the lightest load. To prevent shirking, one or two of the native police who accompanied us watched the proceeding with lynx-like eyes, and, amid much arguing, chattering, and apparent confusion, a long line of carriers would emerge like a black snake from the camping-ground into an orderly string—quaint figures, some of them wrapped in gaudy blankets, and even then shivering in the keen morning air; some with their load on their heads, others carrying it on long sticks, all with the inevitable native vessel, fashioned from a gourd, containing their daily ration of grain.

As a supplement to these carriers, we were also accompanied by the (in Africa) familiar "Scotch cart." In other words, this is a strong cart on two wheels, drawn by bullocks, and its usual pace is about two and a half miles an hour. It apparently possesses the delightful qualification of being able to travel on any road, no matter how rough, without breaking down or turning over; in fact, when travelling by road in Africa, it facilitates matters as much as the employment of a charwoman oils the wheels in an English household, and it is therefore as much to be recommended.

We ride for an hour or so with coats tightly buttoned up, blue noses, and frozen fingers—for the hoar-frost still lingers on the ground—but the air is delightfully exhilarating, and we know that we shall not have to complain of the cold long. By degrees the sun makes itself felt, and we discard first one wrap and then another, till by ten o'clock even light overcoats are not required. And now it is time to "off-saddle" and breakfast. The carriers straggle in more or less in the order they left, but they gladly "dump" down their loads, and before many minutes the fire is burning and the breakfast frizzling. After breakfast comes the midday rest of two or three hours, beguiled by some ancient newspapers or some dust-begrimed book. It is remarkable that, when far away from home, the date of a newspaper is of little import, while none are voted dull, and one finds oneself reading the most obscure publications, and vaguely wondering how or why they reached this distant land.

At two o'clock marching orders come again. This is the hot trek, but there is generally a cool breeze to temper the fierce rays of the winter's sun; and when that sun gets low down on to the horizon, and becomes a crimson ball, tingeing the world with its rosy hue, we look about for our evening resting-place. During our journey to Kalomo, as well as on our southward route a month later, we enjoyed the light of a glorious moon, whose assistance to the traveller cannot be exaggerated when the short twilight is remembered. By the moon we frequently made our camp, by the moon we dined. Those were never-to-be-forgotten evenings, spent on that lonely *veldt* all bathed in silver light. We also had excitements—much lions' *spoor* on the roads by day, many scares of lions round the camps by night, when the danger is that the horses may be taken while the camp is asleep. Every evening our animals were put into a "*skerm*," or high palisade, constructed of branches by the ubiquitous carriers with marvellous rapidity.

One dark night before the moon had risen, just as we had finished dinner and were sitting round the fire listening to thrilling stories of sport and adventure, a terrific noise suddenly disturbed our peaceful circle—a noise which proceeded from a dark mass of thick bush not 200 yards away, and recalled one's childish recollections of "feeding-time" at the Zoo. Not one, but five or six lions, might have been thus near to us from the volume of growls and snarls, varied by short deep grunts, which broke the intense stillness of the night in this weird fashion. Each man rushed for his rifle, but it was too dark to shoot, and gradually the noise died away. The natives opined it was a slight difference of opinion between some wolves and a lion, which animals, curiously enough, very often hunt in company, the lion doing the killing, and the wolf prowling along behind and picking up the scraps.

It was but an incident, but it served as an uncanny reminder of the many eyes of the animal world, which, though unseen, are often watching travellers in these solitudes. Another night, when we were encamped in the very heart of a rumoured "lion country," ourselves and our beasts securely protected by an unusually high and thick "*skerm*," we were, to our regret, left undisturbed; but the aforementioned Scotch cart, which rumbled away from the sleeping camp about midnight, had a series of adventures with *Leo felis*. Sniffing the fat oxen, no less than three lions followed the waggon all night, charging close up at times, and finally causing the oxen to stampede, in consequence of which, instead of finding the precious vehicle, containing grain for carriers and forage for horses, at the next outspan, we did not come up with it till evening, nearly thirty miles farther on, when we learnt the adventures it had had.

The truth regarding lion-shooting in these parts is, that the animals are exceedingly difficult to locate, and the finding of them is a matter of pure luck. The traveller may, of course, meet a lion on the road by broad daylight; but many experienced hunters, who count their slain lions by the dozen, will tell you they were years in the country before they ever saw the kings of beasts, and these are men who do not belittle the danger incurred in hunting them. One old hunter is supposed to have said to an enthusiastic newcomer, who had heard of a lion in the vicinity, and immediately asked the old stager if he were going after it: "I have not lost any lions, therefore I am not looking for any;" but, all the same, to kill one or more fine specimens will ever remain the summit of the ambition of the hunter, and unquestionably the spice of danger is one of the attractions.

At the time of which I write the township of Kalomo consisted of about twenty white people, including the Administrator, his secretary and staff; the Chancellor of the Exchequer, or Accountant, who controlled the purse; a doctor, whose time was fairly well taken up; an aspiring light of the legal profession, who made and interpreted the laws; and, finally, the gallant Colonel and officers of the North-Western Rhodesia Native Police, a smart body of 380 natives, officered by eleven or twelve Englishmen. To Colonel Colin Harding, C.M.G., was due the credit of recruiting and drilling this smart corps, and it was difficult to believe that these soldierly-looking men, very spruce in their dark blue tunics and caps, from which depend enormous red tassels, were only a short time ago idling away their days in uninviting native *kraals*.

I was much impressed in a Kalomo house with the small details of a carefully arranged dinner-table, adorned with flowers and snowy linen; the cooking was entirely done by black boys, and of these the "Chinde" boys from the Portuguese settlements are much sought after, and cannot be excelled as cooks or servants, so thoroughly do the Portuguese understand the training of natives. The staple meat was buck of all kinds; sheep were well-nigh unknown, oxen were scarce and their meat tough; but no one need grumble at a diet of buck, wild-pig, *koran*,[5] guinea-fowl, and occasionally wild-duck. As regards other necessities of life, transport difficulties were enormous;

5. A kind of pheasant.

every ounce of food besides meat, and including precious liquids, had then to be dragged over nearly 250 miles of indifferent roads; and not only groceries, but furniture, roofs of houses, clothes—all had to be ordered six to eight months before they were required, and even then disappointments occurred in the way of waggons breaking down, of delays at the rail-head and at the crossing of the river. To us who are accustomed to the daily calls of the butcher, the baker, and the grocer, the foresight which had to be exercised is difficult to realise, and with the best management in the world great philosophy was required to put up with the minor wants.

As to the climate of North-Western Rhodesia in the dry season—which lasts from April or May to November, or even later—it is ideal. Never too hot to prevent travelling or doing business in the heat of the day, it is cold enough morning and evening to make fur coats by no means superfluous; rain is unknown, and of wind there is just enough to be pleasant, although now and then, especially towards sunset or before dawn, a very strong breeze springs up from a cloudless horizon, lasts about thirty minutes, making the trees bend and tents flap and rattle, and then dies away again as suddenly as it has come. Sometimes, in the early morning, this breeze is of an icy coldness, and might be blowing straight from the South Pole. During the dry season the traveller should not contract fever, unless he happens to have the germs in his system, and in this case he may have been immune the whole wet season, and then the first cold weather brings out the disease and lays him low.

I must now devote a few words to the *veldt* and to its animal life as we learnt to know it during some delightful weeks spent in camp eight miles from the township, where game was then still abundant. There we lived in comfortable tents, and our dining-room was built of grass held in place by substantial sticks. The delight of those days is fresh in my memory. Up and on our horses at dawn, we would wander over this open country, intersected with tracks of forest. The great charm was the uncertainty of the species of game we might discover. It might be a huge eland, or an agile pig, or a herd of beautiful zebra.

Now and then a certain amount of stalking was required, and on one occasion a long ride round brought us to the edge of a wood, from whence we viewed at twenty yards a procession of wildebeeste—those animals of almost mythical appearance, with their heads like horses and their bodies like cattle—roan antelope, and haartebeeste; but as a rule, the game having been so little shot at, with an ordinary amount of care the hunter can ride to within shooting distance of the animal he would fain lay low. Should they take fright and be off, we found to gallop after them was not much use, owing to the roughness of the *veldt* and the smallness of the ponies. Occasionally we had to pursue a wounded animal, and one day we had an exciting chase after a wildebeeste, the most difficult of all bucks to kill, as their vitality, unless absolutely shot through the heart, is marvellous.

When we at last overtook and finished off the poor creature, we had out-distanced all our "boys," and it became necessary for my fellow-sportsman to ride off and look for them (as the meat had to be cut up and carried into camp), and for me to remain behind to keep the *aas-vogels* from devouring the carcass. These huge birds and useful scavengers, repulsive as they are to look at, always appear from space whenever a buck is dead, and five minutes suffices for a party of them to be busily employed, while a quarter of an hour later nothing is left but the bones. Therefore I was left alone with the dead wildebeeste and with the circling *aas-vogels* for upwards of two hours, and I realised, as I had never done before, the intense loneliness of the *veldt*, and something of what the horror must be of being lost on it. Even residents have to dread this danger.

At that season the *veldt* boasted of few flowers, but birds were plentiful, especially the large ones I have mentioned as forming a valuable addition to the daily menu, and flocks of guinea-fowl, which run along the ground making a peculiar chuckling noise, rarely flying, but very quick at disappearing in the long grass. The quaint secretary-bird was often to be seen stalking majestically along, solitary and grotesque, with its high marching action. Then the honey-birds must not be forgotten. They give voice to their peculiar note as soon as they see a human being, whom they seem to implore to follow them; and if they succeed in attracting attention, they fly from tree to tree reiterating their call, till they lead the man whose assistance they have sought to the spot where the honey is hidden, but which they cannot reach unaided. As a rule, it is the natives who take the trouble to obey their call and turn it to account.

The weeks slipped by all too quickly, and it was soon time to bid farewell to Kalomo and its game-haunted flats, over which the iron horse now winds its prosaic course on its way to the dim, mysterious North, bringing noise and bustle in its train. In consequence the hunter and the animal-lover have to travel farther on, but there will always be room for all on that vast continent.

RESULTS OF A DAY'S SPORT NEAR KALOMO.

No matter what paths of life it may be the fortune of my readers to tread, let me recommend those wearied with social bustle and the empty amenities of present-day existence to pass a few weeks in the comparative solitude of several pleasant companions "under the stars" in North-Western Rhodesia, where they can still catch a glimpse of the elusive zebras, with coats shining in the sun like burnished steel, and hear the persistent call of the honey-bird.

At night the roar of lions may now and then cause them to turn in their sleep, and in their dreams they may have visions of the animals that have charmed them during the day—the stately eland, the graceful roan and sable antelopes, the ungainly wildebeeste, and the funny old wart-hog, trotting along with high action and tail erect. Besides gaining health and experiencing the keenest enjoyment, they will know some of the pleasures vouchsafed to those of their countrymen whose fate it is to live, and sometimes to die, in far-off climes—men who have helped to make England famous, and are now, step by step, building up our mighty Empire. Curious are the lives these men, and many like them, lead, cut off as it were from the bustling, throbbing world.

A handful of white men, surrounded by thousands of blacks, with calm complacency they proceed, first to impress on the natives the importance, the might, and the justice, of the great Empire which they represent in their various capacities; then to establish beyond question their own dignity and wisdom; and finally to make themselves as comfortable, and their surroundings as attractive and homelike, as possible, with such means as they can command. They are to be seen superintending a court of justice, looked up to and trusted by the natives, who have quickly found out that the "boss" is just, firm, and that he will not believe a falsehood. The blacks have their native names for all these officials, most of them showing great discernment, and some of quite an affectionate nature.

The commissioners, whose work is entirely among the native population, requiring the greatest tact and patience, besides a perfect knowledge of the language, lead, perhaps, the most arduous, as well as the most lonely, existences. Most of the year is occupied in making tours of inspection through their vast districts; they live continually in the open, in constant contact with Nature, and for weeks together they never see a white man. Almost unattended, they move fearlessly in little-known places, among an uncivilized if friendly people, and to some extent they have their lives in their hands. And yet they do not regard their solitary existence as anything to occasion surprise or admiration; they realise the importance of their mission, and wet seasons, bad attacks of fever, and impaired health, do not quench their energy or their keenness for the great work of development. It is true, indeed, that one and all live in anticipation of the biennial holiday, of the seven months spent "at home," and that all events in their lives are dated from those precious days in England; and then, when the time comes to return to duty, they probably depart without a murmur, and very few, if any, would exchange a life in an office, or that of any ordinary profession in England, for the one, untrammelled and free, they lead in the wilds of Africa.

As distractions in this life which they love, they can only look to the weekly mail and the goodly supply of illustrated papers from home, the attentive perusal of which has made them almost as conversant as the veriest Cockney with all the people of note and the fair women of the time, besides giving them an intimate knowledge of passing events. As hosts they are perfection, and all they have is at their guests' disposal. Their incentive to the great work for ever going on, not only in their district, but in so many far-away localities where the Union Jack flies, is the knowledge that the dark clouds of oppression, plunder, and crime, are, in consequence of their efforts, rolling away as mists disappear before the rising sun.

Appendixes

1

Mafeking Relief Fund

Distribution Committee.
Lieutenant-Colonel C.B.Vyvyan, Commandant of Mafeking.
Mr. C.G. Bell, Resident Magistrate.
Mr. A.H. Frend, Mayor.
Total amount made available for distribution £29,267
Of which the Committee allotted to:

	£
Widows and orphans	6,536
Refugees	4,630
Town relief	3,741
Seaside Fund	2,900
Churches, convent, schools, etc.	2,900
Wounded men	2,245
Small tradesmen	1,765
Hospital staff, nuns, etc.	1,115
Colonel Plumer's Rhodesian Column, etc.	1,000
	£26,832

June 6, 1909.

The "Rainy Day Fund," formed from the balance of the Relief Fund, still exists, and though the amount now in it is small, it is sufficient to enable the Trustees (Mayor of Mafeking and Civil Commissioner) to make occasional grants in cases of distress among those who suffered during the siege, or who have fallen on evil days since.

Mafeking Fund, 1900.

	£
Collected by Lady Georgiana Curzon	24,000
Collected by Colonel Baden-Powell's school comrades at Charterhouse (in addition to gifts in kind)	1,150
Collected by Lady Snagge (£643) and *Birmingham Argus* (£350) for sending nurses, women, and children, to seaside	993

The following sent over £100 each:

Conservative Club, Liverpool.
Melbourne Club.
Luton.
Mr. Butler, of Wellington, New Zealand.
Tunbridge Wells Imperial Association.
Right Hon. C.J. Rhodes.
Swansea, Wales.
Salisbury, Mashonaland.
Mr. J. Garlick, of Cape Town.
Mayor of Brighton.
Raleigh Club, London.
Ilfracombe. Mr. William Nicol.

Sent by Lord Mayor of London from Mansion House Fund	200

Mr. Leonard Rayne, theatrical *impresario*, of South Africa, inaugurated the "Rayney Day Fund," with a view to ultimate calls for relief by members of the garrison in years to come.

2

Imperial Yeomanry Hospitals, 1900-1902.

December 29, appeal signed by Lady Georgiana Curzon and Lady Chesham sent from Blenheim Palace.

President: The Queen.
Vice-Presidents: The Princess of Wales and Duchess of Connaught.
Chairman Of Committee: Countess Howe.
Vice-Chairmen of Committee: Countess of Warwick and
Viscountess Valentia.
Hon. Secretary: Earl Howe.
Treasurer: Ludwig Neumann, Esq.
Military Adviser: Major-General Lord Cheylesmore.

Hon. Civilian Director and Treasurer in South Africa: J.G. Hamilton, Esq.

	£	s.	d.
Subscriptions received between issue of first appeal and issue of interim report in April, 1900, £127,000. During the whole time the subscriptions (including the first) totalled	145,325	15	7
Sale of base hospital realised	15,000	0	0
Government subsidy for prolonging maintenance of field-hospital and bearer company,			
January 1 to March 31, 1901	3,000	0	0
Sale of Elandsfontein Hospital	9,051	9	6
Bankers' interest to December 31, 1901	1,635	12	9

£174,012 17 10

From first to last, various staffs numbered over 1,400 persons, and 20,000 patients received medical aid in the different Yeomanry Hospitals.

When the staff returned to England, medals were presented to them at Devonshire House by the queen.

Deelfontein Base Hospital: Opened March 5, 1900; closed March 31, 1901. Originally with 500 beds, subsequently increased to 1,000 beds. 6,093 in-patients, including 351 officers, were treated there.

Mackenzie's Farm, Maitland Camp, Base Hospital: Opened August 2, 1900; closed March 31, 1901. Originally with 100 beds, subsequently increased to 150. 1,066 patients treated.

Eastwood, Pretoria, Base Hospital: Opened August 18, 1900; closed September 30, 1901. Originally with 400 beds, subsequently increased to 564 beds. 5,227 in-patients, including 466 officers, and 1,095 out-patients, treated.

Elandsfontein Base Hospital: Opened June 29, 1901; closed December 19, 1901. Originally with 50 beds, subsequently increased to 138 beds. 823 in-patients, including 27 officers, and 900 out-patients, treated.

Chesham Convalescent Home At Johannesburg (for officers only): Opened March 1, 1901; closed October 10, 1901. 8 beds. 79 patients received.

Field-Hospital And Bearer Company, with 100 beds, left England in March, 1900; opened at the seat of war in South Africa on April 12, 1900; closed April 1, 1901, having remained three months longer than was originally arranged for. Subsidy of £3,000 received from Government for this purpose.

IMPERIAL YEOMANRY HOSPITALS.

General Committee:

Ninety ladies, whose names are given in the first volume of the Imperial Yeomanry Hospitals Report.

General Working Committee:

Lady Georgiana Curzon (Chairman).

Adeline, Duchess of Bedford.

The Duchess of Marlborough.

The Countess of Dudley.

The Countess of Essex.

The Ladies Tweedmouth and Chesham (went to Deelfontein
in early days of Imperial Yeomanry Hospitals).

Mrs. S. Neumann.

Mrs. A.G. Lucas.

Mrs. Blencowe Cookson.

Mrs. Julius Wernher (later Lady Wernher).

Madame von Andre.

Finance Committee:

Viscount Curzon, M.P. (later Earl Howe).

Mr. Ludwig Neumann.

Adeline, Duchess of Bedford.

Lady Chesham.

Lady Georgiana Curzon.

Press Committee:

The Countess of Dudley.

The Countess of Essex.

Madame von Andre.

The Duchess of Marlborough.

Lady Georgiana Curzon.

Transport Committee:

Assisted by Major Haggard and General Eaton:

Lady Tweedmouth.

Mrs. Julius Wernher.

Mrs. S. Neumann.

Mrs. A.G. Lucas.

Lady Georgiana Curzon.

Gifts and Purchase Committee:

Assisted by General Eaton, Colonel Sloggett and Mr. Fripp, and Mr. Oliver Williams.

The Countess of Essex.

Lady Tweedmouth.

Mrs. A. G. Lucas.

Mrs. S. Neumann.

Lady Georgiana Curzon.

Medical, Nursing, and General Staffs Committee:

Assisted by General Eaton, Colonel Sloggett and Mr. A. Downing Fripp.

The Duchess of Marlborough.

Adeline, Duchess of Bedford.

The Countess of Warwick.

Lady Chesham.

Madame von Andre.

Lady Georgiana Curzon.

The chief workers in Ireland were: The Countess of Longford, Lady Annette La Touche, and Mrs. Pirrie; but they were only on the General Committee, not on any of the subcommittees.

A Lady Trader in the Transvaal

Contents

Preface

The following narrative is a faithful account of my personal experience. The only liberty that I have taken with facts consists of the substitution of fictitious for the real names of persons and farms. These changes have been made for obvious reasons.

Sarah Heckford.

Chapter 1

On a fine breezy morning, early in December, 1878, a number of passengers, and volunteers for the Zulu war, crowded the deck of one of the Union Company's steamships, then lying off the Port of D'Urban, or Port Natal. She had been for some days unable to land her passengers owing to the roughness of the "bar," that terrible difficulty presented by all south-east African seaports; but early on this particular morning the joyful intelligence that the tug was coming was made known, and the excitement, was great in consequence.

The volunteers had all come on board at East London, a very sparely populated and commonplace-looking seaside village on the African coast. They were more or less prepared for what lay before them, for they knew what life in South Africa is; but to the majority of the passengers the low-lying, jungly-looking shore on which the breakers were beating was like the drop-scene of an unknown opera. What lay behind it was a mystery to all those who were then for the first time landing in South Africa—at least one half of the number assembled on deck. Most of them, no doubt, felt this; but there was one, at least, who did not. This was a young gentleman who went by the name of "Dick." He was a strapping youngster of about eighteen, who, I am inclined to think, had been shipped to Africa because nothing could be done with him at home.

The new life before him presented no difficulties to his mind; he knew exactly how he was going to manage. He would buy a horse at D'Urban, put a few things in his saddle-bags, strap his tent on his horse's crupper, and ride to Rustemberg (his destination) with a *kaffir* for his guide. There he would rapidly make his fortune, principally by trading amongst the *kaffirs*, to which end he had, before leaving England, provided himself with a stock of little machines, which (if my memory serves me rightly) are labelled in shop-windows "A cup of tea in five minutes." This invention consists of a piece of sponge covered with wire gauze and encased in a metal cover, so that the apparatus can be carried in the pocket until it is required to perform the part of a spirit-lamp. The contrivance is more complicated than I describe, and decidedly ingenious. Dick had a store of these things in perfect order, and was confident of doing a roaring trade in them amongst the *kaffirs*.

Dick was now, however, troubled with a difficulty; it was this: he had two dogs, one an English bull-terrier—it had cost him 5*l.* to bring the animal from England—the other a *kaffir* mongrel, for which he had paid a sovereign to the owner, who had come on board at Cape Town. The owner was a *kaffir*, and had brought his dog on board without asking any questions, and probably would have taken him off without any being asked of him; but when Dick bought the dog, the captain and chief officer declared that he must pay the full fare for the animal, and on his indignant refusal, threatened to seize his saddle. Poor Dick was in an agony, honestly believing they meant what they said, and being much troubled in his mind as to how his new acquisition, a very large and lively dog, was to be got into the tug.

The method of conveying the passengers from the steamship to the tug was certainly enough to alarm the poor mongrel, and Dick was justified in thinking it likely that he would object to it. A strongly-made basket, large enough to hold three or four persons crouching down, was being periodically hauled up to the side and swung over to the deck of the ship, filled with passengers, and then lowered away, until, amidst much laughter and shouting, its unlucky occupants were let bump down on the deck of the little tug that was bobbing about by the side of her big sister, when they were immediately and very unceremoniously tumbled out if they were men. Women and children were somewhat more gently treated.

It certainly struck me that it would be very easy to break one's legs in the operation, and when my turn came I was very glad to find myself safely on board the little vessel. She was a funny-looking little craft, made expressly for crossing the disagreeable bar, and we were all cautioned to sit fast and wedge ourselves in well, or we might be swept overboard as we passed it. I expected a frightful drenching at least, but nothing at all happened; it was the old story of the mountain and the mouse, and as such, it formed a fitting prelude to life in South Africa, where, so far as my experience goes, everything is exaggerated—dangers, difficulties, beauties, and advantages.

I believe that D'Urban is a pretty town, but it did not look pretty to me, for I was in a bad temper. I had arranged to travel with a party who were going up country to speculate, thinking that it might be difficult for a lady alone, unless blessed with large means, to travel in a country of which the languages and customs were unknown to her. It is, I think, rather trying for any one accustomed to manage for himself to submit to be managed for, unless the management be very good, which in this case it was not. I found it decidedly tried me, and when it came on to rain, and (there being a strike of the *kaffir* porters on that day) my companions piled all the luggage in the middle of a tramway, seemingly unconscious of there being any unadvisability in its being so disposed of, I felt very uncharitable towards them. The result of this disposition of our joint property was, that after a while a number of *kaffirs*, with that beautiful disregard of consequences which is one of the pleasing characteristics of the race, sent a line of empty railway trucks right into it.

The acrobatic and athletic efforts then made to rescue individual boxes dear to the owners' hearts, were amusing to behold; but it would have been a great relief to one's feelings to have been able to vent one's wrath, if only in words, on those unpleasant *kaffirs*, who looked on grinning; but it was no use abusing them, for they didn't understand English, and none of us spoke Zulu or any other *kaffir* language. At last I got into an omnibus which runs between the port and the village of D'Urban, taking "Jimmy" with me. And here, as I shall have occasion to mention Jimmy again, let me introduce him.

Jimmy was a boy of nearly sixteen, whom I had known from the time he was very small. He belonged to the party with whom I had arranged to travel, and was the only member of it with whom I had any previous acquaintance when I went on board the Union Company's ship at Southampton. He was fresh from home and school, and not at all accustomed to roughing it, hence he was permitted to be a good deal with me, and was allowed certain little privileges not accorded to the men of the party, or even to another youngster not much older than Jimmy, but about twice his size and strength.

The omnibus set us down at the best hotel in D'Urban; but that does not say very much. The village consisted of a line of straggling cottages or small houses, some of them with things in the window for sale, a railway-station, and a rather nice-looking building where the post-office was. I say consisted, for it may be much changed since then. The hotel was a cottage standing in a garden. There was a sitting-room with a piano in it, and a *table d'hôte* in an adjoining but separate room; but there were none of the other arrangements which one connects in one's mind with an hotel. The idea it gave me was that a small farmhouse had been suddenly called upon to accommodate several people, and that the owner was doing his best. On the whole, D'Urban did not strike me as a singularly delectable spot, and I was not sorry to leave it.

We departed by the train, which took us to Pine Town, a pretty little place, in the middle of scenery that reminded me of an Indian jungle.

Here we got into an omnibus. We were packed very tight, and had little parcels of various sorts crammed into every available spot. The road was rough, and the horses went at a rattling rate. I suppose it was what some of the people said, "miserable;" but I rather enjoyed it, for the scenery was fine. We stopped for dinner sit a farmhouse, and got into Pieter-Maritzburg at sunset. The town looked very pretty with the evening light on it, lying in the middle of a circle of hills; but it is not really a very pretty place, although I believe its inhabitants think it so. Pieter-Maritzburg in reality is, or was when I saw it, only a large village.

Before I proceed, I must warn my readers, that although I shall have to tell them of rocks and valleys and wooded ravines, &c., they must not picture to themselves anything analogous to what they may have seen in Switzerland or Italy. There are such things in this part of the world, but they are commonplace. It is necessary to come here to understand what a "commonplace" wooded ravine means, but once here one understands it perfectly. I have often tried to make out in what this want of beauty, where there ought to be beauty, consisted, and I think that to a considerable extent it is caused by a want of atmosphere, to use a phrase common to artists. In this part of the world the sun rises, when the sky is cloudless, in a bright yellow halo. It is yellow—not the glorious gold of the Egyptian or Indian sunrise—and the light it throws on all around is simply a bright yellow light. There are no delicately shaded tints, as it fades into shadow, or plays over an uneven surface.

The artist who would portray it need have but few colours in his paint-box. If the sky be cloudy, he need only as a rule have plenty of grey, and enough red and yellow for a streak or two. It is very seldom one sees the beautiful rose-flecked sky which made the fanciful Greeks gift Aurora with rosy-tipped fingers. And then, where will a dweller here find the magnificent colouring of an Indian, or the ethereal blush of an Italian, sunset? The finest he will ever see here will not be equal to many that he will have seen in England.

The colouring of the scenery is monotonous. The grass when it is not yellow is a very vivid green; the trees have not much variety of hue or form; and the sky is very blue—a cobalt blue, deepening into indigo as it nears the horizon, but without a trace of the rose-pink which, when we first learn to put a brush on paper, we are so strenuously enjoined never to omit in an horizon. Even the moonlight is not so ethereal as in other countries, although it is often very bright.

So much for the scenery. Now, as to the life here, I can only compare it to a picture in which there is no central point for the eye to rest on, in which everything is equally prominent. It is moral atmosphere which is wanting, I am inclined to think. Life here is a jumble, to use an inelegant but expressive word. To me, and to many I fancy, there is much in the life which is attractive. It is, I believe, a fact, that people who have been here for some time and have longed to return to Europe, having done so, have come back to finish their days in Africa. But I doubt whether more than two or three of those persons even, could have told the characteristic charm which thus recalled them from their old homes.

CHAPTER 2

Jimmy and I left Pieter-Maritzburg on a fine afternoon, having been there about a week—the rest of the party, together with the two waggons which had been hired by the manager, having gone on in front the men on foot, we on horseback, or rather on pony-back, for neither of our steeds was fifteen hands high. I had found it very hard to get serviceable animals at Pieter-Maritzburg, for at that time all the available, and many unavailable horses, were bought up by the volunteers. Dick had invested in a weedy-looking young mare, and he rode her to death, I heard, in about a fortnight, although he was not in the volunteers. Two of our party had left us to join the native contingent (then being raised) as volunteer officers. They spoke nothing but English, and their men nothing but a *kaffir* dialect; so how they, and many others who joined like them, managed, I do not know. They had also bought miserable hacks. I cannot say much for my own two. One, which Jimmy bestrode, was a rough and ugly Basuto pony, very thin, but with good qualities.

My pony was larger, fat, and handsome; he would have been very good, except for his laziness. I certainly never have seen so lazy a little horse. He would stand stock-still, unless forcibly reminded that he was wanted to walk; and when induced to canter, he would in five minutes fall into a walk. These two animals were the means of introducing me to the common domestic insect of this part of the world, namely, the "tick," or "bush-louse," as it is called by the Boers. There were hundreds on both the ponies, and the groom of the hotel being, as *kaffir* grooms generally are, a useless addition to the stable, Jimmy and I had employed hours in ridding our ponies of the parasites. I had an idea that I knew what a "tick" was, on sheep in England; but the South African tick is a wonderful creature. There are grey, brown, whitish, and striped varieties, besides one exceedingly poisonous kind, yellow-green on the back, with a white line with symmetrical streaks of red on it running round the edge of the podgy little body, and the belly grey. These insects vary in size, from almost invisibility to the bulk of a hazel-nut. They are very agile; and if you happen to be sitting on the grass, you have a good chance of seeing one walk nimbly towards you, with a hungry look pervading his small person. What the creatures live on when they don't happen to fall in with some living prey I do not know, but numbers of them certainly have their habitat in the grass.

Jimmy and I started on pony-back. With a vague idea that I was going into a wild country, and with a distinct one that Jimmy was not likely to afford me much protection, I had a revolver in a case strapped round my waist, and another in a holster on my saddle. The waggons had started in a hurry; and there having been some misunderstanding on my part as to when I was to have all my things loaded up, a good many things belonging to Jimmy and myself had been left behind, and these were crammed into our saddle-bags, and tied on our saddles. However, we started, and having arrived at an even stretch of road halfway up the hill immediately beyond the village, Jimmy proposed a canter. It was not a particularly fast one, but the effect was disastrous. I was a little in front when I heard "*Hilloa!* I say, look what's happening!*" and looking back, I beheld the road strewed with articles which had gradually fallen from Jimmy's various parcels. Jimmy looked disconsolate as he returned, and began to pick them up and tie them on again, while I sat on my pony and laughed. This was unfair, I must confess, for the loading up arrangement had been of my invention, not Jimmy's.

Presently we came up to one of our party, sitting, hot and weary, on a big stone near to a hand-cart laden with miscellaneous articles, which, had not arrived in time to be packed in the waggons. I must here observe, that the manager of our party had contracted for our being taken to Pretoria with our goods by a carrier, or what is here called a transport-rider, and the transport-rider was imperious about when he would "in and out-span," to use a South African phrase for putting the oxen into and letting them out of the yoke. I confess that, being at the time ignorant of the conditions of transport-riding, I thought our carrier unreasonable on this and many other occasions. But experience has taught me that in respect of his treatment of oxen in this one particular, he was altogether reasonable, for in travelling with an ox-waggon, even an inhuman man, and our driver was one, must consider his oxen, or else he will stick fast on the road.

The young gentleman who was sitting hot and weary on the stone, guarding the hand-cart while his companions in misfortune had gone to drink somewhere, must have been a very amiable person if he did not feel something akin to hatred of Jimmy and myself as we rode up, and after a few words rode on. He did his best to look cheerful; and this was creditable to him, although it was a failure, for who could be expected to look cheerful at being harnessed two abreast to a heavy hand-cart, and having to drag it uphill for miles in a broiling sun? Everything, however, has an end. Some time after Jimmy and I reached the place where the waggons were outspanned, the cart was brought in, the articles in it placed in the waggons, and the cart itself sent back—I forget how—to Pieter-Maritzburg. When the oxen were inspanned and we started once more, we felt that we were fairly *en route*; and being so, let me describe the waggons, which were to serve us as houses until we reached Pretoria. The one was an open buck-waggon, something of the same make as our large English hay-waggons, with a tarpaulin, or what is here called "a buck-sail," thrown over it to protect the goods.

There were, I think, eighteen oxen in this waggon, which was driven principally by the Africander transport-rider, a small man, with red whiskers and moustache. The other waggon was also a buck-waggon, or waggon with railings projecting from the sides for the support of goods; but on the back half of it there was a tent, formed of canvas stretched on bent laths, so as to form a complete covering at the sides and top. The ends were furnished with canvas flaps, to be shut or opened at pleasure. With very few articles packed in a half-tent, its occupant, if there be but one, may be comfortable enough; but when, in addition to cases, the entire paraphernalia which a company of twelve men, most of them unaccustomed to travelling, think necessary to keep handy, is tumbled into it, the conditions are altered.

Of course each man had a rifle, and these weapons had to be kept exceptionally handy, although they did not get us more than two or three brace of birds during our whole trek, and not even one buck. The result of twelve men and one woman (myself) having these things "handy "in a half-tent was this. The various articles underwent a rotatory movement every time one of them was wanted, and became well mixed up. Later on I was able to make canvas bags and tie them up to the sides of the tent, and so save my property from the general confusion, but at the out-start my goods contributed to it.

Our evening outspan was on a bleak hill-top, along which a thick, damp mist was beginning to sweep. It soon enveloped us, and rendered the cooking of the evening meal difficult. In agreeing with the transport-driver, no definite understanding had been come to as to what assistance the natives under his control were to render, hence they gave us very little, and the men had to bring water, fuel, &c., and make the fire themselves. This a native will do in pouring rain, but an Englishman, as a rule, is puzzled to do it even in a drizzling mist. Presently, through the mist, up rode the two of our party who had joined the volunteers; they came to bid their companions Godspeed, and then rode off, as it was already late. I don't know what became of one of them; the other was massacred as he lay ill of fever in the hospital at Rorke's Drift.

In the meantime the tent for the men was pitched by them. I had a tent, but I think I only persuaded them to pitch it for my benefit four times, and I forget whether this was one of those occasions. Presently supper made its appearance. The meal consisted of fried ham, bread, and coffee—without milk, be it understood. It does not sound badly, but I will describe it in the words of the man who cooked it: "Rancid tallow candle, with lots of salt in it." He would not eat of it; but I was very hungry, and did, although I confess the description was accurate.

Chapter 3

I shall not give a lengthened description of a journey in or with an ox-waggon, through a country whose leading feature is an utter absence of any objects of interest, except to the eye of a speculative farmer, and even he could not but be disagreeably impressed by the want of water. I will sum it up by saying, that we travelled over many miles of undulating country, starting early in the morning, outspanning in the middle of the day, and travelling again in the evening, during which time we were not particularly comfortable. The men generally walked; Jimmy and I rode. It was very rough, although after our first evening the food improved; but the want of milk was trying. Then, too, it is unpleasant when the weather is very hot not to be able to get a good wash, or to change one's linen often; and these were impossibilities for me, owing to my not being able to induce the men to pitch my tent. The waggon-tent was too much cumbered for even an active person, not to say one who is lame, as I am, to perform satisfactory ablutions in; and the absence of trees made an impromptu dressing-room a thing not to be thought of. Sometimes we came to a little shanty called an hotel, and then I eagerly seized the opportunity for a wash; but these accommodations were very few, and far between.

One duty which devolved on me, many would, I daresay, consider a hardship, but I did not mind it; this was cleaning my horse. I was a new hand at grooming a horse then, having previously only had the brush and comb in my hands *en amateur*, and it is one thing to rub down a well-groomed horse for amusement, and another to clean a very dirty and hot one under a broiling sun; but I cannot say that I disliked this hardship, although I used to wish that our outspanning times were such as to allow of my grooming operations being carried on at some hour when the sun was low. At best, however, a mid-day outspan in a treeless country is objectionable; it is pleasanter to be moving than stationary during the process of being broiled. It is true that under the waggon there is a little shade, but in this case it was not available for me, being fully occupied by the tired men. It is, however, absolutely necessary for oxen to rest in the heat of the day if they are to work well; and, as I said before, our conductor in this respect was a good manager.

The first place that made an impression on my mind was Kar-Kloof. It is approached by a road that winds round a hill-side, and then one is almost startled by the abruptness and length of the ascent in front. It seems almost impossible for oxen to drag a loaded waggon up so long and steep a hill. It is a picturesque place (for Africa), with deep gullies at the side of the rugged road, and with even a sprinkling of trees. On the top of this tremendous hill is a tiny iron house—an inn, and very glad I was that such a thing existed; for hardly were we at the top when a most terrific storm broke over us. There was even a stable, or what served the purpose of one, and in it, to my great relief, I was able to get shelter for the horses. The landlady, a most garrulous and inquisitive old person, was very kind to me; although she apparently regarded my companions as undesirable characters, and came down on them very sharp whenever she could.

The storm ended in a thick mist, through which one of the men thought he saw a buck, and incontinently set forth, rifle in hand. The buck disappeared, and so did its would-be persecutor; the disappearance of the former being for good, and of the latter for the whole night, which he spent in forlornly wandering in continual dread of losing his footing amongst the rocks and gullies as completely as he had lost his way.

Then there was Estcourt, a place that looked pretty by moonlight, but not so well by daylight; and then there was the Drachensberg, or Dragon Mountain. I had heard much of this terrible mountain, and dreadful accounts of what happened to waggons whilst attempting to cross it; I therefore approached it with a certain amount of respect.

The Drachensberg is not a single mountain, but a very long chain, as anyone can see by looking at it on the map. At its foot the road coming from Natal divides into two, one branch leading across the mountain into the Free State, the other going to Newcastle. We were to go by the former, and I now learned that we were to go to Pretoria *via* Heilbronn and Heidelberg. My knowledge of the geography of the country was not up to the mark, but it was sufficient to render this announcement startling to me, the taking Heilbronn *en route* to Heidelberg bringing me some sixty or seventy miles out of my way; however, the conductor said he had to go, and that was considered to be conclusive. I believe the reason he gave was, that having lost many of his oxen on the road, and thinking it likely he should lose more, he had to go to Heilbronn, where his home was, for fresh oxen; in reality, he went to pick up his wife, who wanted to pay a visit to Heidelberg. But whatever was the reason, he said he must go by Heilbronn; and we, having no previous contract as to the road by which he was to travel, had to obey. We left the hospitable little inn at the foot of the mountain in the afternoon. The preamble of our starting was as follows:—

My horse's withers having been touched by the saddle, and Jimmy's pony being also touched on the back, I said I would go in the waggon.

"If that be so," said the conductor, "your young friend had best go with you."

"Why?" I inquired.

"Because very likely the waggon may be upset," quoth the conductor.

What benefit I was to derive from Jimmy's presence in such a case I did not pause to inquire, but, as speedily as I could, descended from my destined conveyance—just in time to see a wretched sheep in its dying agonies, having been killed for our supper by one of the men, alongside of the waggon, to which it was speedily hung.

The innkeeper now provided a light carriage called a "spider," drawn by four oxen, for my benefit, in which I started some time after the waggons had done so.

The ascent of the Dragon Mountain is certainly picturesque, although the lack of trees is very much felt, but the effect of it was greatly marred by a thick mist which came on as evening drew in. Presently we came to our waggons, stuck in the mud amongst a lot of others all in the same predicament. It was a nice pleasant look-out! The spider deposited me in the mud; the men pitched their tent in the mud; and presently up came Jimmy leading the two ponies, all very muddy. The supper was what might be expected under the circumstances. I got Jimmy into the waggon with me, tied the horses to the back of it, and fed them from my hand—for the mud made it impossible to feed them on the ground, and I had no nose-bag for them—and then prepared to go to sleep. My remembrance of that night is, that it was a perpetual struggle to avoid slipping out at the back; for as there was no mattress, but only a blanket or two thrown on a mixed assortment of articles, prominent amongst which were the rifles of the party, and the waggon stood on a steep incline, not only oneself, but all one was lying on had a downward tendency.

Towards morning I heard dismal sounds from a member of our party who had attempted to sleep on the waggon, outside the tent but under the buck-sail, and then a clank which told me that his head must have come in collision with a certain tin box of mine.

"I can't stand this any longer," he groaned; and I heard him descend to where, under the waggon, some of his companions had been sleeping in the mud. This woke them, and they began making comparisons between the relative coldness of their backs, which so amused me that I completely woke up, to find the dawn breaking very sullenly. I found the poor ponies warm under their blankets, but slipping in the mud, which was by this time over their pasterns, and got them something to eat. Then with difficulty I woke Jimmy—who solemnly assured me he had not slept a wink all night—and suggested to him the advisability of saddling, and trying to push on to an inn on the Willow River, which I heard was about twelve miles distant. This we did, passing a waggon, all broken to pieces in its fall, a little way ahead of our waggons, which, with the rest of the party, did not get to our harbour of refuge by the Willow River for two days, having fearful weather on the mountains.

We were now in the Orange Free State, and during my stay at the little hostelry I heard much political talk, adverse to the English, from an old Free-Stater somewhat addicted to the bottle. I also had a conversation with a gentleman of a very inventive turn of mind, who told me some wonderful stories, to which I listened gravely. Whenever something suggested to him that my wonderment was getting too strong, he would appeal in a most artless manner to the memory of a friend of his who was there, and the friend always remembered. These two were dwellers in the Transvaal, but both, with delightful *naïveté*, cautioned me not to trust any Transvaalists, as they were all fearfully acute and untrustworthy.

On the morning after the arrival of our party at the Willow River, Jimmy and I started for Harrismith, the others, with the waggons having gone on before. We found them having breakfast, and stopped for a few minutes with them.

Harrismith looked like a dismal little attempt at a town. I was fresh from European and Indian cities and towns then. Now, after a little more than two years in the Transvaal, I have become sufficiently savage to think Harrismith, whenever I may next see it, quite a respectable attempt at one. There are two inns in the place; the one to which we went was fairly comfortable—at least the sitting-room, dining-room, and my bedroom adjoining the sitting-room, were very good. I could see that the bedroom was the show bedroom, and I don't know what the others were. The stable was large, and crammed with horses—just tied to the manger, without any division between them, and so closely packed that it was difficult to get between them so as to clean one's own horse. And the dirt! The Augean stable must have been a trifle to it!

From Harrismith we were to trek to Heilbronn, and when our party came up it was proposed that I should go there in the post-cart, leaving Jimmy in charge of my horse and his own. I was rather loath to trust my horse to the tender mercies of either Jimmy or any of the men; but I had two reasons for acceding to the proposal—first, that the horses withers were touched by the saddle; secondly, that my companions were evidently looking forward with delight to the idea of getting rid of me, and I felt it would be ungenerous to disappoint them. So it was arranged that they were to start on the morning of, I think, Thursday, and I was to start on Friday in the post-cart.

Just as they were starting, I bethought me that it might be as well not to carry money with me during my solitary drive with the *kaffir* post-boy, and keeping only enough for roadside expenses, I sent the rest of my possessions on in the waggon; and, bidding Jimmy and my pony farewell, I prepared to employ the remainder of the day as best I could. There were a few books on the round table in the sitting-room, none of them worth reading but one, Dickens's *Great Expectations*. With this to enjoy, I lay down on the sofa; and had a thorough rest.

The next morning I remained in bed until my coffee was brought to the door by a *kaffir*; and I was dressing leisurely, when I was startled by hearing a voice I was sure was Jimmy's. I hurried out, and there, in good truth, was Jimmy, looking very tired. In answer to my astonished inquiry how he came to be there, he recounted the following story, which he believes in implicitly to the present day, but to which no one else has ever attached any credit.

He had ridden in front of the waggons, leaving my pony in charge of the men, and although believing himself to be on the right road, virtually lost his way. Being, I fancy, rather glad to ride his pony just as he liked, instead of under my inspection, he rode and dismounted, rode and dismounted, until evening began to creep up, when it occurred to him as odd that the waggons were not coming up into sight. Just about this time he was close to a small stony hill or *coppie*, down which he saw three *kaffirs*, armed with *assegais*, coming. He looked at them with some suspicion, and rode on, looking behind every now and then, when he observed that they were following him. He then cantered, upon which they ran; then, according to his account, he caused his pony to gallop—a feat I don't think the pony was capable of; anyhow, he attained to a pace which appeared a very fast one to the rider, when one of the *kaffirs* threw an *assegai* after him, which overshot him, and stuck quivering in the ground.

Thereupon Jimmy struck across the *veldt*, and cantered or galloped along till night stopped him. He then dismounted and led the pony, feeding himself and his little steed with some gingerbread and other biscuits he had in his pocket; but as he had no idea where he was, it was not much use walking about leading a pony. However, he presently saw a light in the distance, and making for it, found it to proceed from the fire of a friendly waggoner, who told him he was some twenty miles from Harrismith, but far off the waggon-road to Heilbronn, and who advised him to go with him to Harrismith, whither he was bound, and to find me out. He then gave him some supper and a blanket, and tied the pony behind the waggon, so that Jimmy need not stir when the waggon started.

All I can say about the *assegai* story is, that the Free State was far from the seat of war, in a condition of profound peace, and that I was informed that it is unlawful in the Free State for *kaffirs* to carry *assegais*. One thing was evident, Jimmy was there, and so was the pony. Jimmy was tired; the pony completely knocked up. The question was, what could I do? I had my ticket for the post-cart, which was to start at ten o'clock, and a few shillings over what my hotel bill would amount to—and the price of a place in the post-cart was four sovereigns! It was evident that money must be raised, and so I raised it by selling the pony; and then Jimmy and I awaited the arrival of the post-cart, which was supposed to take us to Heilbronn in two days. Its advent was heralded by very loud talking. A gentleman on horseback was alongside of it, who in excited tones drew the attention of another individual to the state of the hulking *kaffir* driver of the vehicle.

"I can't think of allowing a lady to go with the drunken brute," he exclaimed. "We *must* get another driver."

Whereupon he jumped off his horse.

"I'll give you a jolly hiding, and send you to prison, you rascal. You stand there, and take that—and that—and that—and that," and he struck the *kaffir* across the head, arms, and breast, with his heavy stinging ox-hide whip.

The fellow barely stirred a muscle. I could hardly at the time think that he felt much, but *kaffirs* will sometimes bear a beating that *does* hurt in that way. There was a twitch of the mouth each time the whip fell that was all.

"Now you take him away," quoth the excited man; "and you here, you must drive."

You here was a diminutive Hottentot.

"I can't drive," said the Hottentot.

"Oh, never mind that," said the excited gentleman, who probably knew this was not the case; "jump up!"

"And I don't know the road."

"Then you'll have to find it out. You drove the cart some time ago—you must know it; jump up!" and up the Hottentot jumped.

The vehicle into which he jumped, and into which I proceeded to scramble, had once been a dog-cart, but was now a ruin; the system of pieces of leather and cord, ingeniously twisted together, which attached it to the horses, had, I suppose, once been a set of harness; the horses once had certainly been very good, but now they were a pair of vicious, jibbing rips. How they did jib! and when the united efforts of the little Hottentot (who soon proved that he could drive) and some four or five other men had got them to move, how they did rush away with the little cart!

They were just sobering down to a reasonable pace at the outskirts of the village when my driver said, "Will you hold the reins? That's my house; I must say goodbye to my wife, and get my blanket." The small man could talk English. Upon his return from taking a fond *adieu* of Mrs. Hottentot, the horses steadily refused to move. Jimmy had to push the wheels, and there was a great to-do before, with a plunge, they got away again; but alas! there was a *spruit*, or small ravine with a brook running through it, before us!

The Hottentot in the meanwhile opened his heart to me. "It is very hard pressing me like this," he said. "I don't remember the road; and my ribs were broken the other day, and they are hardly well." I don't know whether the effect was that of the broken ribs or not, but as he spoke the little man foamed at the mouth like a champing horse, which was unpleasant when one was to leeward of him, as I was: I therefore discouraged conversation. A few minutes after brought us to the *spruit*, where the operations of coaxing, whipping, and pushing the jibbing horses, had to be resorted to. The road was very uneven, and this had to be repeated at every little hitch, we therefore got along rapidly. I was looking forward with anxiety to the change, but it only brought us even worse horses. Then the harness took to breaking, and was mended with little strips of leather and pieces of twine, produced out of his pocket by the little driver.

Each change seemed to bring us worse horses. At last a pair of almost unbroken colts were put in. It was a terrible battle to get them to start at all, and then they went at a furious rate, but stopped at the first hitch, and plunged the harness nearly off, breaking it hopelessly in one place. The Hottentot's resources were exhausted; but fortunately I had a little hunting-crop with me, and its lash did excellent service.

"We must be near the house where I ought to leave some letter," said the Hottentot at one place; "but I don't know the road."

"Dear me," said I, with my European conscientiousness about letters still unimpaired. "What can you do?"

"Oh, I shall just go on," said the little man. "It isn't my fault. I told him I didn't know the road."

Presently it began to get dusk and chilly. "I can't get to the right place for outspanning for the night," said the driver. "We must stop at the next house."

A Dutch farmhouse is very different from an English one. It is merely, as a rule, a wretched hovel, stuck down in the middle of a waste of grass.

The Free State farmhouses are particularly desolate-looking, owing to the Free State being unfit for agriculture, and given over to pasturing cattle, sheep, and horses. The cottage where we stopped, however, was rather a good specimen, and the people a young man and a pretty woman, his wife—were very hospitable, and gave us a good supper, cleanly served, and, to me at least, a clean bed. There was a nice basin and jug, with a clean towel neatly folded over it, in my room; but they never thought of the water!

I cannot describe the country we travelled through, for there is nothing in it to describe; it is simply a wide expanse of grass, with *spruits* running through it at intervals—*spruits* with quantities of stones, but sometimes only a trickle of water in them. The flocks of sheep, and herds of cattle and horses, are striking features of the scene.

Through this scenery, if scenery it could be called, we took our way once more on Saturday morning. Our hosts would accept of no payment, only thanks. They gave us a cup of black coffee before we started, without either sugar or milk—I suppose the cows were not yet milked—and we were off once more.

Chapter 4

After a long drive we got to a small house, into whose one room a large and very dirty family were crowded. Here the woman gave us a bottle of milk, and a little farther on we got some bread—the man who gave it to us asking for payment, but not getting any, because I had only gold and he had no silver. The horses in the meantime were becoming from bad to worse, Jimmy and our charioteer having frequently to get out to push the wheels, the reins being delivered over to me; and many a laugh I had, although frightened, at the frantic rush these two would make after the cart when the horses at last bolted off, I doing my best to hold them in, so as to allow the little Hottentot (who in spite of his broken ribs was an active fellow) to jump in, and then extending a hand backwards to Jimmy, who had to take flying leaps up to the back seat.

The broken ribs of our driver occasioned him, much to his sorrow, to transgress the regulation laid down that, when approaching any dwelling, the driver of a post-cart is to blow a horn. A Hottentot delights in any row on a thing supposed to be a musical instrument, and our *Jehu* so greatly deplored his inability to perform his duty, that I, not at that time appreciating the true cause of his grief, offered to endeavour to extract sounds from the old brass horn. My endeavours were, however, not crowned with success, nor were Jimmy's. We achieved a great puffing out of our cheeks and a peculiar snorting noise, but nothing more. By nightfall we arrived at a house, which impressed me as the most squalid I had ever seen—I do not mean the combination of poverty and dirt to be seen in London, but squalor in the midst of plenty. This is a common sight amongst the Boers, but it was a new one then to me; and it remains stamped on my memory.

We approached this dwelling by a road which was invisible to me; indeed I had long ceased to wonder at our driver having, as he said at starting, forgotten the "road," for often when he seemed undecided as to which he should take, I could discern none whatever over the bare, dried grass. It was a raw evening with a mist coming on, and the long low-roofed cabin stuck down in the middle of the *veldt*, with three stunted trees near it, looked cheerless in the extreme. Our advent was heralded by a barking chorus from a number of gaunt dogs; this brought out seven men and boys. The little Hottentot whispered "You must shake hands with every one;" and I descended and instantly commenced operations. The oldest of the men led us into the house, where we shook hands with a woman and a number of girls, big and little, terminating with a small baby. All the hands were very dirty.

I leaned against the half-door and looked out at the three trees, wishing very much that I could speak to these people, and turning, saw Jimmy sitting disconsolately near me, whilst ranged round the room on benches, sat the family, regarding us gravely. It was absolutely necessary to say or do something, so I made a desperate effort to form some sounds resembling Dutch out of a combination of German and English. One of the little girls was a pretty curly-headed little creature with large serious eyes. I thought I would make her the subject of my remarks. I daresay that the expression of my face was more intelligible than my words, for the woman looked pleased, and the eldest of the men said something to the effect that she was his daughter.

The Hottentot now appeared, and squatted on the step of the half-door, and he was able to act as interpreter. The family consisted of a man and his wife and their children. It seemed wonderful, for there really appeared to be less than ten years difference between the two eldest men: presently more gawky boys came in and shook hands, until the whole family being assembled, I discovered that there were, I think, fourteen children. They were rich in flocks and herds, and yet all but the father, mother, and two eldest sons were barefooted; none had stockings; none appeared to be possessed of a brush and comb, or of soap!

"I wonder if they are going to give us anything to eat," whispered Jimmy. "Ask them."

I did not like to do so, not knowing whether it might be considered a liberty, as I did not know whether payment for food would be accepted; but I wondered too, for I was very hungry, having eaten nothing but a little bread since morning.

Presently the eldest girl brought me a basin, with a small quantity of water in it, and a not over-clean-looking cloth. I had my own soap and towel, and washed; the same basin and water was presented to Jimmy, who washed; it then passed to the father, who threw the water on his face and hands and wiped them with the cloth, and from him it passed in regular order down to the youngest boy, a lad of about eleven! The girls did not wash. A cloth was now laid on the table, and plates with bowls on them placed on it, a big basin full of milk, and a dish full of a sort of hard, crisp bread, peculiar to this country and very nice, was placed near it. Jimmy, the father, and I had knives, forks, and spoons, the rest had spoons only. It was dark now, and a tallow candle illumined the scene.

The father said a long grace in Dutch, and then the mother helped all to milk and biscuits—the hard bread is called Boer biscuit here—whilst the eldest girl brought in a very small piece of boiled mutton. This the father cut into three pieces, giving one to Jimmy, one to me, and reserving one for himself. I enjoyed my supper, and ended my meat before my host had finished his. Seeing this, I saw him eye me thoughtfully for a minute or so with uplifted knife and fork, then he pushed his own plate over to me. I smiled, thanked him in German, and shook my head, whereupon he drew it back again with a look of relief, and ate the meat that remained on it. And this man had hundreds of fat wethers, and full-flanked oxen grazing on his farm!

I think grace was said when all was done, and shortly after various sheep and goat-skins were spread on the floor, and on a bench by the side of the room; and then the mother signed to me to follow her, and led me into a dark little closet, in which was a big very dirty-looking bed, a number of little *delft* bowls on a shelf, and absolutely nothing else. On the bare rafters various articles, including rags of apparel, were hung. Here she left me, without a candle, the only light I received being from the candle in the sitting-room, which showed over the top of the door. There was a window, or rather a small opening in the wall, with a shutter to it; this was open when I went in, and to it I trusted for light and air; but hardly had the woman left me, ere I heard it being barricaded, in some very secure manner judging from the noise, on the outside; then the candle went out in the sitting-room, and I heard sounds of people lying down.

I lay down dressed, and for a long time listened to such a chorus of snoring that I felt convinced the whole family were sleeping in the sitting-room; and, such was indeed the case, as I learnt next morning from Jimmy. He slept with one of the sons on the bench. None of the party undressed. Boers never do when they go to bed, not even in case of illness; indeed, they think it the height of impropriety to do so—so much so that a Boer who travelled in the waggon of an English Africander, an acquaintance of mine, afterwards said to the wife of the latter,—

"I shall never travel in William's waggon again with him; it is so dreadful of him to take his trousers off when he goes to bed."

My bed was the domicile of innumerable insects.

We had coffee and a wash in the basin, and started early. The horses were of the usual description, the scenery of the usual description, and the delivery of letters of the usual description; and this reminds me that I have not described the operation. On arriving at a place where horses had to be changed, the little Hottentot would request me to stand up, and, opening the top of the seat he and I occupied, would take out a lot of rags and pieces of leather, which seemed to be considered as valuables to be kept, and then pull out the letters, parcels, and papers, and make them over to me to decipher their addresses. The addresses were generally badly written, the names Dutch, and the places unknown to me; hence I think it probable that a great many letters went astray. I know my audience, namely, the driver and a Boer or two, more than once said they did not know the name of the individual I read out.

However, the little Hottentot settled the matter somehow, and I suppose there were no more letters left wrongly on this occasion than on any other. It has sometimes occurred to me to wonder how letters get to their destination at all in the Orange Free State, judging from my experience of the post-cart, and from the fact that I heard from several persons at Heilbronn that the usual driver of the post-cart, namely, the *kaffir* with whom my excitable friend in Harrismith had dealt so summarily, lived in a constant state of intoxication, frequently lying for hours on the ground by the side of the post-cart, whilst the wretched horses grazed, glad enough to be rid of their tormentor, who, when he was in his seat, always drove at a gallop, flogging them without intermission.

I forget whether it was on this day, or on the previous one that we came to a small river with very steep banks, and that the small Hottentot informed us that we had better get out of the vehicle, as he felt sure it would be upset. I concurred in this opinion, although getting out meant fording the river on foot; and indeed, if there had been any weight behind them the horses would certainly have upset the concern; as it was, they jibbed and plunged on the sharp descent, and then bolted through the river and up the other side. How the cart held together during the frantic leaps it had to take over the big stones that strewed the bottom of the river, and the road beyond it, I don't know—the more so as one wheel had been shaky from the time we started. Jimmy and I waded through the river, which came up nearly to my knees, and had to climb into the cart as quickly as we could, and off we went again. It was Sunday now, and we ought to have been in Heilbronn on Saturday evening. We were to have two more changes of horses, and were to pass through the small town of Frankfurt before reaching our destination.

Our last change but one brought us a pair of very fine horses, if they had been in good condition; but they were very thin, their chests raw from the pressure of the chest-strap (collars are not used here), and they looked very vicious. It was hard work harnessing them, and then there was a pitched battle before they would start. It was no wonder, for it must have been dreadful pain to throw their raw chests against the band; the blood was running from them before the poor brutes chose that pain instead of the pain of the flogging they were getting from three men besides the driver. It really was dangerous work driving these horses, for they were very strong, hard-mouthed, and added kicking to the accomplishments of the animals we had before had; in fact, not far from our starting-point one of them sent his hoof through the splash-board in unpleasant proximity to my knee.

It was early in the afternoon when we reached Frankfurt. I was told there was a village there; but all I saw was a small white house, the post-office; another small white house of a shape that suggested to me that it was a church, and which I learnt was one; and I think three little cottages with gardens, in a row at a little distance. There were some children and girls in their best dresses lounging near the post-office, one of whom I particularly remember, owing to the strange incongruity of her attire with both her appearance and her surroundings. She was a podgy young lady of about sixteen, and was arrayed in a white skirt, over which a pink polonaise of some miserable sort of stuff was put on, and a hat with bad imitation flowers in it.

The postmaster, or someone who I supposed was he, came out and received letters; told me also in answer to my inquiries that Heilbronn was not very far, but that we had a very ugly *spruit* to cross. I asked if we could not have other horses; but he said that was impossible—and we started again. We got the horses off well, and were bowling down a grassy decline towards the three cottages before named, when the little Hottentot discovered a letter by his side which he had not left. He pulled up the horses, and the postmaster and another man—a little short man, with black hair and whiskers, a black coat, and a white collar—came running up. Now the question was to start the horses again. They evidently thought that having started once they had done their duty; they had no idea of doing it for a second time, and proceeded to display all their accomplishments.

In the meantime the little black man, who had a very good-natured broad face, favoured us with descriptions of the *spruit* in front of us.

"The cart is generally upset there," he said cheerfully.

"Very often, at least," said the postmaster; "it was upset last time."

"I really think you are bound to find me other horses," I said then. "The persons who have the management of this post-cart are certainly responsible for any damage a passenger may receive, when such horses as you see these to be are kept in it. There must be some other horses here, and you are in duty bound to take these out."

The two men looked somewhat convinced.

"I would ask Mr. —— to lend his horses," said the postmaster, "but they are in the *veldt*, and would have to be sent for, and there would be great delay; you are a day behind time already."

I very nearly laughed.

"Well," I said, "not so much delay as if we are upset and the cart broken in the *spruit*; and you must see that is what will probably take place with these horses."

My listeners seemed suddenly convinced; the effect of my words was magical! It was instantly agreed that the horses should be sent for to the *veldt*, and my cheerful-looking little friend in black requested me to descend and accept of his hospitality. He offered his arm, and asked abruptly whether I was a member of the Established Church? My reply in the negative completely stunned him, or completely satisfied him; he made no further remark, but led me to one of the three white cottages. This reminded me of an English farmhouse, and was a very pleasant relief. Some neighbours, who all talked English, dropped in, and we had tea and bread and butter.

Poor Jimmy had not been asked in, and I felt very sorry for him whilst eating my bread and butter, for I knew he must be very hungry. It was getting somewhat late in the afternoon when we started once more, the owner of the horses which had replaced the vicious pair using his own harness and driving himself, whilst the Hottentot drove his steeds walking behind them. The *spruit* was a very ugly one, but we got over it all right, thanks to this kind Frankfurtian, whose name I forget. He left us at the house where we got our last change. The horses were good, and we got into Heilbronn by dark without farther adventure.

CHAPTER 5

Whatever it may be now I do not know, but then Heilbronn consisted of a square of fifteen small houses, and a few outstanding ones,
stuck on a slope in the middle of a perfectly bare country. If you
walked to the upper side of the village, you could look along a grassy
expanse to where it touched the horizon, whichever way you turned
your head. The hotel was a long low cottage. The entrance door led
you straight into the sitting-room, from whence a step led you into
the dining-room at the back. Two doors at each side of the sitting-
room, each led you into a small bedroom. That is the plan of pretty
nearly all Boer houses that have any pretensions—the architects of
the nation can conceive nothing grander. The size may vary, but the
plan remains. There were other tiny bedrooms built at the back, to get
to which one had to go from the dining-room into the yard. Two of
these were appropriated to Jimmy's and my use.

The people of the inn—a man and wife with a large family—were
good sort of people, I think, and wished to make us as comfortable as
they could. They had two other boarders, unmarried men who had
some employment in the village, and a good many men came there
to dine. It was a strange gathering at meals, and the conversation was
amusing. Very odd, too, it appeared to me, to hear shopkeepers in this
funny little town looked upon as magnates in the land. Of course everybody knew everybody, and was free and easy with everybody, and of
course Heilbronn delighted in gossip; what small place does not?

We arrived two days before Christmas Day, and on Christmas-
eve mine hosts gave a dance in the public sitting-room. Amongst the
guests were the judge of the place, and the magistrate, or *landroost*, a
shopkeeper or two, some of their assistants, and a dressmaker. During
the pauses of dancing a musical box played—the dance music itself
was performed on a fiddle—and there were some songs. But oh, the

dancing! Whilst it was going on, I sat a spectator in the dining-room. They all danced with great gravity and ponderosity, if I may use such a word; but some clung to each other as they hopped heavily round and round to a waltz tune; others charged round savagely with out-stretched arms, to the imminent danger of their neighbours; others held their arms stretched down so tightly that they looked as if they were mutually desirous of dislocating each other's shoulders; whilst one couple, a chubby little man and woman, regardless of the time of either the music or the dancing of the others, with a stolid smile

On each fat little face, turned slowly round and round as on a pivot. I cannot say how they managed it; their progression was very slow, and they seemed quite regardless of the collisions they came in for. I saw them get a thump from one of the chargers which would have knocked a less steady couple down, but only caused them to tot-ter; but the comicality of their appearance at last tickled me so much that I felt I must laugh if I stayed, and so I took myself off to bed.

The entire town of Heilbronn was going out on a picnic (a com-bined picnic) on Christmas Day. Great had been the preparations, and hence great was the woe when Christmas Day broke with a drizzling rain. The great question, to go or not to go? was discussed until ten o'clock, when there being a slight diminution of the drizzle, it was unanimously decided that it was going to clear up, and the whole white population of Heilbronn went off in waggons and carts. Of course there had been great discussion as to who was to go in who's waggon, and who's cart was to take up whom; and the arrangements had been slightly complicated at the last moment by two young gen-tlemen having brought their cart and horses up to the door of the hotel, and there upset it and broken it—leading one to the conclusion that the festivities of the previous night had been too much for them. However, everything was at last arranged, and Heilbronn was deserted for the nonce by its inhabitants. The landlady informed me that she had killed two fowls, picked a dish of peas, and made a plum-pudding, for the benefit of Jimmy and myself, and had given her Hottentot girl strict injunctions to make us comfortable. This was her parting bless-ing, and we were left alone.

There was nothing very amusing to be done. There was the musi-cal box, and it seemed to afford some entertainment to Jimmy, for he kept it playing nearly all day, driving me almost to insanity thereby; and there were some children's stories of good and bad children, and a mutilated copy of *Ivanhoe*. The rain came down heavily after the picnic party had started, and appeared likely to continue coming down. Presently we had dinner, minus the peas, which I suppose the Hottentot girl kept for herself.

In the afternoon, rather late, the weather cleared, and Jimmy and I walked a little outside the village, and I gave him his first lesson in pistol-shooting. As we were returning I was accosted by a man, who asked me if I were not the lady that was going up country with a party of gentlemen who were expected in Heilbronn daily. I answered in the affirmative; and he then told me that he was the proprietor of one of the spans of oxen our conductor had. (I think he was in some sort a partner of his.) He said he heard that many of them were dead of redwater, and that our conductor flogged them cruelly, and had beaten a *kaffir* who was with him severely. I said it was all true. It was this man who told me the real reason of our conductor bringing us to Heilbronn. He asked us to go to his cottage, which stood a little apart from the village; and we went, and found his wife (a pretty young woman) and his baby there. The man was an Englishman with a pleasant English face. He was, as he looked and spoke, of the small farmer class. His wife was colonial born. They were very kind and hospitable, and gave us a very nice tea.

On our return to the hotel we found the party had returned in very bad humour. I should not think picnicking under a tarpaulin stretched between two waggons in a thick drizzling rain on a dead flat likely to conduce to good temper; and then there were all the little jealousies and envyings sure to arise on such occasions—Mr. So-and-so had done this and said that, and so on. The picnic had set the whole little town by the ears!

A day or two after, our party arrived bringing my pony with them. I had heard that the horse-sickness was likely to be bad as soon as we crossed the Vaal, so I sold him at Heilbronn to my pleasant-looking English acquaintance, and resolved to travel thenceforth in the waggon. A good many things belonging to the conductor were taken out of it at Heilbronn, and it was made much more comfortable in consequence.

The evening that we were to start, I went to take tea with the purchaser of my pony, and I have a vivid recollection of the excellent pancakes I was eating, when one of our party tapped at the door and said the waggon was waiting for me. Certainly a kind welcome given to a stranger travelling alone in a wild country, is one of the things the angel who records good actions ought always to make a note of.

I missed my pony very much. To jolt hour after hour in an ox-waggon along a dead flat under a broiling sun is objectionable: and being now always with the waggon, the spectacle of the brutality of our conductor to his oxen, and the fearful language used by him, were very hard to bear.

We crossed the Vaal on New Year's eve, and I shall never forget his wanton cruelty on the occasion. The river separated us, or, powerless as I was, I should have felt called upon to interfere, as no one else seemed disposed to do so.

We were now in the Transvaal, and a day more took us to Heidelberg. We arrived there rather late at night, and I proceeded with Jimmy to the hotel. The waggon was outspanned a little outside the small town, but I was told that I could easily find the hotel by the moonlight, and that it would be open. I followed the instructions given me for finding it, but when I arrived at the house I took to be the hotel, it seemed shut up for the night. It was a nice-looking cottage, standing in a pretty garden. Seeing no light in front, I walked to the back, where I saw a glimmer from a candle through the window shutters. This encouraged me, and I knocked at the door with my whip. After a pause, a very frightened female voice cried, "Who is it?" from within.

"A traveller," cried I; "is not this the hotel?"

Whereupon the door opened, and I saw a very pretty frightened face, with loose hair hanging about it, and a little figure robed in white. "Oh, how you frightened me!" it said; "my husband is not at home. No, this is not the hotel." Of course I expressed the deepest contrition, and the frightened little lady told me where to go to.

Little Heidelberg, sleeping in the moonlight, with the hills around showing brown against the clear sky, looked refreshing after the dreary Free State. We got to the hotel presently. It was shut up, but I was emboldened to knock by two considerations; the first, that I could not go back to the waggon, because the men I knew would already be asleep in it; the second, that I had met the proprietor of the hotel at the Willow River, and he had told me to be sure to come to his house. I knocked, and knocked, until Jimmy said, "How can you go on knocking like that? Well, I never thought you could do such a thing."

At last a man's voice from within asked, "What do you want? Who are you?"

"A traveller," I cried in return. "Can't I have a bed?"

The door was unbolted, and I saw my roadside acquaintance, who had evidently just got out of bed. "I can't give you a bed," he said; "we're full."

"Oh, Mr. Dubois," said I, "don't you remember telling me that I must come here? Do, please, let me in. I can't go back to the waggon, the men will all be asleep in it." Mr. Dubois was mollified. He let me into the room, where I saw a rough-looking man sitting up between the blankets on a sofa-bedstead.

"Here," said Mr. Dubois, "you must put your boots on, and you can sleep in there," pointing to a back-room, "and let the lady have your place." So the rough-looking man tumbled out; and Jimmy said goodnight, and had to go back to the waggon; Mr. Dubois brought me a piece of candle, and I tumbled into bed, and went very fast asleep in a minute.

Nothing particular occurred during our trek from Heidelberg to Pretoria, until we were quite close to the latter place. I think it was at our last outspan that a man, who, in spite of a rakish look, was more like a gentleman than anyone I had seen during my travels, rode up to the waggon, and dismounting, entered into conversation. His manners and address confirmed what his appearance had suggested to me. Long after, I heard something of this individual's story, which still farther confirmed my first impression; the end of it is worth telling, as illustrative of habits and customs out here. It is an odd thing that Boers, although adverse to the English, are very proud if they can induce Englishmen to marry into their families. Our roadside acquaintance, who had earned for himself the sobriquet of "mad" amongst his intimates, was sane enough to make use of this little peculiarity. Being very completely on his beam-ends for about the hundredth time, he wooed and won a young Boeress, whose father was prepared to give a handsome portion. Having used all his fascinations so as completely to infatuate his wife and make her think herself the happiest of women, he suddenly decamped, and had got to the Vaal River, on his way into the Free State, when his father-in-law overtook him. The old gentleman was in an agony of rage and anxiety for his daughter, who of course was doing what old women call "taking on" pretty considerably; the husband was quite cool. He told the story of himself.

"What's your figure?" he asked of his infuriated relative. "Make it high enough, and I'll go back, otherwise I'm off!"

"Will five hundred sheep do?" gasped the old gentleman. The younger shook his head.

"No," he said, "not enough; just consider how dreadfully I shall be bored. Make it a thousand, and I'll say done." And the old fellow made it a thousand.

This individual told us that he was out in command of volunteers, as it was thought that the Boers might break out next day, when they said they meant to come armed into Pretoria. Of course they did not come into Pretoria. Personally I, writing this in the besieged camp of Pretoria, don't believe they ever will do so; but it made one feel a pleasant sort of excitement to think that they might, and that we should be just in time to see them do it.

We came into Pretoria through a *poort*, or opening between the hills, called, I think, Bobian Poort, literally Baboon Entrance. There are no baboons on the hills now, but I suppose there were not long ago. Little Pretoria, with its blue gums and willow-trees, and its surrounding hills, looked very pretty in the light of the fast-setting sun. It was nearly dark by the time we had outspanned on a common at the upper end of the town. I asked the manager if he had inquired which hotel was the best for a lady to lodge at. He said he had; that the "European" was the one recommended; and I started off with Jimmy. I had to ask my way from a gentleman I saw sitting under his verandah on the outskirts of the town, and then to walk down a longish road, with rose hedges at each side, and with a sound of running water to be heard, which, although it was too dark to see them, told me that there must be rivulets at both sides too.

The cottages, standing back in their gardens, with lights in the windows, looked pleasant and home-like, and I was almost sorry when the pretty road ended in the market-square, with an ugly white church in the middle of it. There were lights in two buildings forming one of the corners of this square—low long cottages, and I rightly guessed them both to be hotels. Neither of these appeared to be suited for a lady's lodging—the bar being the leading feature in both, and a number of loud-talking men, in broad hats, short coats, and riding-boots, lounging in front of them. I asked a passer-by which was the "European," and he showed me the one which had a verandah, and appeared the fuller of the two. I could see that it had a public dining-room, which seemed crammed, but the only entrance was through the bar; so, taking heart of grace, into the bar I walked. It was as full as it could be of men of the kind who frequent bars; but, luckily for me, behind the bar itself stood a man who was a gentleman—the then proprietor of the "European," since dead (he was killed by lightning, together with the horses he was driving). I asked this gentleman whether I could obtain a lodging at his hotel, telling him at the same time how I had just arrived, a stranger, in Pretoria, and had been told that the "European" was the best hotel for a lady to go to.

"Well," he said courteously, "you have been misinformed; it is completely a man's hotel. In fact it is not an hotel, but simply a restaurant." I bowed, and asked if he could tell me where to go, as I could not return to the waggon. "If you step into my private room," he said, "I will send you some supper, and I will send round to the "Edinburgh" and "Royal" to know if they have a room to spare." I was only too glad of the offer. Jimmy went back to the waggons, and I had a nice little supper whilst I waited. But alas! there was not a room at either hotel; all were full. Mr. Carter (in this instance I give the real name of the individual) then said that all he could propose was this: there was a small room at a little distance from the hotel, whose usual occupant was absent. Mr. Carter had the key, and I could use it for that night. I forthwith started, with a *coolie* servant for a guide, and was taken to a small room in a stable-yard behind a public-house. There was a stable at one side, and I could hear men's voices in the room at the other side. It was a comfortable little room, and I observed a woman's dress hanging on a peg.

Here my guide left me after he had lighted a candle. I proceeded to investigate the fastenings of the door and window. The former I could lock, but there was no way of fastening the other. It was not very pleasant, for the little I had seen of Pretoria that night had made me acquainted with the fact, which farther acquaintance only confirmed, that it is a very rowdy little village, and that a woman might better walk about late in London or Paris than in that place. I began to wish I had brought my pistol with me; however, there was no use wishing, and so I put a chair on the table that stood under the little window, so as to be sure of hearing if any one attempted to get in, and then turned into bed, and found it very comfortable.

The next morning I had nothing to do but to go to breakfast at the "European." The eating-room was full of men, but Mr. Carter took me into it himself, and seated me at a little table; this he did at each meal as long as I stayed there, for which I am still grateful to him. That whole day I passed looking for a lodging, but could find none, and had to sleep once more in my little room. The next day was the same. In the morning a gentleman spoke to me as I was standing under the verandah of the "European."

"You are looking for a lodging, I believe?" he said. I replied in the affirmative. "So am I," quoth he; "let us go together;" so off we started. Life is very free and easy out here, as will be observed, not only on this occasion but on various others throughout my story. The gentleman told me how he came to be in Pretoria—he was travelling to see the country; and I told him something of how I came to be in Pretoria. We walked about and called at various houses, but fruitlessly; at last, as we were walking along a grassy rose-hedged lane, which in Pretoria is called a street, we saw two fashionably dressed ladies standing under the verandah of a cottage with a strip of garden in front.

"Let us ask them if they let lodgings," said my companion.

"I don't think it would do," responded I; but he evidently thought it would, for he went up and asked, and I thought I might as well go up too, under the circumstances. The ladies were very kind; they did not let lodgings, but they asked us in; my acquaintance soon left us to go in quest of some abode, but I was tired both of walking and of looking for a room, and I stayed and chatted, and had a cup of coffee.

In the afternoon, whilst standing under the "European" verandah, I was accosted by the volunteer officer we had met on the road, and shortly afterwards by the gentleman who had on the night of my arrival told me the way to the hotel. In conversation with them I mentioned my difficulties about finding a room, and also the fact that I had two letters of introduction to ladies in Pretoria, but that I was loath to present them so long as presenting them was tantamount to asking them to put me up. I mentioned the names of the ladies, and one of the gentlemen said he knew them; and with that he walked off, and presently reappeared bringing with him a gentleman, whom he introduced to me as Mr. Farquarson, the husband of one of the ladies, and the son-in-law of the other. Mr. Farquarson took me to see Mrs. Parker, whose house was not far from the hotel; but on the way he heard from someone that she was not at home, and hence I simply gave him my letters of introduction and returned to the hotel; but not immediately, for I took a solitary walk first on the outskirts of the village, and thereby missed seeing the two ladies, who called at the "European" whilst I was out.

Early the next morning I heard a knocking at the door, and the *coolie's* voice outside, saying I must get up at once and clear out, that the Newcastle post-cart had just come in, and brought the rightful owner of the room I was in. As may be supposed, I turned out pretty quickly. But my difficulties were to cease that day, for Mr. Farquarson came in the morning and carried me off to his cottage at the upper end of the town. Oh, how nice it did seem, with its carpets, and sofas, and nice little knickknacks, and, best of all, its pretty mistress, after travelling so long with rough men!

I went afterwards to Mrs. Parker's cottage, smaller but prettier; a very gem of a little cottage, with a small brilliant garden in front, and a well-filled kitchen-garden and orchard behind, and a verandah all overhung with beautiful creepers, and with ferns in pots, and easy-chairs, under it, with graceful young trees standing all round it; and with a pretty setter who gave her paw, and a little springbok, and a cross little prairie-dog, or *meerkat* as it is called here, as its inhabitants, without counting the mistress of all these nice things; mistress also of two of the smallest maid-servants I ever saw—two little Hottentot, or rather Bushman, sisters. They were mere children, but they looked like two pretty little baby monkeys, tripping about noiselessly with their little bare feet, and dressed in their clean little print frocks. The old lady was a relation of old friends of mine in England, and her house and that of her adopted daughter, Mrs. Farquarson, seemed veritable harbours of refuge to me.

CHAPTER 6

We remained a week in Pretoria, during which time all our things had to be removed from the waggons that had brought us from D'Urban, and packed on two others which were to convey us to Rustemberg. This was the destination of our party, and it had been arranged that I was to be lodged and boarded at the farmhouse of the farm they were to work on, and there to remain for a year, during which time I was to receive instruction in the superintendence of South African farming, while I intended to employ my spare time in learning Dutch—or what is called Dutch here, for the Dutch talked by the Boers is such a mere *patois*, with *kaffir*, Hottentot, and even English words, mixed up in it, that a real Dutchman, or what they call here a Hollander, neither understands it nor is understood by the Boers.

When I saw the waggons which were to convey us to Rustemberg my heart sank within me. One was a buck-waggon, the other a long tent-waggon. The buck-waggon was provided with a buck-sail or tarpaulin, the tent of the other was supposed to keep out the rain without any tarpaulin; but as one could see daylight through it, it was not likely to be of much avail. It was so packed that it was impossible for anyone to sit up in it, and only a space of about a foot and a half left at the back to allow of dressing, whilst the flap at the back was so ragged that it was easy to see through it, and impossible to fasten it tightly down. Then my tent, which I had lent to the party at their request during my stay in Pretoria, was lost by them during the loading-up process.

We started about the middle of the day; our oxen were a mixed lot—a very bad thing, for if oxen are to pull well, one must span them in their accustomed places and on their accustomed sides. Many oxen will never make either good fore or hind oxen. Our drivers were a half-cast of the name of William, and a *kaffir*. William drove the tent-waggon. We were hardly out of Pretoria when, at a very small brook, we broke the "*disselboom*," or pole, of one of the waggons, I forget which. This caused a long delay, for William had to go back to Pretoria to get a new one. In the meantime we remained outspanned, in a valley about two miles broad and about sixty long. It runs between the Magaliesberg and the Witt-waters Randt; and if any one wants to know the positions of these big hills, or ranges of hills, let them look at the map. The next day William brought the *disselboom* in a donkey-cart, and we started rather late in the afternoon.

There are three high roads by which one can go from Pretoria to Rustemberg in a waggon. One goes over Mosilikats-nek, commonly called Silikats-nek, one over Commando-nek, and another over Oliphants-nek. We were to go over Silikats-nek, and hence took the turn which leads to it. The tent-waggon was leading, and was well ahead of the other; and the *kaffir* driver of the other went along the main road without troubling himself to look where the leading waggon was. Some of the men were with one, the rest with the other waggon. The blankets of the party were on one, the food all on the other. It was nearly dark by the time we outspanned, and this division of property made the evening and night agreeable for both divisions of our party.

The buck-waggon joined us the next morning, and we got as far as the foot of Silikats-nek by mid-day. The scenery here is fine. The waggon was outspanned under some trees in the middle of thick bush; above us rose the rugged sides of the Magaliesberg, now beginning to show what becomes its characteristic farther down the valley, namely, a precipice of some hundred feet high crowning its wooded sides. This formation is here called, not inappropriately, a *kranz*, or crown. Creepers hung in festoons round the bushes, turning them into bowers or impenetrable barriers, as the case might be.

I rambled about in this refreshing maze of verdure until dinner was ready, and then I determined to walk on over the *nek* in front of the waggon, and so not only enjoy the scenery undisturbed, but avoid the flogging of the oxen and accompanying yelling, which was sure to ensue as soon as the oxen took the hill. I inquired particularly of William as to what road I was to take, and he instructed me to keep to the left. William spoke a little English. Arrived at the top of the *nek*, where the road is, as it were, cut out from between two masses of rock, I looked down on a park-like scene, the well-made road, of a reddish colour, winding through clusters of trees, some of a good size, others small, and most of them festooned by graceful creepers. Leaving an apparently old road to my right, I kept along this pretty road until I saw another one turn off to the right. Here I hesitated, but my instruction having been to keep to the left, I did so.

Presently a sudden thunder-storm caused me to take shelter under a thick bower of trees and creepers. This was, however, not thick enough to prevent my being wet through by the rain, which came down so quick and strong that it soon turned the road into a river. The storm passed, but no waggon was to be seen or heard, and I, although soaking wet, still wandered on, keeping in the grass by the side of the road. I was tempted on by the quiet beauty of the scene, and by a love of solitude, which had been denied to me for some time. Presently a small tax-cart, drawn by two weedy-looking ponies, came along the road towards me. In it were two men, one an oldish man with a big beard, the other a sleek but dirty-looking little fellow in black clothes, with a sanctimonious look about him.

The former said "Good-evening!" as he passed, which made me stop and ask him if I were on the Rustemberg road. He asked where my waggon was; and I told him I had left it at Silikats-nek. "Then," he said, "I think you probably have passed the turn you should have taken, to the right. You can go to Rustemberg by this road, but it is a little out of your way. There is a farmhouse not far off, but I can hardly recommend you to go to it, for the people are not very nice." I thanked him, and he drove on. I now considered that as it was near sunset, if the waggons had taken the other road I could easily pick them up, as they would be outspanned for the night, and that I should be able to know whether they had done so by the fresh marks of wheels and oxen's feet, and hence I determined to walk a little farther, until the farmhouse should come in sight. Commando-neck, with its high *kranz* towering above its brother hills, and showing sharp against a dark bank of cloud with edges gilt by the setting-sun, and the queer piping of some pretty birds with crests that darted in and out amongst the trees, and whose nearer acquaintance I was anxious to make, were too much for me. Presently the small white farmhouse, built in a clearing, came in sight, and I stopped. The thunder was beginning to growl once more, and bright flashes of lightning to light up the dark mass of cloud behind the precipice of the *nek*, whilst the nearer hills and the trees were burnished by the setting sun.

I stood and looked, then turned, but only to stop and look again, although in front of me when I turned the sky looked unpleasantly lowering. Presently, however, a tremendous crash of thunder, accompanied by some very large drops, warned me to be moving. But I had waited too long; before many minutes the sky was as dark as night, the rain began to fall, though not very heavily, and when I reached the road I thought the waggon might have taken, I could only see it by the flashes of lightning. It was evident no waggon had passed there. It was now pitch dark, and I had some difficulty in finding the old road which I had remarked on my way out.

By the flashes of lightning I again discovered that no waggon had been there. I now concluded that the waggon had had some mishap on the *nek*, and soon I heard voices, and came up to the party and to the tent-waggon, outspanned on the very top of the ascent. The buck-waggon with all the eatables in it had stuck half way up. The rain was coming down pretty sharp now. There was nothing to eat or to drink but some rum, of which the men were partaking, and I, being still wet through, thought it best to follow their example before rolling myself up in my damp blankets, for the tent leaked, as I expected.

When I woke the next morning I found it still drizzling, but with a look in the sky as if the day would be fine. If our former conductor insisted on starting early, and ruled our party, William let them do as they liked, the result being that they did not get out of their blankets until long after the sun was up. The waggon on the hill was presently brought up, and we started late. We made but one short trek, which brought us to the Crocodile River, where we did a very foolish thing, namely, outspanned before crossing. It is better even with tired oxen to make them take their waggon through a river at the end of a trek, than try to make them do it just after they are inspanned and before they are warm. It was a very pretty place, with tangled brushwood and tallish trees scattered over the grass and forming a bower over the river in parts. The next morning broke beautifully, and I enjoyed the pretty view, and had early coffee from William's kettle long before the rest of the party thought of stirring, so that it was late in the morning before we spanned in.

The ford, or *drift*, as it is here called, is a nasty one at this place. However, the tent-waggon, in which I was, went through all right. The buck-waggon stuck. There was much flogging and swearing, the end of which was that the *disselboom* broke, and the waggon remained in the middle of the stream. The oxen were then attached to it behind, it was pulled back to where it had started from, and the oxen turned loose whilst the *disselboom* was being mended. This took some time, and when it was at last accomplished it was discovered that the oxen were lost amongst the thick bush. They were not forthcoming till late in the afternoon, when they took the waggon once more into the middle of the stream, where William and the *kaffir* driver between them managed them so well that the *disselboom* was broken for the third time. It was near sunset, and a heavy storm was coming up. William, who said that getting into the water made him ill, and who hence contented himself by dancing about on the bank and shouting, determined to leave the waggon in the middle of the stream for the night, which, considering that in this country, as in many others, an hour suffices to turn a small stream into a roaring torrent, was a very prudent thing to do. No one objected to it, however, as far as I know, and so the waggon remained.

That evening, before going to sleep, I made sundry arrangements in anticipation of the storm that was evidently coming up. I put on my mackintosh, spread my waterproof sheet over me, placed a few articles, which I prized, under me, put a candle in my lantern, a box of matches in my pocket, rolled my blankets nicely round me, and then awaited what was to come.

I was wakened by a rattling crash of thunder, followed by a series of explosions which seemed as if they must rend something in pieces; the lightning was terrific, the wind howled round and battered the wag-gon as if it would overturn it, the rain poured down in torrents, and I could hear the rush of the rising river. I lit my lamp, with difficulty protecting my match under my mackintosh. The sight was absurd! The rain was coming into the waggon like a shower-bath, and after forming lakes and pools all round me, was finding its way through the different articles down to and out of the bottom. Many of the men were sleeping under the waggon, and they presently began to become aware of this; then it was amusing to hear their surprise and disgust. The people in the tent, too, began to rouse up; altogether it was a lively night.

The spectacle presented by our party the next morning was most comical, garments of all sorts being hung about on the bushes in a vain effort to dry them (for the day began and remained very showery), whilst their owners wandered about disconsolately. A new *disselboom* had to be got from a farmhouse at some distance, and it was rather late before the waggon was at last pulled out. The river had risen so much in the night that the water was nearly into it, and the buck-sail having been badly fastened down had blown off, and everything was drenched.

We made a short trek that evening, and outspanned just as the sun was setting. Shortly after, the grey-bearded man whom I had met in the cart near to Commando, rode up and asked us if he could do anything to help us, as his farm was close by. I asked him if he could get me a horse, or any other conveyance, to take me into Rustemberg. I felt sure that we should have some more mishaps before arriving there, and having been now three days without having been able to change my wet clothes, and obliged to sleep in damp blankets, I was getting tired of it. He said that he could not get me a horse, either to hire, or to buy, or to borrow; that the horse he rode was a borrowed one; and that it was very difficult to get horses, owing to the fact of the "horse disease" being so very bad behind the Magaliesberg—so bad that very few horses ever "salted," *i. e.* recovered from the disease. He said, however, that he would do his best to get a trap to drive me over to Rustemberg, and that he would let me know in the morning.

True to his word, my new acquaintance sent a *kaffir* boy early the following morning to show me the way to his farm, where I was to have breakfast, and to find a cart and horses to take me to Rustemberg. I had managed, by taking a little walk, to find a bower of trees suitable for a dressing-room; there I carried some water in a *gutta percha* pail from a neighbouring brook, and was able to make a little toilette; then putting a few things into my valise, I started with the *kaffir*. About a quarter of an hour's walk along a bridle-path took me to a little three-roomed and thatched cottage, built on a grassy slope at the foot of a spur of the Magaliesberg, with luxuriant orchards of orange, lemon, fig, peach, apricot, and quince trees in front of it, whilst a few healthy-looking coffee bushes testified to the mildness of the climate.

Inside, the house was dark and comfortless. Its mistress, a kind-faced woman of about forty—bedridden with a painful and chronic disease—welcomed me kindly, and we attempted a conversation. She understood a little German, and my knowledge of German enabled me partly to understand her Dutch, so we scraped along. Her husband told me that he had had great difficulty in getting a trap for me. The one I was to have, belonged to the sanctimonious-looking little man I had seen driving my acquaintance. He was a Dopper, *i. e.* belonged to a very sanctified sect of the Dutch Church. The sleek little man had shuddered with holy horror at the idea of his committing the impropriety of driving alone with any woman not related to him, neither would his conscience allow him to hire out his vehicle so as to facilitate any such improper action on the part of his neighbour; at last, however, his scruples had been overcome to the extent of consenting to drive me to Rustemberg, provided his neighbour (my new acquaintance) acted *chaperon* to him.

We three, therefore, set forth in the dewy morning through a park-like country. The little Dopper sat in front, and said never a word. Mr. Deckbird, on the contrary, was very talkative. So was I at first, the relief from the dreadful waggon being so great that I really felt in high spirits; but gradually it began to dawn on me that my companion was mad, and I confess that I was very glad that the little Dopper was in the front seat during that day's drive. As I say, I believe that man was mad, but he was very kind for all that; and although I was certainly afraid of him, I shall always remember his kindness with gratitude. We outspanned three times, once near a farmhouse, from whence Mr. Deckbird brought me a basketful of beautiful fruit; once at another farmhouse, where the women came out and insisted on my getting down, and where Mr. Deckbird introduced me in Dutch as his second wife, which, considering that I could not say anything to the contrary, owing to not knowing Dutch, although I understood what was said, and had to confine myself to shaking my head vigorously, was not pleasant. The good people all laughed at the joke, and gave me some very good coffee, and milk, and bread, and sat and looked at me. I, in return, looked at them, and once more observed to myself that many of these Boers, if dressed up in antique fashion, would look like the models from which Rembrandt and others of the old masters painted.

Our third outspan was in sight of pretty, diminutive Rustemberg, and was in the open *veldt*, near, I think, a quarry. The cause of this outspan was original.

"We must outspan here," said Mr. Deckbird. "I must change my trousers before I go into Rustemberg; I know some people there." And retiring to the quarry in mufti, he reappeared in magnificence.

Before we reached the little village I was introduced to a habit common to the Transvaal, and which is not a pleasing feature in the life here.

"You will be sure to meet Mr. Lestrange," said my companion. "A charming man; you will be delighted with him. But you must take care; don't trust him."

This was the first time I heard this; I have heard it now *ad nauseam*. Mr. A. tells you to beware of Mr. B., he is very nice and all that, but to be on your guard; Mr. B. says he sees you know Mr. A., that it is all very well to be friends with him (friends!), but that you must not trust him too much; both Mr. A. and Mr. B. caution you in a friendly spirit against Mr. C., and Mr. C. in the same manner cautions you against them; and this sometimes even when the people who speak thus appear to be on the most intimate terms.

Chapter 7

The village of Rustemberg, from which one can see the last place inhabited by white people, and through whose streets numbers of *kaffirs* and *kaffir* women troop daily, dressed in skins, and adorned with barbaric ornaments, appeared to me to be a sort of *Ultima Thule*. It had some little shops as stores, and a little prison, and a little post-office, and three little churches—for even here the population is large enough for sects to exist; and it had also numerous rose-hedges bounding its grassy streets, and a missionary station, and a mill. Everything looked as if it were just winking between two sleeps. There was no fort then to suggest that poor little Rustemberg was destined in two years from that time to sustain a lengthened siege, the result of which is, as I write, uncertain. Amongst other things that Rustemberg possessed was a little inn, kept by a big, jolly Dutch woman, a Mrs. Brown, by virtue of her marriage with an Englishman.

In this worthy couple's house I spent a month, and if I never see Mrs. Brown again, yet shall I always remember her as the cheeriest, heartiest, most kind-hearted, and sturdiest of housewives. Her heart was open to everybody, whether the body walked on two or four legs. Did she see a half-starved *kaffir* dog look in at her kitchen door or crawl trembling towards the dresser, it was not "*Furtseck*," or "Get out," that she would cry, but "What a shame to starve that poor thing so!" and a piece of bread or meat was sure to be offered. Did she see an ox being ill-treated, she would rush out and interfere. The horses in her stable, whether her own or her lodgers', were well cared for; her oxen sleek, and dire was her anger if she saw marks of heavy stripes on their glossy backs. Her cows all knew her well; and a bevy of dogs, amongst which was one little spaniel she had rescued from a cruel master, sat round her every morning and at every meal, for her to give to each its portion.

Then, as to her own species, she had brought up and portioned one orphan girl, had opened her doors to another, whose mother was dead and whose stepmother was unkind to her, and was talking about the necessity of taking a third because she was so unkindly treated. Her husband was a carpenter; he left her the principal management of the hotel, but was fond of, and kind to, all her various *protégés*; whilst his special favourite was a large tom cat, who always sat by his side at table, and whom Mrs. Brown averred he spoiled by feeding it whilst he was eating himself.

My little room was in a row of small chambers, built outside the hotel but quite close to it, for the accommodation of travellers. The hotel itself was simply a big Boer cottage. It was kept scrupulously clean, and I felt as if in a farmer's family—which in fact I was; it was an hotel in name, but really a farmhouse. There was a gentleman, the doctor of the place, who came there for his meals, and who, strange to say, had known some friends of mine in England intimately during his boyish days; but there was seldom any stranger to break the monotony of the hotel routine. We had early coffee in our bedrooms, breakfast at eight, dinner at one, supper at six, and then a chat in the big sitting-room till we went to our bedrooms.

Often visitors for Mrs. Brown would drop in of an evening, and then I heard Dutch talked. Mrs. Brown could not speak English at all perfectly, and was delighted to hear that I wanted to learn Dutch; she was, however, a dangerous preceptress, for she would teach me all sorts of phrases, assuring me that their signification was so and so, and then, upon my repeating them innocently, her ringing laugh and the wink she would give, showed me that she had been putting me up to say something very different from what I thought. Of course I soon made friends with her four-footed pets; and the little dog "Gip," which she had taken in compassion, got so fond of me that she made it a present to me. I remember one day we passed the afternoon in washing all the dogs in a big tub, and putting them to bed afterwards, rolled up in counterpanes like babies.

But with all Mrs. Brown's kindness and merriment the time at Rustemberg was very trying. On arriving there I soon found that what I had suspected for a long time was only too true. The scheme about the farm was a snare and a delusion; both the men who came out to work on it, and I, who had counted upon getting instruction there, had been utterly deceived. The party arrived some days after I did, and it was a week or so before the whole affair was quite shown up; but when it was so, two or three of the men, and Jimmy, went on to the farm, such as it was, the rest went as volunteers, and I had to shift for myself.

It was evident that I could do nothing in the farming line until I could understand and speak the Boer tongue; evident also that unless I were to earn money somehow, my small stock would rapidly dwindle to next to nothing, for living at an hotel, or boarding, in the Transvaal, is frightfully expensive.

In this dilemma I was helped by Mr. Richardson, the clergyman of Rustemberg, to whom I had brought a letter of introduction from the then rector of Pretoria. He asked me if I would go as a governess in a farmer's family; and on my answering in the affirmative, he said he would write to an English Africander farmer, who had two young daughters whom he was anxious to educate well. This farmer's name was Higgins, he told me, and his farm was about thirty-five miles from Rustemberg, on the southern slope of the Magaliesberg. From all who spoke of Mr. Higgins I heard a good account of himself and his family; and his house, I was told, was the finest farmhouse in the Transvaal. The post only goes out once a week from Rustemberg, and hence there was some delay before Mr. Higgins's reply came. It was to the effect that he would come in to fetch me as soon as he could. My engagement was that I was to be paid five pounds a month, with washing, and that I might take other pupils besides Mr. Higgins's two daughters at any terms I chose to make, while Mr. Higgins undertook to give any such pupils their dinner.

Several days passed, and I neither heard nor saw anything of Mr. Higgins. I used to pass my day in writing a story, without which amusement I should have collapsed under the combined heat, dullness, and anxiety of that time at Rustemberg; but it is wonderful how one can forget oneself and one's own troubles in inventing the joys and woes of creatures of one's imagination! I used to sit up late writing, and so soon as day broke get up to write again. Little Gip was my constant companion now. He would not remain an instant away from me, and many a time his little paw scratching my dress would stop my pen, and call upon me to take the small beast up and give it the caress it wanted; for Gip never cared for being fed, but only for being coaxed and played with. He was a very delicate little dog, having had his constitution undermined, Mrs. Brown told me, by his former owner's cruelty, and was the victim of a species of St. Vitus's Dance, which at times made him go through the queerest contortions.

One beautiful evening, after a very hot day, I was standing at the door of my little room, enjoying the cool air, and admiring two fine grey horses that were cropping the grass in the street, watched by a mischievous-looking *kaffir* boy of about nine. They were evidently fresh arrivals, for I had not seen them before. While I was standing thus and chatting to Mrs. Brown's *protégé*, a fine-looking man, dressed in a riding-suit, with high boots and a wide-a-wake hat, and with a sunburnt honest face, merry blue eyes, and a fine reddish-brown beard, sprang up the steps that led to my little door, and touching his hat said, "Mrs. Heckford, I think; I'm Higgins. I came while you were out," he went on; "those are my horses," pointing to the animals I had been admiring. We settled everything in five minutes.

I told Mr. Higgins that he might inquire about me from Mr. Richardson, who would be able to tell him who I was, and what were my antecedents; but he said it was of no use, that he was quite satisfied with what he had seen and heard of me, and only wanted to know when I could start. I said I should be ready to start early next morning; and so my stay in little Rustemberg, and under the friendly roof of Mr. and Mrs. Brown, came to an end.

CHAPTER 8

Early the next morning I packed all the things I could into the tax-cart with a canvas hood to it which was to convey me to my new home, the farm "Surprise;" my heavy luggage I had to leave behind in Mrs. Brown's charge. Then after breakfast, and amidst much shaking of hands and many good wishes, I got into the cart, climbed on to the back seat—Mr. Higgins and the mischievous-looking *kaffir* imp jumped up in front—little Gip was lifted up to me, and Mr. Higgins having said I might take him, I joyfully tucked him under my arm—and I was launched into my new life.

That asking whether I might take my dog seemed like the first plunge into a cold bath on a frosty morning; it was part of the part I had to play now, and I wondered how I should play it. I had always pitied governesses, and had also always objected to be an object of pity myself, even to myself. I never could see the use of self-commiseration, which to some seems to be so delectable. How I wondered what Mrs. Higgins would be like, what my pupils would be like, what the whole life would be like, and what sort of a governess I should make, as we bowled along the pretty road, over Oliphants-nek, and then along the southern side of the picturesque Magaliesberg once more, into the long valley, up and down which I had looked on the day of our breaking the *disselboom* a little outside of Pretoria, but distant about sixty miles from the spot.

Mr. Higgins in the meantime chatted away pleasantly. He was not an educated man, as he said himself, but he was evidently a very good fellow. He said his children were respectively eleven and nine, the name of the elder was Augusta, of the younger Sarah. He said they had had no teaching to speak of, but that their mother was very anxious they should have good schooling. Then he told me the names of the two greys that were drawing the cart were Sam and Dick, that they were brothers, and that he had another horse, a fine brown horse, called Free State, or, as a pet name, Baby; and then he talked about other horses he had had, and about a little dog his youngest daughter had. We outspanned twice, and twice stopped for Mr. Higgins to pay a little visit at farms we passed, and on each occasion he piled my lap and filled his pockets and handkerchief with peaches. At last, just as the sun was setting, and as we were turning round a spur of the hill all wooded with thorn-trees, Mr. Higgins said, "Now you'll see the house;" and in a few minutes I saw a good-sized red-brick house with a verandah, standing in the middle of the grassy slope, the wooded sides of the mountain and its high *kranz* rising behind it, an orchard of large fruit-trees and a fine stretch of cultivated land lying below it, and a background of mountain range and wooded slope running down into the long valley beneath it.

At the same moment Mr. Higgins said, "There are Mrs. Higgins and the children;" and I saw two tall black robed figures and one small one (the family were in mourning for the youngest child), and a little black and white dog, coming to meet the cart. It was alongside of them in a minute; and Mr. Higgins jumping out, little Sarah was lifted up and took the reins, whilst her dog Fido, who jumped up with her, went through a series of frantic antics ending by nearly tumbling out, all meant for demonstrations of joy at her master's return.

Let me introduce my employer's wife and children. Mrs. Higgins was a very tall, fine-looking woman, with a stately grace about her movements and manners; she talked bad grammar, and misplaced her "h's," but I felt at and from the first that I was in the presence of a lady. Augusta, a child of eleven, was as tall as most girls of fifteen, and looked almost grown up. Slight, with beautiful fine brown hair hanging over her shoulders and down to her waist, with soft almond-shaped blue eyes fringed by long dark lashes and over-arched by pencilled eyebrows, with a sweet but haughty little mouth, and with a white and rose-pink complexion, with long, slender, refined hands too, I thought I had rarely seen such a lovely girl. Everything about her breathed of refinement and indolence; you would have sworn she had been bred in some luxurious drawing-room, and waited on by obsequious servants.

Little Sarah was a contrast to her sister. Small for her age, and with a baby chubbiness still clinging to her; with mischief, wilfulness, and bright intelligence sparkling in her eyes and ringing in her voice; with an expression ever changing, with still unformed features, and with a shock of wild-looking hair hanging about her face, in some ways she reminded me of an unbroken Shetland pony, and in my mind I installed her as my pet.

We were soon at the front of the house—a house not after the Boer model, but built on Mr. Higgins's own plan. A raised "*stoop*," or nagged pathway in front, was covered by an iron verandah, and ended in two small rooms, one used as a visitors' room, the other as a lumber room. Three doors, two of them half glass, and two windows, opened on the stoop, besides the half-glass doors of the end rooms. The two half-glass doors led into rooms which were respectively my bedroom and the school-room. The centre door opened into a passage which led to the dining-room, a long room at the back, with the kitchen and a pantry at one side, and a big store-room at the other, the two former opening into it, the latter having to be entered by a side door outside. Two doors opened into the passage besides the dining-room door at the end of it, leading to side rooms, one the sleeping-room of the family, the other the drawing-room, from which a side door led to my bedroom. The school-room had no door but the one on the *stoop*. There was a fireplace in the drawing-room and kitchen only.

I was taken first into my bedroom, a very pleasant one, large and lofty, with a canvas ceiling under the rafters, papered walls, large strips of a bright coloured carpet on the floor, and a comfortable-looking French bed with white hangings, besides the other furniture of a bed-room in it. From a side window which opened like a double door there was a pretty view of part of the crest and of a wooded spur of the Magaliesberg, and then one looked over undulations in part stud-ded with trees, and across the valley to the distant range of Wittwaters Randt.

There was a big old thorn-tree close by, under which were two little mounds, the graves of two little children the Higginses had lost; and at a little distance, just round the turn of a rose hedge, which here bound the cultivated land, a *kaffir* house could be seen, where farm-servants lived; while between the tree and my window was a sort of dust-hole—a hollow place where refuse was thrown—the outside door of the kitchen being close to it. This place was half overgrown with *stramonium*, a big bush-like plant, with a coarse but not ugly flower. A little beaten path led from the kitchen door up to the cattle and sheep-*kraal*, an enclosure made of bushes of thorn on the side of the hill, and well sheltered from cold winds by the spur of the moun-tain. It was in all a very pretty look-out.

We had supper in the dining-room, and then we went to the drawing-room—a prettily-furnished apartment, with a fairly good piano, and a nice harmonium in it. I got the children to play on the former. They performed a duet from ear—for they did not know their notes—and kept exact time. Then I was asked to play. I had no music with me, the little I had, having been left behind with my heavy luggage, and I had not touched a piano for months, nor practised on one for years. They particularly wanted to hear me play a piece called "The Battle of Waterloo." It was one of those pieces that sound more difficult than they are, and I read it easily enough. Then followed "Shells of Ocean" with variations, and "Home, Sweet Home," and some others with variations, all arrangements new to me, but with which I did my best.

It was very encouraging to hear that I gave great satisfaction—I was so dreadfully afraid I should not; but it was evident that the pleasure caused by my playing was genuine. Then an old copy of the entire opera of "Norma" was brought out. The family did not much care for "Norma;" but, oh! how strange it did seem to listen to that well-known music, which carried one back to the gorgeous Italian opera, and recalled faces and voices some of them passed away, some of them never probably to be seen or heard again in that little drawing-room of the farmhouse on the Magaliesberg, with listeners around to whom the very names that were household words to me, were utterly unknown! Life is a wonderful romance for many of us.

It never struck me more forcibly that it had been so, and was still for me, than on that evening, when, having bid the family goodnight, and having been kissed by the children with heartiness that showed they were prepared to like me, I stood for a while at the open window, with the dark outline of the mountains before my material eyes, but with visions of all that had passed since I had first listened to "Casta Diva," shutting out the present, and substituting for a short while scenes widely different.

Before I went to sleep, however, the present reasserted itself in the shape of Gip. Gip was determined to sleep with his little head touching my shoulder. He had not been accustomed to do so, but I suppose he felt strange in the new house, and wanted a sense of protection. At any rate he was determined on this point. It was useless putting him off the bed; and he would patter on the floor, and scratch at the side of the bed, and make little springs, and whine in a manner that rendered sleep impossible, and I felt that sleep was necessary; so at last I took him up and let him have his own way, although I wondered in my mind what Mrs. Higgins would think of a dog sleeping on her nice white counterpane.

Chapter 9

I woke early the next morning, and took a survey of my new abode, and a stroll towards a wooded spur of the mountain, where I was told Mr. Higgins's father and mother and two young sisters lived, in a little cottage. The road, if road it could be called, passed along the top of some upper cultivated lands, on which a fine crop of Indian corn was standing, and which were shut in partly by a low stone wall, partly by a rose hedge at the top and sides; whilst an orchard of big orange, lemon, peach, almond, apricot, and fig-trees separated these, the upper lands, from the lower lands, which were much larger.

At the bottom of the upper lands stood an old thatched house, used as a stable and outhouse, with two enormous syringa-trees over-shadowing it. This was the oldest house in the Transvaal, and had been built by old Potchieter, who was afterwards made mincemeat of by the *kaffirs*—in days not indeed far distant, but when elephants might be shot on the place where Mr. Higgins's house now stood, and when the cultivated valley beneath me was still covered with bush. A little farther on the road passed over a broad stone bulwark, which served to dam up a rivulet, which, gushing out of the precipitous crown of the mountain, found its way down its side through a ravine overarched by trees, and carpeted with ferns, to a place at which it was compelled to form a big pond or dam.

From this dam as much or as little water as was requisite could be let out, by means of two wooden pipes, to water the lands, *sluits* (or what are here called furrows) having been made on purpose to convey it to different parts. From these furrows it had to be let on to the lands by opening them here and there with the spade, and so directing the various little streams that, without touching each other, they yet wet all the ground. This process is called "letting water," and is a very important one in this dry country, also a very troublesome and tedious one. The stream of water and the dam are the first things to be looked to in buying a farm out here, also their relative position to the ground to be cultivated. The dam has frequently to be made by the purchaser, then he must be careful to see that he can make one of sufficient size above what he means to be his lands.

From the dam the road took me over a little rise, on which some *kaffir* houses were built, and then down towards the valley. It was a pretty walk. As I was returning I observed that the house had a loft, but no outbuildings of any kind. It is the same with all the best farm-houses in the Transvaal. They are comfortable in many ways, but they lack what we consider the commonest conveniences of a dwelling; and this applies to some even of the houses on the outskirts of Pretoria.

The children came to meet me near the dam, and we went in to breakfast. This was Friday 3 and Mr. Higgins said I had better take it easy, and not begin lessons till Monday. My life now seemed settled for a time. I was to give the children what is called a good English education, and to teach them to play the piano, to draw, and to sing. Foreign languages are not much cared for in Africa.

Besides Augusta and Sarah, it was arranged that I was to have Mr. Higgins's two sisters—Alice, a girl of sixteen, and Ada, who was thirteen—as pupils. Their mother, a pleasant-looking old lady, came over from her cottage, and made the arrangement with me. Alice, a small, plump, and pretty girl, with something very sweet and yet determined in her look, and with activity stamped on her every movement, was engaged to be married to a young man who was half farmer and half trader. Ada, almost but not quite so tall as Augusta, was yet a tall girl for her age. She was slight and graceful, with hands as delicate as those of her niece. With a pretty impertinent nose, arched eyebrows, and eyes that could coax you, or calmly overlook you, according to the mood of their pretty owner, with a scornfully-turned upper lip, and a pouting under one—very rosy, and which could part into a delightful smile when she was pleased, or wanted to please—with a prettily disdainful languor in all her movements (except, by the way, when she went in for a romp, at which she excelled), Miss Ada Higgins looked like a little princess in disguise. Like her niece, she had masses of brown hair hanging from her well-set-on head, but her hair was even heavier in its flow than Augusta's.

I had to begin with the very simplest lessons. Even Alice had to learn to spell monosyllables, and be taught the meaning of words which a child of eight in England would laugh at you for asking her to explain. They had no idea of the points of the compass, and had never heard of an article; but they were on the whole very good pupils, and only Sarah was wilful and idle at times, making up for this afterwards by the greatest attention and intelligent comprehension. It was a terrible trial to this small girl to be kept at lessons—she who, up to the time I came, had been allowed to run wild, and romp all day with the *kaffir* children on the property. Many an excuse would she make to escape from the school-room, and forthwith perform a dance with Maikee or Vittaree, or have a sparring-match with Fiervaree, the *kaffir* imp who was supposed to look after Sam and Dick.

Many a day would she pretend to be ill until she persuaded her mamma to let her off school, and then set to, with gleeful enjoyment, to help Sannee, the *kaffir* girl who assisted in the housework, to clean the pots and pans; or turning up her sleeves, and tying her doll on behind her back as the *kaffir* mothers tie their babies when at work, she would get a pailful of cow-dung and water, and proceed to smear the floor of the little lumber-room with it, pretending that it was her house. This smearing operation, unpleasant to English ears, is a necessary part of housekeeping here, where most of the floors are made of mud—or rather, of a mixture of ant-heap and water, stamped and levelled down, and where, without the aid of cow-dung, one would be stifled with dust and eaten alive by fleas.

The life was monotonous, but not unpleasant. Breakfast at between seven and eight, then lessons till one (dinner-time), then lessons again till about five, when there was afternoon tea, then supper at about seven, a chat or a little music, and to bed. I worked my pupils pretty hard, but I tried to make them fond of me, and I think I succeeded. I certainly became fond of them, but little Sarah was always my pet, though I used to make her cry about four days out of the seven. There was a great difficulty in getting books, &c., for them, Pretoria, the nearest town, being forty miles distant, and it was often difficult to explain common things to them, owing to their experience being so very small. It is not easy to convey the idea of a bridge even, to a child who has never seen any nearer approach to it than the wall of a dam with a road over it, or a piece of plank stretched across a furrow; or to convey the idea of a steam-engine, or a steamboat, to one who has never seen anything of the sort; or to create an idea of a large town in one who looks upon a tiny village as a very imposing place. However, all things considered, the children got on well, and their parents were satisfied. Mr. Higgins let me ride "Free State" occasionally, on one occasion taking me to a small *kaffir kraal* that was on his property, where I went into the neat huts and admired the cement-like mud floors.

The *kaffirs* living in the *kraal* were what is called raw *kaffirs*, the men indeed being in some sort clothed in old European garments, but the women wearing skins, and the children being naked. Mr. Higgins, as landlord, had the right to their services for taking the crops off the land, without paying them; and also of commanding their services at other times, for the wage of a shilling a day, at most, to the men, and of something much less to the boys. He also had the right to order the women to weed or to *scoffle*, as it is called here, giving them a basket of peaches in return, during the fruit season, or without payment if there was no fruit. Besides these, he had several families of what are called *urlams*, or civilized *kaffirs*, living in mud houses on his property. These families dressed like Europeans, and had food like Europeans, even to the drinking of early coffee. They also went to school to the missionary station at Rustemberg periodically, and learned a little reading and singing of hymns. I don't think the school did them much good. I heard of one *kaffir* woman saying, that when she came back from school and had been made a Christian, she would sit on a chair and eat with a knife and fork, and not let the raw *kaffirs* eat with her, for that then she would be better than they.

Sannee, the girl who helped in the house, after her return from school refused to help her mistress, who was very ill at the time, saying that the missionary had told her that she must not work for some months, only study. Mr. Higgins was a very kind, indulgent master, partly from good nature, partly from indolence. He could get *kaffirs* to come to squat on his farm when other farmers could not get any; but then they squatted and did little else, except when a sudden fancy to do a little work seized them.

I also rode to old Mr. Higgins's little cottage, a small structure stuck on a very picturesque spur of the mountain, with a big wild fig-tree in front of it. It was simply a mud and stone cabin, with the bare rafters and thatch showing overhead, its one long room divided into three by rude canvas partitions, without a trace of paper on the walls, and with planks supported on the rafters doing duty as shelves. Outside, a straw house did duty as outhouse, stable, cow-house, or anything else, a conical straw hut, with a hole at the top, was the kitchen, and another small straw structure close to the sheep *kraal* served for a fowl-house. There was an old piano, however, in this funny little building, and on it Alice and Ada practised their music. Old Mrs. Higgins kept no servant; she and Alice cleaned the house, cooked, washed in a washing machine, ironed, and made the dresses of the family. Ada, the princess, did nothing, not even mend her own clothes. How Alice managed to do the work she did and learn her lessons I don't know, but she did manage it.

There were no windows to this odd little building, only square holes in the wall, with movable frames stretched over with calico fitted to them, and there was no chimney. Old Mr. Higgins, who had been a great hunter when younger, was now a victim to chronic bronchitis of a very bad type, and how he managed to live in that cabin I do not know. He had not even the convenience of an armchair. He was a small grey-bearded man, much bent, but with a keen look about the eyes that spoke of his hunting days, and with a still easy seat in the saddle—a thorough old gentleman too in all his ways and thoughts, and with a fund of queerly assorted information. Often he has startled me by the things he knew of, having been all his life a great reader, and given to buying books in lots on sales.

Mrs. Higgins the younger did the principal part of her house-work herself, and wonderful was the amount of needlework, or rather machine-work, she would get through in the day besides; yet she never seemed in a fuss or a hurry, never spoke loudly or crossly, but was always stately and ladylike, even with her dress turned up, her arms bared, and a broom in her hand. Augusta, like Ada, did nothing but look ornamental. This was what the two girls were meant for by nature, and they could not, I believe, be useful if they tried; but they didn't try. Little Sarah was already a famous housekeeper, but she scolded the servants well.

There was a wonderful old Hottentot maid, "Khrid," the second wife of a certain Jonas who squatted on the farm—a good sort of creature, who was very helpful in the house, and of whom Sarah was a special pet and persecutor. Sometimes she would spring on the woman's back, and tightening her legs round her waist, pinch her and beat her—in fun it is true, but pretty hard for all that—until the old woman would lie down and roll, to get her off.

In this family I was treated not like a governess, but like a welcome guest. The best of everything was at my disposal without my asking for or even thinking of having it. Whatever there was unavoidably rough in the life, Mrs. Higgins did her best to shelter me from. A stranger would, I am sure, have thought that I was there teaching the children as a friend, not as one paid for it. When poor little Gip got ill and became troublesomely dirty at night, Mrs. Higgins expostulated with me for having cleaned and washed up the things myself; and when my poor little dog died, she got a *kaffir* to dig a grave for it, and in no way objected to lessons being interrupted to attend to it before its death, or to see it buried afterwards. I was dreadfully sorry for the little dog that had been so fond of me when I was a stranger in the land, and it was true kindness to me to indulge me as she did. But it was not to me alone that she showed tact and delicacy of feeling. It was the same with even a raw *kaffir*. The true politeness of quick sympathy and un-selfishness, was always there, for the benefit of any one coming within her sphere of influence.

It must be remembered that all this time the Boer scare was going on. Horrible tales used to be told at meal-times and in the evening as to what the Boers meant to do to the English, or any of the Afri-canders who held with the English; and the Higginses were very loyal. There was even talk of its being as well for the family to go into the Free State. This being the case, I began to feel unhappy about Jimmy, who was away on a farm with three or four other English. This farm was about thirty miles from Surprise, and I had no horse or any other means of conveyance to take me to him. I therefore began to be very anxious to buy a horse, but it was not easy to get one.

The scare had for a time subsided, when one day, while I was in the schoolroom, one of the children cried out, "Oh! there is Uncle Walter," and of course they all wanted to go out to see Uncle Walter an unmarried uncle who, with a bachelor brother, kept a store at Marico. I remained in the schoolroom. Presently Mr. Higgins called me, and said he wanted me to meet his brother. I went out, and saw a fine-looking man standing by the side of a handsome dun horse, and with another horse standing close to him with a rein in its mouth for leading it by.

"That's a nice little horse," said Mr. Higgins; "what do you think of it?"

"It does not look bad," I said, not much prepossessed by the lean animal with a draggly tail, that I was looking down on from the *stoop*.

"Do you think it would suit you?" he asked.

I looked closer at it then. It was a good horse at all points, with a little head, taper neck, and fine ears, which spoke of good blood, better than generally seen. It had been roughly treated, evidently, not over well fed, and ridden hard, and was very dirty, but that time would cure. It was a light-red roan—what is here called a red grey—with white stockings, a white streak down its face, and chestnut mane and tail. The eyes were full, but a little mischievous-looking, in spite of the otherwise very mild appearance of the creature.

"I think it might," I replied, "if the price be not high."

"Would you give twenty pounds?" asked Mr. Higgins.

"Yes, but not more," I answered.

He inquired of his brother whether the horse, which was his, and which he had had for some time, was sound and fit for a lady to ride. He said it was so; and the bargain being struck, my new acquisition, "Eclipse," the grandson of a famous old colony racer, and himself the winner of two races in the colony, was turned loose to graze, whilst Walter Higgins rode off on his handsome dun—a horse whom everybody said was thoroughly "salted," and for whom he had refused sixty pounds, but who died a few days after, it was said from "horse sickness," but I rather fancy from the bots.

Not long after, a neighbour came in. "Have you bought that red-grey horse?" he asked.

"Yes."

"Are you a very good horsewoman?"

"No."

"Then take care; he'll break your neck. Why, he bucked Walter Higgins off him—and Arthur Sturton—and he nearly threw me, only I jumped off. I never saw a horse buck so cleverly as he does."

This was pleasant, the more so as before a day was over I heard further confirmation of it. However, the thing was done, and I had to make the best of it.

Mr. Higgins allowed me forage for my animal, and I groomed him, fed him, and bedded him up myself. No hand but mine touched him. He was stabled in the stable with Dick, Sam, and Freestate, and I now saw how the *kaffir* boys who had charge of these horses neglected them. Anticipating buying a horse, I had brought all the articles necessary for one with me, and Eclipse soon showed his change of owners. At first he was troublesome to groom, but he soon got accustomed to it and fond of me, nor, though a very lively horse, did he ever attempt more than a little playful jump with me; but his character was bad. The Dutch, farmers seeing me ride him would exclaim; and even men who had ridden him could never account for the change in him, although it was easily enough accounted for.

Eclipse knew as well as most horses how to distinguish between a master who treated him well and never punished him except when he deserved it, and one who neglected him and spurred him to make him show off. I certainly felt much happier after getting my horse, although I had to be up early to groom him, and had trouble about his bedding; and although I had no time to ride much—for it is not good during the summer months here to have a horse out of the stable early in the morning or late in the evening—and I was occupied during the day on weekdays. Still many a ride I had, generally with one of the children with me on Dick, and I felt now that if there were danger I could get hold of Jimmy.

Some little time after I got Eclipse—about the beginning of March—it was decided that we should all go over to visit two married brothers of Mr. Higgins (James and John), who had a farm and kept a store behind the Witt-waters Randt, about twelve miles from Surprise. We started early, Mr. and Mrs. Higgins and little Sarah in the cart, Alice on a pony borrowed from her brother-in-law, Arthur Sturton, and Augusta on Freestate. I, of course, rode Eclipse. In parts the road was pretty, particularly at a point not far from our destination, where we saw several monkeys sitting on a low *kranz* above us. Here we had to ford a river three times, owing to its rapid turns. We passed several farmhouses, and at last came to the one we were to stop at.

It was not so nicely arranged a house as Surprise, being, in fact, two houses tacked together. There were several little children playing about, and the hosts were very hospitable and kind to me. Each of the wives had a piano, on which I played in the evening, and I slept on a comfortable bed made up on the sofa in one of the sitting-rooms. Here, too, the mistresses had to do almost all the housework, the *kaffir* servants being either too lazy or too stupid.

The Boer scare now set in again. Plans used to be discussed as to what was to be done in case of an attack, and at last even Mr. Higgins, who generally took things quietly, began to look serious, and to check me when I laughed at the idea of danger—for I thought there was too much talk for anything to come of it. One day a neighbour rode up to say that there was a *kaffir* commando marching on Pretoria, that a son of Cetewayo had ridden through the valley and over the mountain to Rustemberg the night before—that he had told the farmers from whom he had commanded a horse and money, that a great outbreak of the *kaffirs* was close at hand, and that all who did not wish to be murdered had best go into *laagers*. The *veldt*-cornet had ridden late at night to warn some people in his district; all was authenticated beautifully.

Surprise was alarmed: no shame for it, for Pretoria trembled in its shoes at the same rumour. I can't say that I felt frightened, but then it is difficult for any one accustomed to profound peace, and a civilized country, to bring his mind to realize the possibility of a sudden outbreak of savages. The Higginses knew what it was from practical experience, old Mrs. Higgins having had to fly with a child under one arm, and a money-box under the other, alongside of her husband, who was laden with another child and the powder-bag. My employer had seen his parents' property swept away more than once in the old colony by *kaffirs*, and hence it is no wonder that he felt more concern than I.

It was the most absurd hoax that ever was practised, and the *kaffir* who personated Cetewayo's son, and ordered the terrified Boers to give him horses and money must have had a laugh at the success of his piece of fun. Their having obeyed the dictates of a half tipsy *kaffir* was a sore point with the Boers afterwards, and this absurd escapade did not serve to raise my opinion of their courage. But hardly had this blown over, than the Boer scare broke out again. Mr. Higgins wanted to take loads down to Natal, and ride transport up—transport was very high then—but waited and waited for the Beeinkommste, which was then sitting, to break up. Terrible threats were current as to what was to happen to the dwellers on outstanding farms, if the demands of the committee were not listened to, still worse was it to go with us if the English Government attempted to lay hands on the leaders.

Time went by, and at last Mr. Higgins said he could wait no longer, or that he should have too cold weather on his return journey for the oxen; so he loaded a big pistol for his wife, and hung it up in the hall, told her she must do the best she could in case of any disturbance, and on a fine April morning he started off the waggons loaded with wool-bags, and prepared to follow them on horseback. Great had been the preparations for starting the waggons, biscuits having to be baked for the road and other provisions provided. A Mr. King, a small farmer and a great friend of Mr. Higgins, went with the waggons, he came to breakfast before he started, and a starved-looking rough black and white terrier with big beseeching eyes all covered by his long hair came with him. The dog did not belong to him, but was loafing about, and came to Surprise for something to do, I suppose.

We all turned out to see the waggons start. The one with a splendid span of eighteen black oxen in it—their sleek skins shining in the sun, and with their driver, a *kaffir* called Saul, alongside, looking proud of his beasts, and glad of the change—made a great impression on me, and I said to myself, "I will never go down to the coast till I can go with such a span as that." Soon after Mr. Higgins saddled up, and bidding us goodbye, took a short cut after the waggons. We all felt very flat as the last flick of Freestate's tail was seen through the long grass; how I did envy Mr. Higgins to be sure, but we soon settled down, and I began to like being alone with Mrs. Higgins and the children.

The rough black and white dog stayed behind, and in process of time came to be my dog, and developed into a very pretty playful little animal, up to any amount of fun, and a good watch-dog, but with a terror of being lost or stolen from me. He would often go off visiting on his own account, but his dread of being taken hold of by any one strange, and the way he would struggle and bite, were amusing; a terrible dog for fighting too was this Little animal, whom we christened "Rough."

Winter was now beginning, and though I regretted the summer in some ways, I was glad it was gone; for the dreaded "horse-sickness" goes with it. It is strange that no one has ever found out exactly what the "horse-sickness" is; the only thing certain about it is that horses that eat the grass after the sun is set, or before the dew is off, are more liable to it than others. Opinions vary as to whether mere exposure to the night air affects horses in the matter. It is averred that horses that have once had the "horse-sickness" rarely have it again, and if they do get it, have it very mildly; one is told many other things regarding this curious disease, but authorities disagree. I believe that numbers of horses are said to die of "horse-sickness" when in reality they die of bots and of neglect.

In this country, where horses are so seldom kept decently clean, the bots make terrible ravages amongst them. I have frequently been told, and that, too, by people who ought to have known better, that it was impossible to clean the bot-eggs off horses that were roughing it in the *veldt*, and it stands to reason that if the eggs are left on the animals for them to lick off, they will soon be full of bots. I speak now of horses that are ridden. In the case of a herd of mares and colts, it would of course be impossible to prevent harm, grooming in such cases being out of the question.

There are two species of disease called "horse-sickness," one of them is also called "Dick-kop," or "thickhead" sickness. They both come on very suddenly. In the case of simple "horse-sickness," the horse perhaps appears well, and eats and works well, when suddenly it begins to pant and blow, gives a short hacking cough, then a discharge comes from the nose, and the animal seems choked with mucus which it cannot expel. Its distress is very great, and in the majority of cases, death supervenes quickly. In the case of the "thick-head" variety, the head begins to swell first in those hollows over the eyes, which, probably, even my unhorsy readers will have remarked, and soon the entire head is enormously swollen, and the animal appears to die from suffocation. In both cases there is high fever.

No satisfactory cure for either disease has yet been discovered, but even were a cure known, I doubt whether it would be of much avail in the majority of cases, for it would have to be accompanied by more "sick-nursing" than is generally practicable whether with man or beast in this rough country. The great thing, therefore, is, if possible, to prevent a horse from getting the disease, and I was as careful about Eclipse not being exposed to the early or late air as a mother with a delicate baby.

Chapter 10

Not long after Mr. Higgins's departure we were all startled one day by Arthur Sturton's riding up from his farm in the valley to tell us that a neighbouring farmer—an English Africander—had just come back from Pretoria, and had brought the news that Sir Bartle Frere had met the Committee of the Boers—that there had been much angry discussion, and that at last the Boers had leapt from their seats, over-turning the chairs and crying, "War! war! We give you notice that we will march on Pretoria tomorrow." He had told Arthur Sturton that every waggon was being pressed into government service, and that his own had been seized; so that but for a chance he should have had to walk all the way from Pretoria, whither he had gone with a load. Arthur Sturton said that he had sent a *kaffir* to his father's farm (which is halfway between Surprise and Pretoria), there to wait for further intelligence; Moy-plas, as it is called, being on the high-road, and any one coming from Pretoria being likely to call there. He said that when the *kaffir* returned he would send news to us.

Mrs. Higgins and I held a council of war on the verandah that afternoon, and it was resolved that if the Boers came to Surprise, we would receive them civilly, but when we saw them coming, we would put the girls into the bedroom and lock it. The invaders were to be allowed to take what they liked, but if they wanted to enter that room we would first expostulate, saying we had put the girls in there to pre-vent their being more frightened than necessary, and that if the men insisted on forcing an entrance, we would use our pistols and knives; also that we would do the same if they attempted any liberties with either of us. Mrs. Higgins had told me that many of the Boers around had said that they would not kill the women of their enemies; but that they would strip them, and make laughing-stocks of them.

Two days passed, and we heard nothing; the third morning, very early, I was half awake, when I heard what sounded like a very distant cannon-shot. I thought sleepily, "I suppose that is at Pretoria," but roused up when I heard a second and similar sound. I meant to lie awake, but sleepiness overcame me, and I was just dropping off, when I heard a third sound of the same character, after which I went fast asleep. In the morning, however, I told what I fancied at breakfast, and proposed that in the afternoon I should ride down to the valley in search of news. When Alice heard that I was going, she said she would go too. We did get news of rather a surprising character, to the effect that all the inventive young farmer had narrated was pure fiction. My heavy guns have been a laugh against me ever since!

We really felt quite dull after the Boer excitement was over; of the story we had heard, so much alone was true that the Beeinkommste had broken up after Sir Bartle Frere met the Committee. It seemed to me quite stupid to settle down to common-place life again, after talking of pistols and knives; and I know the children had the same feeling in a different way. They quite enjoyed the Boer scare, and once Ada dressed herself in my mackintosh, and girding on my belt with knife and pistol, blackening her eyebrows, and putting on a cork moustache, she gave the *kaffirs* in the kitchen a fine start. Mrs. Higgins and I were still sitting at the tea-table talking after tea, when we heard a violent knocking at the back door of the kitchen; Sannee, the maid, opened it rather reluctantly, being dreadfully afraid of the Boers, when a gruff voice exclaimed,—

"*Var* is Bob Higgins?" and presented a pistol in her face.

Sannee and two little *kaffir* children uttered a succession of unearthly yells, and rushed into the dining-room, where they clung to Mrs. Higgins's dress, hiding their faces, whilst the Boer dashed past, pistol in hand, to search the rooms. We had a good laugh, and Ada was delighted at the success of her scheme.

Winter now came on in earnest, and soon great grass fires were to be seen every evening on the opposite *randt*. One day Mrs. Higgins came into the schoolroom and said she smelt that there was a fire coming our way across the Magaliesberg, and that she had sent some *kaffirs* to see. It did not, however, come close, greatly to my relief.

In the beginning of June, Mr. Higgins came home. For days before, the children, Mrs. Higgins, and the *kaffirs* had been on the look-out for him, and at last a *kaffir* ran in just as we finished dinner, to say that the "boss" was coming. We all went quickly out on the *stoop*, and saw a mounted *kaffir*-boy with a led horse, and Mr. Higgins with another led horse, coming up the short way from the valley. Of course there was great excitement. The new horses were two handsome young black stallions (brothers), for whom Mr. Higgins had exchanged a farm in the *bush-veldt*, and a bay pony for old Mr. Higgins. Freestate had come, too, but so changed that none of us knew him at first. Eclipse was grazing close by as Mr. Higgins dismounted, and I remember his first remark to me: "Eclipse is looking well. I see you *have* kept him clear of bot's eggs" for Mr. Higgins had asserted his conviction that I should not do so. I had already remarked that his horses were thickly covered with them.

I had forgotten to say that during Mr. Higgins' absence, Mrs. Higgins had kindly sent in a waggon to Rustemberg for my heavy luggage, and had allowed it also to call at the farm where Jimmy was, to bring him over to Surprise, with whatever luggage he had—the whole affair of the farm, &c., having come to complete squash—and Arthur Sturton having offered to take him on his farm, where he could learn and make himself useful, in return for his board and lodging.

A few days after Mr. Higgins's arrival, he rode to Pretoria, and on his return rather late in the evening, he said he did not know what was the matter with Freestate; he had seemed so tired on the road. Mrs. Higgins and I were alone when he came in; all the girls and Harriet Sturton, who was paying them a visit, having gone off on horseback and in the cart with Sam and Dick to Fahl-plas, the farm of James and John Higgins. They were escorted by Alfred Sturton and Alice's intended. Alfred was a younger brother of Arthur. The occasion of this festivity was little Sarah's birthday, and there had been great excitement among the young people, for they were to have a dance.

The next day Freestate seemed very ill, standing about listlessly and eating but little, and Mr. Higgins said he ought to have a bran mash, but the *kaffir* never gave it to him. At about two o'clock we were startled by seeing the cart with Ada and Alfred in it, and Alice and Harriet on horseback. I shall never forget the sharp ring of terror in Mrs. Higgins's voice as she greeted them with, "Where are my children?" Little Sarah, they told us, was very ill with sore throat—diphtheria had been fatal in the family—and Augusta was ill too. It was decided to start at once for Fahl-plas, Mr. and Mrs. Higgins in the cart, and I riding, for Mrs. Higgins said she would like me to go to see the children. The two greys did their return journey well. We got in before dark. Little Sarah was very ill with high fever, and her throat dreadfully inflamed—she was almost delirious at times. Augusta had simply a bad cold.

Then, for the first time, did I see the misery of illness in this country. The two houses at Fahl-plas could muster but eight rooms together, counting the kitchens. Into these eight rooms, or rather six rooms, had to be stowed four men, five babies, or children little more than babies, two little girls, and four women—fifteen people! Mrs. Higgins, Augusta, Sarah and I were all in one small room, and its one window had to be kept shut! Its door opened into the dining-room where two of the men slept and it had no chimney to admit air. Then the impossibility of keeping the small children quiet! I remember two little boys inventing a dreadful species of drum made out of an old biscuit tin, which could be heard for miles off, and when it was taken away, their shrieks were worse than the drum itself.

Augusta was well enough in a day to be driven over to Surprise; the rest of us stayed with little Sarah. Her throat ulcerated and was dreadfully bad, but finally the ulcers broke, and she began to mend. Before this, however, Mrs. Higgins expressed a wish that I should return to Surprise, to be with Augusta and Harriet, and great was their astonishment at my appearance alone just as it got dark one evening. Poor Freestate was dead—killed by the bots. I had heard of many things which were suppose to kill bots—one excellent remedy, I had been told, was thick sugar-and-water—also strong coffee. I determined now to make the experiment, and getting a live bot from the stomach of the poor horse, (the creatures had eaten through the stomach in places), I put it into all sorts of baths. Strong solution of tartar emetic—so strong as to be an impossible dose for a horse—alone seemed to make the objectionable little worm feel ill, that nearly killed him, and would have killed him altogether, only that just as he was at his last gulp I put him as an experiment into a bath of strong coffee, when he instantly came to and looked quite lively. Sugar, too, he seemed rather to like; and at last I gave my experiments up, having tried all the medicines in my medicine-chest, besides other simples, such as coffee.

Harriet Sturton was a very pleasant addition to our party, and except for my anxiety about little Sarah, I should have quite enjoyed this time, but I now felt how fond of the child, and still more of her mother, I had grown. I could have cried for joy the day she was brought home.

Mr. Higgins now prepared to leave home for the *bush-veldt*, and here I must explain what the *bush-veldt* is.

Lying towards the northern borders of the Transvaal are large tracts of land, unfitted for cultivation except in parts, owing to there not being much water, and hence given over to nature, and such trees as nature causes to grow there. There are not many parts of this *bush-veldt* where the trees are fine, owing to the constantly-recurring bush-fires; but the *bush-veldt* of Zoutpansberg, which is called the Wood-bush, produces fine timber, and steam saw-mills have been established there lately. Along that part of the Crocodile River which runs through the *bush-veldt* there are some large trees, and I believe in the *bush-veldt*, bordering the Swazee country, trees of good size are also plentiful. The *bush-veldt* generally has few Boer houses in it, although it is divided into farms, whose proprietors live elsewhere in summer, leaving their possessions there either tenantless or tenanted only by *kaffirs*. In winter, however, they trek there with their flocks and herds, also generally with their families, and then the *bush-veldt* is full of waggons and tents.

The Boers greatly enjoy this annual picnic; the men hunting, the women and children sitting and playing about under the trees, and enjoying the verdure, which, to those who live on what is called the high or *Ur-veldt*, a barren but healthy tract of the Transvaal, is a luxury. The *bush-veldt* is fatal to horses during the summer, but is safe for them in winter; and the grass there remaining, as a rule, green under the bushes all through the winter, the oxen and sheep have nice feeding, whereas in the other parts of the Transvaal the grass is either long, hard, and dry, or burnt off by the grass-fires There are, however, great drawbacks to going every year to the *bush-veldt*. Poisonous herbs grow there, one of which is fatal to sheep, the other to oxen. It is easy to lose animals in the thick bush, and when lost they are liable to fall a prey to wild beasts. It is also difficult to keep the herds of different owners separate, and hence the disease called "lung-sick" (which is contagious amongst cattle) often does much damage; whilst a long pod which grows on one sort of thorn-tree has a poisonous effect on cattle that eat it, lowering their condition, and sometimes even killing them.

Many also of the farmers live at a great distance from the *bush-veldt*, and the long journey tells against their animals. On the other hand, if cattle and sheep are to be kept in the higher parts of the Transvaal in the winter, good shelter for them must be erected, and hay and other food laid by for them. This would necessitate outlay and trouble, both things that a Boer detests. He and his wife are so accustomed to the detestable jolting and discomfort of a waggon that they think nothing of the long journey; so much accustomed to the higgledy-piggledy arrangements in their cabins, or small houses, that a tent is far preferable—and indeed a tent can be most comfortable. But the idea of cutting grass for winter fodder, or growing turnips or mangel-wurzel! They would stand and laugh a broad he-haw at such an idea in most cases, only a few being sufficiently enlightened to confess it might be well to carry it out. Their plan is to put a match in the grass when it is dry, to burn it and get rid of it, so that the fresh grass may sprout, and trek to the *bush-veldt*. Grass-fires are very dangerous. Waggons, stock, and dwelling-houses are sometimes destroyed by them; but then it is only sometimes, so what does it matter?

The result of this trekking to the *bush-veldt* is, that for about six months in the year milk cannot be got except in the *bush-veldt*; and the same may be said of butter, for the Boers make butter so badly that it will not keep. They do not, besides, make much, and cheese they never make. In Pretoria milk sells readily at a shilling a bottle in the winter, and butter sometimes runs up to four, or even five shillings a pound; three shillings is considered a moderate price.

Even at the best of times, in this great pasture country (for, as a whole, the Transvaal is that) the cows give very little milk. I have seen over twenty cows give about two buckets when they were in full milk! It is usually said that the cows of this country are bad milkers, and only good for breeding oxen; but it strikes me that even good cows, treated as they are here, would soon become bad. Exposed constantly to the weather, whatever it may be, every night driven into an open *kraal*, sometimes knee-deep in mud, with their calves left close to them all night, only kept from sucking by a barrier of thorn bushes, or a few poles, or at best a stone wall, by which a division is made in the big *kraal*; sometimes trying all night to break through to them; never given any food but grass—what can be expected from them? Boers, too, will assure you that no cow will give milk unless her calf is first allowed to suck, and that if the calf dies she will run dry. Like many other things in this country, a little good management would set it to rights.

Why Mr. Higgins sent his cattle to the *bush-veldt* I really don't know, for he said himself the journey was bad for them, and that they could get as good eating in the *kloofs* (or ravines) on his property as they could anywhere, instancing the fact that the cattle belonging to his *kraal-kaffirs*, that grazed about the mountains in the winter, looked better than his did when they returned from the *bush-veldt*. However, he had sent them under the care of the Nell family as soon as his waggons came up from Natal, leaving only one span of oxen to do the farm work, and one fine ox that was too sick to walk, at Surprise, and now he prepared to follow them. His father and mother had gone before, leaving Alice and Ada at Surprise, and we once more settled down in our quiet life.

Before going farther, allow me to introduce the Nell family. It consisted of a hulking black-bearded father; of a stout garrulous mother, who had unlimited powers of invention, and who could speak a little English; then followed two big sons, and a whole bevy of little boys and girls, ending with an infant in arms. Krishian (I spell as pronounced—I believe his name is Christian) was a young gentleman who wished to be elegant. Whenever he got any money by working—an occupation he objected to—he spent it in making himself lovely in velvet coats, &c., occasionally investing in that most perilous possession in the Transvaal, a horse, but when he had one he took no care of it. As may be imagined, the ups and downs of this young man were frequent. The second son, Dahl—I don't know what his real name was, Dahl being, I heard, his mother's abbreviation of darling—was a big hulking fellow with a baby's face, and the most wonderful talent for romancing I ever met with or heard of, except in Lever's creation of "Potts" in *A Day's Ride*. He was a better fellow by far than Krishian, although dirtier, and worse to shake hands with.

Of the younger members of the family I have no distinct knowledge; to hear their names, you would have thought they were a family of pups. There were Tic, and Tol, and Toss, besides others. The father and mother had come from the old colony, where they had had, and lost, money, and in consequence considered themselves something better than those of their neighbours who were as poor as they, but they let their children, big and little, be on terms of equality with the *urlams kaffirs*.

There was a small one-roomed cabin, situated at the lower end of Mr. Higgins's property, originally built by William Sturton, who, like his brother Arthur, had married a Miss Higgins. He had built it for himself and his wife, before he hired a farm in the valley near to his brother, and since then the cabin had remained tenantless. Just before Mr. Higgins went to Natal, Krishian and Dahl had asked to be allowed to occupy this eligible residence, and to till some ground near to it, in return for their services on the farm. Mr. Higgins had consented, saying, however, that they must come alone! He had had previous and disagreeable knowledge of the whole family as tenants.

"You will see that the whole troop will come so soon as you go away," Mrs. Higgins had said.

"Then I will send them packing, when I come back," replied her husband, causing Mrs. Higgins to laugh in a way that told me she doubted his ferocity. True enough, two days after Mr. Higgins's departure, a waggon was seen depositing the whole family and their baggage at the cabin. How they all managed to pack into that diminutive abode, Heaven only knows! but houses here are wonderfully elastic. They commenced tilling some adjoining ground in a leisurely manner, made themselves very much at home at Surprise in a cringing sort of way, and did as little as possible. On Mr. Higgins's return no change was made; he, an over-easy master for *kaffirs*, was not likely to be less so for people of white race.

Mrs. Nell would sometimes pay a day's visit at Surprise, where her conversation was a mixture of flattery and gossip; she knew everything about everybody, and her curiosity was unbounded. She would follow Mrs. Higgins about as she did her household work, sitting down in the nearest chair and pouring forth a stream of talk. She and her husband were very anxious for Mr. Higgins to adopt one of their small fry, a diminutive but perfect specimen of a Dutchman—chubby, stolid, with little knickerbockers, short jacket, and broad hat, all complete, only wanting a pipe to be quite perfect. I don't know whether he was Tic, Toss, or Tol, but anyhow his parents, whilst giving him an excellent character, were anxious to part with him, partly, they averred on account of his own surprising attachment to Mr. Higgins; Mrs. Higgins, however, resolutely rejected this handsome present. Dahl Nell often favoured Surprise by a short visit, generally asking for a loan of something, which it was difficult to get back again, and enlivening his conversation by stories of doubtful veracity.

Once he gave a touching description of the death of an acquaintance of the Higginses, who was in robust health at the time; but his grandest flight of fancy, that I ever heard of, was reserved for a farmer who lived at some distance. Chancing to meet this individual, the baby-faced Dahl recounted to him that he had been fortunate enough to obtain from old Mr. Higgins the loan of his span of oxen, that he had also got a waggon, and was prepared to ride transport to the Diamond Fields, familiarly called the "Fields." High prices were being given for produce there at the time, and transport was also high, and many a young man's dream was to be able to get a span and a waggon to take loads there. I suppose Dahl as he had trudged along on foot to where he met the farmer, had dreamed a pleasant daydream of how at some future time he might make enough money to afford himself a horse. The farmer pricked up his ears, and the affair ended by a bargain being struck for Dahl to take a load for him to the Fields. How Master Nell got out of his contract I don't know, but as he had no means of fulfilling it he must have got out of it somehow, probably scathlessly, for the Nell family seemed to have a knack of wriggling out of difficulties in safety.

Why Mr. Higgins trusted his valuable cattle to go to the *bush-veldt* under the care of these people I can't say, but the Nell family were delighted to be so trusted. They would have milk all the winter, could make butter, and sell it afterwards if they chose to take the trouble of putting it in jars, or if not eat it themselves; they could have meat too, which was a luxury to them, for they could easily invent a story to account for the death of an animal; and then they were paid into the bargain. They had got an old tent-waggon and departed happy, and by the time Mr. Higgins came up to them had killed a cow. They said she had gone blind! they swore she had—so blind that she could not see where to walk; but it was strange that the *kaffirs* with them had been unable to detect her inability to distinguish surrounding objects. I forgot to mention that amongst other talents Mrs. Nell possessed that great female accomplishment of being able to weep to order, and this always settled the matter with Mr. Higgins.

Chapter 11

I have a pleasant remembrance of winter at Surprise—the bright crisp morning air as I walked through the hoar-frost to the stable, there to warm my hands by cleaning Eclipse; the cheery breakfast of bread and mutton, or sometimes eggs, occasionally pleasantly diversified by hot scones, and which my exercise always caused me to enjoy, although I confess I missed the milk; then lessons. I don't maintain that they were always pleasant—that would be impossible; and the school-room—a bare room, with the rafters showing overhead, a mud floor, and with a big deal table, two forms, one chair, and a big packing-case for furniture—was sometimes bitterly cold; but Mrs. Higgins would bring, or send us in, little iron dishes of hot embers to warm our toes, and we wrapped ourselves up in all sorts of jackets and shawls. Rough would curl up in my lap and act muff; and so we pulled through, and except when little Sarah's grief at not being able to have a good romp instead of saying lessons, became overwhelming, we used to be quite merry over our spelling-books, geography, &c.

Dinner of mutton, pumpkin, potatoes, and sometimes crushed mealies, made a diversion; and then afternoon tea, when Mrs. Higgins generally managed to get an egg to beat up in my tea, and make a substitute for milk. I used to enjoy that tea, I lolling on the table—having been sitting too long for standing not to appear preferable to sitting to me; Mrs. Higgins, always with some work in her hands, sitting on the sofa; and the children running about the room chattering, as children always do when let out of school. The singing lesson generally came after; and then I hastened off to catch Eclipse (for although he would let himself be driven up towards the house by the little *kaffirs*, he would not let himself be caught except by me) and take him to the stable, to give him his evening feed and bed him up.

Just before starting for the *bush-veldt*, Mr. Higgins (having sent the *kaffir* Jonas away) had given me his house as a stable for Eclipse, but before that, I used to feed him outside the old stable under the big *syringa*-trees of an evening, and many a pretty Rembrandt-looking group have I seen of the *kaffirs*, little and big, sitting round this evening fire, which threw fitful lights on the trunks of the surrounding bushes and trees, and on the long grass, also on elf-like little figures dancing some uncouth *kaffir* dance, and chanting some equally uncouth Boer ditty, interrupted by peals of ringing laughter as one or the other played some trick off on his or her companions. Great amongst the trick players were little Sarah (who, free from school, was wild with spirits) and Fiervaree the small groom. Then to walk to the house, and see the light of the bright wood fire in the drawing-room gleaming through the darkness, and know how cosy it would be that evening after our supper of bread and tea, when we would all draw round the fire, and with the three youngest girls curled up on the ground, or sitting in the big fireplace, a petition would be put up by a chorus of young voices for a story, and I had to recall old German *Mährchen* and eastern *Arabian Nights,* and make De la Motte Fouqué's charming "Undine" come forth from the treasury of my memory, to delight these pretty little Africanders, who hung on my words as if I had been a veritable Scheherazade.

There were two additions to our family always in the room; these I had forgotten to mention. One was a *dassy*, or rock rabbit, a round furry little beast, guiltless of a tail, and with the brightest eyes, and the sharpest of white teeth, which it was not slow to use. It was still quite young, but when annoyed was very fierce, and would fly at anyone it fancied meant to offend it, as at any dog or horse that in any way molested it, making a queer snapping noise, and curling up its little upper lip in a savage manner that seemed quite preposterous in such a soft little furry beast. It was wonderfully active, and although its legs were almost too short to be visible, and it had no neck to speak of, and was besides as fat as a plump partridge, it thought nothing of taking the most prodigious jumps up, down, or sideways.

The mischief this little animal delighted in was something wonderful. It had a great taste for flowers; roses it particularly affected; and whether it saw one in a girl's hair, or in a vase on a high chimneypiece, was quite immaterial to it. To jump from the floor on the young lady's shoulder and seize its prey, or to spend a whole afternoon in practising jumps at the chimneypiece, was the same to Master Dassy. He always got the rose in the end. And if there was not a rose, he would demolish whatever in the flower line there was. The numbers of vases full of water that small animal overturned was wonderful; but at times he would become the victim of an insane desire to break something. Once he made up his mind to break a very pretty glass vase. He showed his intention early in the morning, and in spite of the vase being repeatedly placed in positions that were supposed to be safe from his assaults, it was broken before evening.

We were at supper when we heard the crash, and arrived in the drawing-room just in time to see Master Dassy scuttling away, his little black eyes dancing with glee, and the vase, broken in pieces, lying on the floor. At meal-times Dassy was great. He would make one spring from the sofa to the table, and once there he would put one little paw on the side of a dish, and tilt up the cover with his little snub nose, look what was inside, and if he liked it nibble a little, if not put down the cover and go to another dish. I have often looked at him sitting in the middle of the table eating alternately from four dishes. If he was interfered with, he would charge at the offender, barking, and showing his teeth, and if he could not bite his enemy, he would at least fasten on and worry his sleeve. If there was nothing else to eat he would nibble hair or wool mats, and window blinds, sometimes even he would sit on my shoulder and nibble my hair. He and Rough were great friends, and he would curl up on Rough's back, or between his paws, and look exquisitely comfortable. Dassy was a Sybarite.

His slumbers were not to be disturbed with impunity. He generally slept in his master and mistress's bed, and would bite them if they, in moving, interfered with him. In the morning he would have his early coffee, and if it were not given quickly to him in a saucer, he would jump up and upset the cup; then he would hop up to the window, and pop his nose through a hole in one of the panes to try what the temperature was, and if it was cold he would retreat to bed again. There was a thin muslin curtain hung over the lower part of the window which interfered a little with him, so one day he nibbled it away exactly over where it had acted as a curtain to his loop-hole. He was a most engaging little animal; and when at last he fell sick, and his appetite failing, waxed thin, and at last so feeble that he could hardly move, his little face and ways were most touching. He would still try to eat a rose, and if he saw one, would look first at it, and then at anyone who happened to be near him, imploringly.

A few nights before he died I had occasion to go into the kitchen after the family were in bed. Dassy was curled up in the still warm ashes of the fire, and as I came in I was struck by the mute appeal in his eyes. I thought he might want something to drink, and brought water and then milk to him; but he would not touch either, but still looked imploringly at me. I stroked the poor little back, now quite sharp and bony, and puzzled my brains as to what the little thing could want. Suddenly he crawled over to a small piece of half-burnt wood, and took it up, then looked straight at me, nibbled it and put it down. I saw then what he wanted, and got him food, which he ate greedily. I had not thought of it before, for he had persistently refused food for days. During the winter, however, Dassy was still well and mischievous, and Fido, Roughy, the two cats, Dassy, and a little prairie-dog, or *meerkat*, formed members of our evening party.

The *meerkat*, an animal I had often seen in the Zoological Gardens, was even funnier than the *dassy*. With its long black bushy tail, long sharp nose, and bead-like eyes, it looked as if it would be the more active of the two. But the *dassy* beat it hollow in jumping. *Meerkat*, however, would canter along as quick as a horse, and many a time has he even outrun Eclipse as he cantered; when, jumping up on a convenient ant-heap, this little piece of absurdity would stand bolt upright, balancing himself on his tail, and with his fore paws crossed, and his head turning from side to side, would survey his surroundings with the greatest complacency, until the horse, being abreast of him, he would jump down, and with his tail erect make off to the next nearest ant-heap. Sometimes he would lie on his back propped against a stone, with his fore paws crossed, his tail turned up between his hind legs, head thrown backwards, and his eyes cast up in a most sentimental manner.

Really, however, he cast up his eyes to keep a sharp look-out for hawks, of which he was terribly afraid. At other times he would play hide and seek with Dassy, or throwing one fore paw round the cat's neck, sit for half an hour examining her fur in the way monkeys do, or he would compose himself to sleep, leaning back cross-pawed in the chimney corner, or perhaps, after vain efforts at keeping in an absolutely erect position poised on his tail in front of the fire, and after sundry bobs and nods and sudden awakings, accompanied with those demonstrations of great wakefulness which I have so frequently observed and practised during sermon-times in my youthful days, he would suddenly collapse into a little furry ball, and sleep so soundly that he would emit little snores and let himself be handled without awaking. He was as mischievous as Dassy, only in a different way, and having been accustomed in his early youth to follow the fashion of *meerkats* and live in a hole, he was never tired of grubbing, either in or out of doors.

Sometimes our evening's amusements were diversified by making pancakes, or by playing games, such as magic music and friar's ground; and sometimes the children would give me a good laugh by chasing old Khrid as she went about her duties in the kitchen, carrying a lighted candle in a pewter candlestick poised on her head.

Occasionally a chance visitor from the outer world would drop in unexpectedly—strangers travelling through the country for the first time, or people out for a day or two from Pretoria, or sometimes people of the country travelling on business. Whatever or whoever they were, they met with genial hospitality at Surprise. Then, at other times, Jimmy would come up to pay a visit on Sunday, one of the girls and I would ride down to the valley, or I would ride over to the farmhouse where the post was left, for letters.

One hideous episode alone, broke the pleasant monotony of this time. One night I was awakened by a loud tapping at my door and Mrs. Higgins's voice calling me. I jumped up in a fright, thinking that one of the children must be ill, but was glad to hear that it was only a *kaffir* child, the little daughter of a certain Andreas, who lived in a small separate *kraal* on Mr. Higgins's estate. Andreas affected to be something better than the usual *kraal kaffirs*, but his wife was a mere savage, dressed in skins and blankets, and his children ran about either naked or with only a narrow girdle on. Mrs. Higgins took me into the kitchen, where I saw Andreas with the little girl squatted on the floor, and the mother with a baby in her arms standing close by. After examining the child I felt convinced that she had taken poison some vegetable poison; I could not say what.

The history told by her father, and which, owing to my still imperfect knowledge of Dutch, had to be interpreted to me by an old Englishman who was building a stone cattle-*kraal* at Surprise, and who had been aroused from his sleep in the lumber-room by these late visitors, was this. The mother had gone a short time before to a neighbouring *kraal* where the family of Andreas's brother's wife lived. She had taken the girl with her, and from the day she returned she had been ailing. The father seemed greatly distressed; the mother did not seem in the least interested. After doing what I could for the child and leaving the kitchen, I communicated my opinion as to the cause of the illness to Mrs. Higgins. She then reminded me that this very Andreas, shortly after my arrival at Surprise, had been accused of poisoning his brother, Roykraal by name, having administered a certain poison to him which had caused him to go mad.

That Roykraal, a fine lad not long married, had gone raving mad for a time, and had since remained in a half mad state, whilst he looked quite old, was certain. He had deserted his wife, and generally wandered about talking nonsense to himself. Andreas had been accused before the captain or chief of his tribe, but the charge had fallen through in some way. I remembered too that Mrs. Higgins had, at the time, said that Roykraal's people would take revenge. I also remembered that a short time before, Andreas and his wife had had a desperate disagreement, ending by Mrs. Andreas running away to her father across the mountain. This is a usual form of husband-bullying among the *kaffirs*. Girls are sold high amongst these people, an attractive and active girl fetching a considerable price in cattle for a wife. She has to work hard afterwards, for the cultivation of the fields is done principally by the women; but if her husband displeases her she walks off to her old home; and as it is considered a great disgrace to a man for his wife to be in her father's *kraal*, he generally buys her back, paying the father one or more head of cattle to restore her.

Andreas had bought his better half back again, after grieving over her departure for some days; but shortly after she had betaken herself for a visit to the *kraal* of the father of Roykraal's wife, and the eldest of Andreas's children, and his favourite, was ill since then. It struck me as strange that Mrs. Andreas, who was of course well aware of the vindictiveness of her own race, should have chosen Mrs. Roykraal's *kraal* as a place to make an excursion to with her children. I watched the child until early morning, then went to have some sleep. When I saw her later, although still weak and at times light-headed, she could eat with relish; and as it is not pleasant to nurse anyone, especially a dirty *kaffir*, in one's kitchen, I agreed with Mrs. Higgins that the child might be taken to her home. We cautioned the parents that they must not leave her alone a minute.

The day passed as usual. I was very sleepy in the evening and went to bed early. I always slept with my window open, and Rough always lay curled up at the foot of my bed. Some way on in the night I was startled by his furious barking, and jumping up, I saw a black head protruded inside of my window, whilst its owner said, in a frightened voice, that Andreas's child was dying, and that he had brought it. I let the people into the kitchen, and called Mrs. Higgins. It was a frightful scene. The child was in the most raving delirium I ever saw, convulsed in a most horrible manner, and her howls were unearthly, interrupted, every now and then, by the most touching appeals to her father—touching because of the sound of her voice and her action. Her own father could not understand what she said. He had brought her tied on his back, which she had lacerated with her nails and teeth.

The poor fellow had no thought for himself, but with anguish in his face and voice he besought me to save his child. I asked if he had remained all day with the girl; he answered that he had been obliged to go away once or twice, but that the mother had remained with her. That more poison had been administered was, however, certain. I looked at the mother; she was squatted in the chimney corner, rolled up in two blankets, and was looking at her daughter's writhings with a stolid curiosity. Then a horrid suspicion crossed my mind.

The child, after taking some medicine, became quiet, but soon began to get deadly cold. We got all the blankets we could to roll round her, and put hot bricks to her feet and the calves of her legs. The mother never moved. At last, the child still being cold, I ordered Andreas to take one of the blankets off his wife, as she was warm enough with one, sitting as she was by the fire. The patient was just getting a little warmer, and I had turned away from her for a few minutes, when I noticed that the mother moved and began to arrange the blankets round her child. I watched her to see what she was going to do, and was horrified to see that she pulled her own blanket out, uncovering the child, and proceeded to roll it round herself, saying, it was explained to me, that she was sure the girl was dying, and that she could not remain, but was going home.

It struck me that Andreas was afraid of the woman; but I pulled her blanket off somewhat ungently, and again rolled it round the child, telling the woman that she might go without it if she chose; but she crouched up again by the fire. The father again made a passionate appeal to me to save the little girl's life; and Mrs. Higgins having come into the kitchen, I asked her to tell him that I was doing all I could, but that I was combating no disease, but poison, and that it was a poison which I had not the proper means at hand to combat successfully. The wretched man wrung his hands. "Oh!" he exclaimed wildly, "if I could but get to —— (mentioning a *kaffir* name) behind the mountain, he would save her," Saul, the driver, who was standing close by Mrs. Higgins and me, whispered, "That's the man he got the poison for Roykraal from."

I shall never forget that night—the almost dark kitchen, the awe-struck group standing round the child with her father kneeling by her, the witch-like figure of the mother crouched in one corner of the large fireplace, with an impish-looking boy of about twelve—the shepherd—crouched in the opposite one, with a grin on his face, and with his lanky bare arms and legs looking more like a hideous spider than anything else, and the sickening conviction that was growing upon me that the mother was an accomplice to the poisoning!

Towards morning I had so far succeeded that the child was warm, and appeared to be sleeping naturally. I felt quite worn out, and not wishing to disturb the children's routine by sleeping the next day, I told the father to call me so soon as the little girl should awake, and then I lay down on my bed in my clothes. It was already dawning, and it was still very early morning when I awoke. I got up and hastened to the kitchen. All but the elf-like *kaffir* boy were gone; he, as usual, was making early coffee.

He told me that at break of day, the mother had insisted upon removing the child to the old stable near the garden. He said the child had seemed to him better. I drank the coffee, and Mrs. Higgins sent a boy to ask how the patient was. The answer came back that the child was again in convulsions; but on seeing me preparing to go, the boy said it was useless—that as he left, the woman, regardless of Andreas, had rolled her child tight up in a blanket, and had started for her *kraal* with her burden on her back. It was evidently a hopeless case. In the afternoon I rode down to the *kraal*, two small huts in a little yard enclosed with reeds. The yard was lined with women, squatting on the ground and talking, the mother amongst them.

In the principal hut Andreas was seated on the ground, holding his little girl in his arms. She was in a stupor, which I saw at once was the precursor of death; several *kraal kaffirs* were squatted round; one of them, called Old Jas, a relation of Roykraal, with a most diabolical grin on his face. The child died that evening, and amidst much shrieking of the women, amongst whom the mother distinguished herself, was buried in her father's little cattle-*kraal*—the place of honour amongst *kaffirs*—and the huts were deserted as being ill-omened, Andreas and his family going to the big *kraal*.

No farther notice was taken of the matter, but I heard various stories of *kaffirs* having poisoned even white people's children in revenge, which, together with what I had seen, finished the disgust which I already felt for *kaffirs* as a nation. The men who knew the *kaffirs* best, and to whom I mentioned my conviction of the woman's guilt, said they had no doubt that I was right in my conclusions; that *kaffir* women were quite capable of poisoning their own children in revenge upon their husbands.

CHAPTER 12

Mr. Higgins returned from the *bush-veldt* ill-content with the management of the Nell family, but thinking that he had set them on the right path. We had hoped for a little butter, but none was sent. Things went on in much the same way after his return, with the exception that the story-telling came to an end, except when one of the children did not feel well and went to bed early, getting me to sit by the bed-side, or on the bed, and recount tales. I rather think there was a good deal of "foxing" done on little Sarah's part: Augusta never "foxed" about anything.

It was mid-winter, and the grass-fires were wonderful and terrible to look at, as they swept along before the wind. Of course it depends on the strength of the wind whether they 'are dangerous or not, and it has always appeared strange to me how little the knowledge that the wind may rise or veer in a minute, seems to trouble the farmers. One evening I was going to bed, when I observed the whole sky ablaze from an evidently large fire at the other side of that part of the mountain which formed a spur in front of my window. The trees clothing the mountain side, and the magnificent precipice at its top, stood out in effective relief against the flame-coloured masses of smoke which were rolling, not towards Surprise, but, driven by the south wind northward over the mountain. The danger, so long as the wind remained steady, was not to us, for although the lurid light seemed near, I knew the fire could not even have reached the confines of Mr. Higgins's property. However, I called him—he had not yet gone to bed—and showed him the fire.

"It is far off," he said; "don't be frightened, the wind is not blowing this way,"

"But suppose it changes in the night?" said I.

"Oh, it won't change," he answered, laughing, and returned quietly to his rest.

I was convinced Mr. Higgins was not infallible about the wind, and I knew that Eclipse was shut up in a house surrounded by such long grass that it nearly reached to the thatched roof, so I opened my window wide, and resolved to wake several times during the night; this I can do when I choose. The first time I awoke the fire was no closer, it was being slowly driven northward; the second time the wind had changed, evidently only a short time before I awoke (it is possible its change woke me, for there was a slight breeze blowing into my room), and the smoke was pouring over the spur in the direction of the house. I had lain down in some of my clothes in case of emergency, and I immediately hastened through the dressing-room to Mr. Higgins's room, and tapping at the door told him of the change of wind. I had awakened and startled Harriet Sturton and the children, who were sleeping on the floor in the drawing-room.

By the time I regained my room the flames could be seen, dancing amongst the foliage along the top of the spur. I now dressed; and taking a bridle in my hand, I went down to Eclipse's stable, so that in case of the wind rising I might be able to get him out of it and into safety quickly. I did not go in, but waited and watched the scene. It was impressive. The moon was a little past the full, and shed her light on all around; to the north-west she was eclipsed by the fire, that came steadily on, curling round the foot of the precipice, whose projecting crags it lit up fitfully, with its many tongues licking up the long grass, and shooting along the stems of the trees and amongst their branches, until they, instead of standing out black against a lurid background, looked like enormous torches. It came closer and closer, till I could not only feel its hot breath, but could hear the roar of the flames and the crackling of the grass and bushes; then at last some *kaffirs* came from the houses beyond the dam, and extinguished the fire by beating it down with big branches, It broke out again during the day, however; and the next evening, as I was riding back alone from a visit to the valley, I saw its red serpent-like track creeping up and across the mountain.

I was beginning to understand the Boer language now, and even to talk it, having practised it with the little *kaffirs* who used to congregate round me morning and evening while I was attending to my horse. These *impromptu* lessons had become rarer since I had a separate stable for Eclipse, still I had occasional visitors even there. Once I remember a young *kaffir*, the very imp who had reminded me of an ugly spider the night of the Andreas tragedy, standing for a long time, lolling through one of the little windows of the stable, looking at me while I turned up the bedding and cleaned the stall after I had turned Eclipse out; for, strange to say, I had vainly offered a shilling a week to any boy who would do this for me. All were willing to take the shilling, but none would do the work as I chose it to be done, a very small cleaning of a stable going a long way in the Transvaal. The above-mentioned young gentleman watched me with great interest for some time, and I said nothing to him, just to see what was coming (I knew it would not be an offer of assistance), then, turning to a small girl who came to tell me that breakfast was ready, he observed with great unction, "No; thus *I* would never work for a horse."

I was beginning to think that it was time for me to look about for a farm, as I had not intended to remain more than one year as a governess. I had learned a good deal in various ways, too, during the past months, as much as, without neglecting my duties, I should ever learn, and hence, having seen some advertisements in the *Volkstem* and *Argus* which looked promising, and hearing that Arthur Sturton with his wife and Jimmy were going to Pretoria for the races in September, and would take their waggon, I asked leave to go too, as I should be able to send up a dress in their waggon and not be entirely dependent on my habit, as I must be in the event of riding up alone. Mr. Higgins was going to the races also, and upon my getting the desired permission, it was agreed that Mrs. Higgins and the children should accompany him.

Only two events that occurred between Mr. Higgins's return and our going to Pretoria have left any particular impression on my mind, in addition to that made by the fire. The first was the return of the cattle from the *bush-veldt* in the early spring, very shortly before we started. It was a beautiful afternoon when the little *kaffirs* came running with the news that the herd was in sight, but a long way off. We all turned out, lessons being hurried on in honour of the occasion, to see them come up. And a pretty sight it was; the cows, with their calves, born in the *bush-veldt*, trotting beside them, the sturdy oxen, and the frisky young cattle, all coming in a long line across the fresh young grass of the hillside and under the thorn-trees, bellowing a welcome to their old home, and the evening sun throwing their shadows far along the ground.

They no longer found their poor old companion who had been too ill to follow them to the *bush-veldt*. He had got better, and had almost weathered out the winter, but after being left for a few nights of bitter cold rain without any covering, shivering in the *kraal*, into which from old habit he used to put himself at night, he one morning tottered over to the waggon he used to draw, and fell dead beside the *disselboom*, his old place when trekking. I was present when the *kaffirs* skinned and opened the carcass, preparatory to eating it. The poor ox—a valuable one, who, but a short time before he got ill, had, with his mate, prevented the waggon being overturned, by their intelligence in holding back when the rest of the oxen were taking it into danger—died simply of neglected inflammation of the lungs.

The second event was the visit of the Bishop of Pretoria, who came and went on a jolly and evidently petted pony. He confirmed the three eldest girls, also old Mr. and Mrs. Higgins; and I shall never forget the singularly impressive sight of this world-worn couple, kneeling beside their two young daughters and their fair-haired grandchild in the drawing-room at Surprise, and answering from their careworn hearts that they steadfastly believed in that religion from which they had drawn comfort in all their many troubles, whilst the children's fresh lips repeated the same words, without even an idea of what steadfast belief meant.

We used to have occasional religious services in the drawing-room, Mr. Richardson coming from Rustemberg twice, riding; and then a young Englishman (not in holy orders), who was tutor to the children of an English Africander farmer at some distance, being entrusted by the bishop with the spiritual care of the district in which Surprise was the largest farmhouse. On these occasions old Mr. and Mrs. Higgins and the Sturtons, who lived in the valley, and sometimes John or James Higgins and family, would be our guests, also Jimmy; and while I played the piano (for owing to my lameness I could not play the harmonium), the young people sang the hymns. The young amateur clergyman was a very amusing person, and used to convulse us with laughter at his absurd anecdotes of his life at a Boer's where he had at first been tutor. He certainly did not seem to have slept on roses there. Besides being tutor in the English Africander's family, he had to help with a store and mill; at last he found his duties too onerous, and all attempt at church services ceased.

Chapter 13

There were many preparations to be made for going to Pretoria—dresses to be made for the children, and biscuits baked for us all, for we were to live in the waggon whilst there—and the children were in great glee. At last the morning came; the waggon was packed; bedding, and boxes, and provisions, were all put in, and lastly Mrs. Higgins and her children. Then the waggon started, leaving Mr. Higgins and me to follow on horseback. We gave them a fair start; and, leaving the old Englishman who had been building the new stone *kraal*, in charge of the place, and of the dogs and other pet beasts, who all had to be shut up until we were gone, and having locked up the front part of the house, we mounted our horses and followed.

We came up with the waggon about half way to Moy-plas, outspanned just across a deep *spruit*. The travellers were having a tea-dinner, so we off-saddled and enjoyed it with them; then leaving them once more, we rode on. For some distance the road was uninteresting, its chief advantage being that it was good for cantering; but as we neared Moy-plas and crossed the tributary of the Crocodile River, which I had previously crossed when riding to Fahl-plas, we came to a farm which made a great impression upon me. Stretching right across the valley and to the top of the ranges on either side, with water from two tributaries of the Crocodile irrigating it, with its broad lands, magnificent orchard, its outbuildings, and its small but trim farmhouse, it looked the perfection of a Boer farm, and made one picture to oneself what it might be if it were an English one.

The owner of this fine property—a tall, gaunt woman with a pleasant face, the widow of three husbands—was standing by the gate of the little yard in front of her house, a yard trim as a room, with oleander and other trees round it, and shut in by a low whitewashed wall. She received us cheerily, looked inquisitively at me when Mr. Higgins introduced me as his children's schoolmistress, told us that Arthur Sturton's waggon had passed, that he had paid her a visit with Jimmy, and that she thought Jimmy was rude because he did not shake hands all round, but she was delighted at my attempts to talk Dutch, and told me I must pay her another visit. She was surrounded by children of various ages, and all related to her in some way, whose parents lived in some of the buildings which looked like barns. This old lady was a remarkable woman. Hospitable and free-handed to all, of whatever nation they might be, she was yet a frugal manager. She and her first husband had started in life with a waggon and a span of oxen.

I don't know what sort of man he was, but she was a host in herself. If her oxen stuck in a difficult drift, she would tuck up her petticoats, pull off her boots, and leaping from the waggon take the whip from her *kaffir* and drive the team through herself. If labour was scarce at harvest time, or when water had to be led on the lands, she thought nothing of doing the necessary work, but she attended to her household duties withal. She had never allowed her children to take any part in politics, and I don't think any one exactly knew what she thought of British rule. Like all Boer women and men, she regarded husbands and wives as articles so necessary to household comfort that no time must be lost in replacing them when lost; still she was of opinion that there was some limitation as to age in the matter, and I heard a delightful story about her reception of a suitor after the demise of No. 3.

Mr. Higgins was riding home from Pretoria one day when he met a young Boer, so magnificently got up that he knew he must be going a-courting; for Boers array themselves splendidly, and pay great attention on such occasions to the quality and colour of their saddlecloths, a very favourite sort being a large-patterned *drugget* with much green and red in it, and with a broad yellow woollen fringe. The young Boer seemed disconcerted when Mr.' Higgins asked him where he was going, and still more so when Mr. Higgins playfully inquired whether the fair one was Lettie Matersen. This aroused Mr. Higgins's suspicions. Shortly after he had occasion to pass by Mrs. Matersen's farm, and, as usual, went in to pay a visit. He asked if she had lately seen —— (mentioning the young man's name). "Yes," she said, "he had been there;" and then went on to tell how the unfortunate individual had been dealt with by her.

He had come to pay a visit, and the old lady instantly saw through his motives. She tormented him with questions as to whom he was going a-courting to, and as she knew all her neighbours, soon forced him into a corner by making him confess it was to none of them he was bound. She was deaf to his assertion that he was searching for a lost ox (a favourite excuse with a would-be suitor), although he described all its marks; and at last when she extorted from him that she was the object of his hopes and fears, she turned sharp on him with "Ah, ah! You young idiot. You have come a-courting of my farm, have you," &c., &c., until she drove him frantic from the house.

We reached Moy-plas as the sun was beginning to get low, and found the Sturtons' and old Mr. Higgins's waggons there already—for Alice and Ada had persuaded the old people to take them to the races.

I must try to describe Moy-plas. It was a large, irregular-shaped cottage, whitewashed and thatched, and it looked more like an English farmhouse than any place I had seen in the Transvaal. It was approached by a road branching a little off the highway to Pretoria, and the back of the house was turned to this road and to the outbuildings, which partially enclosed the sheep and goat *kraal*. At each side of these were sheds for protecting the animals in bad weather. The front of the house opened on a verandah, from which a step led to a yard like Mrs. Matersen's, this in its turn opened on a strip of grass, with a well-kept path leading to a little bridge across the broad water-furrow (like a rivulet), and into a trim garden and orchard, where you might walk under rows of big orange and lemon trees, and along hedges of figs, pomegranates, and quinces. There were vines, too, kept low and trim, and lots of brandy was made at Moy-plas. Inside, the idea of an English farmhouse was suggested by the wooden ceilings, with their supporting rafters, painted and polished, and the ample cupboards. One apartment, the dining-room, was papered with prints cut from the *Illustrated News*; many of them recalled the ghosts of former days to me, in a manner that was almost pleasant from the sense of strangeness that it awakened in me.

Old Mr. and Mrs. Sturton were already at Pretoria, having gone there on account of Mr. Sturton's illness, and Harriet with her elder sister Maria, and her younger Clara, were to follow them in Arthur Sturton's waggon. The youngest girl, Lettie, was at Pretoria. Two sons—Percy, a jolly young fellow with a ferocious beard, and Augustus, who was still a child—were to be left in charge of the farm, which, like Mrs. Matersen's, stretched from the top of the Magaliesberg across the valley to the top of the opposite range. William and Alfred, the two remaining sons, were the one on his farm, the other at school near Fahl-plas, his tutor being the amateur clergyman.

During the afternoon two rakish-looking men rode up, and were introduced to me as I sat under the verandah: they, too, were going to the races. One was an Englishman I had often heard of, Charlie Harris; the other, a Boer, whom, however, I took for an Englishman, as he spoke English perfectly, and I did not catch his name, Van der Veer, when he was introduced. I must here remark that it is far more the custom to talk of people by their Christian and surname together, than to use the term "Mr." It is very common, indeed, to use the Christian name alone. These individuals did not stay long, not even off-saddling. The Sturtons made me have my meals in the house, but the others cooked beside their waggons, and I had a picnic tea by old Mrs. Higgins's camp fire.

Our waggon came in late, and in the very early dawn it and its occupants, together with Arthur Sturton's and old Mr. Higgins's waggons, and many accompanying waggons laden with forage for the Pretoria market, were got under way. They were to outspan for breakfast immediately after they had crossed the Crocodile. Mr. Higgins, Arthur Sturton, and I, waited for early coffee, and then started after them on horseback, Percy Sturton riding with us so far as the first outspan.

Very pretty the wooded *drift* of the Crocodile looked that morning, the river flowing past it towards the deep cleft through which it winds its way to the back of the Magaliesberg. All but one of the waggons were already outspanned on the opposite side, and the camp fires alight, the ladies and children standing in groups looking down at the one forage waggon which had stuck in the *drift*. I rode on, and Mr. Higgins and Percy Sturton, dismounting and taking the whips, soon drove it through.

We outspanned that evening close to Dasspoort, and within two miles of Pretoria, which lies on the other side of it. The name is derived from the number of *dassies* that used to live in the rocks at either side; none are to be seen now, but the name remains.

The next morning we inspanned early, and Mr. Higgins rode on before the waggons so as to be early on the market with samples of his forage. We all followed in the waggon, Eclipse being led. I thought Dasspoort looked very pretty in the early morning light, the road being cut out of the face of the rock a few feet above the course of the Apis River; and even before we outspanned on the outskirts of the village, I remarked that it had greatly increased in size since I had seen it last, and that a great deal of building was going on.

CHAPTER 14

The great excitement during our stay at Pretoria was the races, but other things, too, made an impression on my mind. First of all, the sleeping in the waggon. Mr. and Mrs. Higgins slept in the back part with little Sarah; a curtain divided them from Augusta and myself; and Sannee made up a sort of bed for herself on a box which stood across the fore part of the waggon, called the waggon-box, from which she had a tendency to roll down on my head in the night. Our washing arrangements were very limited; and camp life, though jolly in its proper place, is a bore on the outskirts of a village, particularly when the village calls itself a city. However, we rubbed along. We found old Mr. Sturton very ill, and the arrangements for taking care of him were such as made my hair stand on end. A bare room had been hired at an enormous rent, in a house whose owners did not trouble themselves much about the illness of their tenant.

A few things had been put in hastily, and there he lay, in danger of his life, with the cooking having to be done in his room, or outside, in a sort of yard, into which the refuse from all the neighbouring houses was thrown. There were no means of keeping the rooms fresh and clean—no comfort which an invalid requires. On the arrival of his daughters another small room (also bare) was hired, and here the girls slept, and sometimes sat, on mattresses spread on the ground; all this discomfort was not caused by want of money, but because the necessary accommodation was not to be had.

I, of course, saw my kind acquaintances again at Pretoria, and then there were the races. These were much better than I expected. The horses looked more up to the mark than I thought they would—the jockeys, also—and the running was not at all bad. Eclipse, remembering his old racing days, I suppose, was in a great state of mind at the first start. I rode with Mr. Higgins to see that, and then we separated, and I presently fell in with Mr. Van-der-veen at the Higgins's waggon, which was drawn up in a line with many other waggons. The scene was characteristic of South Africa—the ox-waggon element predominating—but there were also traps of various kinds drawn up in line, a little grand stand, with the ring close to it—refreshment and other tents, a number of men on horseback, and two women besides myself. Mr. Van-der-veen proposed to go with me to see another start, and told me that one of the horses in this particular race belonged to an old Boer who believed greatly in him.

He said he was glad to see Boers doing this sort of thing—it approached somewhat to civilization—in short, he talked altogether so much as if he had nothing to do with the Boers in general, that I was much surprised when I heard afterwards that he was the son of a Boer. He and I then went to the Edinburgh Hotel, where I had put up my horse during my stay at Pretoria; there we had lunch while the horses had a feed. I had been rather amused at Mr. Van-der-veen proposing this proceeding, although I thought it a very good one.

By the end of the day the male portion of the community were getting very lively, and rows were plentiful. Poor old Mr. Sturton participated unpleasantly in this part of the day's programme, for while the noise outside his window was unceasing, his hosts favoured him with snatches from "Bonnie Dundee," and other ballads, until a late hour; and Mrs. Sturton would not interfere, or allow me to interfere, because she thought it likely that if we did the invalid would be told to march the next morning, in spite both of his illness and the high rent he was paying.

The next day I did not go to the races, as I thought the surroundings of the course would be too lively; and on the third the waggons started on their homeward way. I remained behind, having affairs at Pretoria which, owing to all places of business being shut during the first two days of the races, I had been unable to get through before. I picked up the waggons at their first outspan, and had tea. Mr. Higgins had already arrived on horseback from Pretoria, and before we started James Higgins and his wife, with Alice and Harriett Sturton, in his covered-top cart, drawn by two good horses, came up; and, after a short rest, I started for Moy-plas in their company, but on horseback. Half-way we stopped at a Boer's house, where I was asked to prescribe for the children, who were very ill with whooping-cough; and by night-fall we reached Moy-plas once more. The waggons came in the next morning; and in the afternoon Mr. Higgins, Arthur Sturton, and

I started for home, leaving the rest to follow.

Two events had taken place during our absence, both of them unpleasant. A neighbouring farmer, Do Krüger—brother of the well-known Paul—had been murdered by one of his *kaffirs*; and a tremendous grass fire had swept up to within a yard or so of the house Surprise, and to within about three feet of Eclipse's stable; it had even destroyed part of the rose hedge bordering the upper lands.

The circumstances of Do Krüger's (pronounced Kreer) death were singular. He had an old quarrel going on with some *kaffirs*, who lived in a little *kraal* just where his property touched Mr. Higgins's. Of late the quarrel had been getting worse, the *kaffirs* being very disobedient. They had lands given them to cultivate for their own use in lieu of payment (a common arrangement in the Transvaal), and the natural consequence was that they wanted to work on their own lands when their master wanted them to work on his. The letting of water was the immediate cause of dispute. Do wanted water let on his lands, whilst the *kaffirs* persisted in spending their time letting it on theirs. At last Do, having made up his mind to go to the *bush-veldt* to see how his cattle were getting on there, thought he would make an example. He called on some of his neighbours, amongst others on William Sturton, to ask them to accompany him to the little *kraal*, as he meant to give the *kaffirs* a good lesson.

This was a common practice amongst the Boers before English rule. William Sturton declined, but several Boers agreed; and the next day, saddling his horse and bidding goodbye to his wife, he started for the *bush-veldt*, intending to settle his quarrel with the *kaffirs en route*. His friends joined him at his own house, and having all reached the little *kraal*, Do called the *kaffirs*. One only came out of the hut, to whom Do said that he must immediately let on water to the land. The *kaffir* replied, that he would do so after he had watered his own, no doubt speaking disrespectfully as well as disobediently. Upon this the Boers leapt off their horses and made a rush for the huts, forced their way in, overturning a small child, and seized the man who was particularly obnoxious to them; but just as Do entered the house, a man of the name of Manell hit him over the head with a stick with a heavy knob at the end of it, here called a "*knobkerrie*," and felled him.

His friends were intent on belabouring the man they had caught; but Do called out, "Leave him alone and help me out—they have killed me." He walked a short way towards his house and crossed a *spruit*, then he said he must sit down. A large blood tumour had already

311

formed behind the ear where he had been struck. He soon became unconscious, and died shortly after he was carried home. Strange to say, he received his death-blow on the very spot where his father had cruelly killed a *kaffir*. His wife, a very fat woman, had seen her former husband brought home dead, killed by lightning. She went into convulsions and wept unceasingly, and did all the proper things to testify to the intensity of her grief on the occasion of Do's demise, and married for the third time six months after. The two men—Manell, the one who killed him, and Paul, the one who was going to be beaten—on hearing he was dead, ran away to Pretoria. They got there whilst we were there, and were caught whilst sitting by Mr. Higgins's campfire. After a long imprisonment Manell was hanged.

The pretty farm of Surprise was a mass of black, with the ashes still lying on part, and the whitish effect they gave to the otherwise black prospect made it almost ghastly. Fido and the other animals were all right, except Rough—he was gone. It appears that he had got into one of the rooms when we were locking up the house, and had been shut in. The *kaffirs* hearing him whining had, after two days, forced a window open and let him out, when he immediately rushed off to Eclipse's stable, and then down towards the valley, the way I used to ride. I therefore concluded that he had gone back to Mr. King's, whom he had left to come to me, and this was the case. Mr. King came up the next day, and told us that he had seen Rough sneaking about his cottage; but I had not time to go down for him. The day after Mr. King came again, and brought his big dog. This dog knew me, and must have told Rough on returning home that I was at Surprise, for that very evening Roughy came running in at the door, and up to me.

The old life began again, disturbed only by my constant inquiries about farms. There were, of course, plenty of people willing to sell if they could induce me to pay exorbitantly; but none of the Boers in the vicinity, who had good farms, were disposed to part with them at all. At Pretoria I had not been able to arrange anything.

Shortly after our return the dreaded "lung-sickness" broke out among the cattle. Investigation proved that an ox had died of lung-sickness in the *bush-veldt*, but the fact had been hushed up by the Nell family, who swore it died of what they call here "heart-water," in order to save themselves trouble; for it is of the utmost importance when a case of "lung-sickness" occurs, to inoculate the grown cattle, and to drench the young ones. They take the disease after these operations, but have it slightly and become "salted," that is, are not liable to have it again; whereas if they take the disease naturally (and if it once breaks out in a herd it is sure to run through it) they are most likely to die of it. It was also found that the Nells had let some of Mr. Higgins's cattle get into the *kraal* of a man whose *bush-veldt* farm touched Mr. Higgins's, and had let them remain there a whole night, although it was well known that there was lung-sickness in it.

The worst part of the whole was, that when the disease broke out at Surprise they said it must have been caused by the malice of this very man (who was on bad terms with Mr. Higgins), for that he had buried the intestines of the cattle he had lost by "lung-sickness" close to the place where Mr. Higgins's cattle went to water. At first Mr. Higgins believed the story, but subsequently found it to be untrue. I had now an opportunity of seeing the operations of inoculating and drenching. The lungs of a "lung-sick" animal are smashed up, and the liquid from them strained through fine gauze. It is necessary to kill the animal in order to obtain the lungs in a proper state. For drenching, the liquid thus obtained is mixed with about two parts of water, and given to the animal as a drink—about a bottle-full being used.

For inoculation, a strip of linen, or more commonly cotton rag, is threaded through a packing-needle, dipped in the liquid, and drawn through the lower part of the tail like a seton; or the tip of the tail is split, the rag inserted, and the wound bound up. Great inflammation ensues, the tail generally rotting off, more or less. I have seen oxen with no tails at all. Sometimes the inflammation produces swelling of the parts above and around the tail, and then the animal generally dies in great agony; one of Mr. Higgins's oxen died thus. If at the time of the operation these parts be well smeared with tar, and in case of the inflammation spreading very high, the animal be bathed every morning with salt and water, death seldom ensues; but few masters take so much trouble. The day when these operations took place at Surprise was a regular field-day, Mr. King, and Arthur Sturton, and the Nells coming to help. Some of the oxen and other cattle were very restive, and it was dangerous work for the men; still, on the whole, I was surprised to see the business done so quietly.

CHAPTER 15

In the beginning of November I at last decided to accept an offer Mr. Higgins had made me of buying half his farm, including the small house his father had hitherto occupied. I need not enter into the various reasons which induced me to do this, but need merely say that, all things considered, it appeared the best thing I could do, and that I bought the farm conditionally. I was not to pay the purchase-money for some months, and was to be free to leave the farm, if I chose to do so, before that time. I was to take Jimmy to live with me, as he and I had agreed; and besides, I had engaged the services of a young Englishman who, with another, had come to Mr. Higgins's place looking for work. It was much to be suspected that they were deserters; however, the one had evidently been a working farmer, and the other a groom; so Mr. Higgins arranged to take the former, and I the latter.

Before I left Surprise I was called upon to doctor one of William Sturton's children, the baby, who was dangerously ill with inflammation of the lungs. It had been ailing for some time, but not much notice was taken of its illness until one day, when, having ridden over to see the sick wife of a neighbouring Boer, I took William Sturton's on my way home, and was shown the child. It was very ill then, but before two days were over it was so bad that I remained with it and Alice, and, later on, Mrs. Higgins came to nurse it. That was not my first experience of the misery of illness in this country, but yet I must revert to it, it made so painful an impression on me. A small house, consisting of two rooms and a kitchen; one of the rooms used as a store and general sitting-room; a father, mother, and three young children; no servant but a dirty, more than half-savage *kaffir*; no convenience of any sort!

Fancy nursing a baby, choking with inflamed lungs, in a room where, if the window was opened, the draught could not do otherwise than come on the bed; where the door into a draughty passage was being perpetually opened by the two elder children, who, when not quarrelling, were always crying, and both of whom had sore eyes and no one to look after them. If the window were kept shut the heat was stifling; and so it became necessary to open a window at the top of the gable, which had been intended as the door of a loft, but which, owing to the ceiling not being put in, still opened into the room.

I remember this was decided upon late in the evening when we were all suffocating, and to do it an enormous, roughly-made ladder had to be brought in by William Sturton and the *kaffir*, and left in the room, so that we might be able to get up to shut the window if necessary. Even with this window open the heat was dreadful, and I felt the fever I had had badly in India, and the approach of which I was only too well acquainted with, creeping over me and prostrating me. After two days of incessant care, the baby so far recovered that it was out of immediate danger; but I was obliged to lie by for a day or two—and even then I felt weak.

On the 19th November, I at last moved into my new abode, old Mr. Higgins and his family going to live at Pretoria. I bought his flock of sheep, and old Mrs. Higgins's fowls and two pigs; and Ada, much to her regret, had to leave me her two cats, for the good reason that they positively refused to be put into the waggon. One was a fine grey-and-white tom, the other, Tom's mother, was a very ancient specimen of the feline race, with a crooked eye, and the most surprising voice a cat was ever gifted with. I was not able to afford as yet to buy a waggon or oxen, wishing first to feel my way, and there not being any immediate necessity for oxen, as it was not time for ploughing. I also tried to do with as little furniture as possible, and as few servants. A small bed and a dressing-table and washing-stand, made of old cases, together with a chair and a box, made up the furniture of my bedroom. The bed was lent by Mrs. Higgins.

A deal table, three old chairs, and a horizontal piano, which had been old Mr. Higgins's, and which I used as a table, adorned the sitting-room; while planks, supported on the rafters, gave standing room to various articles, and others of a very miscellaneous character were hung on nails and lines round the walls. The third little apartment, partitioned off like the others with canvas, was a lumber and forage room, and here Barrie the groom slept—Jimmy sleeping sometimes in it, sometimes in the sitting-room. As I mentioned before, doors there were none, except the outer one. A curtain hung over the entrance into my room alone; windows also there were none, only large square holes in the wall, which could be closed at will by shutters of stretched canvas. Goat and sheep skins did the duty of carpets, and the skins of two tiger-cats and one wild cat which had been killed at Surprise, hung on an old folding armchair, completed the Robinson Crusoe look of the place.

After experience of the same, I think a Robinson Crusoe cabin is nicer to read about than to live in; and yet sometimes of an evening, with the light of a dip made from the fat of my own sheep, lighting up, in the feeble manner of dips in general, the motley ornaments of bridles, saddles, bits, fire-arms, tools of various sorts hanging on the walls, and faintly showing the dogs crouching on the floor and the cats' heads peering from off the rafters overhead, I used to think that it would not make a bad picture of an African-squatter's "interior." It will be observed that I say "dogs," for besides my own Rough I generally had two visitors; one was a half-bred brown pointer left behind by old Mr. Higgins—a dog of an undecided character, who never could make up his mind to whom he would belong. He was not one of those independent dogs who decline to belong to anyone—but go on visits to their friends; on the contrary, he was a very slavish, poor brute, addicted to yowling piteously if any one raised a hand to him; but he was always running away from one place to another, and kept in a circle between my place, "Grünfontein," the Nells, and the *kaffir kraal*.

The other visitor looked like a half-bred turnspit. He had belonged to James Higgins, at whose house I had first made his acquaintance, and bestowed on him the name of "Moustache" for he had a ferocious pair at the time. He was afterwards presented to a *kaffir* of the name of Mangwan, who in his turn made him a present to his son and heir, called Magaliesberg. This young gentleman and his father valued the dog highly, in spite of his preternaturally long back, nose and tail, the shortness and crookedness of his legs, and his generally ridiculous appearance. The only thing Magaliesberg objected to was his moustache, and that he cut off. They failed, however, in awakening corresponding sentiments in the ugly quadruped's breast, for he always ran away to me whenever he could, and had to be fetched home again, looking the picture of dejection. Considering that he got next to nothing to eat, and that the deficiencies in his feeding were made up by plenty of beating, it is perhaps natural that Moustache preferred Grünfontein to his master's *kraal*.

I had a great deal to do at Grünfontein, before it could be called a farm. Old Mr. Higgins had indeed made a diminutive dam, and had a good piece of cultivated ground lying beneath it; also a splendid orchard, but the place was terribly neglected. I began by cleaning out and enlarging a tiny dam which was near the cabin; and by making a rough bridge over the large drain from this dam, which was also to serve for a drain from the large upper dam, which I had not as yet commenced.

I must give a little description of the property I now called my own. It was perhaps as pretty a property as one could see in the Transvaal. It was bounded to the north by the precipices of the Magaliesberg, jutting out in bold bluffs and receding into clefts, which rendered it very picturesque, the ground, at first broken and covered with trees, ran abruptly downwards, then up again, forming a sort of upland valley, and then sloped sharply down to the valley, having reached some little way across which, my property ended. A sharp wooded spur ran out from the mountain side, about halfway down the incline, and here the cabin and funny little outhouses had been built between masses of rock and tangled brushwood, while the water, diverted from a rivulet, came babbling down to the tiny dam near the house, making a path for itself sometimes between the rocks, and, until I made a drain and bridge, occasionally made a swamp quite close to the cabin.

A rough road led from the cabin round the lands to Surprise, but the shorter way was by a narrow path through the orchard, and across a piece of ground that I afterwards cleared and tilled, and which then went by the name of the Upper Lands, to where it suddenly dipped into a deep and rugged ravine, down which a rivulet from the side of the rock high up, gurgled pleasantly beneath tall ferns and overhanging trees. Some stepping-stones lay in the water to help passers-by, and then the path, climbing up the opposite side of the ravine, brought one to a grassy and partially wooded slope, which, being passed, the boundary of Grünfontein was also passed, and that of Surprise entered. A pretty scrambling path it was, which, if you took it on horseback, necessitated much bending of the head, and putting aside of boughs, and gave the rider the chance of picking luscious figs and soft peaches without dismounting, by merely stretching out his hand; and many a time Eclipse has been startled by the birds he himself had startled from feasting on the fruit.

And oh! what a quantity of fruit there was. How it lay in heaps under the trees that still were overladen! *Kaffir* girls came in troops to gather it in for me to dry and make vinegar of it; little *kaffirs* from Surprise came to steal it; any and all who came to Grünfontein might eat as much as they cared for; the Nell family sent their children daily to pull a big basket full; the pigs ate of what fell to such an extent that they waxed ridiculously fat without getting any other food; and still such quantities went to waste before it could be gathered or eaten off the ground, that one trod on masses of fruit when walking through many parts of the orchard.

The boundary of the other side of Grünfontein was another deep and wooded ravine, even prettier than the one near the garden; but the prettiest spot in the whole property was just below where the cabin had been built. Here the spur of the mountain terminated in a small, level platform, round whose outer edge the rocks formed a sort of low wall, breaking off suddenly, and falling in jagged masses first to another smaller and lower platform, then in all manner of rough grotesque shapes into the sloping valley beneath. On the upper platform stood a beautiful *syringa*-tree; the rockery below was thickly interspersed with shrubs of different sorts intertwined with the beautiful wild clematis.

Standing on either platform you could look up the valley for forty miles. On a clear day you might catch sight of a white speck where the house at Moy-plas was, and could see as far as Dass-poort; or you could look down the valley until it ended in the undulations which one rode over going to Fahl-plas. Many an evening have I stood gazing at the changing light on the valley, on the opposite mountains, and on the nearer range of the Magaliesberg, and have tried to conjure up what Grünfontein would look like on the evening when I should at last have made it fit for the reception of the guests I hoped to bring to it. Then a pretty cottage should stand near the *syringa*-tree; then the natural rockery should have been made still more attractive by flowers and ferns interspersed between its graceful bushes; then the land below should be waving with crops; then the old cabin should be my calf-house, and a herd of sleek cows should be lowing on their way home to their well-kept sheds; and then Eclipse and other horses should have an English-kept stable, and not a straw-hovel, to eat their evening meal in.

The high road from Pretoria ran through the valley portion of my property, and I used to think how I should point out the house when it first came in sight, and so on, like a great many dreams a great many people have doubtless dreamed in wild homes, which they are trying to shape into civilized ones.

In the meantime it was rough work at Grünfontein. Besides Jimmy and Barrie I had only a *kaffir* woman, called Reva (Manell's wife) to help during the day—she went away early in the evening and came late in the morning—and a little *kaffir* boy to mind the sheep. I rose at early dawn, called the little shepherd, who slept in the straw kitchen, to light the fire, roused Jimmy and Barrie, and generally got to work before the sun shot his first rays upwards behind Witt-waters Randt, where it intercepted the eastern horizon.

As I wanted to push on with the work as fast as I could, I did as much as I could myself, so that Jimmy and Barrie could get on with what I could not do. The cleaning of the horse and stable, the looking after the sheep that were lame or sick, often the skinning and cutting up of one of them, fell to my share, at times also cooking, and cleaning the house, and other domestic duties—when Reva gave herself a holiday—besides superintending the work. Then there was the fruit-drying; and this was an important business, for dried fruit, besides being useful for one's own winter use, sells well in the Free State.

Parties of *kaffir* girls used to come from different *kraals*, some thirty miles distant, to pull the fruit and spread it on things made of wood and reeds, called *stellassees*, that look something like stretchers. Each girl would bring a large conical-shaped basket on her head; into this she would pull the fruit, and she expected to be allowed to fill it once for her own benefit as payment. These young savages looked very picturesque, with their necks and arms and ankles ornamented with beads, gay handkerchiefs, or a gay strip of cloth bound round their heads, skins or blankets loosely hanging from their often shapely shoulders, walking in single file, with their baskets poised on their heads, or sitting in a circle cutting the fruit up and spreading it on the *stellassees*; but they had to be kept in order, or they would eat more than they plucked or cut up, and would talk their time away instead of working.

Once or twice I had even to threaten them with my whip. The peaches and apricots alone have to be cut up; the figs have to be peeled, and gradually flattened out as they dry. When the fruit is all settled on the *stellassees*, they are placed on poles fixed in the ground, and the fruit left to dry in the sun. It has to be continually turned, and some experience is required to know when it is dry enough to put in a sack. Of course it must not be let get wet, and many a time the *stellassees* had to be brought into the house, and piled on the rafters or wherever a place could be got for them.

Then there is another way of preserving peaches and apricots without sugar, when they are too ripe to dry well. They are squeezed in the hand to a pulp, and the skins and stones being thrown away, the remainder is spread upon a plank previously smeared with fat. The paste dries quickly in the sun, and can then be folded up like thick paper, and is very nice to eat. I made a quantity of dried fruit, and in consequence I was kept hard at work, for the turning, and flattening, and squeezing, and the hunting away of the fowls—they would flutter up and oftentimes upset a *stellassee*, if not watched—devolved of course on me, although in the last-mentioned part of my duty Rough and Moustache were valuable coadjutors, making sorties from where they would be lying in the shade, at my cry of "*Sah! Sah!*" accompanied by much barking and whisking of tails, to the confusion of the assembled fowls, who would rush off in dire confusion for a few yards, then stop and begin picking about in an apparently innocent manner, but with a tendency to come stealthily closer and closer to the *stellassees*.

I have often amused myself watching their tactics. There was one hen of a more enterprising turn of mind than the rest. She used to go on picking away, keeping her eye on me all the while, always coming nearer and nearer. I used sometimes to pretend not to see her; for an instant she would stand, with head erect and a little on one side, looking at me, and then come picking along in a straight line for the *stellassees*. If I moved she would at once turn and take a circuitous route; but if she caught my eye she would give a frightened cackle, and make off as if the dogs were behind her, but only to commence operations again. Those fowls were altogether rather a nuisance, for they insisted on coming into the cab in, showing as great pertinacity about that as about the fruit, and when in, they would get on the table. This was particularly agreeable, if, dinner being laid, I had just gone out to call to Reva to go for Jimmy and Barrie, and on returning found a party of fowls picking in the dish; or if the dough for the bread was left uncovered for a moment whilst Reva and I went out, and the result was, its being all trodden upon and picked. Jimmy used to take their disregard of our wishes as something personal, and call them "insulting creatures," and throw broom handles, brushes, and boots after them.

Having but one servant, it was impossible in such an establishment as mine to keep up the usual distinctions between master and man. Barrie had his meals with us and passed the evening in the common sitting-room.

He was not either a bad-looking or a badly-educated young fellow this Barrie (not that Barrie was his name; I don't know what his name was), that is to say, if by education one understands book-learning.

He wrote a very good hand, read fluently, and was fond of improving himself, reading history by preference in his leisure-hours. But I am afraid he was but a bad sort of a fellow, or was on the road to become one. He had a great talent for deception, and gloried in it; he had a favourite theory that dishonesty was the best policy; he was very sharp, very lazy, very noisy, very violent, but a good-humoured, merry fellow nevertheless.

He never showed his violence to me or to my animals, except by a vicious look, but the look told of what was going on within; and one evening, when Eclipse, who hated him, made him run about three miles to catch him, and then had to be caught with Mrs. Higgins's assistance, I heard that he confided to the latter that if he had been his horse he would have shot him had a rifle been handy, "but that the missus was that particular as he daren't touch the brute." On the whole Barrie restrained himself creditably, for his language, although certainly inelegant, never became intolerable while he was in my company; and this must have cost him an effort. If he kept up a certain respect of manner towards me, he was inclined to be the reverse of respectful in his manner of talking of, and even to, the Higginses and Sturtons, and had to be periodically checked about it.

It is certainly demoralizing for English servants to come to this country. They may begin fairly; but even serving under one whom they acknowledge as undeniably their social superior, their ideas of master and man are liable to become confused after a time. The master cannot refuse to associate, on what appears to be terms of equality to the man, with Africander farmers both of English and Dutch origin, many of whom are in no way superior to the servant, whilst many are his inferiors, and only a few his superiors. They may be rich people, but the English servant knows well enough when they belong to the two first classes; but often when he remarks that those of the last class have no more "book-learning" than he has, he classes them with the former, although in their breeding they may be infinitely far removed from him.

It is not easy to keep up the proper distance between master and servant when the very people whom he is called upon to bring in coffee to whilst they sit on a visit to his master, and behind whom he is expected to ride as long as his master rides by their side, are ready to drop into familiar conversation with him the next moment, or if they do not do so with him, will be on familiar terms with someone who is on familiar terms with him. For this reason, and others also, after many trials, I have come to the conclusion that it is more comfortable, and better in all ways, to have coloured servants than white ones. The *kaffirs* are bad as a rule; but there is a class of half-castes between white and Hottentot blood, here called "bastards," in which very excellent servants may be found.

To return to Grünfontein. My sheep caused me a good deal of trouble, the tick tormenting them terribly, and several catching a sort of fever which is very fatal in this part of the Transvaal. My neighbours lost largely by both causes; but I took great care of my sheep, often working for two hours in the *kraal* with them, and I lost hardly any. I became quite an expert sheep-doctor, and could throw a good sized lamb alone. There was one splendid wether, a pet from his lambhood, which I had bought with a promise not to kill him. He was quite too nice a beast for me to think of such a thing, even without the promise. He would trot up to me and hunt all over my hands and pockets for salt, and then run to the door, or inside if he could, and refuse to go out till he got some. His name was Hans. I say *was*, for I fear my poor old sheep has been butchered by this time by the Boers.

Many a time some Boer visitor has said to me admiringly, "Oh! there you have got a fine wether!" with a truculent expression of face and voice, indicating carnivorous tendencies. Of horse-disease, as long as Eclipse grazed on my own property or that of Mr. Higgins, I was not much afraid, these farms forming a sort of healthy oasis in the midst of an unhealthy country although all along the southern side of the Magaliesberg the mountain grazing is pretty safe; besides, I heard from several people that Eclipse had marks about him of being surely salted, and I began to suspect that I had got him cheap on account of his viciousness, although, as I said before, he was gentle enough with me.

CHAPTER 16

Shortly before Christmas the Boer scare broke out again, and Mr. Higgins and Arthur Sturton determined to go into Pretoria. The morning the waggon left Surprise, Mr. Higgins rode up to my cabin from the high road. "Goodbye!" he said, shaking hands as he stood by his handsome black horse Wellington. "Don't be frightened; no one will hurt you." I laughed, and thought it was a very needless piece of advice. I was not at all frightened. A day or two after, Jimmy had occasion to go to the valley; he came back full of the news he had heard from William Sturton and Mr. King. The Boers had declared war; they were going to break out on the outstanding farms, and every Englishman, woman, and child was to be killed. There were all sorts of circumstantial proof of the truth of this piece of news, which interested me too little for me to remember it.

However, Jimmy and Barrie seemed impressed. A waggon was going up from the Sturtons to Pretoria, and I told them if they liked they might go up with it. However, they said they would stay; but they were not altogether comfortable. I think it was two days after, while I was busy about the *stellassees*, I heard an exclamation from both of them as they were working at a little distance from me at the small dam and bridge.

"Look there! What's that" And then Jimmy cried out, "There is a commando riding to burn Surprise" (an old threat amongst our Boer neighbours).

"Nonsense," said I.

"But you should go and look," persisted Jimmy. "Barrie says too that he can see a party of horsemen riding over the *veldt* to Surprise; they must be going to burn it."

Barrie thereupon expressed his belief that such was really the case. Now in my heart I believed Barrie to be a deserter, so I thought he might know something about what mounted men looked like, and I said, "You're sure they're not oxen, Barrie?" Barrie was sure they were not; so I went to look—but they *were* oxen nevertheless.

I think it was the next day that a young man, a brother of Alice's future husband, rode over from Fahlbank, to ask me to ride back with him to see John Higgins's baby, who was ill. Giving Barrie many instructions as to the proper carrying out of the bridge he was making, we started so soon as the sun began to decline a little. We had to call at Mr. King's, in the valley, for some medicine which he had, and which I had run out of; and as we saw that a storm was brewing we pushed along briskly, but it caught us just as we touched the top of the *randt*. How it did come down! In a few minutes the horses could with difficulty keep their feet in many places where the nature of the soil rendered it slippery. I had forgotten my waterproof, and was soon wet through, and before long it was pitch dark.

Fortunately my companion knew the country well, and by a detour saved crossing the river at the deepest drift. It does not sound pleasant, does it? but I was getting sick of the monotony of Grünfontein, and the slowness with which the work seemed to progress, my feeling of weariness being increased by the fever, which kept hanging on, and I enjoyed it. The baby was not very ill after all. I slept in the room with the child, its mamma, and its little sisters, and the next day rode back alone to Grünfontein. The bridge was finished, and Barrie was triumphant at its fine appearance.

"If it is as good under as it is above, Barrie," said I, "it will do nicely." I rather doubted the fact in my heart.

"You may trust to me, missus," said Barrie. But the trust would have been misplaced had I done so, for a few days after Mr. Higgins's return, Wellington put his foot right through the bridge, and it had all to be pulled to pieces, and made again under my own inspection.

The new year came, and with it talk of the Higginses going on a visit to the old colony, where Mrs. Higgins's relations still live. The weather was intensely hot, and there was a great deal of sickness about. The fever was steadily taking hold of me, and Jimmy was laid up with a slight attack; but everything went on much as usual, until one day we learned, through the paper that used to come to Surprise, that Pretorius (called Pretors) had been arrested at Potchefstrom. The next day Mr. Higgins started on horseback for Marico, where he had some business; he was to take Fahl-plas *en route*.

Before leaving, he rode over to ask me to go to Surprise, as Augusta was ailing, and her mother felt anxious about her. I found the child not only ailing, but very seriously ill. Mrs. Higgins and I sat up all night with her. The next day we were surprised at Mr. Higgins's return. This time the Boers had fairly broken out, he told us. He had met numbers the day before, riding through the pouring rain to Potchefstrom, armed. He had spoken to many of them. They all said one thing. Pretorius must be given up to them, or they would fight—aye, if they had to die for it. They would rather die than leave their leader under English arrest. Mr. Higgins said he felt sure they were in earnest now. He would like to put Mrs. Higgins and the children into the waggon and trek quickly into the Free State; he had turned back on purpose.

They would have gone, had it not been that pretty Augusta lay dangerously ill; such being the case, they had perforce to stay. That there was a general ferment this time among the Boers was certain. There was great saddling in haste to ride to Potchefstrom, although when those who saddled in haste got to Potchefstrom they began to repent at leisure. Many Boers who had not horses talked about the desirability of having them, and some suggested borrowing them from those who had, but did not, on this occasion, use them. The next day Augusta was better, and I returned to Grünfontein in the morning, but rode over again to Surprise early in the afternoon. I had not been there long before a sound something like a cannon-shot was heard.

Of course everybody cried out "What's that?" and everybody but myself said it was a cannon-shot. We heard it three or four times. Mr. Higgins stood on the *stoop* with a field-glass in his hand. We were in quite a state of excitement, still I did not believe that it was a cannon-shot. Presently a *kaffir* appeared, who told us all about it, he knew even where the shots came from. Pretorius was being taken under heavy escort to Pretoria. The Boers had attacked—the fighting was sharp. He could not tell the result, but he knew the place of the battle exactly; as to how he knew it, he was a little hazy.

Mr. Higgins brought Wellington up from the stable, and put him into the store for the night, fearful that under these exciting circumstances some enterprising Boer might steal him, or as they say here "jump" him at night. The same idea struck me with regard to Eclipse. I asked if I might put him too in the store; but hearing that if I did he would have to be left loose as well as Wellington, I desisted; for Wellington was very fond of biting and kicking other horses, was shod all round, and was a much bigger horse than Eclipse. When I left Surprise in the evening, Mr. Higgins was still on the look-out, field-glass in hand, and perched on the top of an old stump.

As I rode up to where Jimmy and Barrie were working at the upper dam I was making, I was greeted by "Did you hear the cannon?" I remarked that I did not believe they were cannon; and Jimmy scouted me.

Although sceptical as to cannon, I thought horse-lifting was possible, so I determined to mount guard on Eclipse. The little straw outhouse was divided into two apartments by a rough partition, the stable was the inner one. I directed Barrie to take up bedding for me and also for himself to the outer one, and then taking arms for both of us with me, I camped for the night there. Jimmy wanted to go instead of me; but Jimmy and Barrie as sentinels would have been like two logs—the one slept sounder than the other. The dogs of course came and lay near me. Towards one or two in the morning they woke me by their growls. I sat up, and thinking I heard a stir in the bushes below, I called Barrie—not loudly, because I did not want to give the intending thieves, if there were any, notice of my being ready to receive them.

A snore was the only answer. I called again softly, and pushed him a little with my foot after I stood up—a groan and a mumbled remonstrance was all I got from him; it was evident that if further roused he would remonstrate loudly before thoroughly waking up, so I left him alone, and cocking my revolver took a cautious survey. All seemed quiet, and although I waited and watched for some time, I neither heard nor saw anything, and so went to sleep again. I had a good laugh at Barrie in the morning, who didn't like it, and pretended to feel ill after a night of sleeplessness and discomfort. I was amused at the fellow's absurdity, but when he said he felt too tired to act guard the next night, I contented myself with saying that he could sleep in the house if he liked; it would have been the report of my revolver that would have first wakened him in the stable, it would probably also waken him in the house.

He was annoyed, but persisted in his assertion that he was so dreadfully tired he could not act guard. Poor fellow, he did not know how near his fate was upon him! Jimmy now insisted upon being my companion on guard; and although I did not much like to expose him to danger, if there should be any, still it was so clearly the right thing for him to do that I acquiesced. Nothing, however, disturbed the tranquillity of the second night, except the rain, and that was less than the night before. The front compartment of the outhouse, I must remark, was not perfectly water-tight, still one could keep fairly dry in it.

The next day was Sunday, and I was cleaning the stable, preparatory to getting dressed for going to dinner at Surprise, when a delicate, gentlemanly-looking man, in a sort of blue serge blouse, ran up the little broken pathway leading to the stable, and raising his wide-awake, said he had heard that I was looking for brickmakers, that he and his mates were brickmakers and builders, and would be glad of a job. I glanced at his slim fine-skinned hands, and putting his appearance and mode of speech together, I said to myself "*You're* not, whatever your mates may be." I said aloud that I was in want of bricks, and that I thought of building, and asked where his mates were. He pointed to the cabin, and then I saw a sturdy-looking man of about forty, who looked every inch a tradesman, and a rollicking-looking fellow with a lot of yellow hair about him, who looked anything chance might require him to be, provided it did not ask him to attempt anything polished. I descended from the stable, pitchfork in hand, to greet them, and invite them inside.

The tradesman, whose name was Williams, told me they had been thinking of coming to the cottage late the preceding evening and asking for shelter, but that knowing of the Boer scare, they thought they might frighten me, and so slept in the *veldt*. Of course I knew they were very hungry, and I had eaten up the last bit of meat that very morning; the bread was nearly done; I had no milk, no eggs; Reva was away, and I did not know what to do. So, retiring for a minute, I set Barrie to work to make flat cakes, and despatched Jimmy to get some milk and meat at Surprise, if he could, and to ask Mr. Higgins to come over after dinner. The result was that I engaged the men to make bricks at the rate of fifteen shillings a thousand, burnt out, and that they were to cut the wood themselves, and with the agreement that I was to get the brick-moulds made as soon as possible by a carpenter who lived at Fahlbank, and that until their completion the three men were to work at the dam at the rate of half-a-crown a day; I was to feed them into the bargain, and they were to sleep in the outhouse.

The next morning early the three men went to work at the dam, and I, leaving Jimmy and Barrie to settle the *stellassees*, which had been taken in during the night, was walking up through the long dewy grass to see how they were getting on, when I saw Mr. Higgins and a man in a white mackintosh and cork helmet, push aside the branches of the fig hedge of the orchard and ride through. They were some distance from me, but I perceived in a minute from his seat that the man was an officer, and his horse I knew to be an English-bred and groomed horse. A momentary thought that it might be some old acquaintance come to look me up, struck me, but in a minute I felt sure that it was for Barrie the officer had come.

"Where is Barrie?" asked Mr. Higgins, after a short "Good morning."

"At the house."

"Well, I am afraid you must lose him," said Mr. Higgins.

"I thought so," said I; and continuing my walk up to the dam, I left them to carry out their disagreeable duty. It seems that Barrie swore to the last that he was no deserter, and became so violent that the officer had to draw his pistol. It was all over in a minute or so; when I returned to the cabin, in ten minutes, they were already gone. Mr. Higgins's servant was also captured, and from that day to this I have never heard more of them.

It appears that the party of soldiers accompanying the officer had struck terror into hearts of many a Boer on the road they passed along. It had been generally known the day before that the great Potchefstrom demonstration had come to naught, and the Boers thought this was a party sent out to catch other members of the committee, some of whom lived close to us.

Fat old Hermanns Potchieter slept in a *sluit* on the night which they passed near his place; and the equally fat Cornelius Vanroy slept, or rather tried to sleep, in a tree. I don't suppose he succeeded.

The first day's work at the dam showed me that the man who had first accosted me was not worth half-a-crown a day at such work. I told him so, politely, the next morning. He said that he had been on the point of speaking to me much to the same effect, and asked me whether I would allow him to help me in such ways as he could, without payment, until the brick-moulds were made. To this I agreed. On the second day the rollicking-looking man sprained his back, and had to have poultices applied, and to lie by. This was not very pleasant. However I made Mr. Letheby useful in the fruit-gathering and drying business, and soon learned that he was the son of a manufacturer in the north of England, had been a clerk in the office, had had a disagreement with his father, and had come out here. He had not got on—met with his present mates in Pretoria—could do lots of things a little—didn't mind what he did. It was the old story, that of hundreds out here. I could not call him Letheby, he was an educated man; so I called him Mr. Letheby, and then had to call the others "Mr." too, to prevent envy, hatred, and malice. These soon showed themselves without any extra incitement.

The two workmen hated and despised their social superior after their manner, and he reciprocated the feeling after his; but they made a butt of him, and he was too yielding, and not sharp enough to be able to reciprocate; besides, they were coarse, and he was not. He used to amuse me by his *naïveté*. I think after his many struggles he had quite made up his mind to the advisability of marrying a rich Boeress if he could; he told me so, in fact, more than once, candidly admitting that all he should absolutely require was money, youth and beauty he should like if they could be got. He did not, I must say, assert that he was ready to take this course, but he used to discuss its advisability in a manner so personal to himself that it was hard for me to keep from laughing, At last, after Williams had been more rough than usual to him, and just when the brick-moulds arrived, he determined to break his ill-assorted partnership, and departed with a letter of introduction from me, which got him a place as tutor in a neighbouring Boer's family. There, I heard, he got on very well.

The yellow-bearded man being restored to a salubrious condition, he set to work at the bricks with Williams, but after a day or two took his pack on his back and silently departed. I heard that he objected to getting meat only once a day, to not having butter on his bread, and to having occasionally too little milk in his coffee. Mr. Higgins wondered why he had not complained to me; but I thought he showed his sense by not doing so, as it was evident that he would have gained nothing, for the good reason that butter there was none, that milk was scarce, and that as I had a limited number of wethers in my flock, I could not kill *ad libitum*.

Besides all this, he knew that he fared exactly as I did. I was not left alone with Jimmy and Williams this time, however, for two days before the discontented one departed, three men had come tramping up to my door while Mr. Higgins was at tea with me, and having declared that they wanted work "bad," and "didn't mind hard work or hard grub neither," and that they "was men as was used to roughing it," accepted the wage of half-a-crown a day, and set to work on the dam. Very rough men—the greatest stretch of politeness could not have extended "Mr." to one of *them*. Jimmy and I had our meals together now, then Mr. Williams, and then the "Philistines," as I called them.

They did not work very hard unless urged thereto, but they ate very hard without any urging. They were respectful and obedient to me, but I felt that they were dangerous, and must be kept well in hand. Jimmy told me certain things he heard them say; and other things which they said to me, without thinking about the impression they were producing, made me aware that they were familiar with violent measures. They, of course, had all been volunteers, as had the others,—you can hardly meet a man in this country who has not been a volunteer,—and they certainly impressed me with the idea that it would have been unpleasant to have been in a farmhouse to which they had access, in their volunteering capacity, unless a very strict officer happened to be with them. One story, in which they greatly gloried, was of how, having been rudely spoken to by an unfriendly Boer, they had caught one of his sheep in the *veldt* and cut its throat, not to eat it, for they had to run away so as not to be found out, but as revenge.

The weather was very wet, and Williams being singlehanded got on but slowly with the bricks; but he was a thoroughly good work-man, and a straightforward, honest fellow, and he made more headway than I expected under the circumstances. His idea and mine from the beginning was that he was to build as well as to make the bricks, but I found it hard to get him to state for what sum he would contract to execute my plan. I had drawn this plan before agreeing to buy the place, and Mr. Higgins had estimated the cost for me.

In the meantime Mr. Higgins and his family were getting ready to go to the colony. It was to be a great emigration, for they took a large number of cattle with them, some to sell, and also spare oxen. I felt that it would be very desolate after Mrs. Higgins and the children went away, and the increasing fever did not raise my spirits. Most of my fruit was dried, and packed away in sacks, ready for my friends to take with them to sell in the Free State; but a peculiar sort of yellow peach—a fruit unknown in England but common in Italy—had yet to be dried, and I was hard at work gathering it in, and spreading it on the *stellassees*. The weather had now become dry again, and the heat was very great—greater than usual. I sometimes felt as if I should break down unless I could have either entire rest or some violent excitement.

One day Mr. Higgins rode over early to my place, and said that he was off to Fahl-plas, and proposed that I should go with him, so as to reply quickly to a letter of interest to both him and me, which I expected to find there—the post being fetched at that time from the distant farm where it was left by John Higgins. I jumped at the idea; it would be a change.

"You look too ill to do it, though," said Mr. Higgins. "You won't stand the ride."

But I knew better, the programme being only so far changed by Mr. Higgins, that instead of riding there and back in one day, I was to dine at Surprise, start immediately after dinner for Fahl-plas, sleep there, and return early on the following day.

It was a very pleasant ride; the day was not too warm, and we got in just in time for a pleasant supper with the James Higginses. The next morning we idled about and talked, and did not saddle up until late, when a fearful storm soon drove us back. We saddled up after early coffee on the next day, and got to Surprise a little after breakfast—so we had our breakfast alone—and as we were talking about how things would go on with me while the Higginses were away, Mr. Higgins said if I chose he would sell me his black span and the old waggon. The span, that had been of eighteen, had now dwindled to fourteen, but it had been twice down the dreaded Natal road, and all that remained were, I knew, salted with both red water and lung sickness. The sum asked was twelve pounds apiece, but I knew the oxen were worth it, and clenched the bargain. I felt perfectly delighted at getting possession of those oxen.

The Higgins family were to start in the early days of February, which were now quite near; and as I was anxious to see the last of them, I arranged to go with them as far as Fahl-plas, going in the waggon with Mrs. Higgins. Mr. Higgins was to lead Eclipse, who would carry me back.

The day before they started I turned out all my dry fruit in the sun, and sorted it well. The weather was frightfully hot, but I knew a great deal depended upon the fruit being perfectly dry and free from insects before it was put in the waggon. I slept at Surprise that night, and felt very ill—I was not quite sure whether from fever or from the anxiety I felt at being left quite alone; and yet in a certain sense I was glad, for I knew that I depended a great deal on Mr. Higgins, and I knew too that I should never really succeed so long as I was not completely self-dependent. I should be so by the time the Higginses came back. We started the next morning; it was very hot, and by the time I got to Fahl-bank my bones ached so severely that I had to go to bed, or at least to lie down on the bed the whole afternoon. The next day, Sunday, I was better; but that evening, as we stood looking at the comet, I felt the premonitory shiver of the real set-in of fever. It was curious how much that comet affected even the Higginses. They were really afraid it was going to do something, and many coupled it with an old rhyme of Mother Shipton's, much talked of here, in which it is set down, in doggerel verse, that after certain curious events happening, all described in allegorical language, the world is to come to an end in 1881.

The next morning we all sat on the *stoop* having early coffee, and waiting for breakfast, the Higginses to get into the waggon (Wellington stopped at Surprise), I to saddle up for my return journey. I felt very ill, but hardly expected to do what I did, *viz.*, faint away at a moment's notice. I know of no more annoying thing than to faint in another person's house, particularly when the performance is followed by such prostration that one has to be supported to bed, and has to be lifted up in bed like a baby. Yet this was what happened to me.

Mr. and Mrs. Robert Higgins would not start: they said if I did not get better they would not start at all, but take me back to Surprise and nurse me—but I well knew what a dreadful disappointment that would be to Mrs. Higgins and the children. I ordered myself quinine, but I knew that there is not much use in taking quinine when this sort of jungle fever, which is remittent but not intermittent, is at its height. Robert Higgins asked leave to doctor me, saying he knew a great deal about African fever; calomel was the thing for it. I knew that he had had experience in the matter, for he was an old elephant and ostrich hunter, and many a time of an evening had I listened eagerly to his graphically told stories of adventures, in which fever sometimes had its share; so I obediently said that I would take calomel, although I don't believe much in it, but I would have taken anything they suggested just to show that I was ready to try to get well.

Robert Higgins administered the calomel, and the effect of it was that I kept his wife, who slept in my room, awake all night by my half-delirious talking. Robert Higgins was surprised at my being worse the nest morning. I think he would have liked to administer another dose; but then James Higgins said no, he could cure me—homoeopathic aconite was the thing! I assured him I should be delighted to try it. I did take it. He said I was to take four drops, but I altered his prescription by doubling the dose on the sly. It did me good, whereby I learned something in medicine that I had not known before.

All this time I was being nursed with the utmost kindness in James Higgins's drawing-room. John Higgins and his family were away, but they came back; and then Mrs. Robert Higgins carried me into their sitting-room, which was more adapted for a sick-room than the other. I remember how everyone laughed at a suggestion made by Mrs. John Higgins as to how I could be moved, for walking was impossible and I objected to being carried.

"Do you think *you* could carry me?" said I to Mrs. Robert Higgins.

"Well, if she can't," said her sister-in-law, "at the worst, there's the perambulator."

This suggestion conveyed such a comical appreciation of my smallness that I laughed heartily, in spite of my weakness. Two days afterwards I was so much better that I induced the Robert Higginses to start. It was very hard to part with them—in my then weak state it was quite a wrench—but the Higginses of Fahl-plas did all they could to make me comfortable; if I had been their own sister they could not have done more, and although it is a dreadful feeling to be ill away from home, still I admitted to myself that it was well for me that I was with them—not at Grünfontein.

On the Monday after the Robert Higginses' departure, Jimmy, having heard of my illness, rode over on a borrowed horse to see me. His account of the proceedings at Grünfontein was the reverse of satisfactory. On finding that I did not return on the Monday, Jimmy imagined that I had gone on to Potchefstrom with the Higginses, and communicated his ideas to the men. The result was a mutiny next day. The Philistines struck for meat twice a day. Jimmy told them he could not go beyond my orders as to the allowance of meat, but that on his own responsibility he would give them no food at all if they did not work. They held a consultation upon this, and repaired to the dam, where they pretended to work, but in reality hardly worked at all; in the meantime, Jimmy having gone to the valley to ask if any news had been, heard of me, they stole the meat that was drying in a tree, and a whole bottle of brandy which Jimmy had removed from where I left it, but thought he had carefully concealed in the bedroom.

"They swore by all that was holy they had not touched the meat," said Jimmy, "and looked me straight in the face; surely you don't think they can be so wicked as to do that when they knew they had really taken it?"

I assured Jimmy that such was my opinion of human nature that I believed it capable of even that depth of wickedness; and remembering that I had thirty pounds locked up in a desk that might happen to take their fancy, I suggested to Jimmy that the best thing for him to do was to return to Grünfontein before night.

He left me more anxious than before. So innocent a boy was not likely to have much control over the Philistines, and any attempt on his part to enforce his authority might lead to violence. My only hope was Williams. I seriously thought of trying to ride home, but as I could hardly crawl, the thing was impossible. Then James Higgins, seeing my anxiety, offered to drive me over the next day, but the next day his wife was seriously unwell; then torrents of rain set in, which rendered the river impassable. Two day after, the three Philistines presented themselves, and asked for payment, saying they would not work any longer. They swore the strongest oaths that they had worked as hard as men could during my absence, and that the dam was finished.

Of course I knew they were lying, and I also knew that they had no legal right to payment, for they had engaged for a month, and the month was not out; but when they saw that I was not going to be bamboozled, they changed their tone, said that they saw I did not believe them, and that Jimmy had been "a poisoning of my mind;" farther, that they would know how to settle with him if they did not get paid. Now I thought it very improbable that Jimmy would know how to settle with *them* in case they returned to Grünfontein with that amicable intention, so I considered for a few moments, weighing the following facts and possibilities in my mind.

There was a canteen in the *poort* near the river, but on the other side of it; there was also a small river between the canteen and Grünfontein, a mere nothing generally, but which the rain, still pouring down, must have converted into a deep and rapid stream. If I did not pay these men, they would have to pass the canteen, with bitter longings for a glass, setting their angry passions ablaze, for they had not a penny in their possession. They would reach Grünfontein in a murderous frame of mind; the consequences might be terrible. Against that, if I paid them, they would certainly get drunk at the canteen, and then they would either stay there drinking so long as the money lasted, and that being expended, until the inevitable "horrors" were over, or they would try to go to Grünfontein with no good intentions, for they were likely to feel rancorous towards Jimmy in their cups; but then there was that conveniently swollen little river. I felt almost sure that a tipsy man, if he tried to cross it, must inevitably tumble into it; it was not very improbable he might be drowned, and in any case he would hurt himself considerably, and be incapable of walking to Grünfontein after his bath. All these things duly considered, I paid the men, and determined to get to Grünfontein as soon as possible myself.

It seemed destined that the work at Grünfontein was not to make progress; but the next evening a note was brought to me by an Englishman, who said he had come from Pretoria. It was from old Mr. Higgins, and told me that this man's name was Richard Hall, that he was the discharged soldier who had spoken to Robert Higgins about coming to work on his farm; and that old Mr. Higgins thought, if his son was gone by the time the man reached Surprise, I might like to engage him. I remembered to have heard of this man from Mr. Higgins, who said he had reason to believe he thoroughly understood farming, and that he bore an excellent character.

Mr. Higgins had greatly hoped that he would come; and now he was there, and I could engage him, at least for a time, I felt very glad. It had been arranged that James Higgins was to drive me to Grünfontein on the following day; the difficulty had been as to how Eclipse was to be got there, but now I determined to let this man ride him over. In the meantime Richard Hall was taken into the dining-room, and given something to eat. He was a fine, stalwart young fellow, and had a mongrel pointer puppy with him, of which he seemed very fond; but he was too free-and-easy in his manner towards the Higgins, for me not to see there would be the old difficulty there.

We started the next morning. Eclipse was rather disposed to tricks when the man mounted him, but quieted down when I spoke to him and petted him, and we all reached Grünfontein safely, passing the Philistines dead drunk at the canteen. Jimmy and Williams welcomed me back heartily, and little Rough was overjoyed to see me; but the fruit I had taken such pains to get settled on the *stellassees* before I left was all spoiled or destroyed. The horses of Hermans Potchieter had come over one night when the *stellassees* had been left out, and had knocked many of them down and eaten the fruit, the rest Jimmy had piled one on another during the rain and covered with a waterproof. He had not uncovered them for days, and even the *stellassees* they were on had rotted in consequence; the fruit was a mass of black corruption.

Roughy, too, had been seriously hurt in some way, and was very ill; the cats looked miserable, and were wild and frightened. It was a damp evening, and the discomfort of the house sent a chill through me, in spite of my desire not to feel it. The truth is, I was still so weak that objects had a tendency to waver before my eyes, and Grünfontein was not a place for nursing oneself. Perhaps the worst part of this species of fever is, that so long as it hangs about one, painful sores are constantly making their appearance on different parts of the body; when one crop vanishes another appears; the least scratch turns into one of them, but if there be no scratch they will come of themselves. My hands, legs, and feet were particularly affected by them, and the pain almost crippled me. There was no use in lying by, however, and I began my usual routine next day.

Richard Hall said he would not remain for less pay than six pounds a month, and although Mr. Higgins had told me, when I was making my calculations about farming, that good European labour could be got much more cheaply, my own inquiries subsequently showed me that it could not. It was evident that I must have some one besides Jimmy and the shepherd boy—and none of the *kaffirs* on the property could be induced to work—so I said I would engage Hall for a month on trial. He spoke very confidently as to his own knowledge of farming operations, and remembering what Mr. Higgins had said of him, I thought he might be worth the money. His first task was mere labourer's work: *viz.*, finishing the dam which the Philistines had left unfinished, so I could not at once judge of his skill as a farmer.

Chapter 17

At this point I must digress to relate a *kaffir* idyll. It concerns Mangwan, the father of Moustache's proprietor.

Mangwan was the son and heir of the great and powerful *kaffir* chief Mosilikatz, who only a few years ago held sway as far south as the southern slopes of the Magaliesberg. The Higginses, then dashing young hunters, and their father, an experienced one, used to pursue their game in his territory for months, and were on friendly terms with the old chief, with whom they exchanged visits and presents. Mangwan, too, used often to come to their waggons, and his brother also. At last old Mosilikatz died. The Higginses' waggons were not far from the place at which he expired. The old chief had many wives, but one was his special favourite. She not only fascinated the father, but the son; and on his father's death Mangwan persuaded her to fly with him to the Higginses' waggons. By *kaffir* law, a son who appropriates one of his father's wives, forfeits both her life and his own, and loses his inheritance, but Mangwan and the girl were ready to risk all for each other.

Old Mr. Higgins hid them, and kept them hidden, until he brought them to a place of safety. The property at Fahl-plas was then his, and he settled them on it. For a time Mangwan kept up state. He did nothing himself, nor would he allow his wife to do anything; he had *kaffir* slaves who attended on both (even to cutting and cleaning his nails), but now that his dependents no longer supplied him with food, skins, money, &c., his store rapidly diminished, and old Mr. Higgins pointed out to him that as he had determined to forego his rights as chief for the sake of the *kaffir* girl, he must now work for his livelihood. To this Mosilikatz's son could not bend. His flocks and herds dwindled, but he would not work.

A son was born, whom he called Magaliesberg, and who grew to be the prettiest *kaffir* boy I have ever seen. Little by little the slaves of Mangwan became reduced in number until he had but one, a wretched little girl who was starved and beaten, and made to sleep outside the door of the *kraal* in all weathers. When the child was dying of privation Mrs. Higgins pointed out to Mangwan the wickedness of letting her sleep in the cold and wet, without even a covering.

"Surely," said Mangwan, "the place for a dog to sleep is outside his master's door."

The little two-legged dog did sleep there until she died, and then the wife had to begin to work in a lazy fashion. When Robert Higgins bought Surprise he asked his father to come and live at Grünfontein, and told Mangwan he might build himself a *kraal* in the valley beneath. Both invitations were accepted, and so when I bought Grünfontein, Mosilikatz's son became my tenant.

He was an old man then, and very skinny and ugly, and the woman he had given up his kingdom for was a hideous specimen of humanity; but Magaliesberg was a very pretty, active, and graceful boy—also a disobedient, idle, and mischievous urchin. He would order his father about instead of obeying him, and he was the apple of his father's eye. He was supposed to tend the cattle and goats, but he never did so. Mangwan never worked, and he was not above begging, yet, as he walked along with an old blanket thrown over his shoulders, there was a certain stateliness about him. He never mixed with other *kaffirs*, and he always spoke Zulu. Dutch he did not understand. In spite of his poverty he managed to marry two other wives, but the youngest ran away from him, and he never got her back. I suppose she thought the magnificence of his *kraal* hardly corresponded with his rank.

But although Mangwan took unto himself other wives, his first wife was the one he always clung to; and the only time I saw Mangwan's serenity disturbed, was when a *coolie* servant of mine, who understood Zulu, after enduring her taunts and shrieks, and the snapping of her fingers under his nose, for about an hour, endeavoured to push her forcibly out of my domains at my order be it understood, for I was fairly tired of the termagant's vociferation. Then Mangwan, who had previously been sitting quite unconcernedly on a heap of stones hard by, leapt up, and throwing his blanket from him with quite a tragic air, gave one yell, and sprang at the *coolie*. They both rolled down the hill together.

Mangwan arose with his nose bleeding, and his old bones sadly shaken, but still looking defiance. Magaliesberg, however, strongly advised him and his mother to keep the peace and retire to their *kraal*, and this they did. The next day the *kaffir* presented himself before me. His dignity as well as his nose had been injured. He was very sad: indeed, I always felt sorry for the old man. Whether to a European or a *kaffir* the sense of having to ask for favours when you once dispensed them, to obey where you once commanded—the feeling of dependence upon a stranger—must always be bitter. Mangwan, looking down from my little eyrie on the cultivated valley below, which had once been a wild bush, and his own hunting-country, must in a miserable blind sort of way have felt something of what the exiled French princes experienced when they looked across the channel to the distant shores of France.

Mangwan, climbing from his wretched little *kraal* in the valley to sit down in front of the door of my cabin, hoping that I might give him a little coffee or the feet of a sheep, or let him pull some fruit out of my garden, must have felt also, in a blind sort of way, the bitterness of the great Italian poet's heart when he climbed the stairs of others! I always treated Mangwan with respect, and the old man felt this, I know. On the occasion to which I refer I fortunately had Saul the driver with me when he arrived, and I made him translate into Zulu what I considered a neatly turned speech for Mangwan's benefit. I alluded to the fact of his being Mosilikatz's son, and of my wish to treat him with respect in consequence, but I distinctly forbade Mrs. Mangwan's reappearance near my cabin. I saw that the allusion to his illustrious birth pleased the old man, and his peace of mind was restored by a present of some carbolic oil wherewith to heal his nose. He proceeded to smear on the oil with great satisfaction, and I added the gift of half-a-crown! Mrs. Mangwan was thenceforth no more seen at Grünfontein.

Mangwan had a great liking for the possession of animals, although he never took care of them when he had them. When the *kaffir* Jonas was sent away from Surprise he left his cat behind for Mangwan. But the cat preferred its liberty, and would not let itself be captured by Magaliesberg. Thereupon Mangwan undertook to catch it, and the way he carried out his undertaking was by every morning for about a fortnight, walking up in a stately manner to Surprise with a sack (destined to receive the cat) on his shoulder, and perambulating the vicinity of Jonas's hut for about an hour. He never looked for the cat—that would have been beneath his dignity—but held his head erect, and if he looked at anything it was at the sky. It is hardly necessary to remark that the cat retained its liberty.

On Moustache he set great value. Moved to compassion by the entreating looks the poor little beast used to cast at me when Magaliesberg would come to drag him away, I offered Mangwan two shillings for him. I thought it a handsome offer considering the dog's surpassing ugliness; but Mangwan shook his head, and ejaculated "Pond," by which he meant that a pound was the value he set on the animal. During the Higginses' absence, however, Mangwan began to feel the pangs of hunger, for he used to get subsidies from their kitchen, given, not stolen—I don't believe Mangwan would steal—then he would often come to me and say, "Bow-wow, bow-wow," and hold up his ten fingers. That meant that his price for the dog had come down to ten shillings. I thereupon shook my head and held up five fingers, intimating that I raised my offer to five shillings.

At last, one day, when Mangwan was very hungry, we struck a bargain for six shillings, and the absurd antics whereby Moustache testified his delight when Mangwan and Magaliesberg went off without him, quite repaid me for my extravagance. And so Moustache became a member of my household, much to Roughy's disgust, who, although much the smaller dog of the two, maintained his supremacy in a most lordly manner—flying at his rival and shaking him by his long drooping ears, until they bled profusely, whenever he thought his right of precedence was in any way interfered with.

Mrs. Mangwan never forgave me, but used to scowl in a most vicious way whenever she saw me. She was a terrible virago; and it was impossible to imagine in what her fascinations had consisted. Dressed in skins not more shrivelled and brown than her own skin, she used to inspire Augusta with horror, when she insisted upon kissing the girl's hand, on the occasions of her visits to Surprise. I have seen my pretty pupil run round and round the table, the old witchlike-looking creature pursuing her until she caught and mumbled over the fair soft hand that formed a curious contrast to the brown, skinny paw of Mrs. Mangwan.

The old savage always called Mr. Higgins "Bob," the name by which she had learned to call him when he used to hunt in Mosilikatz's territory. Her great delight was to be taken through the rooms at Surprise. She was never tired of admiring their splendour, and would clap her hands from time to time, and cry out, "Oh, Bob, Bob!" meaning thereby to convey an idea of her appreciation of what a wonderful man Mr. Higgins was, to have been able to amass such treasures.

CHAPTER 18

Shortly after Hall's arrival, Jimmy informed me that he was going to seek his fortune elsewhere, and departed, with his saddle-bag slung over his shoulder, by a bridle-path which led over the mountain to Rustemberg. The day after, three *kaffirs* came seeking for work, and I engaged them. I told them I would give them two shillings a day and their food, but that I expected them to work hard. Mr. Higgins had told me that I should always be able to get *kaffir* labour for one-and-sixpence a day, and that I could feed my *kaffirs* on nothing but mealie meal; but times, I suppose, were changing quickly. I found that it was almost impossible to get a *kaffir* labourer for less than two shillings, and that the vast majority of them demanded meat at least three times a week, many insisting on having it every day. This was the experience of the Sturtons, as well as my own. Mr. Higgins never employed any *kaffir* labour other than his *kraal* afforded him.

I set these *kaffirs* to work under Hall's orders at the dam; but I was not very well satisfied by the way he made them work or worked himself; they all required supervision. Hall was rather a fine-looking young fellow, and addicted to giving himself airs. He was much coarser of speech than Barrie, although he looked less rough, and was also much more ignorant. I soon came to the conclusion that he would not suit, for I felt sure he was a bad fellow, in spite of the character I had heard of him; but thinking that, for all that, he might be a valuable man on the farm, I gave him plenty of rope, so as to let him hang himself before the month was out, if hanging was to be his fate. Under this treatment he developed rapidly. In the meantime he and the *kaffirs* worked at the dam.

One evening, some time before sunset, I went up to see how they were getting on. Hall was at work, the two *kaffirs* lying on their backs smoking. I asked them why they were not at work; they answered that the sun was gone. That was so far true, inasmuch as the dam, which was on the side of the mountain, was in shade, but the valley and opposite range were still in bright sunshine. I pointed to the valley and bade them get to work again at once. They hesitated a little, then, shouldering their spades, got into the dam and commenced operations. I stood by, until the last rays faded away from the valley; then I told them they might go. I stood guard over them towards sundown every day after that until Saturday. This was pay day, and having received their pay after their work was finished, they bolted without giving me any notice. But the dam was finished; that very evening the finishing touch had been given to the embankment that shut up its narrow outlet; the lower pipe and the drainage pipe were fixed, and I let the water in. This was a very great mistake, but I was in a terrible hurry to see how my dam would act.

The *kaffirs* in the meantime were gone; my shepherd-boy had taken French leave, because I had had him whipped, after repeated warnings, for letting the sheep get astray, whilst he played with some of Mr. Higgins's little herds, who, now that he was away, never looked after the animals in their charge at all. Williams had that morning told me he was too ill with fever to work, and I could see he spoke the truth. The time for ploughing was come; the work must be done, or Grünfontein would be a dead failure. That evening I told Mr. Williams that I must have a decisive answer as to the contract for building. He, after some hesitation, named a price far exceeding that at which Mr. Higgins had estimated the cost, and much higher than I could afford. I told him so, and then he said he would not like to make bricks for another man to build with. He was too ill to walk to Pretoria at once, however; and so, of course, he and I had to make up our respective minds to his remaining until he regained his strength.

I sat up a long while considering the position. Hall had told me that there was a man of the name of Egerton, at Pretoria, who had expressed a wish to obtain work on a farm; he said he believed he knew something of farming, and that though he was drinking hard in Pretoria he might be steady on a farm. He had also told me that he knew a *coolie*—a capital gardener, and accustomed to farm-work—who would, he was sure, be glad to come. My meditations ended in my resolving to saddle up early next morning, and ride to Pretoria to look for workmen, for it was clear that workmen I must have, and at once too. There was, however, the difficulty of my hunting up workmen unassisted, and there was also the difficulty of taking Hall with me, and this for two reasons—one that I had no second horse, and the other that if he came with me, Williams must remain alone at Grünfontein. I must here mention what I omitted before, that my oxen were herded and *kraaled* still with Mr. Higgins's.

I thought it best, however, to trust the farm to itself, and take Hall with me; and the matter of the horse I managed by determining to take the loan of Wellington as far as Moy-plas, and, leaving him there, to ask the Sturtons for the loan of one of their salted horses to Pretoria. It was the unhealthy season for horses, and Pretoria is a very unhealthy place. Mr. Higgins, while regretting that Hall had not come before his departure, had mentioned, as one cause for his regret, that he could have exercised Wellington, so I felt no qualms about letting him ride the horse: and no case of horse-sickness had occurred in the valley, so that I was not much afraid of leaving Wellington in the stable at Moy-plas. I told Hall my plan early, and then went up to look at the dam. Alas! the embankment had sprung several leaks. I opened the pipe, and let the water run out, and while doing so I was standing on the embankment, when I felt it shake, and stepped back just in time to escape from falling, with the part I had been standing on, into the dam. I felt dreadfully disappointed, but there was no time for regret.

I returned to the cabin, where I met Fiervaree, who had brought me some milk. I told him I wanted to see his father, that he was to come back with him as soon as, possible. They arrived shortly after in company, and I persuaded the father to allow his boy to undertake to look after my sheep while I was away. He was to get a shilling a day provided he lost none of them—so far for the father; but Fiervaree had a will of his own, and a separate bargain had to be made with him. He was howling, and saying he wouldn't mind the sheep; what was the money to him? His father would keep it. At last he was induced to name his price, a toy flute and a pound of sweets, always provided no sheep were lost. I then counted them out of the *kraal* to him, and, Wellington having arrived, I told Hall to saddle up.

Hall was delighted at the idea of riding the handsome black horse. He rubbed up Jimmy's stirrups, and the snaffle and curb of his bridle, before putting them on his steed; he was determined he should look decently bitted for once, he said, alluding to the rusty state of Mr. Higgins's bits and stirrups. All his preparations being made, we started. We were not fairly on the flat, and I had only just began to canter, when Hall called out,—

"These stirrups are too small for me, missus."

"Oh," said I, cantering on.

Presently I heard an angry ejaculation behind me.

"What's the matter, Hall?" asked I, looking round.

"It's these —— stirrups," replied Hall. "They're babies' stirrups, not men's; and the brute jumps so I can't stick on with such stirrups."

"Well, take them off, and ride without them," quoth I.

Hall had always spoken of himself as a good horseman. He got off, not looking much pleased.

"Where can I put the things?" he asked.

"Across your saddle in front;" but Hall declared he couldn't do that. "Well," said I, "tie them on to my saddle; anything to push along;" and off I started so soon as they were fastened as I directed. In a few minutes Hall was alongside of me.

"I don't know what's the matter with the brute," he exclaimed; "I never saw a horse go on as he does."

Wellington was evidently very uncomfortable; his rider was mismanaging him; and besides he clearly disliked the snaffle together with the curb—he was not accustomed to it.

"Take off the snaffle," said I; and we stopped, and took off the snaffle. Then we started again. Wellington was fresh, and felt that his rider was not master over him, and it was all Hall could do to hold him in, whilst bumping up and down on Jimmy's small English saddle. The bumping was evidently becoming trying; he shifted his position continually, and at last attempted sitting on his one hand whilst he checked Wellington too sharply with the other; at last—

"D—— the brute and this confounded saddle!" he exclaimed; and I very nearly burst out laughing.

"Gently," I said. "What's the matter?"

"Why, who ever saw such a saddle?" exclaimed Hall. "No *man* could ride on a thing like that; it's a child's saddle;" he had been admiring it greatly while he was girthing it on.

"Well," said I consolingly, "perhaps I shall be able to get you a big Boer saddle at that house yonder," a house belonging to Boers, who, though adverse to English rule, were very civil to me whenever I passed that way.

Poor Hall! How he did wriggle about and abuse his horse and his saddle, and everything but his own bad riding, until we reached the Boer farm; and then, oh, woe! all the saddles were in use.

"You have often ridden bare-backed, have you not?" asked I. "Barebacked, with a blanket strapped over the horse, would perhaps be better?" Yes, Hall thought it would be better. We set off again.

I was cantering sharply, but Wellington shot far ahead of me.

"Steady," I cried.

"I can't stop the horse; I never saw such a brute," cried Hall in reply, tugging at the reins in a very unhorsemanlike fashion.

He was beginning to get angry with the horse, and the horse with him. I knew Wellington to be a very pleasant-paced horse, and to have a very tender mouth, having ridden him myself, so I administered a little admonition to Hall as to keeping his temper. Presently, when I stopped and walked, I saw Hall deliberately get off Wellington and begin to walk by his side. I requested to know what he was about, and elicited from him that he intended to perform the rest of the journey to Moy-plas on foot. Now between Moy-plas and the place where we were was a farm, where there was an exceedingly savage dog. Few dogs are savage with me, but this dog made no exception in my favour; and I had an unpleasant remembrance of a certain solitary moonlight ride home from Mrs. Materson's, whither I had gone on business, when this dog had pursued me for more than a mile, sometimes leaping at Eclipse's throat, and sometimes only kept from biting his legs by the horse's kicks, while I had to keep the brute from fastening on my habit by using my long hunting crop freely.

If Eclipse had not known me and been fond of me, and withal been an intelligent horse, I knew he would have thrown me that night, and the dog would have worried me. I should not have been the first person who suffered from him, for he was the terror of all passers-by that way. I had counted on Hall as being able to cause a diversion in case this pleasant animal should attack me, and I was by no means disposed to forego his company before he had escorted me beyond Mr. Cucumoor's farm. I therefore summarily ordered him to mount, and once more started off at a smart canter.

When Cucumoor's farm was passed (without the dog being seen, by-the-way) I let him dismount, and leaving him to lead Wellington, pushed on for Moy-plas myself. How wretched he did look! I knew he would make no fresh attempt at riding Wellington, so that it was quite safe to leave him.

When I rode up to Moy-plas I found Arthur and William Sturton there. I believe the first thing I said was, "Has there been any horse-sickness here yet?" I heard that there had not been, but that horses were dying fast in Pretoria. I told my story, and asked the loan of one of the two salted horses belonging to Percy. He said I might have my choice.

In the meantime Arthur and William saddled up their salted steeds, and prepared to start home. They had been gone about an hour, when Harriett Sturton suddenly ran in from outside, exclaiming, "Oh! what *can* be the matter? Here is Arthur coming back again, leading his horse." Arthur soon told us. The salted horse had nearly fallen under him; it had the horse-sickness. I felt greatly alarmed, thinking of Wellington, who had just come in with Hall. Arthur had to borrow one of Percy's salted horses to ride home on.

In the evening Harriett and I went for a walk. Percy had ridden over to where his father was having a mill built. We had not gone far when I said, "Look at that horse; it looks ill." It was a brown horse walking to meet us on the road, and looking very mournful.

"Why, it looks like Tommy," said Harriett, "but Percy is not riding him." In a moment, a turn in the road showed us Percy carrying his saddle. The horse was the salted Tommy, and had fallen ill under him. Both horses died the next day, after I left for Pretoria. Hall had now no choice but to follow me on foot, to his great disgust.

I put up at old Mr. Higgins's in Pretoria. He had a little cottage on the outskirts—a miserable-looking place outside, but snug inside; and he had a little stable, into which he kindly let me put Eclipse. Hall arrived late at night, very cross. The next day he found Sam and a brother of his, Mosam—he was doubtful about finding Egerton and these two I engaged. I could not get them to come for less than four pounds a month. In the afternoon I was riding towards the market-square, and Hall was walking beside me, when, just as we passed a public-house, he turned and spoke to a man, then called to me, and presented the individual as Egerton. He was a man of apparently about five-and-thirty, with two black eyes, and a face whose general pallor betokened late heavy drinking and consequent illness. I did not want any more servants, having engaged the two *coolies*, and the man's appearance as he stood before me in a battered wide-awake, torn and dirty coat and trousers, and apologies for boots, was not prepossessing. I had, however, heard that Egerton had said, when Hall was leaving Pretoria, "I would to God I could get out of the place," and so I thought I would see about it.

"You would like to get employment on my farm?" said I. He answered in the affirmative without raising his eyes. "Can you do farm work: do you understand it?"

He answered he had worked on a farm for nine months; but, in reply to my questions as to whether he could drive oxen or plough, he said he could but try. It did not strike me that he would be a very valuable acquisition, but I saw that there was some sort of painful struggle going on in the man; and, although he answered almost monosyllabically, his voice sounded refined.

"What wages do you ask?"

He hesitated a little, then said six pounds a month.

"No, I could not give you that," said I. "I give it to Hall, because I got him with a character of being a steady man, and one who thoroughly understood farming; I should not give it to him otherwise."

"And I have no character, or a bad one—this," said Egerton, raising his hand to designate his black eyes. "Would you think five pounds too much for me to ask?"

What trifles one is sometimes swayed by. A moment before I had almost determined to let the man go, but there was something in his voice and manner as he said this, that reminded me of the voice of a friend, of the manner which, had misfortune and his own fault placed him in Egerton's position, would have been his; it was a very faint resemblance, but it told me that there was something better in Egerton than what appeared, and I said I would give him five pounds, and that he might walk down to Grünfontein the next day in company with Hall and the two *coolies*. I told him to call later in the day at Mr. Higgins's to sign his contract with me. He did so, and then went away. I was busy in the meantime getting offers for the contract for building my farmhouse and out offices.

To my surprise I found that I was known by name to a great many people in Pretoria whom I did not know at all, was indeed a small celebrity as a rich and enterprising farmer. I, of course, knew that there were unexpressed additions to these two adjectives, *viz.*, "inexperienced," "green," and "fair game." I could get no offer for the execution of my plan which did not enormously exceed Mr. Higgins's estimate. I also heard much talk as to the large price I had paid to Mr. Higgins for my farm; when I said that I had not paid for it at all, and that he would let me throw it up if I chose, people laughed, and said I "had better try him." Of course I was offered other farms, which were all described as far more desirable than the one I had.

The next day the rain poured down in torrents, and the third day also. On the first rainy day, Egerton, who, together with his companions, was unable on account of the rain to set out for Grünfontein, came to Mr. Higgins's house. I think he must have been there standing outside for some time before I happened to go to the door. "Could you ask Mr. Higgins if I might sleep in the stable," he said, "it is so very wet?" The question told a terrible story. He slept in the stable, and the Higginses gave him some food. I had been obliged to put Hall up at the Edinburgh at ten shillings a day, I could not get him boarded for less. The next day the men started; I had given them provisions for the road. Sam celebrated his exit from Pretoria by getting gloriously drunk.

I remained behind for two days, partially on account of Mrs. James Higgins having come up to Pretoria for a fourth little baby's advent. Her husband had had to hire an unfurnished house, and bring up furniture for it in his waggon. She liked me to be with her, so I stayed. The fever was yet hanging about me, and I was still troubled with the fever sores, and did not much enjoy the idea of my ride home; however, on Saturday at about half-past three, I saddled up, having managed to get through my various engagements at last.

It was rather late to start on a twenty-four miles' ride in the early part of March; however, I was too anxious to get Eclipse away from unhealthy Pretoria, to wait longer than necessary, and although I felt very tired, having been walking all the morning, I cantered sharply until I reached the farm which is situated midway between Pretoria and Moy-plas. I had calculated that if I could do the distance in three hours and a half I should get in just before dark, for there was no moon. I had kept time so far, but I could not hold out. The pain of those dreadful sores was becoming unbearable when I cantered, and I felt almost too weak to sit in the saddle. Eclipse, on the contrary, was very gay and festive, and as the rays of the declining sun glanced on the sticks or stones he passed, he would pretend to be frightened, and shy in play. It is tedious as well as tiring to walk twelve miles on horseback.

The last faint streaks of day lighted me across the Crocodile; then it became pitch dark. I could hardly see Eclipse's pretty little head as he tossed it up and down impatiently; as to guiding him it was out of the question. But my little horse was quite able to take care of both of us. Winding about, now down a steep and stony ravine, now up the other side, turning cleverly round bushes and trees, he brought me safe to near the backdoor of Moy-plas, where he was assailed by a troop of dogs, whose barks and yelps soon ceased at the sound of my voice, but who heralded my arrival to the supper-party inside.

Old Mr. Sturton, as he stood by me while I ungirthed Eclipse, said,

"I suppose you know about the black horse?"

"What? "I exclaimed.

"It's dead."

I felt that I turned deadly pale; the horse was worth a hundred pounds, and I could ill afford to lose that sum. Mr. Sturton saw my face by the light of the lantern. He began to laugh. "It's my son William's black horse," he said, "not Bob's."

After giving Eclipse his supper in an outhouse, I went in to my own.

Very cosy the long, low room, with the well-spread supper-table looked, after my dark and weary ride, very cheery were the familiar kind faces of those seated round it, and very pleasant was their hearty welcome. Little did we all think that evening, when, forgetting my fatigue under these varied influences, I sat telling the news from Pretoria, that before that day twelvemonths, all that would remain of that comfort—hard won comfort, too—would be the bare walls, which may perhaps even yet fall victims to the revenge of the Boers!

There was one unfamiliar face, however, amongst my listeners. It was that of a little man who sat back from the rest—for supper was just over when I entered—and who struck me as being a stranger to the Sturtons as well as to myself. He was apparently between fifty and sixty, chubby, self-possessed, apparently on very good terms with himself, and engaged in a close scrutiny of everybody present, with a way of putting his head a little on one side in order to assist his investigations. This little man was so strikingly like a little cock-sparrow, that when he made any observation it almost sounded like a chirp.

The next morning at breakfast there was talk about my intended buildings, about what had been asked by the contractors I had spoken to in Pretoria, about the servants I had engaged, and who had passed by Moy-plas the previous day. There was a general impression that Egerton would be found worth nothing, the *coolies* worth little, but Hall worth a great deal. Mr. Sturton had let him have Wellington to ride home on, much to my horror, for I knew that he was not fit to be trusted with a horse. Egerton had gone on alone, the *coolies* remaining half a day behind him to prepare and discuss a curry, for which purpose they had bought a fowl from the Sturtons. Mr. Sparrow listened to all this with his head on one side.

After breakfast I loitered about. I always feel lazy on Sunday mornings, and besides, I was tired. Harriett had got a little pig as a pet, a jolly fat little beast that trotted about everywhere after her, and was very good-tempered, except when anyone but Harriett happened to inconvenience it, then it made furious onslaughts on the offender's legs. There was the garden to look at, but after a while I became interested in some remarks Mr. Sparrow made to me about farm-buildings: they betokened that he knew something about such things, and we began to talk seriously. Presently he asked me whether I would show him my plan; I did so, and then he pointed out various faults in it, and I saw that he was right. He gave me several valuable hints, all in the way a benevolent sparrow might have done, and at last said, that if I would allow him, he would draw me a plan which would, he thought, please me better—quite disinterestedly—just because it was such a pleasure to see anyone so enterprising—so energetic; he was engaged in carrying out another contract, for he was an architect; indeed, he was in such request, because of his superior knowledge, that he had no spare time, that his head—his head, and he shook it a little as he thought of his sad case—was overtaxed; still, for a lady, and such a praiseworthy energetic lady, he would put on the strain. All this, and much more that was eulogistic of himself and me, did this benevolent specimen of the sparrow tribe twitter forth, whilst I thought to myself what a sly old bird it was.

However, disinterested or not, Mr. Sparrow evidently was a great deal more advanced than anyone else I was likely to meet with, in knowledge of the sort of building I was anxious to erect. In the midst of the abundance of his self-laudatory and adulatory twitters I could see that he was also an original, and he amused me greatly; so I accepted his offer, and we parted very good friends.

CHAPTER 19

I saddled up after dinner, but alas! my first short canter showed me
that I should have to make Eclipse walk the eighteen miles home. It
was a dreary look-out, but there was no help for it. Soon I saw a slight
figure walking towards me, the figure of a young fellow dressed in
coat, trousers, and wide-awake—a white youngster too. Who could he
be? None of the young men at Lettie Matersen's farm, I knew; neither
was he any of the Sturtons of Moy-plas; he was not one of the Nells:
who could he be? It is unusual to see a Boer walking at any distance
from his house, and the pedestrian was evidently of the well-to-do
classes. The figure and I were diminishing the distance between us all
this time, and then I saw with surprise that the youngster was Jimmy.
He had terminated his wanderings by getting employment as tutor to
two small Boers. The paternal Boer was going out trading, taking his
youngsters in his waggon; Jimmy was going too.

The waggon was outspanned for a short time at Mrs. Matersen's.
Jimmy had been to Grünfontein; had heard of how his riding accou-
trements had been dropped along the road; had picked up bridle and
saddle at Grünfontein, whither Hall had taken them, and was now
going to Moy-plas to pick up his stirrups. I wished him Godspeed in
his new life, and we parted. I had yet to pass Cucumoor's dog. I saw
the brute sitting on the top of the rise across which the road went, and
no sooner did he spy me than he began to bark and wag his tail—in
a fiendish manner it appeared to me. I had heard that the Cucumoors
were adverse to the English, and that they would encourage the dog
to assault any one belonging to our race; but I suddenly made up my
mind to beard Cucumoor in his den (a mud-hut), and turning Eclipse
off the road I cantered towards the house, whereupon Mr. Dog did
the same.

Then I saw three small Cucumoors running towards me. The cause of their *empressement* was that a baby related to some member of the Cucumoor family had the thrush. They expostulated with the dog, and introduced me to a wonderfully large family, of several men, still more women, a good many hobbledehoy girls, a troop of small children, and a sprinkling of infants, all related in some inextricable manner, and all capable of being compressed when necessary, like "Alice in Wonderland," judging from the diminutive size of the house compared with the number of its occupants.

During the day they only enter it by relays, so the eyes of the uninitiated are not favoured with a view of them in a compressed condition. Cucumoor's household was no more surprising in this respect than many others, but the family was the largest, as compared to their house, I had yet seen. They were very friendly. They gave me coffee, and I gave them a prescription. They asked what they were to pay; and when I said, "Nothing," they beamed. They laughed at my absurd efforts to speak their dialect, and I laughed too; and we parted excellent friends, after I had learnt the name of the dog—or rather dogs, for there were two of them. The savage was a jolly dog when you had a personal introduction to him, and his name was "Docks." This was supposed to be an English name, and was derived from the English word "dog." I heard it was a favourite name for a dog amongst the Boers.

It was nearly dark when I reached Grünfontein. Williams was better (he went away soon after). Several sheep were missing, but I afterwards recovered them; and there were two English brickmakers awaiting my arrival, anxious to get the job to go on with the bricks—a desire in which I gratified them. I began work in earnest now. The next day I went for my oxen. I had a plough already. Mosamma was a very fair driver, and a splendid cook; he was also conceited, lazy, and good-for-nothing, but his curries were delicious! Sam was not a bad fellow, but he was for some unknown reason the bounden slave of his younger brother. Egerton worked hard and spoke little, and Hall continued to develop quickly; he also in a very short time showed clearly that he could not hold a plough properly, or drive a *span*—he was in short an agricultural Mr. Winkle.

He was greatly disgusted at my clear perception of his ignorance, and put on extra bumptiousness. Then I administered a rebuke, the result of which was that the next morning he said he wished to leave me, and as I had meant to send him away, we agreed perfectly. I had been lately in the habit of having my meals in my tiny bedroom, while

Hall and Egerton had theirs in the sitting-room, the *coolies* of course eating outside. I had often listened to Hall's loud talk, and observed Egerton's reticence and different mode of speech. I had no doubt now that he was a gentleman by education and early association, although fallen from that estate. So on Hall's going away I took my meals with him.

I had one difficulty with respect to him. The *coolies* called him "Jack," as Hall had done. It was evidently out of the question for this to be allowed, if Egerton was to be treated as a gentleman by me, and after a few days of more intimate acquaintance with him, I saw that it would be unjust to treat him otherwise. I knew, however that the two bumptious *coolies*, though respectful enough to me, would rebel at this, and probably leave me at the end of the month. However, I took heart of grace, and with a regretful eye at the finishing of the dam, the ploughing, the cutting of poles for fencing in the land, &c., I told them that henceforth he was to be called Mr. Egerton. They looked glum, but obeyed. In the meantime, about a day after Hall's departure, as the sun was setting, and as I was getting the table ready for tea, a German, of the thorough good working German type, presented himself at my little cabin door. I knew my man at once, and engaged him on his own terms, six pounds a month, and he was worth even more.

Quiet, quaint, like one of the figures in some German etching il-lustrative of German country life, doing everything he did thoroughly and unostentatiously, with a love for a quiet chat over a pipe when work was done, careful of any animal whether belonging to him or committed to his charge, shrewd, business-like, strictly respectful, but with a thoroughly good opinion of himself,—my new acquisition, in his respectable dress, his enormous flat hat, under which his kindly and merry blue eyes twinkled, with his rugged face and greyish mous-tache, and his talk about fatherland, conjured up pleasant visions of my childish days before me. He had been many years in Africa, but had fought in the Franco-Prussian war, and had also fought the *kaffirs* as a volunteer. So had Mr. Egerton—in fact, as a rule every man you meet here has been a volunteer and they had had some slight acquaintance with each other.

The men who were making the bricks an old man, Joe, and a young man, Jim—had also been in the volunteers at Secocoonee's, and so all were more or less acquainted. They all called Mr. Egerton by his surname, and I left that alone. The work, all but the dam, now got on well; but I had to give up the idea of making the embankment of the dam until I could build it up properly, and for that I had no lime; a second attempt at an earthwork embankment failed also. Pigsties had to be built, for so soon as the crops began to come up, the pigs could no longer be left to wander about. A large water-furrow was taken out, leading through the large dam to the small dam, and thence down to the new lands below; the garden had to be got into order; the poles cut for the wire fencing which I intended to get fixed round the upper lands; and the ploughing and sowing had to be done.

In the midst of all this, one evening Jimmy made his appearance. He had tired of teaching, but was going to help in the Higginses' store at Fahl-bank; until they were ready for him he had come to me. He had to sleep with Mr. Egerton in the sitting-room. The German slept in the stable by preference, and of course he helped in various ways—Grünfontein was no place for idlers. Reva no longer came, except to do the washing, and the *coolies* cooked, so that we had much better dinners, a change which Jimmy appreciated. On the whole we were very jolly.

Mr. Sparrow appeared one morning with his plan—and a very good one it was, vastly superior to mine; and at last we arranged that he was to have the contract for the house, I was to find material, he labour. He said he would send me his partner shortly, who would give me a specification of what would be required, and of the probable cost; that he had arranged so as to be able to do my work; that he must ask me to send my waggon to bring a few things from where they were, behind the mountain, to my place. He kept up the fiction of his suffering head, and his disposition to sacrifice himself, to a certain extent, for my advantage—spoke of how he would not do so for a man—oh, dear no! (and the head was shaken gently), kept it up delightfully and as it seemed an agreeable pastime to him I never interfered, but seemed to accept it all as gospel.

The brickmakers in the meantime got a *kaffir* to help them, and progressed well. I paid them at the usual rate, a pound per thousand, and they found themselves. Joe was nothing remarkable; but Jim was a fine young fellow, and when I was at times in want of help, showed himself to be a good practical farmer. He kept his own place, was never pushing, but had a frank hearty manner that was very taking.

A few days after Mr. Sparrow's departure I had ridden to and from the valley, and coming back late, long after dark, owing to having to go out of my road considerably in order to avoid a grass fire, I remarked that Eclipse was ill. He carried me well, but I knew even before I got off him that he was going to have an attack of a peculiar and danger-ous kind such as he had had a short time before. I got him into the stable and applied all necessary remedies as quickly as I could; but the poor horse was in terrible agony, and at last I thought I should certain-ly lose him. We all—the *coolies* excepted—sat up in the little anteroom to the stable, and at length, after a heavy dose of opium, he got better, and we were just thinking of leaving him and going to supper—it was about eleven o'clock—when we heard a scrambling sound amongst the rocks and bushes below where we stood, and then a voice asking if this were Grünfontein.

On our answering in the affirmative, a man and horse made their appearance, and the man presented himself as Mr. Sparrow's partner. He had ridden on in front of the waggon I had sent under the charge of Mosamma and Dahl Nell to fetch him and his things, and had lost his way. We all adjourned into the little sitting-room after I had seen his horse given food, and after supper the German retired to the stable, and Mr. O'Grady made up a bed for himself in the house, in company with Mr. Egerton and Jimmy.

Mr. O'Grady was an Africander, and a very singular person. He had a perplexing habit of answering at random at times, like a person who is deaf or who is listening to a foreign language; yet he was not deaf, and he habitually spoke English. He was fond of using long words, and had a disposition to laugh in an unreasonable and unaccountable manner. He might have been taken to be very simple, or very deep. He affected rather to patronise Mr. Sparrow, who in his turn spoke of him in like manner. He was certainly very obliging and good-natured. He informed me that Mosamma and Dahl had got drunk together, and had behaved very badly, on the road. The waggon came in the next day, while Mr. Egerton and I were at work thatching the pigsties.

I called Dahl Nell up to me, and in Mosamma's presence gave him a good blowing up, laying stress on the fact, that disgraceful as it was for a man to get drunk at all, the disgrace was still greater when a black man was his boon companion. I did this, partly because I knew it was a rebuke Dahl would wince under, partly because I saw it was neces-sary to snub Mr. Mosamma; not because I thought there was really any sense in what I said, but then it would evidently have been throwing pearls before swine to have taken high ground in talking to my two auditors. They were both very angry, and yet felt very much humili-ated, which was just what I wanted.

A few days after Jimmy complained to me that Mosamma had

called him "Jimmy," and had been disrespectful to him; and on my speaking to my friend on the subject, he got into a terrible fury, and said that I was his mistress, and that he would always treat me with respect, but that as to the others he was as good as they were, with all their masters and mistresses! This, from a low-caste Indian, who knew that I knew what he was in his own country, for I had spoken to him in Hindustani, was strong, and I put him down pretty smartly. The result was that two days after, having finished their month, the two worthies departed (I heard them as they passed Jimmy and Mr. Egerton say derisively, "Goodbye, Mister; goodbye, Master"), and Jimmy having to leave for Fahl-plas the day after, I was on the eve of being left in the lurch once more for want of labour, as two men cannot manage ploughing, and sowing, with oxen.

CHAPTER 20

It was evident that something must be done under the circumstances, and that quickly. The German said he knew where he could get good *kaffirs* to work, at a missionary station. He told me the name. It was eight hours on horseback from Grünfontein. I sounded him a little as to whether he would walk there to get them; evidently he was not disposed to do so. I had no horse but Eclipse, and he was not well; besides, even without its being horse-sickness time, I had no fancy to trust Eclipse to a stranger; I knew he would make a battle of it between his rider and himself at some part of the journey, and if he were the conqueror, where should I get my *kaffirs*? If the rider were the conqueror, it would only be after severe punishment had been inflicted, and I did not care for my horse to be punished by anyone but me. However, the horse as it was could not go; he was still weak from his attack of colic. In this dilemma I bethought me of Mr. O'Grady, and of his horse—a sorry brute, but if there be any truth in the theory of salting, it certainly was salted.

It had been through the Zulu war, had had horse-sickness, and had recovered. I asked him if he would lend me the animal, I of course taking all risks; and he very kindly consented. The German set forth on a Saturday, and the next morning Jimmy too bade me goodbye. So Mr. Egerton and I were left sole possessors of Grünfontein. There was plenty of work for him in the garden, and for me in various ways. I had no one to help me now, for Reva had gone, as I think I said before, and she only washed for me, and I had been unable to get any boy to mind the sheep. There were several who would have come, and played noisily all day near the house or in the garden with other little *kaffirs*, whom they would have invited to spend the day and have dinner with them, but there was not one who would mind the sheep, so I preferred doing without them.

Mr. Higgins's sheep were constantly coming astray by twenties or thirties into my *kraal*, and his cattle were constantly causing me damage by trampling down the sides of the leading water-furrow. Numbers of Mr. Higgins's sheep got lost on the mountains, and at last one of his *kaffirs* asked me to go and count them out of the *kraal* one morning, to see how many were away. I did so, and found more than a hundred missing. I cleaned the house and the pots and pans, and washed up the dishes, counted the sheep out of the *kraal*, cleaned Eclipse and the stable, cooked dinner, calling Mr. Egerton from the garden occasionally to look after the sheep when they wandered to an unhealthy part of the *veldt*, or to help with lifting the big pot and kettle, for the fire was on the ground, and I had a tendency to tumble into it if I had to move anything heavy; then towards evening, after I had washed up the things, I cut Eclipse's bed for the night, or helped in the garden at clearing the weeds. After supper Mr. Egerton and I played chess on a small pasteboard chess-board which I made, with absurd little chess-men that he had cut out of wood, and we talked of all sorts of things of which I had not talked since I came to Africa. Mr. Egerton was very fond of painting, and of reading, and I think it was as pleasant to him as to me to meet with a person to whom he could talk about anything except every-day topics.

Days went on, and the German did not return. On Friday, Jim came to the cottage to buy some meal.

"Strange that German not a coming back," said Jim.

"Yes," I said.

"I'm a thinking he must a taken the wrong road," said Jim.

"Why what wrong road?" asked I; "he knew the road. I don't think he can have taken the wrong road."

Jim's eyes twinkled, "Well, I was a thinking as he might a taken it on purpose," said Jim.

"What!" I exclaimed.

"Well," continued Jim in a stolid sort of way, although with a twinkle in his eye, "I said to my mate when I saw him a ridin' off on that there horse, as how he'd never come back."

"Do you really think he has stolen the horse?" I asked.

"Lor bless you, ma'am, yes," said Jim, smiling at my simplicity. "I did say to my mate as how it would be well if we was to offer to let our *kaffir* go for you to get boys from his *kraal*; but then, you see, I said it certainly was no business of ours."

"I wish you had warned me, Jim," I said. "I never thought of his stealing the horse!"

"You have to be very particular in these parts, ma'am," said Jim, "more especially with them furriners. I knew a Frenchman as jumped a horse"—and he paused reflectively. "No, ma'am, I've no manner of doubt as how he's in the Free State now with that there horse."

This was pleasant. I went down to Mr. O'Grady's little canvas house below the spur where the hut stood. Mr. O'Grady still believed in the German's honesty. So did Mr. Egerton. But days went on; Saturday came, and Sunday, and passed. Jim was triumphant; we had all given up the missing German. He had asked me to give him some money for the road, saying, he had none of his own, and what I had given him amounted to his wages—the things he had left behind were of no value. I gave him up at last, and I told Mr. O'Grady that he must name his price for the horse. He said that there was a salted horse for sale, in the valley, for twenty-six or seven pounds, and that, if he liked it when he saw it, he would ask me to buy it for him. He was to see it on Tuesday.

On Monday evening Mr. Egerton and I had finished supper and were playing chess (Mr. O'Grady lived in his canvas house), when the dogs jumped up and barked, there was a sound of horses' hoofs and the German rode up, with three *kaffirs* following him. He had been delayed owing to the difficulty of getting *kaffirs*. He said he knew that we should all think he had jumped the horse. He was very good-humoured about it when we confessed we had thought so, made us each a present of a handkerchief he had bought at the missionary's store, and ate a hearty supper. Two days after I engaged two other *kaffirs*, and the work went on quickly and well. Jimmy used to come over of a Saturday to spend Sunday, when we used to be very merry, carrying our conversations on sometimes until after we were all in bed—at least if Mr. Egerton's and Jimmy's blankets could be called bed, the partition between my room and the sitting-room not in any way impeding it. Mr. O'Grady, in the meantime, drew a multiplicity of plans and elevations and diagrams of doors and windows, and partitions of stalls, &c., but I could not get him to give me the specification I wanted; he said he must wait for his partner—and his partner was not forthcoming.

At last one afternoon he appeared. He was full of importance; he twittered and chirped, and said now everything would go on delightfully. I pressed him for the specification, and at last a very detailed one was offered for my inspection. I went over it carefully, and got Mr.

Sparrow to give me estimates as to cost. It ran up much higher than he had led me to suppose it would. It was very hard to bring things to a clear understanding, for he twittered and chirped so much about his head, and how overtaxed his brain was, and made so many digressions about the society he was used to, and so many polite speeches to me, that time went by, and I was often obliged to interrupt our business talks, to go about necessary household duties; but at last I pointed out things I should wish cut out, as merely unnecessary luxuries, and the specification was taken back to be revised.

It was drawing near the time when the Higginses were to return, and at last I got a letter telling me when I might expect them. They had left me the key of Surprise, and sometimes on Sundays I would walk over there to air the house; or sometimes, if the moon was up, I would go after work was over, and play on the piano. On one of these occasions I remember being struck by Mr. Egerton's delight at seeing a carpet which I had stretched out in one of the rooms. He said he had not seen one for years, that it was quite refreshing. It was also refreshing to me to hear anyone say, as he did, when by chance I happened to turn over a waltz and play it, "Oh, don't play that stupid thing; go on with Norma, or Mozart's Twelfth Mass."

Looking forward to the Higginses' return, I was often struck by the curious gulf that lies invariably between the European settlers in this country and those born in it—a gulf which is rendered wider, doubtless, when the European settler has been bred amongst all the refinements of European life, but which exists even when he is of the lower middle, or even of the labouring class. To the European, life here is an excitement—it is a race after wealth. There is something of the spirit of the gambler in all who try their fortunes out here. They may work in the fields sowing crops, or they may tend their herds and flocks unexciting occupations you would say but all this represents a portion of a game on which they have generally staked all they have; and to all, there must be something of excitement in such a game, whether it be dice or oxen, cards or seeds of corn, that are the counters.

Then further; until a settler here becomes demoralized, he always looks forward to something beyond what he has—it may be to go home; it may be to bring some dear one out to him; it may be to become very rich for the mere sake of being very rich; but there is always something. How different are this man's thoughts, as he glances over his cultivated lauds, and at his live-stock, from those of the Africander farmer, who, standing perchance by his side, thinks of all his possessions as things that he has perhaps won by toil, but with which, now that he has them, he is contented, looking for nothing beyond. His crops will realize a price which will enable him to live as he is living. If they fetch a higher price than usual, he can perhaps get a new waggon, or indulge in a half-bred English horse; or perhaps, if he be a very enterprising character, he may think he will sometime take his children to Natal, and let them behold the sea, and the great ships that he would be afraid to trust himself on, though, may be, he has faced a lion in his day; his cows will calve, his ewes will lamb, and he will every year mark some of their little ones for his own little ones, so that when they are men and women they too will have flocks and herds, without having to take away from their old father.

The two talk of the market-prices, and of the oxen, &c., as if they had a common interest; but they are as far separated from each other as a gamester is from the man who plays a quiet rubber of whist for sweets, with his wife and children of an evening. Of course if, joined to this, there be in the one the existence of a remembrance of all the artistic culture—the refinement—the romance—the historic remains—which can be the portion only of him who has lived in old countries, and which is denied to one born and bred in South Africa, the gulf is enormously widened. Once this had struck me forcibly at Surprise, when Mr. Higgins, looking at a representation of an angel on the cover of a photograph-book that was lying on the table, said to me, "What a beautiful thing! I wonder if there can exist such beautiful things."

"I don't think that is so very beautiful," I said. "One can easily imagine a more beautiful angel than that."

I remember the look in his eyes as he said, "Yes, I dare say you can. But do you know, I don't think any of us Africanders can imagine much; we haven't got the training; we never see anything."

I felt so sorry for what I had said, but his words were a commentary on what I said before as to the commonplaceness of the country. What training more than that which Nature gives him does an Italian, or a Swiss, or even many a German or Frenchman want, to render him capable of imagining things of beauty? What taught the Greeks to become masters of the beautiful to all succeeding ages? Mr. Higgins was a man capable of admiring nature; his wife had a most sensitive appreciation of natural beauties, but they had never seen beauty. The greatest beauty Mr. Higgins ever saw, by his own confession, was a sunset lighting up the valley that lay below Surprise. I remember, one evening, his asking me in good faith if I had ever seen anything to surpass it in all my wanderings.

The consciousness that this great gulf lay between the Higginses and myself, struck me painfully now. It was irremediable; but as I looked forward to their return, and felt how delighted I was that I should soon see them, I could not help lamenting in my heart, that our friendship should have this flaw in it.

One evening after dark, Fiervaree came to the door of the cabin to say that Mr. Higgins had come, and wanted the key of the house. The waggons were to come in next day. I had just got the specification from Mr. Sparrow, and he had brought me the contract to sign as well, but I declined signing it until I had gone to Pretoria to see about the prices of material. Mr. Sparrow had urged me to go quickly, and said Mr. O'Grady could go with me, that he would give me every opportunity of getting things cheaply, and would save me a great deal of trouble. Mr. Sparrow was disturbed in his mind about one thing. Mr. O'Grady was, he twittered, a very young man—a good young man; he did not like to expose him to the temptations to be met with at Pretoria; could not I suggest any place where he could stay with some kind, respectable family? Mr. Sparrow was paternally interested. It struck me that as Mr. O'Grady was considerably over twenty, and had been in the volunteers, he must have seen sufficient of this wicked world and its doings, for his innocence not to suffer much from a three days' stay in Pretoria.

I said I was sorry, but I could only suggest that he could sleep at the waggon. Then there was one other little point that Mr. Sparrow was uneasy about. He was subject to palpitations, and he wanted a bottle of brandy, but he did not like to put temptation in a young man's way, although Mr. O'Grady was sober—oh, yes, a strictly sober young man indeed, said the little bird, shaking its head at me as if it had discovered me in a mental doubt as to the young man's virtuous disposition with regard to alcoholic drinks. Would I be so good as to bring him a bottle of brandy? Thinking that Mr. O'Grady must be a very odd young man if he found no difficulty in refraining from entering the public-houses of Pretoria, but was liable to fall into the error of uncorking and drinking out of a bottle of brandy belonging to somebody else and entrusted to his charge, I replied that I would bring the brandy myself with pleasure.

I passed the day before I was to start, on horseback, for Pretoria with Mr. O'Grady as my companion, principally at Surprise, taking the plans with me. I went there also in the morning on the day of my departure. Somehow Mr. Sparrow seemed to take it ill my showing the plans to Mr. Higgins; and he and his partner had some disagreement, in which they were mixed up with some men they had hired to work, one of whom I had cautioned them against, as belonging to the drunken trio I had had working on the dam. They seemed irritated, and talked a great deal, until I was obliged to cut them short and saddle up. I gave Mr. O'Grady a little start of me. As I bade Mr. Sparrow goodbye, he laid his hand impressively on my horse's neck. "Now remember," he said, "you need do nothing, absolutely nothing. Mr. O'Grady will save you all trouble. You must just let him know where he can find you whenever he wants you, at any moment, and he will do everything." I said I felt much obliged for Mr. O'Grady 's benevolent intentions as to my comfort.

The German had already started for Pretoria in charge of the waggon. He could not drive, but had a *kaffir* as driver, and also a *kaffir* foreloper, but of course I wanted a responsible man in charge. I only hoped he would not become irresponsible at Pretoria.

I had promised to see on my way to Moy-plas, where I meant to sleep, the wife of a certain Fenter, an old Boer, whose house was not far from Cucumoor's. Fenter had ridden over to Surprise that morning to beg of me to do so, and I had promised; but the little Sparrow and his partner had delayed me, and it was rather late when I started. Added to this, Mr. O'Grady's sorry little pony was not up to keeping to a quick canter, although his master insisted he was. He would not let me leave him and ride on alone; he said he was afraid of losing the road; and he protested that his horse was so fresh he absolutely had to hold him in; although, if I cantered fast for any time, I could hear the poor little animal blowing behind me, and hear a cut given to it every now and then; and once, when Eclipse got far before it, it lifted up its poor little voice and whinnied for him to stop.

Of course after that I kept Eclipse at a very slow pace, and so by the time we had to take the turn for Fenter's house it was nearly dark. The house was a very small one, built of unburnt brick, and, as is general with Boer, or even English Africanders' houses, stuck down in the *veldt* without any attempt at making its surroundings pretty. Hearing the horse's tramp, Fenter, a small, thin, delicate-looking old man, came out. He was surprised to see me so late, and surprised, too, to see me with a companion. I introduced Mr. O'Grady as a builder, which explained everything; and then I told how I had been delayed, and asked old Fenter whether he could give me stabling for Eclipse. He said "Yes, for both horses." I did not ask whether he could put O'Grady and me up, for, arriving late at a Boer's house on such an errand as mine, I knew that to be unnecessary; some sort of shakedown was sure to be provided.

After I had cleaned Eclipse, and given him his forage, I adjourned to the house. There old Fenter introduced me to Mrs. Fenter. As is very often the case amongst the Boers, the lady's proportions made up for what was wanting in those of her lord and master. If old Mrs. Fenter had been asked to sit in a stall at the Italian Opera, I don't think she would have been able to get in. She was a jolly-looking woman by nature, but just then she looked somewhat woebegone, having *erysipelas* in her face not badly, but doubtless enough to be very uncomfortable. Old Fenter was deaf. Mrs. Fenter having tied up her head in numerous bandages, was so artificially. O'Grady sat on the edge of his chair, and grinned at nothing in particular, occasionally varying his amusement by a chuckle, also at nothing in particular. Old Fenter occasionally asked a question of me, or made remarks about O'Grady and myself to his wife—not offensively; personally I have seldom found Boers offensive—but from a sort of natural rudeness which is in the race, and with which, being natural, it would be absurd to get annoyed.

A little girl who helped in the house, and who I suppose was some sort of relation, looked covertly at me, and when she caught my eye smiled pleasantly and rather shyly, whilst I endeavoured in bad Dutch, to converse—or rather, to hold a soliloquy. This was a thing I was getting accustomed to—not very amusing, but good as practice. My auditors were generally much what they were in this case, only the number of fat women and shy little girls with pleasant smiles was sometimes multiplied, and a hulking young man or two, or a young matron already running to fat, thrown in. The soliloquy always had the same headings—the big dam I was making (the biggest dam in that part of the country, some one would always remark parenthetically), the fine span of salted oxen I had bought from Mr. Higgins, at which some one would always say, "Are you sure they *are* salted?" and when I said I had been at Surprise when they salted, they would wag their heads and say, "Ah, yes, that is right," and ask the price, and wag their heads again, and say, "Ah, yes, that was not too much for salted oxen, real salted oxen—oxen that had had redwater and lung-sick."

Then I would tell what crops I was going to put in, and ask advice about it (the Boers like an English person to ask advice from them);

and then I would tell of how I thought I might get manure from Hermann Potchieter's old *kraal*, which would lead to a little discussion between members of the family I was talking to, and give me time to think what should be my next heading; and then I would tell how many sheep in my *kraal* had had fever; and when I was running very low, I knew I could always make the whole party laugh by saying how I had tried to make bread myself, and how bad it was. That point was always a success, and led to my being asked whether the Boer bread was not nice; and that led to my saying how very nice the Boer biscuits were, and that we did not know how to make them in England; and that was always a second success. I flatter myself that my Boer neighbours thought me rather agreeable. They certainly thought me cracked, but that did not matter in the least.

Supper on this occasion caused a pause in my soliloquy. It was the usual bread and mutton and coffee. Old Fenter said grace. Presently I saw preparations being made for a bed on the floor of the sitting-room—there were only two rooms besides the little kitchen in the house. Then old Fenter signified to O'Grady that he was to sleep in the sitting-room, and Mrs. Fenter lighted a candle and took me into the bedroom, which was doorless a curtain doing duty as door. It was a small room, with a four-post bed at one side, nearly occupying the whole side. This bed had hangings of white calico, which shut it in and made a sort of box of it. At the other side of the room was a trestle bed. Mrs. Fenter pointed to this as mine. Now, as I had intended to sleep at Moy-plas I had taken no nightdress with me, for I knew I could get one there, and I had sent up all my small amount of luggage in the waggon to Pretoria. As Mrs. Fenter had not given me any garment of the sort, I simply removed my shoes, and lay down on the bed. I knew that Boers never undress at night, even in case of illness, so I was prepared for this; but what I was not prepared for was to see old Fenter toddle into the room.

Mrs. Fenter had just removed her upper dress, and then rolled into bed, raising the curtain to do so. The little girl had lain down near the foot of the same bed. I lay quietly watching old Fenter's operations. I rather wondered what he was going to do. There was a light hung on the wall at the other side of the four-poster, and I could see the portly form of Mrs. Fenter cast in shadow against the white curtain. Old Fenter divested himself leisurely of his coat and of his *feldt-schoons*, or field-shoes, made of untanned leather; stockings he had none; and then (having apparently an idea that going to bed was a process which demanded a certain amount of privacy, although compatible with having a small girl in bed with Mrs. Fenter and himself, and a strange lady in the same room) he, instead of boldly raising the curtain, like Mrs. Fenter, proceeded to creep in from the bottom of the bed, very cautiously, on hands and knees. A few minutes after, portentous snores proclaimed that the three occupants of the couch were fast asleep. I went to sleep, too, and slept till dawn.

I cleaned Eclipse (I always carried his brush and comb with me), had early coffee, and O'Grady and I up-saddled in the still dewy morning, and departed.

We had breakfast at Moy-plas, where I found Harriett's pig still flourishing; and after a short rest, saddled-up once more.

I had postponed a little of my talk on business with O'Grady, until I should be taking this ride to Pretoria with him, for the Sparrow and he, being fond of frequent digressions from the main subject of discourse, were apt to take up a great deal of time before coming to the point, and time was precious at Grünfontein. O'Grady seemed troubled in his mind. He at last asked me whether I really meant to let him and his partner carry out the contract? I said, certainly I did; was I not going to Pretoria on purpose to get materials for them to work with? He then repeated the kind offer Mr. Sparrow had made in his name, to save me all trouble if I would only let him know where he might find me at any moment. I suggested that this would be difficult, as I had a great deal of business on hand, and should be here, there, and everywhere during the day. I asked if it would not do for me to tell him some particular hour when he would be sure to find me at some appointed place. O'Grady seemed surprised, he had not known that I had business in Pretoria.

"Not about getting estimates, &c., for material?" I asked.

O'Grady thought that *he* was going to Pretoria for that purpose. If *I* were going to do this business, what was the use of his going also? I suggested that two heads were better than one occasionally, as also proverbially; to which proposition O'Grady, with a look of thoughtfulness, agreed.

We off-saddled half way to Pretoria, against my usual custom, but I was sorry for O'Grady's pony, and we reached Pretoria late.

O'Grady left me, to go to the house of an acquaintance, where he had arranged for himself to put up, so that I conclude his senior partner's anxieties on his account had been allayed. I rode on, anxious to find the German and my waggon, and discover whether he had been drinking or not. I found the oxen grazing on a piece of common land towards the middle of the town. The *kaffirs* were with them, and one of them took me to where the German was, with the waggon, on the market-square. I then went to the house of my kind friend Mrs. Parker, where I had an invitation, and sent Eclipse to the stables of the "European" under the German's charge.

In the ensuing days I found out satisfactorily that the cost of material would enormously exceed anything that it had been estimated to me at. I found out, too, that the German could be as thorough in getting drunk, as in doing anything else. This did not surprise me; the former discovery did. Of course, I heard the same talk about my purchase of Grünfontein as I had heard before. In the meantime, O'Grady seemed gradually getting excited, and at last one evening called on me, and after much beating about the bush told me that he found he and the Sparrow had been mistaken, that they could not execute the building for what they had said, and handed me an estimate for nearly double the stated amount. The result was, that he went down to Grünfontein next day to tell the fact to the Sparrow, while I remained a day behind to attend the weekly auction on the market-square. I had never attended an auction before, and I had a vague idea that I was doing something very disreputable.

I knew that in my new character of an enterprising farmer, auctions were in my way; but I felt rather nervous in taking to this clearly-defined line. The German, being sober, looked respectability itself, and I kept him close to me, hoping thereby to cover myself with a little of his aegis of propriety. I wanted a second horse, and the German confided to me that he wanted to buy a horse, if I would buy one for him, and let him work for it; in the meantime I could use it, he said. I thought I saw a way to killing two birds with one stone. In the meantime, one horse after another was brought out; they were none of them good horses, some miserable brutes, but the German was caught in the excitement of seeing horses, and hearing the bidding; time after time he almost begged me to bid for some animal: "Its legs are swollen, yes, but they will come all right," or, "Its chest is narrow, but that won't matter." He was a good judge of a horse, I think, but he was excited

At last a very thin, dirty, shaggy brown pony was brought out; nobody seemed to fancy him, and it was hard to get the bidding up to fifteen pounds, but he was a thorough good little horse for all that. I was hesitating whether I would tell the German to say "sixteen," when William Sturton, who happened to be there, said, "If you want a horse, that one is salted. I happen to know he has come from Dammerland." This decided me, and the German walked off quite pleased with his prize.

I left Pretoria early next morning, as early at least as the opening of the "European" stables (seven o'clock) would allow. The waggon had gone on a little in front, but I soon picked it up, and had breakfast at the first outspan. Then leaving it to follow, I rode on. I had much to think of, and not very pleasant thinking either. From the time when I arranged to buy Grünfontein, I had known that to make it pay a certain class of buildings would have to be erected on it. It was not a farm, to the best of my belief, that could be made pay by working it in the hugger-mugger fashion of the country. I had been careful in making all my calculations before going in for it, believing that I was making them on trustworthy data; now I found that I had been grossly, although I do not mean wilfully, misled. The meaning of all this to me was, that I must give up Grünfontein or be ruined.

Of course I chose the former alternative, but it was very painful. I dreaded parting from the Higginses, and going as it were out into the unknown again. I knew that Mr. Higgins would be greatly disappointed at my not buying the place. I had worked so hard to improve it; had counted labour and hardship as nothing if I could but push on the work there; it was such a pretty place for this country! However, the truth was too obvious; to me Grünfontein meant ruin. I was sorry about Mr. Egerton, too. I knew that breaking up Grünfontein would very likely throw him on his beam-ends again, and that meant probably ruin to him. Then what was I to do? Of course I had to look for another farm, but in the meantime what was I to do with my oxen, with my sheep, with little Roughy and Moustache? I found Moy-plas bright and home-like, and the usual cheery welcome awaiting me. I started after breakfast the next day, and it was early in the afternoon when I rode up to Grünfontein.

Mr. Egerton, who was working at a large new fowl-house that I was making, came to meet me. He had been expecting me, having heard I was coming from O'Grady, and had something ready for my tea. I had hardly finished telling him the result of my visit to Pretoria, when Mr. Higgins rode up on Wellington. I felt I was in for it, and I told him, too. I watched him anxiously. People in Pretoria had said I placed too great trust in his high-mindedness in money-matters; I was putting him to the test.

If this were not a history of mere facts, without embellishments of any sort, or any flights of imagination—if it, moreover, were written for the sake of amusing or merely making money, not with a further object of giving anyone who reads it a truthful conception of this country, I should be much tempted to make Mr. Higgins what I had imagined him; but as it is, truth compels me to say that he fell a little short of my ideal. He did not oppose my leaving Grünfontein, but he did ask for compensation beyond the improvement of the crops, and the bricks that I left on it. If I had not received much kindness at his wife's and his hands—kindness which it is not likely I shall ever have it in my power to repay—I think my natural pugnacity would have asserted itself; as it was, I paid the compensation, feeling more sorry that he had asked for it than that I had to pay it, although I was hard up for money too.

Only when I was leaving Grünfontein for Pretoria, there, as I well knew, to have the whole matter discussed, and to be forced into speaking of it myself, did I tell Mr. Higgins that I thought he had not acted quite rightly—told him exactly what I should say to anyone who might force me to express an opinion on the matter, but told him, too, that I hoped we should ever remain friends. In truth, I believe there is not a man in the country who would have acted better than Mr. Higgins, and few who would have acted as well. South Africa is a bad training-school for high class morality in money-matters—or indeed, in any matter whatever.

CHAPTER 21

Before I left Grünfontein various arrangements had to be made, amongst others the disposing of the wool of my sheep, which I had had lying by for some time. I arranged with James Higgins that he was to buy it, and I sent it over to Fahl-plas on the waggon, with the German in charge. I had discharged the brickmakers, Jim promising in case I wanted his services, in any capacity, to come to me, and I was only waiting for a few days before discharging all the *kaffirs* but two, who were to act as driver and foreloper to the waggon. I had determined upon going to the *bush-veldt* to trade amongst the Boers. The winter was drawing near again, and the migration to the *bush-veldt* was beginning. I thought I would go first to Pretoria and meet some goods that I expected would be soon there, as I had sent to England for them some time before—whatever was deficient I could buy wholesale there; that I would go to the *bush-veldt*, taking with me the German, Egerton, and the *kaffirs*; that, if I were fortunate enough to get rid of the goods quickly, I could leave the German in charge of the waggon and oxen, at some place where the grazing was good, and, with Mr. Egerton, could ride to Pretoria, and when there look out for a new farm. All I should require would be a third horse, to carry a blanket or two and the saddle-bags.

Accordingly, I sent off the wool to Fahl-plas, telling the German that I would follow on horseback for I had other business there. I saddled Eclipse towards evening. He had been hurt by the saddle, and was not quite well, but I arranged the saddle on him so that it seemed not to touch the sore, before mounting. At the end of a sharp canter he seemed uneasy, and I stopped to see if anything had gone wrong. Alas! the sore on his back was bleeding. I had no choice but to return home. The question now was what was to be done? When I reached Grünfontein, it was too late for me to ride to Fahl-plas that evening on the brown pony, even if I could ride so far on him at all; but my saddle did not fit him, and I knew a long ride on him would give him sore withers. It was, however, necessary for me either to go to Fahl-plas myself or send a message. I could of course send Mr. Egerton, but there was an objection to this. I had an idea that the German was covertly jealous of my treating Egerton as my equal when work hours were over.

Now if I sent Egerton to Fahl-plas, Jimmy would be sure to take him into the house and have him to dinner, &c., whilst the German would be left outside with the waggon; besides, I should have to let Egerton ride the pony—Eclipse could not bear the saddle—and I did not know if this might not annoy the master-in-prospect of the other quadruped. Mr. Egerton came to my assistance by proposing to walk, saying he thought the German might dislike his riding the pony; however, I would not listen to this. The risk had to be taken, for I was absolutely obliged to send a message where I could not go myself. Egerton started on the pony the next morning early.

In the evening I saw the waggon coming along the road at the foot of the hill. The German was walking beside it, and even from a distance one could see that he was all bristling with rage. He hardly waited a moment after he saw me before his wrath found utterance. From living amongst Boers and English for so long, he always talked a mixture of German, Boer lingo, and English, difficult at times to understand; but when wrath quickened his utterance he became quite unintelligible. I never knew the immediate cause of this outburst, although I could easily divine it; but the outcome of it was, that he vowed he hated Egerton, couldn't—wouldn't bear with him—and that if Egerton were to stay he wouldn't remain another day—that I could keep the horse myself.

Of course when an one tells you that you must send someone else away if you mean to retain the services of the speaker, it means either that there is a legitimate cause of complaint, or else that the speaker must go. There was no particular cause of complaint even by the German's own admission. His complaint was founded on generalities, and so, although he was a valuable servant, I said of course if he couldn't agree with Egerton he must go as he said, but that he couldn't go immediately, unless he wanted to forfeit his month's pay, as he was engaged by the month, and his time was not yet up. He saw this, like a practical man as he was, although he was in a rage.

Egerton came home on the pony soon after. It had been just as I said. If Jimmy had not been at Fahl-plas I dare say the German's pride might not have suffered so much, but the English-bred boy made a sharp distinction between the respectable servant and the gentleman's prodigal son. The former had been given brandy in the store, and had bought more drink. Farther than that he had been taken no particular notice of, as he had the waggon to sleep in, and his food and means of cooking with him. The latter had dined with the family, and had coffee under the verandah. Egerton was not a careful master for a horse—he was not very careful about anything, himself included—but on this occasion I afterwards heard from Jimmy that the pony had been treated just as I should have treated it myself; still, I dare say the idea of his prospective pony having been ridden by the man who was treated as his social superior, added to the German's anger.

I was now in a difficulty. Egerton could not manage oxen at all, to say nothing of driving, and it was necessary to have somebody besides the somewhat raw *kaffirs* to manage the oxen, for I am physically incapable of working with such very unwieldy beasts. In this dilemma I bethought me of "Jim." He, I knew, could not only work somewhat with oxen, but could drive them fairly well. I sent him word that I wanted him. In the meantime I arranged with Mr. Higgins that my sheep should be herded with his until such time as I could send for them. I was sorry, for I knew how little he looked after his own sheep, and I could not expect anything better for mine.

Still I could do nothing else. I had nowhere to leave my flock except with him. The German did whatever I wanted of him punctually, but I could see him talking a great deal to the two *kaffirs* I had kept, and at last he came and told me confidentially that they had told him that they did not wish to stay. On questioning the boys myself, however, I found that they were quite willing to go with me to Pretoria, and they even said to the *bush-veldt*. I was content so long as they would go to Pretoria.

On Saturday Jimmy made his appearance as usual. Jim was with him, and had a little donkey, that he had bought and trained while with me, packed up with his various traps. As they came up I noticed that Jim had got himself up very smart, and I was disagreeably surprised by his putting out his hand to greet me in Boer fashion. I hate snubbing a man publicly, and the German and Egerton were near me when he came up to me, besides Jimmy, so I took the proffered hand, reflecting that he must have been getting spoiled since I had last seen him.

It was drawing towards evening, and presently Jimmy, Egerton, and

I had supper. The German had long before asked me to give him board-wages, and let him cook for himself. I then called Jim to supper, but he said he was going to have supper in Eclipse's ante-room with the German, and would make his bed there. Jimmy was eager to come with me on my trading expedition; but my prospects were too unsettled and uncertain for me to consent to this, as he had a very good berth at Fahl-plas: we sat up late, discussing plans for the future. The next morning we were having an early breakfast, when Jimmy, who was sitting so that he could see through the open door, said suddenly,—

"I say, you had better go and see what's up; there's Jim packing up his donkey."

I went out immediately. Jim and the German were standing under the wild fig-tree with the donkey ready packed.

"Why, Jim," said I, "what's the matter? I was just going to call you in to breakfast."

Jim looked a little this way and a little that way. Then it came out. "He had heard—heard things—he saw he shouldn't get on," &c.; but I was determined to get to the bottom of it, and the bottom of it was that the German and he had been talking, and that he had heard that Egerton was treated differently from one of them, and that he wouldn't stand it. He admitted that he knew that Egerton was a gentleman by birth and education; he admitted that I made no difference between him and any other man while they were at work, but still he would not stand it. Once that I made him speak out—and spoke out myself—he was quite reasonable, and perfectly respectful. He took his own view of the matter; it was one I could understand. With Jimmy he said he would work side by side, and treat him as a young gentleman; but Egerton had brought himself down to his (Jim's) level, and there he should remain—he had lost his title to social superiority. Jim was very ignorant, and he expressed this in his own language, which is very different from mine; but that was the meaning of what he said.

I said that I could not take his view of the case; that Egerton was doing his best to work well, and to redeem himself; and that I was bound to stand by him, such being the case.

"I'm afraid, ma'am, as you'll be the loser by it," said Jim.

"I'm afraid I shall, Jim," said I; "but right is right, whatever comes of it."

"Yes," Jim assented. "You be right there, ma'am; but I couldn't work with him like that—it would be no use my trying; but I wishes you all success, ma'am, as I am sure you deserves it."

And with that Jim and I shook hands, and he and his donkey departed down the hill.

I had moved from under the tree to the bridge, as I spoke to him, so as to be out of Egerton's hearing. I took a stroll in the garden before I returned. That spiteful little German had determined to pay me out for discarding him rather than Egerton; and he was doing so.

When I returned to the cabin Mr. Egerton interrupted some remark I made as I opened the little half-door.

"Mrs. Heckford," he said, looking very pale, "I must leave you—I am ruining you."

I said, "Nonsense;" but I felt there was a good deal of truth in what he said.

"No," he went on, "you may say that; I knew you would; but as an honourable man I have no choice in the matter, and can leave you none. You must see this yourself."

There was more truth in this than even in his former remark, and yet it was but superficial truth after all—such truth as passes current in the world—but not real truth; for ruin can never come to anyone through doing what is right, and it is undoubtedly right for one weak human being to stand firm against the tide of ignorance and selfishness which will always set in against any other weak human being, who having once fallen publicly, tries to rise, even though it may be by dint of hard labour, and though his efforts may be made in a spirit of all humility, as were Mr. Egerton's. Surely there can be no dictate of honour which should tell such a one that he must cast aside the help that is voluntarily held out to him by one, who, fully estimating the cost of what he does, is prepared to do it fearlessly.

It cannot be honourable wilfully to throw away the chance of redeeming oneself; and if anyone here is disposed to say that a man ought to be able to do so without some external help when he has once fallen, I would advise that person, before he is quite sure in the matter, to come out here and see whether, after studying life in Pretoria for a little, he will not change his mind.

It is not easy to make all this evident to a man of delicate susceptibilities, with the usual ideas about honour, which, however strong they may be, are in nine cases out of ten very vague in men's minds, and who is smarting from a severe and recently-inflicted wound. I almost despaired of dissuading Mr. Egerton from packing up his small stock of goods, and starting then and there for Pretoria; but I gained my point in the end.

Jimmy remained with me until I left Grünfontein. I could not let him go; it was hard enough to have to bid goodbye to him and to the Higginses at all, without dividing the goodbyes. I paid off the German, and let him go; packed the waggon, killed one pig, and sold the other; loaded up my fowls for the Pretoria market; counted my sheep, with poor Hans and my pretty little pet ram, to Mr. Higgins; commended Ada's cats to Augustus's mercy; and then, having bid goodbye to the Higginses and to Jimmy, and started the waggon off, Mr. Egerton and I mounted our horses, and left pretty Grünfontein with little Roughy and Moustache as our companions.

Moustache cared not a pin, but Roughy evidently felt much as I did—that he was going away from what he knew into a dreary un-known region, where there would be no more little *kaffirs* to bark at, as they danced on moonlight nights; no more fowls to chase, no more trots over to Surprise and games with Fido. Poor little dog! A presenti-ment of evil seemed to have taken possession of him. He could hardly be got to leave the place, and when he at length followed us, it was with a drooping tail, and with a little miserable yelp every now and then, as if he was crying for pretty Grünfontein and homelike Sur-prise. I could have cried as I turned my back on them, if crying had been of any use.

CHAPTER 22

It was a bright afternoon as Mr. Egerton and I rode towards Pretoria; and as I looked at the waggon with its indifferent driver, and utterly untutored forelooper, at Mr. Egerton, who knew as little about oxen and waggons as I did, and at the span of splendid oxen committed to our joint charge, I wondered in my heart whether I were not a great fool to go in for the undertaking I had just entered upon. But, as I have said, it was a bright afternoon, and if there was risk in what I was about to do, there was also the excitement that always attends risk; and before I was many miles from Surprise I felt that the whole thing was rather enjoyable. We outspanned for the night near to Cucumoor's farm. There was a new moon; and although it was chilly, it was still pleasant for sleeping out. The waggon was too full for me to be able to sleep in it, if I had wished to do so; but I dislike sleeping in a waggon when there are horses and oxen to be looked after, unless I have very trustworthy attendants. My *kaffirs* were not trustworthy, I knew, and Mr. Egerton, when he was once asleep, was very hard to waken.

I had my blankets spread near to where Eclipse was tied to the waggon—for he had an objection to being tied, and was accustomed to a loose stall, and I thought it probable he might require my ministration during the night, which, in fact, was the case. It was a long time since last I had slept in the open air, and I enjoyed it. The next day, early, we passed Moy-plas, where I paid a visit. John Higgins was there; he laughed as he bade me goodbye. "You'll be well salted by the time you come back from the *bush-veldt,*" he said. I picked up the waggon and Mr. Egerton a little before we had to pass the Crocodile. The oxen took the waggon, through well; but I could see that the driver was not up to much. That evening we outspanned close to Dasspoort, so as to be able to get in early to market next morning.

I had forage and seed oats, pumpkins and fowls for sale. As I sat on Eclipse, close by the waggon, waiting for these various articles to be sold, two or three persons whom I did not know, spoke to me by name. Presently one man, who seemed to know me quite well, though I had not the least remembrance of him, was accosted by a very good-natured-looking man with a brown beard. I saw them both looking at me, and then heard the man with the beard ask who I was.

"Oh!" said my unknown acquaintance, "don't you know? that's Mrs. Heckford; let me introduce you;" and so he did. The man with the beard was Mr. Hans Felman, and his introducer told me if I wanted to hear about farms he was the very man to tell me about them. Mr. Felman then spoke very politely, saying if he could be of any use to me he should be most happy. I asked where I could see him if I wanted information. He told me where he lived, and asked me to call on his wife. I had much to do, having after the market to deliver the things I had sold; then to find out where my English goods were, and to load them up (they had just come up to Pretoria, and were still on the waggon that brought them); then I had to select and buy other goods, so as to have a fair stock to take to the *bush-veldt*.

Then I had to unpack all these goods, and write out a list of their selling prices; besides, I had to get a third horse. The packing out and pricing of the goods I did at a farm close to Pretoria, belonging to a young Englishman, where I had obtained leave to outspan. There was very little grass to be had; but on his farm the grazing was still pretty fair. I slept in the *veldt*, and we had our camp-fire, and cooked for ourselves, of course. Indeed, the house was at some distance from where my waggon was. It was a house of only two rooms, and a little kitchen outside. In it the young farmer with his young Boer wife and two little children lived.

I got through all I had to do at the end of a week. My new horse was a big, bony, unkempt colt, barely three years old, and only half-broken. He had excellent points: but one thing I saw would always spoil his beauty, he had a fiddle head, so I called him Violin. He was very thin, and rather depressed in spirits, as well as in condition, but he had a vicious way of rolling his eye back, and an equally vicious way of flicking his tail straight up and down, as if he had a hinge in the middle of it. Mr. Egerton hated him from the first, and prophecied that he would turn out badly; and Violin, I suppose in consequence, never liked him. He soon learnt to know me, and would let me handle him as I liked; but he was a troublesome beast with most other people.

After some bargaining, I bought this animal for fifteen pounds, and I was now ready to start.

Mr. Egerton and I were eating our supper by the campfire; I had been showing him a photograph of myself, which I had had done in Pretoria at Mrs. Higgins's request. I had a presentiment of evil hanging over me, and the look of this photograph displeased me, and strengthened it. It was a very nice photograph as a pleasing representation of myself I was more than satisfied with it—but the individual represented in it struck me, as I looked at her, to be absurdly unfitted for a "Smouse," as a trader in a waggon is called here. Looking at that picture, it struck me that I was not only doing a foolish thing, but a ridiculous thing. Mr. Egerton had told me that he had heard some talk between the boys about wanting their pay raised. In the midst of my meditations they broached the subject. They said if their pay was not raised they would not leave Pretoria.

I knew their game. They had waited to tell me this till all was ready to start. The time for the *bush-veldt* trading was going by; other traders were getting in before me—they thought they could extort money—for drivers were scarce in Pretoria then—*kaffirs*, as a rule, not liking to go away from their *kraals* in the winter. I told them plainly that I should not raise their wages a penny; and we all turned in for the night soon afterwards. The next morning my friends said they were going. They hung about, however, apparently waiting for something, I meanwhile saddled up to ride to Pretoria to look for another driver, leaving Mr. Egerton in charge of the waggon. Then they asked me to pay them their wages, but I pointed out to them, that when servants left one at a moment's notice, even though towards the end of their month, they forfeited all pay.

They knew well enough that I could have them put in prison, so they held their peace, and I rode off on the brown pony Dandy. I had arranged the saddle so as to fit him as well as Eclipse; and he was a better horse for work in Pretoria, Eclipse being too larky to be left standing alone if I had business indoors. Dandy was full of spirit; but although quite young, he was quietness itself.

All that day I hunted for a driver, and other people kindly hunted for me, but I could get none. Day after day passed; every morning I saddled up, and bade Mr. Egerton goodbye: every evening I rode back to the waggon, to see him waiting by the camp-fire, that showed me in the half-darkness where the waggon stood, as I cantered over the *veldt*, always to tell the same story. I rode over to neighbouring *kraals*:

it was of no use.

I had got the gentleman on whose farm I was outspanned, to have my oxen herded with his oxen. Mr. Egerton and I slept by the loaded waggon; got up early; and while he lit the fire and made early coffee, I cleaned the horses alone, until, coffee being made, he took his share of the work. Then I saddled up for my hopeless search. It came on bitterly cold; every morning the grass was white with hoar frost, and so were our blankets. In the middle of all this, one evening I felt unwell, and the next day I was choking with a violent attack of bronchitis. I went on my quest as usual that day, and for several succeeding days—but I could hardly speak.

The nights were very bad. I would have gone into town to sleep at a friend's house but for two reasons, one, that I had the horses to look after; I was afraid of leaving them altogether to Mr. Egerton's care. He had been so long in South Africa that he had acquired a good deal of South African carelessness as to horses; besides, I thought, as he must remain at the waggon, it was only right I should not shirk roughing it. I shall never forget that man's kindness at that time; how he would get up when he heard me coughing, and get me whatever he could to relieve me; and how jolly he was over it all, as if it was the pleasantest thing in the world to turn out of his bed and walk about in a bitter cold night. He did all this in such a perfectly natural and unaffected way, so that it seemed as if it were an everyday occurrence for him to have to act nurse to a bronchitic lady in the open *veldt*.

At last, after I had spent about a fortnight there, I determined to try to go into Pretoria, instead of remaining on the farm—I seemed no nearer than before to getting a driver. I got the gentleman on whose farm I was outspanned to lend me a driver; Mr. Egerton acted forelooper, and I led Violin and Dandy, and rode Eclipse.

I had, some days previously, called on Mrs. Hans Felman. She received me very kindly; and she and her husband did all they could to help me out of the dilemma I was in. Mr. Felman was a Boer from the old colony, his wife a Transvaal Boer. They had three children—two girls and a boy. Their house, on the outskirts of Pretoria, was built after the usual fashion of Boer farmhouses. It stood on a large piece of ground, or *erf*, with fruit and other trees round it, and would have been a very pretty house and place only that numbers of *kaffirs* were allowed to congregate there, in return for their doing a little work, and they kept the whole surroundings of the house in a mess with the heads of oxen, a favourite dinner with them, partly because it is rather a cheap dish, and partly, I think, because it gives them plenty of fiddle-faddle work to prepare it. I may mention, incidentally, that I have seen *kaffirs* throw away the brains as nasty, although they will eat the intestines with the dung just pressed out! The horns of these numerous heads, old bones, and old rags, bestrewed the Felmans' otherwise pretty *erf*.

One evening, by moonlight, I happened to walk across it: it looked like a *charnel*-house! In one corner of the *erf*, the farthest from the farmhouse, was a diminutive house of one room, measuring about nine feet by seven, but with a fireplace. As it was impossible for me to put up at any hotel in Pretoria, and desirable that I should have some place of abode (for the waggon was too full to accommodate me), I arranged to take this eligible domicile for thirty shillings a month. It was not a very inviting-looking residence. It had a small window, closed by a shutter, and the door opened directly upon a swampy sort of pond. It was a peculiarly damp and low-spirited-looking spot; one where, if you dug a hole for a stake, the chances were that a frog would hop out of it, and that a series of other reptiles of the same species would periodically make their appearance from it, whilst the stake would decline to become fixed. The liveliness of its general appearance was enhanced by a gap in a neighbouring quince-hedge having been filled up with the skulls of oxen. The fact that this place commanded a rent of thirty shillings a month, tells sufficiently plainly that house-rent in Pretoria was rather high. Its advantage to me was that the Felmans allowed me to bring my waggon into their enclosed *erf*; also to let my horses graze in it—and these were two things of great advantage to me, particularly as most audacious stealing goes on in Pretoria.

Of course there was no furniture in the room. Mr. Egerton and I rigged up a table, and made seats of packing-cases. My bed was made on the floor. Mr. Egerton slept outside—and a funny picture it would have made of an evening, when Mr. Egerton was cooking our evening meal, whilst I lay on the blankets on the floor, playing with the dogs and talking. But coming to Pretoria did not seem to bring us any nearer to procuring a driver; neither could I hear of any farm likely to suit me; so at last, in despair, I began looking about for a house in Pretoria.

Houses of five or six rooms sometimes fetched more than that number of hundred pounds; and I know of one nice cottage of five rooms, standing, it is true, in a very large and productive garden, which, shortly before the war, fetched two thousand five hundred pounds. I did not find it easy to get a house to suit my taste and my pocket. At last I heard of one which had a stable attached, a thing I was particular about; and just at the same time a gentleman, previously unknown to me, called at my funny little abode, and told me that he heard that I was in want of a driver, and that he could recommend me a good one, a bastard or half-caste, who had served with him while he was the Government transport officer. I was really delighted.

The man came to be inspected a fine-looking man with a good face, and who spoke English: his name was Hendrick. I engaged him at the wages he had been receiving from his former employer, *viz.*, half-a-crown a day. He brought me a Hottentot of the name of Hans, who, he said, was a good forelooper, and to whom I was obliged to give one-and-sixpence a day; and Hans besought me to engage a small Hottentot boy (also a Hendrick) who had been left to his charge. This I eventually did, at ten shillings a month. I was now ready to start, when suddenly I got an offer of a very nice farm close to Pretoria, at the rent of sixteen pounds a month. There were some law difficulties in the way of my concluding the bargain—the lease had been mort-gaged. I was in too great a hurry to get the waggon out of the village to stop, (for drivers and foreloopers have a pleasing habit of getting drunk in Pretoria,) so I arranged that I would take it out a day's trek, leave it in Mr Egerton's charge while I rode back with Hendrick to settle matters, and then rejoin the waggon.

It was a beautiful moonlight evening towards the end of June, when at last, after so many troubles, I started for the *bush-veldt*. I was more than a month later than I ought to have been: however, I was glad to be off late though it was. We outspanned for the night about three miles out of Pretoria, and I was wakened out of my first sleep by a lively riding-party from the town going out to a farm-house near. The next morning early we started again, and outspanned for breakfast at Derdepoort—a pass through the Magaliesberg—where we were almost cut in pieces by the sharp wind which seems to be always blowing in this spot. Here I met two men coming from Water-berg with waggons loaded up with leather. They bought some pipes and some sugar from me, and I remember them particularly as having been my first customers.

We inspanned after breakfast, and a long trek brought us, towards evening, to a missionary station, where there was a good-sized *kraal* of *kaffirs*, supposed to be Christianised. Whatever progress they may have made in Christianity, they had made but little in civilization in general.

Their *kraal* was on a bare slope towards a small river. There was little shelter to be got from the cold wind—but we had a good supper, and were all soon asleep.

I started the next morning by the light of the setting moon for Pretoria. It was bitterly cold, but as long as the moon lasted I did not mind so much, for we could canter. At last, however, the moon failed us, and, as the dawn was yet about half-an-hour off, we had to walk. Just before the waning light of the moon failed altogether, I had felt my watch-chain, which was tucked inside my habit, get loose, and before I had time to put it in again, it swung as I cantered, and seemed to catch on something. When at last the day broke sufficiently for me to be able to distinguish objects clearly, I found that it had broken, and that some keepsakes I had on a ring, through which the chain was passed, were lost. I suppose there is a lurking superstition in all of us; anyhow, I confess that I could not help feeling that the loss of these trinkets that I had carried with me for years, which had been my companions in many vicissitudes, and which, of no great value in themselves, were dear to me from the memories attached to them, was like a bad omen.

I reached Pretoria just as the Felmans were going to breakfast. I was perished, and sat by the kitchen-fire sipping some hot coffee with great gusto, whilst kind Mrs. Felman got me some bacon and eggs, which I thoroughly enjoyed. The treaty about the farm fell through, and I had only just time to leave word with an agent, that he might offer four hundred pounds for the house in Pretoria, which I previously mentioned, before I had to start out to the waggon. It was already late in the afternoon, but we pushed along sharply, and got to our destination about half-past nine, very cold indeed.

Mr. Egerton had shot a hare and had some hare-soup awaiting me, which I, and Hendrick, also enjoyed; and so I was fairly in for my *bush-veldt* experience, for we were to start early next morning, and to get to the outskirts of the *bush-veldt* the day after.

CHAPTER 23

We made but one trek the next day, and outspanned by the Apis river, in a thick and rather pretty bush, near to the other waggons— one, the property of a Boer, going to Pretoria with a load of planks for sale; the other, belonging I think also to a Boer, but an Anglicized Boer. The former gentleman was very fat, and toddled about like a barrel on legs (a common thing with the Boers) . He bought some trifle, I forget what, and told me that his wife was dead, and that he had always to take his little boy about with him. The said boy was a shy bright-eyed child, with a strongly developed taste for sweets, in which his fond parent somewhat sparingly indulged him; whilst I, prompted thereto by his motherless condition, indulged him freely. The other people outspanned at this place also came to the waggon and bought something; but I remember them chiefly because, later in the evening, a spanking pair of horses in a spider, brought the sheriff from Pretoria to serve a writ on them.

The night was very dark, and I was almost startled as we sat round our camp-fire to see an individual suddenly illuminated by its ruddy light, who asked in English (and Hibernian English too) where was the nearest water. He and his companions, he told us, were old Australian gold-diggers—they were going to Zoutpansberg, gold prospecting; they were travelling alone, except for their donkeys, and none of them could speak Dutch or *kaffir*. I sent one of my boys to show the way to the water, and afterwards this man sat and talked for a while, and had a cup of coffee.

Early in the morning we inspanned. We had to make a long trek that day to get as far as the Eland River for the evening outspan. Our gold-digging acquaintances were just putting the packs on their donkeys; they were going a different road from us. I was looking at the way that one of their packs was padded, so as to avoid any chance of the animal's back being hurt by it, when Mr. Egerton uttered an exclamation of delight, caused by his having discovered two birds, and, jumping off Dandy, he threw the reins to me, and before I had time to gather up the assembled reins of Eclipse and the two led horses, he fired, quite close to them. I certainly was greatly gratified at the manner they all stood fire, but, whether it was owing to his finding a report close to his ears disagreeable or not, I cannot say, but, after that Dandy never would stand still when his rider dismounted to fire, but would instantly trot away with his head well in the air to prevent his tripping over the bridle, and refuse to be caught.

He had a comical way of looking behind him to see the exact time when he must quicken his pace so as to avoid being caught; and many a time after that, was poor Mr. Egerton's temper tried by Dandy's antics and my amusement thereat. After this we slightly lost our way, but coming to a farmhouse, were directed rightly, and crossing the Pinaar's River, on a very rickety bridge, we outspanned for breakfast. The bridge was made of logs and sods, and the Pinaar's River was only a small affair then, but, as. I afterwards saw, could become a tremendous torrent in an hour.

When we started again we were fairly in the *bush-veldt*, and very uninteresting *bush-veldt* it was. Thick bush was on either side of our narrow road, but there was no fine timber; and as all the trees were thorn-trees, the effect was infinitely monotonous. There was no game of any sort to be seen; once we heard a sound of an axe, and going in search of its proprietor, found a young Boer cutting firewood, with his horse browsing beside him. Of course he looked a little surprised at seeing a lady, and asked who we were, and was farther a little surprised at hearing that I was a "Smouse." He told us that there were a lot of traders on in front, and that trade in the *bush-veldt* was slack.

We reached the Eland River about an hour after noon, much in advance of the waggon, and off-saddled. Mr. Egerton took his gun and went off; I lay down to watch the horses browsing, and to look at the view, there being nothing else to do. A long line of tall reeds marked the course of the river between high banks. The ground was clear of trees for about a hundred yards on the side where I was sitting, but on the other for much farther. On my side the ground soon began to undulate, but on the other the hills were a long way off. Sheltered amongst the scrubby trees on my side, and about a hundred and fifty yards off from, where I lay, were tents of Boers, stationed there with their flocks and herds. The grass was very dry, and near where I lay it was much eaten off, it being the usual place for outspanning, being near to a drift, where the cattle could easily go down to water. After I had had two or three half-dozes, and had watched a large flock of sheep being driven towards the tents by a *kaffir*, and when the sun was getting low, I saw the waggon emerging from the bush. This meant dinner, whereat my soul rejoiced.

The next morning early, I made up my mind to ride over to the tents and inform their occupants that I was a "Smouse." I did not particularly enjoy the prospect of doing this, for novelty is not always charming, though it certainly was something quite new to me.

Moustache and Roughy of course announced my approach by a little skirmish with some of the Boers' dogs. Boers are not very demonstrative: they generally stand in a stolid manner near the tent, and say good-day in an equally stolid manner, although they may be really dying of inquisitiveness about a stranger. The individuals in the first tent I went to did this exactly, and when I told them that I was a "Smouse," and asked if they wanted anything, they said "No," in a manner so completely exhaustive, that I felt it would be useless to attempt conversation, so I rode on to the farther tent. Here I found two women and several children. Both the women were big, strapping, peasant-like women. They asked me into the tent.

The men of the family, they told me, were in Pretoria, and they expected them out next day. They gave me coffee, asked numbers of questions as to what had brought me out to this country; whether I was married; whether I had any children with me; whether I had ever had any children; who the white man with me was; and a great many others of a similar nature. They said they would come to the waggon and buy, and they displayed all that they had to display, namely, their little children and their pets—two little night-apes: funny small beasts, all furry and soft, and with such big eyes and ears, and such long tails, that they remain on your mind as having eyes, ears, and tails, and nothing else. The night-apes are very agile, and the Boers are fond of them as pets; the orthodox way of displaying them to admiring friends being, to swing them about by a piece of string attached to a collar round the small beast's neck. The Boers say the animal has no objection to the proceeding—in fact, rather likes it—but perhaps they may be in error. The springs the little ape makes, whilst undergoing the process, are very surprising, considering that it has nothing to spring from.

I was very glad to perceive that I could make myself fairly understood by these women, and could understand them fairly. I was not only anxious to be able to do so because it was necessary for my success in trading, but also because I was desirous of knowing something of the people. Up to the time of which I am now writing, my knowledge of the Boers was small. I had seen numbers of them, and had even been kindly received at their houses, but our conversation had been necessarily very limited. I had been able to observe that most of them are dirty and untidy—even the relations of the famous Paul Krüger, living in a state of dirt and disorder, that reminds one of an Irish hovel; while at the same time, I had heard many accounts of their absurd ignorance—of how they believed the earth to be flat, and that the sun and stars were made expressly as lamps for our benefit, &c.; and I had been amused to learn that Paul Krüger had privately expressed his opinion, that the footman of his noble English host was both a better dressed and better mannered man than his master!

Horrible tales had also been told to me of the brutality this Paul Krüger and others were capable of, when left to themselves, by men who had, in the olden time, served under or with them against the *kaffirs*: of how they had taken little babies, too young to be easily reared, away from their mothers, who had perhaps been slaughtered, and had thrown them all into a heap in a *kraal*, and, covering them with dry grass and bushes, had set fire to it; of how they had shot nursing mothers in cold blood, and let them linger in misery for days, if the shot had not proved immediately fatal; of how children had been dragged from their mothers' arms and taken away as slaves, the mothers being shot if they ventured to run after the capturers, and annoy them by their despairing wailing. I had heard that the Boers were a treacherous, lying, hypocritical people, with all the faults but with none of the virtues supposed to belong to rough peasants; and I had even spoken to a Boer who, a very few years ago, dragged a *kaffir* to death tied to his horse. I thought I would now begin to learn a little of them from my own observation.

I had not long returned to the waggon, and I was sitting on the grass, when the two women came up. They sat down by my side, and asked me if I had some cotton of a particular size. I said I would look. Then they asked if I would take eggs in exchange. Having expressed my willingness to do so, they asked if I had needles of a particular size; and I said once more that I would look. Mr. Egerton had to do the looking, by-the-way, and did not much enjoy it; my department was the talking business! My customers now expressed their desire to see some "*kommekies*" (be it understood that a "*kommeky*" is a small bowl used by the Boers instead of a cup—handles being inconveniently given to breaking on trek); I said I had, and then they asked what was their price. I named it, but my visitors threw up their eyes in horror. "Oh!" they said, "that is more than we give in Pretoria." I ventured to remark that the *bush-veldt* was not Pretoria. Then they asked what would I give for eggs. I said a shilling a dozen.

Once more they were seized with surprise and horror; they had never heard of such a low price; all traders gave more. But I was obdurate. How those women did haggle over a penny more or less in the price of a few "*kommekies*" and a few eggs; the penny having to be subtracted in the former and added in the latter case. At last, to get rid of them, I let them have the coveted little bowls at almost cost price, and got the eggs at my own. But my customers were aggrieved—they rose to depart, and, as they wished me farewell, the elder woman patted her pocket fondly.

"Ah!" she said, addressing her companion, "I have plenty of money in it—I wanted to buy—but the woman gives so little for eggs, and her things are so dear! "

Mr. Egerton and Hendrick were indignant, and I made them worse by laughing at them; but the best of the joke we had to find out afterwards—half of the eggs were addled!

Not long after this, two Boers, father and son apparently, rode up to the waggon and dismounted. The father held his hand out to me across the *disselboom*, evidently expecting me to get up to take it, but I was too comfortable lying down.

"I can't reach so far," said I.

"No more can I," quoth he. "Have you any boots?"

"Yes."

"What is their price?"

"Eighteen shillings."

"You must not tell lies," remarked my visitor.

I assured him I was adhering strictly to truth; upon which he said I might show him the boots; but they were not strong enough for his fancy; and he and his son rode on to another trader, who was, I heard, stationed not far off.

Then Mr. Egerton's wrath against the rudeness of Boers in general, and of this Boer in particular, burst forth, regardless of my endeavours to point out to him, that, as friends and relations, in Boer-land, constantly recommend each other (in a friendly spirit) not to lie, the expression was doubtless only a playful allusion to the fact, that traders are in the habit of making as good bargains as they can.

Soon after we inspanned, and Mr. Egerton and I riding on in front, we presently came upon the encampment of the trader we had heard of. He was stationary there for a time, and had set himself up very comfortably. After a few words we rode on, following the right bank of the Eland river, towards its junction with the Elephant river. The bush was thick, and the banks were so steep, that although we were close to the river the whole time, we were not aware of it; and here I may remark that it requires to get one's eye accustomed to the *bush-veldt* before one can discover where the course of a river or the source of a spring lies, and also where a Boer encampment lies, for the Boers draw up their waggons and pitch their tents often in the midst of thick bush; and a trader's eye must often be as practised as a hunter's, to see the little white speck they present amongst the green foliage.

Mr. Egerton and I overshot many at our first outset, giving Hendrick a laugh at our want of experience when he came up with the waggon.

The next day brought us to a *kaffir kraal*. The river ran between it and us, but I halted the waggon, and sent Hendrick over on Dandy to ask if I could get mealies for the horses, and whether the *kaffirs* would care to buy. He soon returned, escorted by a troop of whooping and yelling children, all nearly, and many quite, naked, who evidently looked upon the arrival of a "Smouse" as a delightful interruption to the monotony of their existence. They were closely followed by numbers of men and women: the former dressed in every variety of attire, from a worn-out European suit to a strip of rag round the loins; the latter wearing girdles of leather, fringed, and more or less ornamented with beads or brass buttons round their waists, without any other covering in the case of their being young girls; the married women had in addition skins thrown round their shoulders or passed under one arm and fastened over the opposite shoulder. Many carried baskets containing mealies, pumpkins, &c., on their heads, and babies in their arms.

This motley crowd of men, women, and children, literally besieged the waggon, chattering and screaming like so many monkeys, and clambering up on the wheels, and jumping backwards and forwards across the *disselboom* in an ape-like manner. As their excitement abated, and as they fell into groups, the *coup d'oeil* was effective—the women, in their quaint costumes, and with their arms and legs decorated with beads and bangles, being the leading feature in it. Many of the men spoke Dutch, but none of the women could speak that language, so that I lost the fun of hearing their observations. One of the women was very graceful and pretty, with a turn of the head and neck that reminded me of the hunting Diana in the Vatican. She was quite conscious of my admiring glances, and took advantage of the knowledge they conveyed to her, to wheedle me into buying a pumpkin at a preposterous price.

I never saw so grotesque a caricature as these *kaffirs* presented, of scenes I have observed at Swan and Edgar's, and Howell and James's. Some absurd-looking savage in a blanket, would ask to see a shirt, or a coat, or a pair of trousers, or perhaps a hat. The assembled multitude would become all attention. He would be turned round and round, the critics would fall back a pace or two, and look at him with deep thoughtfulness, while he watched their faces anxiously: no, there was a bulge in the back! or the brim was a little too narrow—he must try another. Or perhaps when the critics were satisfied, the purchaser would screw himself round, and gazing down his own back, say, "Don't you think it would be better if it were a little more this or a little less that?" and his friends would discuss the matter, gravely walking round him with their heads on one side, until it was settled to general satisfaction.

The trying on of boots was very fine—the would-be purchaser often having very little on him except the boots. After pulling them on, he would promenade backwards and forwards in them, trying how they felt. When the purchase, whatever it might be, was concluded, the purchaser frequently celebrated the event by a "break-down," amid universal applause. I stayed at this amusing place until the next morning, and then continued my route along the Eland River.

We passed several Boer encampments, the tents being pitched a little away from the path, and close to the river. I rode over to them to ask if their inhabitants wished to buy anything, but none of them did. They were very civil to me, however. One gaunt old lady, at whose tent I dismounted and had some coffee, was much interested in politics, as well as in all my private concerns; and farther wished to induce me to buy an ox at an exorbitant price.

"Why," said I, "you are asking war prices; no one will give you ten pounds for an unsalted ox in peace times."

"Ah," said she cheerfully, "we all mean to keep our oxen until the *kaffirs* break out again: they are sure to break out—quite sure."

We outspanned for breakfast near the encampment of an old in-firm Boer of the name of Prinsloo, who had a very jolly-looking wife. Prinsloo himself looked like a gentleman, and they seemed nice peo-ple in their way. They came over to the waggon, after I had paid them a visit in their tent, and bought a bottle of brandy from my private store; for I had none for purposes of sale.

It was near this place, but I forget exactly where, that two waggons laden with planks from the wood-bush came along while we were outspanned. With them was a tall young Boer, who evidently had a very good opinion of himself, and thought it the correct thing to swear most villainously in all the English he knew. This prepossessing specimen of young Boerdom halted his waggons, and, swaggering up to Mr. Egerton, asked him his name; then whether he was the owner of the waggon.

Mr. Egerton pointed to me, upon which my friend swaggered over to where I was sitting on the grass, and proceeded to survey me as if I were a curious animal of some unknown kind. Then he said,—

"So, you are a Smouse, are you? Well, you will howl."

(N.B. The same word "*heul*" is used in Dutch for either crying or howling.)

"Indeed," said I.

"I want some brandy," said he.

"I'm sorry for that," said I; "because I can't give you any."

This disconcerted him, and he called to his oxen, and departed, swearing at them in English as long as he was within hearing.

For the next few days nothing remarkable occurred. We passed several encampments and one trader—and once I was most agree-ably surprised by finding Mrs. Farquarson in a tent instead of a Dutch woman. Her husband was surveying neighbouring farms, and she, with her baby, was enjoying the free *bush-veldt* life as a change from Pretoria. I kept along the Eland river still, but I found that trade was bad, a great many traders being just in front of me; and so I deter-mined to change my route, and turned across, past Schildpotsfontein, towards Waterberg.

Schildpotsfontein is a very muddy fountain in the midst of a large *kaffir kraal* or town. The chief is named Andreas Mayepee (I spell as the name would be pronounced in English), and the principal feature of the place is sand. I never saw such a sandy place; you waded through sand wherever you went, you were in constant danger of getting your waggon stuck fast in the sand, and had to pilot it in its course to the outspanning place, as carefully as if it were a ship amongst shoals. If there was a breath of wind you were choked with sand; but, although not otherwise an inviting place, it recommended itself to me by its inhabitants doing a good trade with me, although another trader came there a few hours after I did, and also did a good trade. The chief was but a poor specimen of a chief, and kept a general store. His subjects paid him scant respect, and said his store had not much in it, and what little there was, was dear.

The *kaffirs* here were not half so amusing as those at the Eland River, although laughable enough. There were *kaffirs* in European dress, and *kaffirs* in blankets, and *kaffirs* in shirts. I don't remember any naked *kaffirs* here, and the women, girls, and children, were attired, or not attired, like those at the Eland River. The men mostly spoke Dutch, but the women only Kaffir, or rather "Makatees;" for there are many *kaffir* languages. I may here remark that the Makatees' language is a very unpleasing *kaffir* dialect, and that the Makatees people are, by universal admission, a very nasty *kaffir* people.

I remained here several days, and then went on a short distance to a Missionary station. Here the women and girls wore European dress, and many of even the little children were clothed. I think it was here that I was amused to hear Mr. Egerton trying to convert a *kaffir* to republican principles. The fellow admitted that Andreas Mayepee was, so far as he knew, of no particular use, and yet that all his subjects had to pay him tribute; but there he stuck fast. "One must have a chief— some chief—we couldn't get on without a chief," he said; and farther than that he could not be got by any arguments.

We had a long-trek without water between this place and the next water at Marullo-kop, or Marullo-hill, so-called from a picturesque hill crowned by a large *marullo* tree near the spring of water. Oxen do not care to drink late at night, or early in the morning, so, as one is obliged to outspan once between the Missionary station and Marullo-kop, we started late, in order to outspan after dark. The trader I mentioned before (Mr. N.) trekked along with us. I left Roughy in the waggon, for he was rather footsore, and Mr. Egerton and I rode on; but to my dismay, when the waggons came up, I heard that the poor little dog had jumped out, and run after me as the boys supposed but in fact had lost himself. It was pitch dark, but I hoped he might find his way to the camp-fire. Morning, however, came, and no Roughy. I could not keep the waggon waiting, for there was no water for the oxen, and it was useless to ride back to the *kraal*, as, even if I had found him there, he was too heavy to carry far on the horse, and too bad a runner to run after me, so I regretfully had to leave him to his fate, and go on.

We saw several spring-bucks as we rode along, but none near enough to allow of Mr. Egerton trying his skill as a marksman; and early in the day we got to Marullo-kop. The little precipitous hill rises suddenly from the flat thickly-wooded plain, and the spring of water makes a very little lake at its foot. Tucked in among the trees were some Boer tents; saddles, skins, and dried *quagga* flesh were hanging on the trees close to them, and various implements, strewed around, showed that one at least of their occupants carried on the trade of a blacksmith and a mender of waggons.

This individual came to greet us, as Mr. N——, Mr. Egerton, and I rode up. He was a fine, sturdy-looking fellow, with an open smile and a yellow beard. After greeting him, I led my horse to where I wished the waggon to outspan, off-saddled, and sat down, while Mr. Egerton departed with his gun. Presently the pleasant-looking Boer came over from his tent with a glass of wine in his hand, and accompanied by Mr. N——. He said, that, at home, he would have offered me something better, but here in the *bush-veldt* he had nothing else to offer. I thought more of this attention afterwards, when I learned from himself and others that he was a leader amongst the malcontents. His name was Barend Englesberg. I went with him to his tent, and was introduced to his wife, an enormously fat woman, with a very merry face, also to his daughter-in-law, Liza, and to several other women and girls— relations of his.

The waggons soon came up, the goods were spread out, and a great deal of bargaining ensued; also a great pulling about of goods, during which we had to keep our eyes about us; for it is a well-known thing amongst traders that Dutch women and girls are very light-fingered.

Barend Englesberg told me there were numbers of wild *quaggas* about, but that they were shy and difficult to get close to. He also told me that there were several lions, and that they often came down to the water at night. He evidently wished to frighten me. In the evening he even took the trouble to send me over word that he had heard a distant roar, and that I had better be on my guard; but that was all I heard of a lion during my stay.

On leaving this place Mr. N—— and I parted company—he taking one road into Waterberg, and I another. My road led through thick bush until we crossed a chain of hills and descended into a wide valley, intersected by the "Nilstrom," or Nile River, and saw, in front of us, the magnificent, solitary, and precipitous hill, called "Kranz-kop" whilst, across the valley, the view was bounded by the range of the Waterberg hills (for they cannot be called mountains).

We outspanned for dinner near to a *kaffir* house in the valley, whence a woman came with a cup of coffee for me, and told me, she had seen me while I was with the Jennings. She had relations living on their place, and had been there on a visit. She was dressed in European costume, and talked Dutch. She told me she belonged to the Mission station, which I could see tucked away in a fold of a hill just opposite, where she informed me I should find a very nice lady, the wife of a German missionary, who had passed me on his way to Andreas Mayepee's while I was outspanned at Marullo-kop. She said also that I should do a good trade, not only at the Mission-station, but at the *kaffir kraals* round Kranz-kop.

It was sunset as we rode up to the pretty little Waterberg Mission-station, which will ever remain impressed on my memory, with its little cluster of white huts, its mealie gardens, its rambling parsonage, shaded by blue gum-trees, and its little church with a tiny spire, all nestled in amongst the hills—as the prettiest although not the most striking picture I have seen in the Transvaal—a picture that was sadly pleasant, as reminding one of home.

CHAPTER 24

The next morning I went to pay a visit to Mrs. B——, who received me most kindly. The whole house spoke of true homely comfort; the face of the mistress of it beamed comfort at you, although she was still crippled from the effects of the fever which had desolated Waterberg that summer, and which had made her desolate by the loss of her baby; but she had many older children, and they looked as if they had just stepped out of a German "*Randzeichnung*," or of Retzsch's etchings to the "*Lied von der Glocke.*" There was something wonderfully refreshing and wholesome about the whole establishment, and the *kaffirs* in this place were certainly the best I came across—mainly, I fancy, from the good influence of Mr. B—— and his wife, of whom I heard a high character from everyone, and of whom I can only say that it is a sad pity there are not more missionaries like them.

Their flock were certainly fond of them; but Mrs. B——, and afterwards Mr. B——, told me that the *kaffirs* were very disobedient, lazy, deceitful, selfish, and grasping in their dealings, even with them; and that many whom they had helped at great personal inconvenience at the time of the fever epidemic, had afterwards refused to assist them in putting their land in order, even for pay. They never varied in their kindness, however, towards these people, although they were firm with them. This was the character I heard of them from their neighbours among the Boers, and my own observation certainly tallied with it.

On returning from my visit I found Mr. Egerton and Hendrick doing a roaring trade; and this was kept up for the whole day, and for some succeeding days, *kaffirs* coming in from the neighbourhood to buy. Some of these were "Knopnäse," perfect savages, with tassels of fur tied on to their woolly heads, and a girdle, with a fringe of wild cats' tails, as their only garment: We spent Sunday here. The service in the church was conducted in the Makatees' language, and some of the girls and young men came out very smart. After a few days we moved down the valley, trading at various *kaffir kraals* and Boer farms (for now we were out of the *bush-veldt*), then crossed the Nile River, and traded amongst the wild Kranz-kop *kaffirs*, until I had no more *kaffir* goods left. I remember being greatly amused one evening, at the astonishment and delight caused by my appearance on horseback amongst some girls and women we met on their way to a *kraal*. They clapped their hands and danced about the horses (I was leading Violin), crying out, "Oh, the missus! the pretty missus on the horse!" And when I broke into a canter, their screams of delight, as they ran after me, made me laugh so much, that I had to interrupt the performance, and return to a walk.

Having got rid of all my *kaffir* goods, I thought I would try to get rid of a few more of my Boer goods before returning to replenish my stock at Pretoria. I therefore passed through the mission station again, and followed the course of the river towards Makapans-poort, thus once more getting into the *bush-veldt*.

At one of my outspans I came across a man who lived near Noit-gedacht. I was riding Eclipse and leading Violin, and Mr. Egerton was on Dandy, when we rode up to his encampment He asked me if I would sell Eclipse; and on my saying that I would not part with him, asked me if the other horses were for sale. I said he could have the pony for thirty, the colt for eighteen pounds—that the pony was salted. He said I asked a dreadful price; but later on, after he and some other Boers had done a little trade with me, he said a friend of his, De Clerc, wanted Violin. There was a deal of bargaining, for he wanted me to exchange him for two oxen, and at last we struck a bargain. I was to have the oxen and some money to boot; but in the morning he changed his mind—he would have Dandy instead.

I insisted upon having the full sum in cash for Dandy, and this was a sore point. It turned out that it was not De Clerc who was buying the horse; he was buying him for his son-in-law, Willem de Plessis. He tried every way to get me to lower the price; but I was really sorry to part with the pony, and I stuck out. They had him up, and asked me if he would stand fire, upon which I told them he always trotted away when his rider dismounted to fire; so young De Plessis tried him, and found my statement to be correct; but he still wanted the pony. At last the money-bag was pulled out, and the counting out began. He got up as far as twenty-eight pounds, then his courage failed him. He asked could I not take twenty-eight pounds? I said I could not. He said it was all he had got. I said that was all right, then; I should keep the pony. He got up from the *disselboom*, on which he had been sitting alongside of me, and going to another Boer who was standing a little way off, brought the two sovereigns, and gave them to me.

"Give him the pony," said I to Hendrick. "Take off the saddle and bridle."

"Oh, but you will include them in the price," said he; but I shook my head. "Then you will let me have the stable head-stall?"

"No, not unless you pay for it."

"But the knee-band you will give in?"

(It is the fashion in Africa to spancel a horse by tying its head to one of its legs, and a knee-band is often used to prevent the leg from being frayed by tying the rein round it.)

"No," I said; "not unless you buy it."

"You will, at least, let me have the rein?"

I let him have that. It was worth about sixpence. He looked at the gold lovingly as I put it into my bag.

"You will give me a written guarantee that he is salted?" he said ruefully. "It is a terrible lot of money."

"No, I won't," said I.

"Then, at least," said De Clerc cheerfully, "you will sell us a bottle of your brandy?"

"Yes, if you will pay me ten shillings;" and they did so, and departed rejoicing.

I did not go much farther along the river, for I met Mr. N——, who told me that there was no trade to be done with the Boers farther up; and, as I said before, my *kaffir* goods were exhausted. My last outspan, before I turned back, was close to the encampment of an old woman of the name of Nell, related to the De Clercs and Engelsbergs in some inextricable manner, as is often the case with Boer relationships. This is natural, when it is the custom for people of both sexes to marry so often as they do in Boer-land, for each succeeding wife to call her actual husband's mother "ma," her former husband's or husbands' mother "ma," and her husband's former wives' mothers "ma." The husbands observe the same rule, one that includes the various fathers as well, who are called "pa" by a variety of people hardly related to them according to our ideas. The relationships become still more bewilderingly intricate, when one considers that the "pa" and "ma" may marry half-a-dozen times themselves, and may thus multiply their children's fathers or mothers, and grandfathers, and grandmothers to an appalling extent. I once made, or at least attempted, a calculation of the number of grandmothers a Boer might have, but I felt that to grapple with the subject was to court insanity, and so desisted.

The old Mrs. Nell had had several husbands, and it was an endeavour on her part to make me understand how a certain individual I knew was related to her, through his being related to some relation of a former wife of one of these husbands, that started me off on the above-mentioned calculation. She was an old woman who wished to do business, and evidently thought me very verdant—as I was in those days—still her expectations were beyond my merits, for when she wished me to purchase an old and rather vicious bull, and explained to me that all I had to do to get him to walk along with my waggon was also to buy a cow or two—I respectfully declined. A grandson of hers was a boy with a sharp turn for business, which I suppose he had inherited from her. I had bought a young falcon and a pair of turtle-doves at the mission station, and I conclude the fame of that purchase had reached this young gentleman' s ears.

On riding up to old Mrs. Nell's tent I remarked a sort of magpie tied to the stump of a tree close by. In the course of conversation Mrs. Nell directed my attention to it, and said her grandson had caught it. I said it was an amusing pet; and she said that it was so indeed. Some little time after she hinted that perhaps if I liked to have it her grandson might be induced to part with it, but I took little notice of the remark. Later on she came with the grandson and the magpie to my waggon. I admired the bird, to please the boy as I thought, but was rather amused when he suggested that I should give him a bottle of sweets for it. I assured him that if I had the misfortune to own the bird, I would give him a bottle of sweets to take it away. This disconcerted him, and I heard him whisper to his grandmother, "If the aunt" (Little Boers call all women "aunt") "won't buy it, what shall I do with it?" He then returned to the charge, and at last came down to begging me to give him threepence for the bird.

Finding that I would not give him anything, he walked off looking very sulky, carrying the poor bird; and I heard afterwards from Mr. N—— (who was at Mrs. Nell's tent when he returned) that he said it was a horrid shame of the aunt not to buy the bird when he had caught it expressly to sell to her—and forthwith proceeded to wring its neck. On my way back I traded two cows, which I sold afterwards at a gain, but otherwise trade was very slack.

Mr. N—— picked me up on horseback, as I was riding in front of the waggon on my way from the missionary station back to Marullo-kop. His waggon was on in front, and shortly after we caught sight of a large herd of wildebeests, and chased them. It was a magnificent sight to see them bounding through the bush, with their tails flying, the bulls tossing their long black manes. They do not look like animals of the antelope species when thus seen.

Mr. N—— had no gun with him, greatly to his regret and my delight. He raced after them farther than I did, and we parted company in consequence. I then remarked how very easy it would be to lose oneself in the bush. In the excitement I had not remarked which way I was turning. I only knew that I had left the road to my left when I darted into the bush; and when I found myself alone (having pulled up owing to Eclipse putting his foot in a hole), I should not have had any idea of where I was had it not been that the line of hills I had just crossed, with the top of Kranz-kop looking over them, gave me my direction. When I got to Marullo-kop I found Mr. N—— already there, and he and Barend Engelsberg had made up their minds that if I did not soon arrive, they would set out to look for me, as they said lions had been seen close to where he and I parted company. For the truth of this statement I should be sorry to vouch, although Mr. N—— believed it.

The Engelsbergs gave me a hearty welcome, and Liza felt that her acquaintance with me had developed sufficiently, to allow of her asking me to lend her some money, to buy jam from Mr. N——. I suggested that as there was no knowing when we might meet again the transaction was likely to be a losing one to me; but she cheerfully answered that I should no doubt come again that way, and then she would see me.

A little Engelsberg, of about twelve, with a very innocent face, also distinguished herself by taking Mr. Egerton in. She came up to me as I was walking away from the waggon, and asked me if Mr. Egerton might get her an article which cost two shillings. She knew the price, for she had asked it before; so I said "Yes." She then went to the waggon, and on Mr. Egerton handing her the article she tendered one shilling, telling him that she had just asked me if she could not have the thing for a shilling, and that I had said "Yes." Mr. Egerton having seen her speak to me, believed her, and she took her purchase away, no doubt much pleased with her adroitness.

Mr. N—— and I came into Andreas Mayepee's *kraal* together, and found there another trader, a very jolly young fellow, who spent the evening by my camp-fire, telling stories of hunting adventures and smuggling adventures in which he had been engaged. My driver, Hendrick, had served the firm to which he belonged for a long time, and Mr. S——, the young trader, gave me a very high character of him, and told me one of his great recommendations was that he could be trusted to go trading alone with a waggon amongst the *kaffirs*.

I inquired here about my little dog, but all I could hear, was that he had been seen some days after I left. I felt pretty sure that he was hidden away in some *kaffir* hut; for *kaffirs* have a great fancy for pretty little dogs.

We three traders parted company the next day, and I took my course once more towards the Eland River. That evening I rode over to a Boer encampment to ask if I might outspan near it for the night. The owner, a fine-looking man, who was just putting his sheep in the *kraal*, answered courteously in the affirmative, and, after I had ridden back to the waggon and told Hendrick where to outspan, I cantered once more towards the tents, with a view to paying a visit to their occupants, when I suddenly saw a little black and white dog standing looking at me and flourishing his tail in a most surprising way. It was my Roughy! I jumped off the horse and caught the small beast up. He screamed with delight as he cuddled up to me, then suddenly leapt down and performed a frantic dance round me, letting off such a volley of little barks that I thought he would have choked, whilst the Boer family looked on in high satisfaction.

It seems that, some time before, the poor little thing had come across the river to their tent, thin and so footsore that he could go no farther, and they had taken him in and cared for him, and had refused to sell him once, because they wanted to find his true owner. The name of these good Samaritans was Briet. Very nice people they were, clean and tidy in all their arrangements, and keeping their little adopted child (a rosy urchin of four, with laughing black eyes) as neat and fresh as any English child could be—very unlike the generality of Boers, whose children are filthy.

I stayed there the whole of the next day. They told me that, owing to the want of rain causing the grass to be dry, their sheep and young lambs were dying. Just across the river were the broad lands of an enormously rich Boer, a man who counts his cattle by thousands, as also his sheep, who has numbers of large farms, and plenty of money in hard cash besides. His name is Erasmus, and he is know in Boerdom as the "rich Erasmus." Now it so happened that, some time before, the grass on the other side of the river had caught fire, and he had sent to ask the Briets to help him in putting it out. They had done so, toiling all through the night with might and main. The burnt grass had now shot forth sweet green leaves, such as sheep delight in, and the Briets asked if they might hire a run for their starving flock—but were refused it by the old miser! I heard that this enormously rich man refuses himself sugar in his coffee, and wears his coats until they almost fall into rags.

There were some pretty young girls, relations of the Briets, in a tent close by. When I was starting the next day, one of them in a pretty coaxing way asked me to make her a present as a remembrance of me. She was too pretty and too young to rebuff, so I said I would give her something, I forget what.

"No," she said, holding my hand, "you must let me choose my own present."

For the same somewhat unreasonable reason as before, I said she should do so, when judge of my astonishment as she tried to draw a valuable ring off my finger, saying "You shall give me this!"

"No," I said, "I can't give you that."

"Oh, but I don't want anything else," she answered; and she looked very much disappointed when I explained to her that the ring was a keepsake, and under no circumstances could be removed from my finger.

CHAPTER 25

Nothing worth relating occurred on my road to Pretoria. When close to the town, I rode to a house built close to the road, and situated on a farm where there was very good grazing, to ask whether I might outspan the waggon, and let the oxen feed there, while I was in Pretoria. It turned out that the farm had been lately leased by an Irishman, who had served in the volunteers along with Mr. Egerton, and who now was trying his hand at a *kaffir* store and a suburban hotel, together with farming. He asked me in, and I stayed for some days at his hotel, riding into Pretoria to do my business, and was much amused at his efforts at keeping his house, and a partner he had, in order. It was a decidedly bachelor's establishment, but was also decidedly preferable to any hotel in Pretoria; and my host did all he could, with true Irish hospitality, to make me comfortable. However, I soon moved into Pretoria, and my own house being let, pitched a tent in the Felman's Erf, where I still retained possession of the eligible residence I mentioned before. This, however, I did not now occupy, but used as a store-room.

I had determined upon parting with Mr. Egerton, as, in the life I was now leading, I no longer required his services. I think we were both sorry to say goodbye; and I was the more sorry, because I could not see any chance of an opening for him. He got an employment of a very laborious nature before I left Pretoria once more, and I left him the key of the eligible residence, which he determined to use as his domicile, so as not to incur the expense of an hotel. And this brings me to what has been my reason for recounting so much of Mr. Egerton's history; a reason which, if he ever reads this record of my adventures in South Africa, I believe he will deem a good one. His story points the moral of what I am about to remark.

For two years before I bade goodbye to Mr. Egerton, and, as an act of friendship, offered him the key of that miserable little hole, wherein to eat his meals and make his bed, subscriptions had been asked for and obtained for the erection of a new church for embellishments of that new church—and even (if I mistake not) for an organ for it; and from its pulpit had been thundered forth denunciations of the drunkenness and consequent vices, only too common, alas! amongst the dwellers in Pretoria. These denunciations were so frequent, that they became the topic of general conversation, and reached the ears of even those who, like myself, never heard them from the pulpit; but no effort was made to provide the means to enable men (not exceptionally determined) to avoid being dragged into the cardinal vice.

It is not an easy thing for a man to avoid frequenting a canteen when he comes as a stranger to Pretoria. He cannot get furnished lodgings—there are not such things to be had—the nearest approach is board and residence in a family; and not only is there no comfortable reading-room to be found in the hotels, but the bedrooms are small and uncomfortable. The natural and almost inevitable resource is the "bar," where he can find companionship.

If he does not get employment at once (which is very possible) , or supposing that on arriving in Pretoria he has but a very little money in his pocket (which is often the case), then, not being able to afford to stay at an hotel, he must try to get a bed or some sort of shakedown at a canteen, where he is bound to drink or he would not get the shake-down.

If he does succeed in procuring employment, but without getting introduced to some quiet family where he can board and lodge, the difficulty of spending his evenings anywhere but in a "bar" remains, for there is nowhere else to spend them if he does not sit in his bedroom. If he does not succeed in getting employment, or can only procure work for which he receives pay too small to meet his daily expenses, (even rough living is expensive in Pretoria,) then it is not easy for him to avoid, after a time, finding it expedient to take his blanket and make his bed upon fine nights under a rose-hedge in the vicinity of the town, so as to save the expense of a bed; and when in the chill, damp morning he gets up, I personally do not wonder that the temptation to have a "tot" at the canteen is too strong for him. The time may very easily come when he cannot afford to look whether the night be fine or not, before making his bed under the rose-hedge, and then the morning "tot" seems still more alluring, I fancy—and so on, and so on, until he becomes one of the denounced.

Would not (under these circumstances) a subscription to start a cheap but self-supporting lodging-house, with a restaurant and reading-room attached, be more to the point than a subscription for an ornamental church, from whose pulpit the poor homeless victims to a strong temptation may be denounced, after a hymn has been sung to the accompaniment of an organ also bought by subscription?

As I regretfully shook hands with Mr. Egerton, in the market-square of Pretoria, with the moonlight streaming over it, and turned after my waggon, once more on my way to the *bush-veldt*, I wondered whether, were I he, I should have the strength of mind to go back to that dismal hut by the swamp, every evening, to cook my dinner with wood I should have to gather and blow into a flame after a hard day's toil, and, having eaten, to sit down on a box to read, by the light of a single candle, unless I spread my blankets on the ground and went to sleep, amidst the litter of a store-room. This too with a dreary consciousness, that I should wake up in the grey morning, to discomfort, loneliness, and toil—while, all the time, there were lights and there were warmth and rest to be had in many a canteen, and something to drink—which meant to feel jolly for a little time, and to go to sleep without thinking of the morrow.

I believe it is a fact that gentlemen's sons go more quickly and certainly to the dogs in this, and I suppose in every, colony, than the sons of working men. Putting aside that they cannot obtain work so easily as the latter, the reason is self-evident; they cannot battle so strongly against the privations and discomfort they are exposed to, and hence they are more liable to seek temporary solace in drink. The habit once formed, will hardly be abandoned, even if the origin of it ceases.

I do not mean to say that all the drunkenness which prevails in Pretoria is originally caused by a desire to forget discomfort, but I am confident that a great deal of it is, and that much misery and vice might be prevented by the adoption of some such plan as I have suggested.

Before leaving Pretoria, I had dismissed Hans, my leader—he was too fond of smoking "*daccha*," an intoxicating leaf, the constant use of which drives its votaries at times almost to insanity—and in his place I had engaged the services of a Zulu *kaffir* called Pete, recommended to me by my driver, Hendrick. The boy, little Hendrick, remained with me by his own desire; and I was glad to keep him, for he was a bright, intelligent, and yet wonderfully innocent-minded child. When he first came to me he used to amuse me by turning out of his blankets of a morning without a scrap of clothing on him, although the sharp wind might be blowing, and the hoar frost be lying thick on the ground, reserving his dressing arrangements until after he had lit the fire and set the kettle on to boil, for early coffee; but by this time, he was beginning to think it incumbent upon him to put on his shirt before he performed these duties.

Another change had come o'er the spirit of my dream. I was now the possessor not only of a house in Pretoria, but of a small farm, about twenty-five miles from Pretoria, going the shortest way, and which carried with it the right of free grazing and water on the large farm of which it originally formed a part. The place was noted as being healthy for horses and sheep, and was an excellent stand for a Boer-store; and I got it for a price which even the Boers near considered cheap.

My load consisted principally of *kaffir* goods, and I had a barrel of Cape brandy up as well. This speculation I had been recommended by many who knew about trading, and I had been asked for brandy so frequently by Boers, that I thought I would try it. So I took out a bottle licence. This reminds me of an absurd old magistrate who gave me the said licence, and who took me up very sharp for wanting a bottle and not a retail licence (I think that is the correct name for a licence to sell by the glass).

"I don't want to sell by the glass," said I.

"Oh! don't you?" quoth he; "but I am very much afraid you will." And he held up a long finger, and shook it and his head, in a manner that would have suggested to a bystander, that I already stood convicted of several similar offences.

"It is not probable," I remarked, "that I should like to have a lot of tipsy *kaffirs* round my waggon." But up went the forefinger again, and with a terrible shake of the head he answered,—

"Well, mind, if I catch you at it, I shall fine you heavily—very heavily."

"I will give you permission to fine me as heavily as you like, when you catch me," said I, pocketing my licence; and I conveyed to my old friend, doubtless, the idea that I was a hardened sinner, up to all the dodges necessary to evade the law successfully.

There was another thing about this brandy which amused me. A friendly store-man at the store where I bought it, who had previously given me many little hints about trading, beckoned me aside when it was loaded up.

"When you get well out from amongst the Boers," he said— "for I understand you are going right in amongst the *kaffirs* this time—just fill up the cask with water; the *kaffirs* won't remark it. I wouldn't advise you to put tobacco into it; that I don't think right. But just fill up with water; it won't pay well enough if you don't."

I thanked him and departed.

This time I took my way through Buckonoo's Kloof (I spell as pronounced in English), instead of through Derdepoort. It was a very pleasant change; the gorge, or *kloof*, with its craggy sides so thickly wooded that only here and there a bold mass of grey rock could be seen, jutting oat at some curve of the river, or of the road that ran between them, looked quite delightful in the morning light; and I several times stopped to look at the pretty picture the waggon made, as, with its long team of oxen, it wound its way through the chequered sunlight and shadow. There were thousands of monkeys in this leafy retreat, and they hooted at us as we went by, not coming close, however, but affording an immense amount of excitement to the dogs and to little Hendrick, who was riding with me on Violin.

On emerging from this gorge we came to several pretty farms; at one of them I was hospitably received by an old Dutchman and his family, who were in favour of English rule. They had a farm on the *high-veldt*, and used this farm only as a *bush-veldt* farm. I went along slowly, trading as I went, at the various places I had visited before, and at last got to Marullo-kop. The Engelsbergs seemed very much pleased to see me, and I met young De Plessis there. He had come over to have something done to a waggon of his, and had brought his wife and his youngest child with him. As I sat in the Engelsbergs' tent, waiting for the waggon to come up, the men—amongst whom, if I remember aright, was De Clerc—talked much of the *Beeinkom- mste* that had just been held, to discuss the advisability of starting Boer stores, the goods to be imported direct, so as to oust English traders from the Transvaal.

Barend Engelsberg said he had promised to subscribe 100*l*., and mentioned the names of some other Boers, who were going to subscribe different amounts. There was a doubt about whom they should import from. They said that the Americans and the Germans had made very liberal offers. My friends in the tent seemed to think that the American offer would be accepted. I had been listening to the men talking, while the women chatted about their babies and other domestic topics. I doubt whether they thought I understood much

405

of what they were saying, so that there was a little hush of surprise when at this point I said "I think the plan you propose, or that has been proposed at your *Beeinkommste,* is a very good one, and you will, I dare say, get your things much cheaper than you now do, but I would advise any of you who may have any influence with the committee you speak of, to avoid dealing with the Americans; they are first-rate men of business, but they would be too sharp for you probably. I think it would be much safer for you to deal with the Germans."

It was a great surprise to them, in more ways than one, to hear me say this; and some time after De Clerc asked me if I was born English. I said, "Yes, I am born English—at least an English subject; but I was born in Ireland, and my parents were both Irish." Upon which he said, "Ah!" as if he were making a note of it in his mind.

The next morning, as I was sitting by the waggon a number of girls of various ages came over, and sitting down, after they had made some purchases, talked to me. One of them, who seemed rather a nice girl, had bought a pair of gloves I remember, and she laid them on the grass between herself and her two little cousins. These two little girls bade me goodbye before she did, and, when she rose to go, she missed her gloves. She searched everywhere for them in vain. At last she said, "Oh, I remember; they were close to my cousins; they have taken them." And I saw the tears in her eyes.

" Well," said I, "then you can get them back; they will have found them amongst their things."

"Oh, no," she said simply; "you know of course they will keep them. That was why they went away so soon."

"Then tell their mother," I suggested rather indignantly, "and get them given back to you."

The girl almost laughed at my ignorance. "Why that would be of no use," she said. "She would never give them to me, even if she knew they were there."

I found that the beauty of Eclipse was a constant theme among the Boers, and that my prowess in riding him was greatly extolled. On one occasion Barend Engelsberg brought another Boer over to the waggon, expressly to admire the horse, and to ask me to show how I could do anything I liked with him without his kicking me. Boers as a rule are very fond of horses, although they are somewhat careless of them, as indeed they are of themselves and their families, and our common taste soon established a sort of freemasonry between us, the men being always ready to listen to all I had to tell of my horses, and to recount long tales of their past and present horses in return.

When I reached the mission station I found that Mr. B—— had resigned his position as missionary, and was just removing to a farm at some distance, called Sandfontein. He came to see me at the waggon, but I did not go to the house, as I was very busy trading and had no time. Pete, my leader, distinguished himself by getting drunk on *kaffir* beer while I was here, and sitting under the waggon the following day, loudly deploring his headache and general wretchedness, caused partly by the drink, and partly by the disgrace I kept him in.

My way now lay past some warm springs, of which there are several in Waterberg, to Makapan's-poort. On my way I once more passed the encampment of the De Clercs and young De Plessis, the size of which was increased by the addition of several tents and waggons belonging to Boers who had been encamped further along the river, but were now on their way from the *bush-veldt* to their farms on the *ur-veldt* or elsewhere. Amongst these Boers was old Mrs. Nell, who had tried to sell the bull to me.

The stories about lions being in the vicinity, and having killed horses and cattle, belonging in some cases to Boers whom I knew, were so numerous, and so well authenticated, that I thought it best to keep fires burning all night, and that we should sleep in a ring round the horses, leaving one boy to sleep by the fore-oxen. I saw Dandy again, and he knew me, and could with difficulty be got away from the waggon, but he was evidently well cared for and kindly treated. I must describe his master and his master's family. They are the best Boers I have come across.

Young De Plessis himself—a man of about middle height, wiry, and full of energy, with bright laughing eyes, a merry mouth, and clustering hair, with a manner in accordance, bold and free, and with something pleasantly boy-like in his way of enjoying a joke or asking a favour—was known amongst his mates as a sure shot, a daring hunter, and a first-rate horseman; yet always ready to help his wife with the baby (she told me herself he always weaned the children for her), and withal a most diligent and energetic farmer. He was the only Boer I ever saw who groomed his horse regularly every day.

His wife was tall, and made on a large scale; but her every movement was graceful. Her face, with its regular features, large steady eyes, with long dark eyelashes and pencilled eyebrows, was a picture of serene cheerfulness, and the set of her well-shaped head on her finely-formed neck and bust was statuesque. I have seen her doing all sorts of little domestic work with the air of a Juno, except that Juno, according to Homer, never can have looked serene. She was always dressed neatly, with a fresh kerchief folded across her breast, and her hair was always tidy, her hands always clean, and she never seemed disturbed or hurried about anything. Her tent was a model of neatness, and her children never looked dirty.

The baby was a delightful baby, with big brown eyes and round cheeks; and it was always speckless. I am sure I don't know how she kept it so, but I never saw that infant otherwise than spotlessly clean from the top of its head to the tip of its little pink toe; and its garments always seemed to have been just put on. There were two older urchins—one a handsome dark-eyed fellow, as brown as a berry, and full of mischief; the other blue-eyed and shy, with a tendency to hold by his mother's apron and put his fingers in his mouth when in the presence of a stranger, but a pretty child. These youngsters were often superficially dirty, but one could always see their little white shirts peeping out at their collars and cuffs, and when, at meal-times, they were told to wash before sitting down, a very little soap and water made them look refreshingly clean.

I have described this family, not as a type of Boer families, but because it is the only Transvaal Boer family, amongst the many I have seen, of which all these nice things could be said, unless I except the Briets, and the Briets were rich, whereas young De Plessis was very poor. I dined one Sunday in the De Plessis' tent, and had a very nice dinner, of wild buck's meat and a sort of sweet suet-pudding with cinnamon in it, served up with thick meat-sauce. Several neighbours came in, and we were very merry. De Plessis and his friends were laughing over a "grand spree" they had had the night before, when, as a finish up, they had smeared each other's coats all over with fat. Some very distinguishable marks of the practical joke yet remained. Trade was good here, and I stayed for some time.

There was one man, of the name of Jan Smith, who was always coming to the waggon to beg me to sell him a "tot," and when I said I could not sell one, begging me to give him one. It was wonderful how these Boers would beg of me to infringe the law, and assure me that they would never tell of me, and that no trader minded adhering to it. I soon began to be sorry I had got brandy up, for, when they found that I would not sell them "tots," they would club together and buy a bottle, drink it in a surprisingly short time, and come back for more, until the whole encampment was several sheets in the wind.

They were only gay and festive during the day, but at night I rather think they used to quarrel; and in order to get rid of the liquor, which I saw would prove a bother to me, I offered it to the whole encampment at cost price, and said I would trade it in cattle. They were much inclined to take it, but could not quite make up their minds as to how they would manage to bottle it off, and so, much to my regret, the thing fell through.

One day my driver Hendrick told me, in a very mysterious manner, that young De Plessis had got the plumage of an ostrich, which he would like to sell to me, taking three quarters of the payment in goods. I said he could bring the feathers, and let me see them. Then Hendrick said he would bring them that evening, but that I must be very careful not to let anyone see them. I asked why, when he informed me that as a rule Boers were very envious of each other, and that if it were known among young De Plessis' friends and relatives that he had had the luck to shoot an ostrich, he would be annoyed by them. In the meantime the feathers were brought and approved, and young De Plessis, with his wife and her mother, Mrs. De Clerc, came over in the evening secretly, chose the goods, and got payment, and also showed me how to pack up the feathers nicely, this process being performed very secretly in my tent. Before he left I asked him the reason why he observed so much secrecy, for I did not believe Hendrick's version.

"You see," said De Plessis, "it is against the law."

"Indeed."

"Yes, it is breeding-time now, and although it is true that that cock bird had lost his mate, yet I should be liable to a fine of 500*l.* if it were known I had shot a bird during this season. Besides, my father-in-law promised that he would shoot that bird for Mr. L—— (a trader), and if he knew I had shot it he would persecute me. So pray don't say anything about it, for I should be utterly ruined if I had to pay 500*l.* In fact, I could not pay it, for I have not got it."

"Well," said I, "I am sorry that I have helped you to do an unlawful act; however, as I have, I will keep your secret, even if I have to depart a little from the truth. It is no secret of mine, and I should be sorry to harm you—"

"Oh, but," said he, "it is your secret as well as mine. You are as guilty before the law as I am."

"Oh!" said I; and in my own mind I thought that altered the case very much. However, I resolved to keep the feathers until I came back from Makapan's-poort. I knew I should see De Plessis on his farm in Waterberg as I returned, and I need tell no lies, nor talk about the feathers until I got to Pretoria, and wanted to dispose of them.

De Clerc used often to come with other Boers to my waggon. He was an oldish man, but handsome in a rugged sort of way, was a bold hunter and a good horseman, and a leading man amongst the Waterberg Boers, being a fairly well-educated man for a Boer, and having held office under the Boer Government. He used often to talk politics to me, and always introduced me to his friends as an Irishwoman. Once one of the friends remarked that the Irish hated the English; upon which I told him that I did not, and that although I thought that in many ways the English Government had behaved badly to the Boers, yet that if ever it came to war I should take the English side. De Clerc said he understood my feeling; that he believed it was best for the country that the English should govern it; that England was a strong and rich country, and that the land would be more secure and more prosperous under her auspices than it would otherwise be; but that yet in his heart he felt sore about the English dominion.

He went on to say that he always dissuaded his friends from any thoughts of fighting; that he meant to bring up his boy as a friend to the English; that he believed that fighting would only end in a complete overthrow of the Boers; but yet—and I could see his dark eyes flash under his shaggy brow—that, if there was fighting, his life and all he had should be thrown into the balance for his own race. "I quite understand that," I said; "it would be the same with me were I a Boer."

"But you are English, and of course if war comes you will go with your nation, as I with mine," he answered.

One evening I walked across to the Boer encampment, crossing the river by a little plank thrown over it. I found De Clerc paying a visit to a very fat and rather old woman, who had just presented her husband, an old man with a white beard, with a first baby. There was an attempt being made to galvanize a sentiment about this unfortunate infant, but as its parents had had husbands, wives, and children before, the attempt was a failure. However, I gave the mother a present of a bottle of brandy and some raisins, and everybody was very much pleased. The invalid was in the waggon where the baby had been born, the happy father was sitting at the back, and De Clerc and I sat on chairs in front of him. It was a beautiful afternoon, and the trees, the river, the green grass near, the waggons and tents peering out from the foliage, and the blue sky, made a pretty picture, and put me into a very good humour.

"Well," said De Clerc, "we are going to have a lion-hunt this evening or tomorrow. A cow has been killed close here, and we must find the lion and kill it."

"Oh dear," said I, "how I should like to see the hunt"

"What do you say to my proposal?" said De Clerc. "We will bring you the body of the lion just as it is killed, and you shall give us 5*l*."

"And the skin?"

"Oh, no! If I give you the skin you must give us 10*l*."

I laughed at the absurd demand. "No," said I; "it is nothing to me to see a dead lion, for I have seen many live ones in cages, and I don't much care for his skin. But I'll tell you what I will do. Take me with you on the hunt, and I'll give you 10*l*., and a bottle or two of brandy to have a spree with afterwards."

"Done!" cried De Clerc. "What will you ride?"

"Eclipse."

"But is he accustomed to lion-hunting?"

"I'm sure I don't know," said I. "If you can spare me a horse that is accustomed to it I should prefer it."

"You can have my horse, and let me have Eclipse."

"No, no," I answered; "no one rides my horse but myself, particularly where there may be danger."

"Hear her!" exclaimed De Clerc; "that is how an Irishwoman speaks. But are you sure you won't be frightened?"

"I'm sure I shall be frightened, horribly frightened," said I; "but I'm sure I shall do whatever you tell me to do, and that I shall not run away, or scream, or do anything of that sort."

Then there was some talk between the men as to how the hunt was to be arranged, and during this I observed that De Clerc was envious of De Plessis, who was the sharpest and boldest hunter among them. Presently two youngsters rode up at a canter.

"We have got the spoor (or track), but we cannot follow it; we can only make it out in one place. Shall we get the horses up, and try again all of us, as it is not too late?"

It was agreed that it was too late, and that they had better wait till morning. As I went back to the waggon I said to De Clerc, who walked a little way with me, "You won't deceive me, will you?"

"Oh, no," he answered. "I think you had better be ready about nine. By-the-way, there is one of those nice hats you have; I want one so much, but I have not the money to buy it. Won't you give me one as a remembrance of my taking you with me on the hunt?"

He had asked me to bring the hats over that he might choose one, but had not fixed upon one, and little Hendrick was still with me, with the hats in his hand. I saw through the old fellow, and was inclined to say that he should have the hat when I returned from the lion hunt; but I still had clinging to me some of the politeness which was instilled into me in my youth, but which it is advisable to discard in Boer-land, unless you mean to be victimized at every turn; so he took his hat and departed.

I waited there for several days afterwards, but no lion-hunt took place.

Before my departure I bought Dandy back again, giving Violin and some money for him. De Plessis was in want of money to pay off a debt, and I found that Dandy was a great loss in Pretoria. Violin was a capital horse for a gallop, but, with anybody but me, he was inclined to be vicious, and required careful breaking in to become a good horse, whereas when I had but him and Eclipse I could hardly ever ride him, and the boys were spoiling him by riding him badly. Dandy seemed delighted to be once more with me. The last I saw of De Plessis was after I was already on my road, when I heard a "Halloa!" behind me, and turning, beheld him coming along at a gallop on his new acquisition, flourishing a black bottle in his hand. He was delighted with Violin's performance, and said he must buy one more bottle of brandy just to let them all have a spree on my going away. So I stopped the waggon, and, while he was getting his brandy, poor Violin, for the last time, searched my pocket for bread.

I was now approaching the last tent belonging to white men. After passing one of my old acquaintances near to the warm baths, I entered a country prettier than any I had traversed before. I rode along a wooded valley, skirting the hills that bounded it at one side. The scene was a mixture of wildness and resemblance to an English park. There were many very good trees, the bush was thick, and there was a sprinkling of tropical-looking and enormous cacti or cactus-trees. One day I came on a group of *kaffirs* on their way to the diamond-fields, sitting under a spreading tree. I knew that I was near water—the horses were very thirsty—but I could not make out where the spring was; the course of the rivulet coming from it, was in parts dry, and in parts spread out into a half-marsh thickly overgrown with reeds. One of the men volunteered to show me the way. The spring was some distance from the spot, deep and clear, and Eclipse plunged into it eagerly.

"I have brought you to the spring," said the *kaffir*, while I sat enjoying the enjoyment of my horse and little Hendrick and Dandy in the cool water. I took out a small piece of money to give him.

"I did not want any money," he said; "I merely said I had showed you the water." And he seemed quite satisfied with thanks. I afterwards gave him and his companions some brandy, and one man came forward after they had all drunk, and said they wished him to thank me very much. These were very raw *kaffirs*, and could hardly speak anything but *kaffir*, but they were wonderful in the matter of courtesy; for *kaffirs* generally are either rude like monkeys, or like Boers—and the latter is a very bad and disagreeable form of rudeness, characterized by much staring, talking of and laughing at anything which may strike them as unusual in a stranger.

My last outspan by a white man's tent, was on a beautiful evening, and the scene struck me very much. I emerged from a thick wood on a delicious greensward, almost like an ornamental lawn, interspersed with a few fine trees. The road wound through this, and it was bounded on one side by the thickly-wooded hills, on the other by the forest. A large herd of cattle were making their way to three white tents pitched on the border of this, and partially concealed by its foliage; and the last rays of the sun, as it sank behind the hills, were tinting all near objects with gold, while in the distance the hills of Makapan looked blue and misty.

The family from these tents soon came to see me. Three of the men had been severely injured by fire. They had been hunting on the hills, and had set fire to the grass to hunt out the animals; but the wind suddenly rose, and, in rising, changed its direction, so that the fire hunted them out instead.

Early the next morning I passed the last white habitation; the owner was a woodcutter, and had pitched his tent under a superb tree, not with the intention of cutting it down, however. Close by I saw a very curious animal. It was an enormous lizard, so large that it was like a little crocodile. It was close by the path when I saw it, and I frightened little Hendrick very much by riding up to it. He assured me that it had extraordinary power in its tail, and that if it struck Eclipse it would kill him. The little beast looked at me for a moment, then, slashing his long scaly tail in a most extraordinary manner, ran away with extreme agility, the tail vibrating from side to side all the time.

I followed it on Eclipse, but it suddenly disappeared, I suppose down some hole. Our mid-day outspan was by the side of a rivulet, and in such thick bush that, no sooner were the oxen and horses loose, than they were lost to sight. It was said that there were lions close to this place, and thieving *kaffirs* also, so I cautioned Pete and little Hendrick to keep the animals in sight, whilst Hendrick prepared the food. When it was prepared, and he went to call them to eat and make a fresh start, they were nowhere to be found, and neither were the animals, and it was some time before they came up. I had eaten, and was impatient to start, so I told them to up-saddle and inspan at once. I rode Dandy and led Eclipse this time, and I did not look specially at the latter until I had ridden a little way, then I saw he was sweated, which excited my suspicion. It was late when I reached Moer-drift, the place for outspanning. The valley here begins to narrow, and the hills of Makapan's-poort can be plainly seen; the valley itself is but little wooded, but the hills are covered with trees, and the effect is very pretty. I off-saddled, and it was not till almost dark, that the waggon came up.

Pete was running in front of it, and a glance showed me that he was quite drunk. The oxen were hardly outspanned when he fell down under the waggon and went fast asleep. I perceived also that little Hendrick was tipsy. I asked Hendrick how this was, and he told me that Pete had taken little Hendrick to a *kaffir kraal*, instead of minding the animals at the last outspan, and had given him some of the beer upon which he himself had got tipsy. I said nothing about Eclipse, but I felt sure now that Pete had either ridden him, or hunted him very hard on Dandy. I called up little Hendrick and told him that I would give him something to make him remember that the after-consequences of drink were disagreeable, and ordered Hendrick to give him some good cuts with a *reim*; Pete had to be left till morning. In the early dawn I saw him arise, wrap a blanket round him, loose the oxen and take them off to graze. ' "He is trying to get into favour," thought I. I also heard little Hendrick laugh at him slyly for having been thrown by Eclipse—so I was quite sure about my affair now. The boys thought I was asleep, for I did not move.

I had breakfast, but no Pete appeared: At last I sent Hendrick on horseback to look for the oxen. He found them far off, but Pete was missing. However, I had no mind to wait for him, so inspanned and got on near to a settlement of Knopnäse *kaffirs*, where I outspanned and was trading with them when Mr. Pete slinked up. I was too busy to speak to him then, and presently inspanned to go on to Makapan's-poort.

It was a pretty ride, and when I got to the place itself I thought it a very pretty place. Right in the middle of the pass, a precipitous hill, crowned with Makapan's *kraal*, forms a sort of natural fortress. A small river (the Nile River, I think) winds round its base; trees of various sorts cluster round, and are scattered over it, and the ruins of a once large mission station, and the pomegranates, *syringas*, and other shrubs of the garden that used to be, add a charm to the scene. Numbers of women and children stared at me as I crossed the river with the two horses, and waited for the waggon to come up, for I did not know where to outspan. Hendrick could not talk the pure Makatees, spoken by these *kaffirs*, sufficiently well to trust entirely to him, so I had taken a *kaffir* from the mission station to act as interpreter and guide. This *kaffir*'s name was Nicholas, commonly called "Clas."

So soon as the waggon arrived, Clas showed me a pretty little dell at the foot of the hill, where we outspanned. I sent him to the *kraal*, with the present of a bottle of French brandy to Makapan, and a message that I wished to have his permission to trade with his tribe. And in return the chief sent me his thanks, and said that he was glad I had come, and would protect me.

CHAPTER 26

Makapan, or rather Clas Makapan, for the latter is only his surname or family name, is the son of a chief who, after a fearful massacre of the Boers, was at last reduced to submission by them. Clas was taken as hostage, and brought up in a Boer family. When his father died the *kaffirs* determined to get the child back, and, fearful that the Boers would not give him willingly, they stole him one night, and having got him, made peace with the Boers by paying for him in cattle. One of the old *kaffirs* told me that the little Clas had been very much frightened when he found himself a prisoner amongst the *kaffirs*, and had cried and kicked to get away.

I soon found that unless I traded for corn, I should be able to do but little here, for the taxes were just being called for by the government, and the *kaffirs* were very much afraid of not having money to pay them in, as cattle were taken at a ridiculously low value for the amount, if the cash was not there when called for. I determined therefore to trade for mealies and *kaffir* corn, as I got them very cheap, and they were likely to fetch a good price in Pretoria. When I made this intention known, the *kaffirs* came in swarms, the men walking in front, followed by the women and girls, bearing on their heads baskets filled with grain. There were hundreds assembled, between those who came to trade and those who came to look on; it was hard to prevent their crowding too close to the waggon, and many a time had Pete to rush at the ever-narrowing circle formed round it, with a big whip to keep the intruders off.

It takes a long time trading for grain, for the grain has all to be measured off into sacks, or sometimes by buckets-full; besides this, one has to examine its quality. The din of all these savages, talking, yelling, laughing, was deafening, and at the end of a day's work, which lasted without intermission from seven o'clock in the morning until

416

the same hour in the evening, I was not only tired in body, but I felt nearly mad. This lasted several days. It was amusing, however, and I had a good opportunity of observing the *kaffir* in his natural state. The women were dressed much like those at the Eland River, except that they had two long, thin pieces of leather hanging from their girdles behind like tails. These were ornamented with beads, brass or white buttons, &c., according to the taste or means of the wearer, and the young ladies were in the habit of holding one of these appendages in one hand and switching it about.

I may here remark that Makatees young ladies are as fond of flirting as any other young ladies I have had the pleasure of studying. The girls were rather graceful, and had a way of entwining their arms round each other and falling into groups, which was absolutely artistic. I remember one group which seemed to have arranged itself with a consciousness of "The Graces." These three young ladies had rubbed their bodies and their hair or wool with a mixture of fat and red earth which, although it does not sound nice, was by no means unbecoming. Mother's darlings were also to be distinguished from urchins who were not darlings, by the former being reddish-brown and the latter of a natural black colour. The girls wore a variety of ornaments, some very prettily made—of grass and wire, also of beads. A disease much resembling scabies—called, I believe, *kaffir*-pock—was very prevalent at Makapan's-poort, and I observed that the persons of those who rubbed themselves, or were rubbed by their fond mammas, with the unguent I have described, had escaped it.

The men wore all sorts of costumes. Some of the aristocracy of the place wore European dress, others skins curiously sewn together and prepared, others blankets, others girdles fringed with the tails of wild cats, others again a shirt, sometimes tied by its sleeves round the neck, sometimes properly worn; while many had just a rag or a little strip of soft leather round the loins. Many had their wool ornamented with little rosettes made of the tail of the rock rabbit, or by *meerkats'* tails, tied on like tassels. I often saw the men going out hunting, armed with *assegai* and tomahawk, and often with a rifle. They would start off early in the morning, whooping and dancing, with a troop of dogs after them.

One day I noticed a girl who was quite pretty, and also modest-looking, in the crowd that surrounded me, but at a little distance. I took aim at her with a small circular looking-glass, and successfully. She was delighted when she saw herself, but after giving me one beaming smile, she turned shy, and ran away.

From that moment I had no peace. The girls were not so bad as the women, who had no excuse, for they were all ugly. One old wretch who, although she had been brought up amongst the Boers for years, and had been accustomed to dress, now wore a fringed girdle and a skin over her shoulders, pestered me every day for a glass. At last I said, "You ask me why I gave that young woman one, and won't give you one? That is easily answered. She is pretty, and has some use for a looking-glass; whereas you are old, and if you had one, would have nothing pretty to see if you looked in it: when I was young I often looked in the glass, but I don't now: looking-glasses are for young people."

How that woman laughed, and clapped her hands, and laughed again. Then she called several of her friends, and told them; and they cried out, "True! true!" and laughed until I began to feel that I had perpetrated a wonderful witticism. They were, however, quite as anxious to get a peep into a looking-glass afterwards as before, though no elderly female ever asked me for a glass again as a present.

I had almost forgotten to tell about Pete.

On the evening of our arrival at Makapan's-poort, I went over to the camp-fire where the boys were sitting, although it was very warm, and the moonlight was as bright as day, and said, "Pete, this is your second offence; and you made it worse by attempting to ride my horse without my permission; now remember, I never speak three times; the third offence I punish; and as I object to punishing either a servant or an animal, I never punish either, unless I give them something they are not likely to forget in a hurry."

Pete stared hard at me, and said, "Yes, missus;" and I walked off. I may here remark that although I have always found the giving of a certain grace a good plan with European servants, I have found it a bad plan with African servants. I think personally that they are too much like animals to be treated in this way, and that the best way to manage them is to punish severely the first offence (I mean, of course, an offence whose culpability they understand) just as one does with an animal one has to train. At the time of which I am now writing, however, although I greatly doubted whether a *kaffir* ought to be treated otherwise than as an animal, I thought it right to give him the benefit of the doubt.

The heat even at night was now very great; and the irritation caused by the biting and crawling over one of microscopical ticks was very great. I found it difficult to sleep at night, and I have often got up and walked about in the moonlight, or watched the sleeping horses lying comfortably by the waggon, and sometimes giving little ghostly neighs in their sleep that testified to their dreaming. I never slept in the tent, for I was always afraid of some robbery going on, and once my suspicions were aroused by missing Pete from where he ought to have been sleeping. He turned up shortly after, however, so I thought no more about it, as I noticed nothing else remarkable.

A serious difficulty now began to claim my attention. I had been led to believe that I should be able to get meal from some of the Boer houses in Waterberg (at the other side of the mission station), but I had not been able to procure any, and in consequence of finding very little game and no meat towards and at Makapan's-poort, the meal I had was beginning to run short. I could buy but very little milk; and the coffee was getting low. I determined to start for Pretoria, but deferred my departure a little in order to be present at a grand feast which Makapan was about to give. He was to "make rain" for his clan, and there was to be a grand dance.

Although brought up amongst the Boers, Makapan has not adopted any substitute for the superstition of his father and his tribe, and he has a pronounced objection to missionaries. He came to pay me a visit the day before this feast. He is a big man, with coarse features. He was dressed in a short coat, riding-breeches, gaiters and boots, and a felt hat. Of course I gave him a "tot;" and gave one also to his head-man, called "Stürman," who was dressed like himself. He said he hoped I would visit him before I left the place; that he had heard that I said that I would not visit Makapan before Makapan visited me, and that now Makapan had come. I said I would go to his *kraal* the next day. I was greatly surprised to see how unceremoniously his subjects, and even my driver Hendrick, were allowed to treat him, and felt that it was difficult to know how to treat as a chief, a man who allowed my driver to shake hands with him; however, I promised to go, and then Makapan asked for another tot. I have heard that such chiefs as Cetawayo and Sekocooni are approached by their subjects in an abject posture, and are never spoken to by them unless permission has been given. I can only suppose that chiefs like Makapan, who have adopted European costume, are by degrees losing the consideration of their subjects.

The morning of the great feast-day broke splendidly, and, before the sun was up, groups of young warriors, dressed in their best, came past my encampment on their way to the chief's *kraal*. I was no sooner dressed than I ordered the horses to be saddled, and taking Clas as my companion, started for the *kraal*. I had been told that one could ride up, and indeed I had seen that Makapan and his suite had ridden both up and down. After turning a little round the hill we began the stony ascent, through a maze of little *kaffir* huts, from which the children came forth yelling, at the sight of me, followed by their mothers, some trying to stop their clamorous vociferations, while others did their utmost to add to the din. At last, after a desperate scramble, which landed me on a shelving piece of rock with boulder after boulder rising above it, I declined to endanger the horses' feet any longer, and dismounting, told Clas he must lead the horses back, and give them in charge to some decent *kaffir* until his and my return.

At this moment, however, I saw Makapan descending from his eyrie to greet me, with a staff in his hand, which he offered to me to assist me in climbing. Having passed within the low wall that bounds his *kraal*, I found myself in a labyrinth of huts, each with an enclosed yard attached, and traversed by narrow paths. Makapan led me past a large stockade, and through various enclosures, each with a hut in it (his *harem*, or whatever it may be called in *kaffir*), to his own house, a cottage built of bricks, and with a verandah in front. He took me into his bedroom (the house had only two rooms, I think) and asked me to be seated.

The dark and dirty room was furnished with two or three chairs, a little table, and a common bedstead, on which were thrown a mattress, some gaudy blankets, and a *"caross,"* or large mat made of skins curiously stitched together, and with the hair left on. He asked me if I would have coffee, and brought me some in a cup; then, after talking about various things, he said he hoped that I would make him a present of a very handsome rug I had for sale. I did not like to refuse, but I said I thought he ought to make me a present too; he said he would do so gladly, and sent one of his officers to get me an ostrich feather—a very indifferent specimen. I then asked him if I might attend the feast that he was about to give that day.

He seemed much pleased at this proposal, and said that I should be surprised at seeing what swarms of warriors would be there. He also told me that he should kill an ox in the course of the day, and that he would send me some of the meat; this, for aforesaid reasons, I was very glad to hear. He asked me several times whether I was not surprised to see such a large place as his *kraal*; whether I did not think it very strong; and told me that I should be surprised at the number of his warriors. Before I went away he asked me if I would not have something to eat, but this I declined. As he was escorting me to my horses, we met a singular-looking old *kaffir* carrying herbs. Makapan said, laughing, "That is my doctor, and those are his medicines; he will help me to make medicines for my *kaffirs* today." He seemed to think the whole thing rather amusing; and indeed I doubt whether he was not aware, as I was, of the absurdity of his conjuring away diseases and conjuring up rain.

Chapter 27

It was still early when I got back to the waggon. The dance was not to begin till noon—a curious time, by-the-way, for a dance, for the heat was very great. In the meantime I had ample opportunities of observing the different costumes of the savages, numbers of whom came over to talk to my boys before taking their way up the hillside to the *kraal*. Some of the young men presented a very picturesque appearance. Their loins were girt with leathern girdles, fringed with magnificent cats'-tails, their heads were decorated with rosettes and tassels; a warhorn—beautifully and curiously worked in brass, copper, or tin wire, sometimes all three together—was hung round their necks and thrown behind them; a bright coloured scarf thrown over one shoulder and passed under the opposite arm; their legs were covered with buskins made from the white skin from under the belly of a buck, and each carried an *assegai*, often ornamented with wire embroidery on the handle, a short club, also ornamented, a tomahawk or a rifle, or sometimes an assortment of these different articles.

At a little before twelve I took Clas with me, and began the ascent of the hill. I went by a different way this time, one which led me in and out of rocks and boulders, overhung by trees, a scrambling, delightful way, giving one pretty glimpses of the valley and of the *kaffir* huts clustering at the base of the hill. Every now and then some of Makapan's warriors would rush by me with a leap and a bound, and as they scaled the hill rapidly I could hear their yell and the discharge of their rifles as a salute to the chief's stockade as they entered it. Groups of girls also passed me, their arms intertwined, chattering and laughing until they saw me, when they would stare for a minute and then go on.

About halfway up I discovered that Moustache had followed me. He had kept in the background until he thought he was far enough from the waggon to avoid being sent back; he now came forward with a conscious air, wagged his tail, and gave an awkward sort of hop, as much as to say, "I hope you won't be angry; but I'm here, and you can't send me back now;" and trotted on in front. He distrusted those men with rifle and *assegai* though; he did not bark at them, and rush furiously after them, showing his white teeth by a vicious curling up of his nose, as was his wont with *kaffirs*; he put his head on one side, drooped his tail, cocked his big flap ears, and endeavoured to take in the situation, but unsuccessfully.

We at last got near the outer wall of the *kraal*, and heard a hum as of a mighty bee-hive, broken every now and then by a yell and a discharge of fire-arms. Moustache began to keep very close to me; we were inside in a moment, and at the same moment amid a throng of excited men, women, and children, who filled up the narrow alleys through which we made our way to the stockade; the hum was getting louder and louder; I caught up Moustache, who looked around savagely as he sat up in my arms.

Makapan met me at the entrance of the stockade, and spoke to me, but I could not hear what he said for the din. Lining the stockade was a dense mass of women and children, talking, laughing, singing, yelling, and clapping their hands. Makapan made way for me to the front ranks and got me a chair. Just opposite to me there was a crowd of men, some dressed as I have described, some with bright coloured shirts, some with a waistcoat and a girdle of cats'-tails, some with only a woollen comforter crossed over their breasts, and a rag round their loins as their holiday costume; others again in half-European dress, and others painted, some to represent skeletons, some merely daubed with colour, but all armed.

Ever and *anon* one or more of these would rush into the area of the stockade with a yell, and dancing the war-dance, then enact some scene of warfare, casting himself on the ground, looking around cautiously, taking aim, firing, then perhaps tomahawking or *assegaing* his imaginary foe with such savage exultation, that it made my blood curdle, while the women clapped their hands, yelled, and even— sometimes becoming over-excited—rushed into the arena and did a frantic war-dance. Then after each exhibition there would be a race of a group of girls from one side to the other, before the next performer stepped forth, evidently to compare notes with friends as to the relative merits of the dancers.

Four men particularly attracted my attention, not by their costumes, but by their good acting. One of these acted alone. His play was that he was defending the stockade from enemies who were creeping up through the mass of rock and tree below. He would look over the stockade, taking cover carefully, peer hither and thither, then swiftly level his rifle, and fire. He always killed his man, and then the haughty way in which he would throw up his arm as he turned on his heel and pretended to reload (for I conclude they were firing blank-cartridge) was more expressive of defiance and satisfaction than any war-dance. The other three acted together. They were defending themselves from enemies who were close around them, but their imagination had transformed the stockade into brushwood, the sand that strewed it into long grass. I then, for the first time, saw what we have all read of at some time, I suppose, in some novel about the North American Indians—I mean the snake-like movement of a savage as he draws near his victim.

These three savages darted into the arena and looked cautiously round, then suddenly dropped on the ground, their every muscle tense, their eyes strained; suddenly one, raising himself a little, appeared to catch a glimpse of something, his eyes literally seemed to start from their sockets, and as he grasped his comrade's arm with one hand, and pointed with the other towards some imaginary object, he trembled with excitement; then each grasping his arms they all moved—how, I really cannot say—they did not rise from the ground, they wriggled quickly along it like snakes; in longish grass all that one would have seen would have been a slight waving; now they were close to the stockade; to bound up, fire, and fall prostrate once more was the work of a moment. These men were actors by nature. Sometimes their fire told, sometimes it did not; sometimes an enemy would fall near them, and they would tomahawk or assegai him with savage delight, but with no waste of time; at last one of them was wounded; he crawled painfully back, and was helped by his comrades; and that ended their play. But numbers now were rushing forward; the arena was a mass of yelling, whooping savages; and Moustache began to think affairs looked serious.

Just then Makapan asked me to excuse him, he said he had a dog of a friend of his under his charge, that he had just heard it had broken loose, that no one could catch it but he, and that he must go and do so. As he was turning away, my attention was suddenly arrested by seeing a gentleman, apparently an Englishman, step from the crowd and speak to him. Makapan shook hands with him, and clapped him on the shoulder, then turned, and introduced him to me as Mr. N——. He was a trader coming down from far upcountry with oxen, cows, and sheep, which he had traded. He was an Austrian, not an Englishman, and an educated, gentlemanly man—a wonderful person to meet in this out-of-the-way part of the world.

As Makapan left me he clapped his acquaintance once more on the shoulder, and I blessed my stars that I was a woman, for I suppose it was owing to this fact that Makapan did not testify his friendly feelings to me in the same manner. I do not remember what became of Mr. N——, for my attention was occupied with the savages; I imagine he went away. Not long after, one of the men, painted like a skeleton, made a set at me: first he glared at me till he caught my eye; then he took me as his imaginary foe, and ended by bringing his *assegai* within half an inch of my nose. I think he was disappointed that I did not scream. Another savage thought he would try whether I should be proof against a rifle brought into close proximity with my head; finding that I did not faint, he turned it towards a group of girls, who screamed loudly enough to satisfy anyone. I regret to state that Moustache's nerve failed him at this crisis—he made a violent effort to bolt, and had to be held, cowering and trembling, under my chair for the rest of the time I stayed in the stockade.

Shortly after this, the sun being very hot, the odours from the crowd oppressive, and considerable monotony prevailing in the performances, I rose to depart, when the woman who had asked me for the looking-glass, and who could speak Boer dialect, told me I ought to remain until Makapan led his guard, the flower of his warriors, into the stockade; *that*, she said, would be a very splendid sight. I waited accordingly. Presently there was a lull amongst the savages, and the crowd opening nearly opposite to where I sat, a band of fine-looking *kaffirs*, all be-cat-tailed, armed to the teeth, and with their long shields slung on their arms, advanced, dancing their slow war-dance, singing the accompanying war-song, and rattling their *assegais* against their shields.

There is a peculiarity about this dance and song. I had seen and heard them once before, performed by some *kaffir* levies on their way to the Zulu war. The dancers move very slightly, and their song is a chant more than a song, but it gives one the creeps to see and hear it; it looks like the movement of men held in a leash, impatient for it to be slipped; and it sounds so threatening, like the muttering of a storm: one can imagine the yell that would burst forth if the leash were slipped and the blood-hounds let loose. They advanced thus into the middle of the arena, a hundred men perhaps; then opening their ranks Makapan and Stürman jumped forth from their centre. Oh! such a pair! Makapan was carefully attired in a gentleman's morning wrapper—brown, edged with red—and the girdle with its tassels bobbed up and down behind him; under this he had a riding-suit and heavy boots with gaiters; on his head was a white French hat, very narrow in the brim and well turned up, with three ostrich-feathers stuck in it, all pointing straight forward; a *kyrie* (or short club) in his hand, completed his "get up," and in this attire he did the clumsiest "breakdown" I have ever witnessed, dancing opposite to his admiring subjects, and followed by his savage guard, who I think must have despised their leader.

Stürman, in the meantime, dressed in a riding-costume, booted and gaitered, with a pith helmet on his head, a red handkerchief round his throat, and a *kyrie* in his hand, did a very frantic breakdown—indeed so frantic, that it made him very hot; so he pulled off his neckerchief and threw it aside, then flung away his helmet; and the last that I saw of Mr. Stürman in the arena, just as I left the stockade, was that his attire had diminished to his shirt and breeches the former article of dress having been freed from its confinement in the latter. The breakdown was as frantic as ever.

Moustache's delight when we got outside the precincts of the *kraal* was very great, but he showed it in a chastened manner, not by leaps and frisks, but by rubbing himself against me, looking at me wistfully out of his little pig's eyes, and waving his absurdly long tail in an undulating manner. He was evidently offering up a canine thanksgiving for a special deliverance!

As I was going down the hill I met some women coming up, and they spoke to Clas. I asked him what they had said, and he hesitated. This of course made me inquisitive, so I pressed the point. Then he told me that these women had said that the feast was not yet ended; that as a finale an ox was to be killed; that one of its fore legs and one of its hind legs were to be hacked off at the hip and shoulder, and that then it was to be goaded until it died. This was to be the finale of the scene of which I had been a spectator. This was to be the culminating-point of the entertainment I had participated in—the *bonne-douche* reserved for the people I had spoken to in friendliness!

I could not attempt to describe my feelings. To do Clas justice he expressed utter horror of the hideous idea. He said he had learnt better things since he knew the Christian religion—that he knew it was a sin to torture an animal; and although I am certain missionaries have done a great deal of harm in some ways in Africa, if they only did this one piece of good, taught but this one lesson—they have certainly done one great work.

When I reached my encampment I found a good many *kaffirs* assembled talking to my boys, many of whom understood Boer dialect. I told Hendrick what I had heard.

"Mind," said I, "if Makapan sends me any beef as he said he would, send it back, and say that we English do not eat the meat of an animal that has been tortured to death, or let it be eaten by our servants; that we would rather starve than encourage such an atrocity as he allows to be committed in his *kraal*."

Hendrick remonstrated in a low voice, to the effect that it was not prudent to offend Makapan; but I was too much disgusted with the savage and his savages to care; and, as from Hendrick's remarks I became aware that the *kaffirs* understood what I was saying, I said something stronger for their benefit. The result of this was that Makapan sent me some goat's meat, and a message to the effect that not only was it not his custom to kill oxen as above described, but that he had killed no ox at all on this occasion—only a goat. I knew this was a lie told to calm me down, and I said so to Stürman who brought the message. As to the meat, I let the boys eat it, and contented myself with some fat pork I had bought the day before—and horrible greasy stuff it was.

CHAPTER 28

I had traded too much corn to take on one waggon, but I heard that I could get a waggon and oxen at the Mission Station to bring it up to Pretoria for me. I bought several large closed baskets of a curious manufacture special to the *kaffirs*, to store what I had to leave behind me in, and Makapan promised to take care of it for me. He and Mapeela, a greater chief than Makapan, who came to visit him, rode down to my waggon the next day. Makapan wanted me to lend him one of my horses, but I told him I never lent my horses. The chiefs and Hendrick had a shooting-match with their rifles and my rifle for a bottle of brandy; Hendrick, not I, to stand the brandy. I think Mapeela won; I do not quite remember whether it was he or Makapan. I left them to their own devices, as they thought fit to let my driver enter into competition with them. Mapeela pretended not to be able to understand Boer dialect, but he could both understand and speak it.

Hendrick informed me that he wished to buy Eclipse; I could see in his eye that he coveted the horse as he looked at him; but whether he offered a hundred pounds for him as Hendrick said, I do not know, for I refused any offer that he might make. I fancy his offer was a high one, for he looked surprised at my refusal. At that moment I admitted distinctly to myself that trading was not my *forte*. Fancy a "Smouse" refusing to make eighty pounds clear profit! After this I found that it was a standing joke amongst Boers I passed, that I would not sell Eclipse for any money. I think they somehow respected me for it, probably because it gave them an idea that I was very rich—I don't think it could be for any other reason.

Thinking of Eclipse, I was very near forgetting to describe Mapeela. He is a big, sensual, and violent-looking man. He was dressed in a riding-suit and a white French hat; wore his waistcoat a little open, and showed a white shirt; had a necktie and a pin in it, white cuffs, and a ring on his finger. He affected more airs and graces than Makapan, and I liked him less.

And now, before leaving Makapan, I must record two things: one, that it struck me that Hendrick was a little afraid of these wild *kaffirs*; and secondly, that my brandy gave me a great deal of trouble. The difficulty I had to prevent myself being forced into doing what I had said I would not do, was a constant worry. It was impossible to sell by the bottle, for the good reason that my purchasers had no bottles, or at least very few. They had old tins that had once had paraffin in them, and old oil tins, and tin mugs, and little and big gourds hollowed out, and sometimes they had small medicine bottles, or old sauce bottles. Then they would worry me perpetually to sell them sixpence worth of brandy; but this I always refused to do; and I used to hunt them away from the waggon when they wanted to drink brandy there.

"We won't tell," they used to say. Of course I knew that. "Every trader sells us 'tots'—what is the law here?" they would say. Of course I knew that too. One old gentleman, after vainly begging me to sell him a sixpenny "tot," paused, then said, "I want to make you a present," and offered me a sixpence. This is a common way of evading the law; you don't sell, you accept, and give a present! I astonished the old gentleman by dismissing him summarily. He was a curious specimen. He had been brought up amongst the Boers, had lived amongst them and dressed like them for years, and now he was accustomed to walk about in the most outrageously light costume, not from poverty but from choice.

The day I left Makapan's-poort, as I was crossing the stream after the waggon, which had gone a little ahead, I heard horses' hoofs coming rapidly after me. The riders were Makapan and an attendant bearing an empty paraffin tin. He wanted another pull at the brandy! He got it; shook hands with Hendrick and Clas, then put out his paw to me, as Mapeela had done the day before. That affair about the ox made me extremely dislike to touch the savage; but one can hardly refuse to give a man one's hand when one has voluntarily gone into his territory; so I held out mine, which he shook heartily; and turning our horses we cantered away in opposite directions.

The *bush-veldt* was now a desert, all the Boers had trekked to their farms. It was getting late in the season, the weather was very hot—so hot that it was impossible to trek in the middle of the day. At noon one lay under a bush, or under the waggon if one could not get a leafy bush (and most of the bushes are thorn and don't give much shade), and panted. Under these circumstances, to be reduced to eat rice and pig's fat, and drink tea without milk, for breakfast, luncheon and dinner, is the reverse of agreeable, but there was nothing else to eat.

One morning as I was riding in front of the waggon I saw Mr. N—— outspanned and having early coffee. I rode over, and as I did so a young zebra frisked up to Eclipse, and turned up his pretty little nose at him with a vicious grin, which affected Eclipse's nerves so much that he pretended he was going to rear. Mr. N—— asked me to dismount, and while he was giving me some coffee the zebra tried to upset the sugar-bowl, and being hunted away, watched his opportunity, kicked the little table over, and having broken some crockery, and sent the sugar-bowl flying, ate up the sugar, and then trotted up to his master in a perfectly artless way, and rubbed his taper white nose on that gentleman's coat. Mr. N—— had a young leopard there who excited Roughy's curiosity, and who nearly caught hold of Roughy's tail, to the great discomfiture of the latter.

A little farther on we met a Boer, going, I think, to the wood-bush. Hendrick managed to get some Boer biscuits from this man, who came over afterwards to my waggon, and to whom, at his request, I gave some pig's fat. He, and a friend who was with him, had not tasted anything but biscuits for several days, so the fat was a luxury to them, and the biscuits were a luxury to me.

A little farther on Mr. N—— picked me up. He wanted to buy some *kaffir* corn and came to my waggon. His zebra came with him, and thought he would like to taste the corn as it was being measured out; so he put his head in the sack and twirled round and round, with his head representing a pivot, kicking the whole time until he had gratified his fancy. He kicked even at his master, whose feelings were so hurt that he asked for the whip.

I rode into the Mission Station with Mr. N——. We met a young missionary, to whom I bowed, and asked him whether Mr. and Mrs. B—— were still at the station, or had moved permanently to their new farm of Sandfontein. He said they had moved. It happened that I had heard Mr. N—— speak in German to him before I addressed him, and so I spoke to him also in German. He was the new missionary; judge of my astonishment, when I heard from himself and others that he could speak neither English, Dutch, Boer dialect, nor any *kaffir* tongue; and yet he had been some time in the colony and was a missionary!

While I was at this place, an incident happened which gave me some concern. One evening Hendrick asked me if he might go a-visiting, and I gave him leave. Then little Hendrick asked me if he might go and play with some friends, and I said he might on one condition. The hut or cottage he was going to was not far from the waggon, and I told him I should hang up a piece of candle at the back of the waggon in the lantern, and that when he saw that it was burnt out he must come home and go to bed. These two had not long departed when Pete asked me if he might go. I said he might not; that I objected to being left alone, in case of anything going wrong with the oxen. He submitted with a good grace, and to show him I was pleased with him, I said, "I know it is a little hard on you, Pete, as this is the last night you will be here, but it can't be helped. You have been behaving well lately, so here is a 'tot' for you, and go to bed."

I drew him a "tot," then lay down on my own bed, which I had made just behind the waggon, near the cask of brandy, and also near the horses. I heard Pete lie down towards the front of the waggon. I remained awake, for I made it a rule never to go to sleep if any of the boys were away. Little Hendrick came back so soon as the light was put out, and lay down alongside of Pete. Shortly after Eclipse got uneasy. I called Pete, but getting no answer I got up and went to ascertain what was the matter with the horse. He had been apparently startled by something. I thought that I would go and see whether Pete was in his place. It was very dark, but at last I made out that he was not. I woke little Hendrick after waiting for a while, but found he was too stupid with sleep to understand anything. I did not like to leave the waggon, so waited until Hendrick came back, which he did soon. I saw he had had rather too much *kaffir* beer. He was not drunk, but excited. I told him that Pete was missing, and added, as I was going to lie down again,—

"It seems he is determined to get his five-and-twenty."

At this moment Pete himself emerged from the darkness, and said—

"Oh! am I to be punished for no offence? I only went away for a minute to that Boer's waggon that is outspanned there."

The waggon was at a very little distance.

"You have been some time away, Pete," said I, "and if you had only been to that Boer's waggon, you would have heard me call you, for I called you repeatedly. I am quite certain you are telling a lie, and that you went away to get drink; but you have not been very long away, and you are not drunk, so I will not punish you this time, for I have no absolute proof against you. It is a lucky thing for yourself that you failed in getting drink, or when I trekked out of the village tomorrow I should have had you tied up and given twenty-five lashes. I never told you what my punishment for you would be. Now you know it, and will, I hope, remember it. Now go to bed."

But instead of going to bed I could see Pete by the flickering light of the lantern dancing and shifting about in the most remarkable manner, and with an expression of very great dread on his face.

"Don't make a fool of yourself," quoth I, "but go to bed at once, unless you wish to make me angry with you."

"*He* is going to beat me with the double whip," he said, still dancing about.

I turned, and there I saw Hendrick with the long driver's whip in his hand also dancing about. I saw their tactics then. Hendrick was trying to get a sly cut at Pete, and Pete was taking cover. *I* was his cover. Hendrick, in his excited state, looked rather demoniacal; but I could hardly keep my gravity in spite of the unpleasantness of the situation; for those two savage looking wretches dancing about in the dark, and the idea of how the group would look if I could only see myself between them, tickled me amazingly.

"Put that whip down, Hendrick," said I. "You must not touch Pete without my orders."

"He is my forelooper," quoth Hendrick, "and I must correct him."

And the dancing went on.

"That is not the way that I allow my servants to speak to me," said I. "Give me that whip directly."

He hesitated a moment, then with a sullen look gave me the whip.

"Now both of you go to bed at once, and do not let me hear a sound from either of you," said I.

And I saw them both in their blankets before I lay down again; but hardly had I done so when I heard Hendrick's voice.

"You had better be quiet, Hendrick," said I, "or I shall punish you."

"Pete is only waiting for me to go to sleep to knock my brains out with a *yoke-skey*," said he.

"It's a lie," growled Pete.

"You've got one ready in your hand," cried Hendrick.

I stood up once more, and went over to the two worthies. I found that Pete was up again. He said that he was afraid of Hendrick, and he looked as if he were. If he had had a *yoke-skey* in his hand he had none then. I stooped to try if I could find any missiles in his bed, and my eye was caught by a hat, which was unlike any hat belonging to my boys, lying close to Pete's blankets.

"Whose hat is this?" I asked, on the point of taking hold of it, when a dark face peered from under it. "Who are you? Get out of this at once!" I exclaimed. But the face scowled, and the figure it belonged to rose gradually. "Quick with the double whip, Hendrick," I cried. "You shall get it hot! "

Hendrick was by the side of my bed where the whip lay, and back in an instant; but the fellow was too quick. He had bolted into the darkness, and to my astonishment not only he, but another ruffian, who rose from my very feet. I must almost have trodden on him. Of course Pete was astonished, and Hendrick was astonished. There was no proof, but it did not look nice. I suspected Pete, and Hendrick averred that he did.

The next morning I had business at a farm lying at some little distance. Just as I was saddling, the Boer whose waggon had been out-spanned near mine asked me to sell him two bottles of brandy. I drew the brandy for him, and mounted my horse. Now I always carried the key of the tap of the brandy-cask and the key of the waggon-box in a leather pocket on a broad belt which I wore day and night, and it was so much my habit to put my finger in this pocket every time I mounted, to see that all was safe, that it had become purely a mechanical movement. I cannot absolutely remember whether I did this or not on that occasion, but I have little doubt that I did.

I rode to and from the farm pretty sharply, for I was in a hurry to get back to the waggon. When I got back I found the keys were not in my pocket. I looked everywhere for them fruitlessly, but at last I discovered that the stitching of the leather to the belt had given way in one part, and although it would have been difficult for the keys to slip through, still I had ridden at a very sharp canter, and it was possible. This was vexatious, but it could not be helped.

I started the next day for Pretoria, taking the direct Waterberg transport road. I found that I could not get a waggon to return for the corn left at Makapan's-poort, and I had only to make up my mind to return for it from Pretoria, after selling what I had up. I started the waggon, and rode over to Sandfontein myself to bid goodbye to Mr. and Mrs. B——. After having no one to talk to except Boers for a long time, it is refreshing to get amongst such people as the B——s. I remained to dinner, and then delayed, talking and thinking very little of the time, until the rays of the setting sun shone into my eyes through the window, and awakened me to the fact that I had a long ride across country before me, and a country that I did not know into the bargain, and that I had not an hour of daylight, or even twilight to count on. I was off as soon as possible. I knew that I had to keep in towards the Waterberg hills, until I came to a road running close to their base through thick high bush. The wind had become very high, and there were heavy clouds gathering swiftly. I rode as fast as I could, but it is not easy to ride very fast over a *feldt* full of holes, covered with long grass, and thickly studded in many parts with little thorn bushes; besides, it was soon pitch dark.

However, I got the road, and, soon after crossing a stream, I saw a light which I knew must be in the farmhouse of Jan Steen, near which my waggon was to outspan. After a few minutes more I was greeted by Hendrick and Pete. The camp-fire was made in a hollow of the ground to try to keep the wind off, but it was blowing a hurricane now, and the fire had become so disorderly that cooking was not to be attempted, and Hendrick had cooked and kept my supper for me in the house of an old *kaffir* "Swartboy," Clas's father, and a retainer of De Clerc's and De Plessis, whose houses were quite close to Jan Steen's. Young De Plessis came over to the waggon, and asked me to sleep in his house but I felt too anxious about the waggon; besides that, in such a storm, the horses, or at least Eclipse, were likely to get frightened, and to listen to reason from me alone. So I slept close to the waggon under an enormous tree, and sheltered by its trunk. Behind it I could not sleep, the sand was driving so furiously before the wind. During the night the dogs seemed restless, but I could neither hear nor see anything. To say the truth the wind roared so much, and the darkness was so dense, that it would have been strange if I could.

The next day it was evident that rain was near—heavy rain too. The Boers were very unhappy about my having lost the key of the tap, because I could not get them any brandy. They tried to put an old tap which had a key into the barrel, but it did not work. Then they showed me a way of displacing the tap, drawing off a bucket of brandy, and replacing it without its appearing to have been removed; and this suggested certain novel ideas to me. They got their brandy, however, and were happy. There was a perpetual trotting backwards and forwards from their cottages to the waggon. A Boer or Boeress delights in buying by driblets, thus spinning out the amusement.

On one of these occasions I asked De Clerc if he could sell me a sheep. He said he would consult his wife. After a time he came back, and said that sheep were scarce, but as he regarded me as a friend, he would let me have one for a pound; and of course I had to give him the pound, which he pocketed, assuring me all the while that if his father had not taught him that he ought to help travellers he would not have let me have the sheep at all. He then asked me to give him a "tot," but as I found that the giving of "tots" was a very losing concern, I declined. He looked very angry.

"Well," said he, "it is of no consequence. I have plenty of money to buy with; but if you do not help others you cannot expect others to help you. Who can tell? a little act of kindness done to me might pay you in the long-run," &c., &c.

He evidently wished me to see the giving of "tots" in the light of a Christian duty.

"Now," he went on, "I let you have that sheep."

This was rather too much.

"I think, Mr. De Clerc," said I very politely, "you forget that I let you have that hat for nothing, for you did not even take me to the lion hunt, and all because you said you had no money, but wanted it very badly."

The old fellow collapsed at once.

"You are right," he said, looking very sheepish. "Let us talk no more about it. I will buy a bottle of brandy."

He did so.

"Now," said he, "let us drink to our friendship."

"I will pledge you in water, if that will do," said I. So we pledged each other.

I have not described De Clerc. He was a tall, athletic man, with a trace of his French origin still lingering about him. A handsome man, with grey beard and hair, a well-cut nose, fine, rather cruel-looking lips, and blazing, black eyes under shaggy eyebrows.

A little later on he was lolling against the waggon, and some remark was made by me as to the untruthfulness of the *kaffirs*. I think I was guilty of uttering some platitude to the effect that honesty is the best policy.

De Clerc turned his black eyes on me, and said in an undertone,

"Then how about this treachery between you and Willem?" meaning De Plessis.

"Oh!" said I, "I thought you were supposed not to know about those feathers. You mean that, I suppose?"

"Don't talk so loud," said he. "I will keep your secret."

"Thanks," said I, "there is no secret of mine to be kept. It is De Plessis's secret, not mine; for now that I know that it was unlawful in me to buy them, I shall either declare them, or not keep them."

"You had better not do that," said De Clerc. "I will keep your secret."

"What you had better do," said I, "is to come over to Willem's, and hear what I have to say to him about the feathers. I am going there now."

De Clerc said he was just going home, and departed. I went to De Plessis's cottage, not a stone's throw from De Clerc's, and awaited him there, but he did not come.

I must say a word about this cottage. It was a mud-hut, of small dimensions. The little bedroom was only curtained off from the other room—that is to say, there was but one room in the house; but going into that hut you felt as if you were in a drawing-room. There was very little furniture, and it was very simple; but everything was clean and fresh.

Having waited for a time I thought I had better begin about the feathers. I said, —

"Your father-in-law spoke to me about those feathers this—"

"My father-in-law!" gasped De Plessis. "What, does he know of them?—"

"Didn't you know he knew?" asked I.

Poor De Plessis's face was sufficient answer. In this dilemma they (Willem and his wife) sent for Mrs. De Clerc. The old gentleman had kept the matter dark from her as well as from them. I began to suspect that he had some deep game in hand, but I said nothing. His three relations were in dismay.

"Now," said I, "you see I did not know that I was doing an illegal act when I bought those feathers. I know now that I am liable to a fine of 500*l.* if it is found out that I did buy them. When I get up to Pretoria, and want to sell them, people will ask where I got them."

"You can say you bought them in driblets from the *kaffirs*," suggested Mrs. De Clerc.

"Unfortunately that would not be true," I remarked.

"Oh! it don't matter about that," said De Plessis, quite simply. "You have only to tell them so; they won't find out."

"Unfortunately," said I, "I have an objection to telling lies."

"It's a mere matter of business," said De Plessis.

"It may be your way of doing business," said I; "it is not mine. That being understood, I will tell you what I am going to do, and then you can tell me what you are going to do. I am going to do one of three things. I will return the feathers to you if you will return the money to me. I know you worked hard for that bird, and that you have a struggle to keep up this nice little home as nicely as you keep it; therefore, I will take off whatever profit I made on the goods, and let you have them at cost price. If you will do this the affair ceases to have any farther interest to me, as I shall be rid of the feathers. Or, if you choose, I will go with you to the Landrost of Nilstrom, and we will tell him the story as it stands. You say you can swear that the bird's mate was dead. Perhaps that makes a difference in law, and he may decide in our favour, and let matters stand as they do. If you don't like either of these plans then I shall go to the Landrost of Nilstrom, and tell him that I bought the feathers without knowing that I was doing an unlawful act, and ask what I am to do with them, and whatever he tells me to do I shall do. I shall not mention your name unless I am forced to do so; but I may be forced."

The three looked very blank. Then there commenced a grand powwow. It is no use denying that this paying back of the money was a very serious affair to poor De Plessis. He was still in debt—and in debt to his father-in-law; and it seems that the father-in-law used to make himself unpleasant about the debt. Living as these Boers did, and as most Boers do, all squeezed up together—seeing each other constantly—with the terrible habit of running in and out of each others' houses, developed to an alarming extent, an unpleasant father-in-law assumes the same proportions as an unpleasant mother-in-law in better regulated communities.

I was very sorry for De Plessis. He, on his part, was overwhelmed by his misfortune, and to do him credit, he seemed to be most deeply affected by his father-in-law's perfidy. "He wants to ruin me," he went on saying, "and I never have done him any harm." Under these circumstances the two women took the matter in hand, and the deliberate advice given by two very excellent specimens of the female Boer—a people, we are told by themselves, and some others, remarkably Christian was, that De Plessis should go with me to the *landrost* and swear—take his solemn oath—that he had found the ostrich dead in the *feldt*. They urged this as the best and safest proceeding, using all the little arts they knew of to make it out a very venial deviation from the truth.

Willem and I sat listening to them. I assumed a "know-nothing" expression; De Plessis listened eagerly. When they had said all they had to say, he sat quite still I could see his face working; there was a great struggle going on; then his eyes filled, and with a catch in his voice he said,—

"No! I cannot forswear myself for sixteen pounds! Mrs. Hedwick (his version of my name), I will pay you the money; send the feathers back secretly tonight."

("I am so glad you say that," was my reply; "I should not have liked to know that you were not an honest fellow, Willem. Now you understand why I would not tell a lie about those feathers; a lie to me is what a false oath is to you."

De Plessis said, "Yes, I understand," and we shook hands. "But," he added, "never again do I go into that man's house. He may come here, but I won't go there."

He did go, however, but I don't think it was willingly.

I had not done with this little incident yet, for I had made up my mind to have it out with De Clerc; so, after leaving De Plessis, I walked over to De Clerc's house. This was very different from the one I had left. It was much larger, and there was more furniture in it. I think there were two rooms, but it had the frowzy look common to Boers' houses. I found De Clerc alone, which was just what I wanted. He was delighted to see me, and we sat down and began to talk. After a while I said,—

"Oh! about those feathers."

"Don't let the matter trouble you," he replied; "you can trust me, but still, if you really think it better and safer for you not to keep them, you can let me have them and I will give you fourteen pounds." (*N.B.* Two pounds less than De Plessis had asked for them. This had been his game all through.)

"Thanks," said I; "I have just been speaking to your son-in-law on the subject, and we have settled the matter satisfactorily. Although it is unnecessary to give particulars, I may say that both he and I shall lose by our arrangement, but that we shall have the satisfaction of knowing that we have behaved honestly."

The old fellow looked at me.

"But," I continued, "this is not what I wanted to say with regard to the feathers; do you remember a conversation we had before I went to

Makapan's-poort, when you asked me where one could find a more Christian nation than your nation?"

"Yes, I remember."

"Well," I continued, "as an influential member of that nation, I should like to know whether you consider it Christian-like to spy out your son-in-law's errors, and afterwards, instead of speaking of them to him, to try to make mischief by talking of them to a stranger like myself?"

De Clerc began to stammer out excuses without looking me in the face.

"It is no use trying to get out of it, Mr. De Clerc," said I; "what I want you to tell me is, whether this is the sort of thing that the Bible tells you is right? Look up to Heaven and tell me whether you think that in doing as you have done by your child's husband you believe you have done right in the sight of God?"

De Clerc hesitated, then said,—

"No."

"And now," said I, "do not you think that it is very disgraceful of you, who, you told me yourself, are a leader amongst a nation that prides itself on its Christianity, to require a lesson in Christianity from one of a nation which you hate, and consider beneath you in this respect?" He had tried to interrupt me, saying,—"Pray let that be," but I went on. For a moment he sat silent, then he said,—

"Yes, I thank you for the good lesson."

I put out my hand, and he took it. I said,—

"We can shake hands now. Do you remember that we pledged our friendship a little while ago? If I had not pledged you, perhaps I should not have spoken to you as I have just done; but having once called you my friend, I could not do otherwise."

I believe the man understood me, and I know he seemed to like me much better after this affair, but it did not prevent his calumniating De Pies sis and trying to make me dislike him. He told me that De Plessis had neglected Dandy while he had him, had overworked him, and given him no mealies or forage. He knew this was a tender point with me.

His wife was present when he said this, and she immediately said, "He lies. Willem gave Dandy forage every day."

I said, "You must not tell me that, Mr. De Clerc. I only required to look at the horse to know that he had not been overworked, and that he had been fed well while Willem had him."

I may mention that I incidentally found out that Dandy had once belonged to De Clerc's brother, who had taken him to Dammerland, and there sold him to the man who put him up to auction. His name had been "Rennevinn" in those days. I think it was in the afternoon of this day that I rode over to the farm of a neighbouring magistrate, a very respectable Boer, descended from a German family. His wife, who was similarly descended, was a very good woman, and the children were all well brought up. They were not at all like Boers; quiet, gentle people, very superior in every way. Their farm was very pretty to look at, but was spoilt for practical purposes by the failure of water. Some years before, it, in common with the rest of Waterberg, was well watered. Now all the springs are drying up. This is, perhaps, due to some of those curious caprices observable in volcanic countries, for Waterberg is very volcanic. In many places signs of this are obvious, without taking the hot springs into account.

On returning late from this farm I missed Pete, and on asking where he was, I heard that he had left the oxen committed to his care, to stray where they would, and had disappeared. Now at this time of the year a plant grows in certain parts of the *feldt* which is poisonous to oxen, and I was very much displeased. He did not come back either that night or the next morning. On cross-questioning little Hendrick, he said that he had heard Pete's voice in a large *kaffir kraal* which was on Jan Steen's farm. I felt sure that he wanted to hide away until I had gone, being afraid of punishment, so I went to the magistrate I have mentioned above, and requested that Pete might be caught and punished. Two *kaffirs* were despatched secretly to the *kraal* to catch him, in the meantime I looked at some oxen, and arranged to buy them.

The magistrate was at De Clerc's house paying a visit, and two of the oxen were his. Presently there was a general stir noticeable among the *kaffirs* hanging about the place, and I knew that Pete was coming—and the next minute I saw him running, with his hands tied behind him, in front of the two *kaffirs* who had been sent for him. I felt I was in for it now. I had said that this man was to have twenty-five lashes the next time he offended, and he had offended very grossly; of course, he must have them, but it was the first time I had ever seen a man flogged. The instant that Pete reached the waggon, looking like a hunted baboon, Hendrick flew at him, tripped him up, and had him tied to the *disselboom* by his wrists in a twinkling of the eye.

The demon in the man was loose, he looked as if he would have liked to tear Pete to pieces, and he scowled at me when I made him untie the prisoner, and told him to wait until the magistrate should come. In the meantime I explained to Pete that he was going to get his twenty-five lashes all the same. How that fellow did grovel to me, to be sure! How he called me his dear missus! his good, kind missus! How abjectly he twisted himself about before me! At last he started the happy thought that he would pay a fine to me, which was absurd on the face of it; for he had to my knowledge no money, having drawn on his wages for clothing until all I owed him was about four shillings.

In the meantime the magistrate and the other Boers, besides a crowd of *kaffirs*, had arrived on the scene of action. Jan Steen, a funny-looking man with a crumpled up face, bristling black hair, and bead-like eyes, looked like a weasel that has caught sight of a rat; De Clerc had a bloodthirsty look about him, and gloated hungrily on Pete; even Willem De Plessis looked excited. The magistrate alone was calm. He began to examine Pete, and asked him whether he had any complaint against me. Pete said,—

"No; never have I had such a good mistress; I eat the same food that she does; and even the other evening she gave up some of her own dinner to me because she thought I had not had enough."

The men sent to fetch him deposed that they had found him in the *kraal*, and that he had pulled out a knife and resisted fiercely until they tied his hands. Of his repeated offences there could be no doubt; it only remained to be decided what his punishment was to be.

"Twenty-five lashes," said the magistrate.

There was an eager movement amongst the Dutch; Jan Steen seized him.

"Sir! sir!" cried Pete; "I will pay—I will pay."

"Stop," said the magistrate; "what did you say, that you will pay?"

"I will pay three pounds," cried Pete.

"Don't let him! off with him! flog him!" snarled the assembled Boers.

"He can't pay," said I, "for he has no money."

"This man will lend me money," cried Pete, pointing to a *kaffir*, who that very morning had assured me that he had no money and wanted me to let him have a pair of boots on credit.

"Stay," said the magistrate, "by law, Pete, if you can pay three pounds you can escape the flogging."

The Boers were furious, and between them and the *kaffirs*, all of whom were talking at the top of their voices, it was very difficult to make my voice heard.

"Have I, as Pete's employer, any voice in this matter?" asked I.

"Of course you have," shouted the Boers; "flog him!"

"But have I by law?" I asked again.

The magistrate hesitated, then said, —

"Yes; you can insist on his being flogged if you choose."

"Then," said I, "I do insist,"

"I daresay he will be better in future," said the poor magistrate, whilst the assembled Boers scowled at him.

"I don't think he is likely to be improved by finding that I don't carry out my threat, or by another man paying three pounds to get him off," said I; "you have said I can choose his punishment, and I choose twenty-five lashes; the quicker he gets it, the quicker this painful scene will be over."

They were round him in a minute those Boers and Hendrick, like hounds round a fox. They tripped him up, they pulled him about and yelped over him. Jan Steen was the foremost. It was a disgusting spectacle.

"Look here," cried I, in a rage, "if you don't leave that man alone I'll send every one of you away from my waggon; he is to be punished not tortured; stand back all of you."

A very cool speech, as it struck me afterwards, considering that my waggon was outspanned on these men's ground, but they stood back. He got his five-and-twenty. I waited to see him get up before I made up my mind as to whether I would keep him in my service or not; as he stood up, he turned savagely to me, —

"Thank you, missus," he said, "give me something to drink; I am almost dead."

He had not had a severe beating by any means, but his rage was almost killing him I could see.

"Give him some water quickly," I said, but he dashed it from him.

"I want brandy, brandy," he said hoarsely, and then in Zulu he said, what I understood (and rightly) to be, that he would complain of me in Pretoria, which under the circumstances was of course absurd.

I took the money I owed him out of my purse and gave it to him.

"I may stop, may I not, missus?" he said.

He was cooling rapidly.

"No," I said, "you have had your punishment and been insolent— now go," and he went.

I was sitting by the waggon in the evening, at the camp-fire, little Hendrick and a few *kaffirs* from the *kraal* were squatted chatting. They were talking Boer dialect, and as I sat apart from them they probably, if they remembered that I was there at all, thought I could not understand them. A little time before I should not have understood their gabble. One man was telling how Pete had bought a goat, and some fowls, and how he had seen him pull a handful of sovereigns out of his pocket. I let the fellow go on until he changed his subject; then I called to him and asked him to repeat what he had said about Pete. He instantly shuffled, but as I told him that I had understood what he had said at the fire, he repeated it all correctly to me.

I then sent him back to the others, got out my account-book, and examined my money. It was all quite correct—the inference therefore was, that Pete had been robbing the waggon, and selling. I knew that he had no money, honestly come by, and this discovery only corroborated a suspicion I had conceived when his friend offered to pay three pounds for him. I said nothing, but the next morning, instead of starting, I told what I had heard to the magistrate, and he agreed that Pete should be caught again and examined. The *kaffirs* said they were afraid to go to catch him, and the gentle magistrate was obliged to ask me to bribe to the extent of half-a-crown each if they brought him; to this I agreed.

This time there was a grand conclave in Jan Steen's cottage—a cottage as large as De Clerc's, but more untidy and dirtier. The whole Steen family, although related to the De Clercs, were very low-class Boers. The magistrate had papers and ink, and witnesses were called, and everything was supposed to be going to be conducted in a strictly business-like manner.

After the prisoner was brought in (in a very defiant state of mind) everybody began talking at once; then the magistrate called to order, and in the course of examination—the examination being conducted by all the assembled Boers according as an idea struck them—Pete called De Clerc "uncle," upon which De Clerc remarked he was not his uncle—Pete, while there was a pause in the proceedings, owing to one of the witnesses being absent, sat down on a chair, and was indignantly told to stand up or squat—Hendrick, who was present as a witness, and old Swartboy, who was present as a spectator, began to chaff each other; Jan Steen joined in, and no order at all could be restored until I told Hendrick that I should send him out of the room if he were not silent. He was the chief offender on this occasion, but yet, as I looked at him, I could not but admit in my mind that he was the most gentlemanly-mannered man in the room.

After a sitting of several hours, it was made evident that Pete had stolen articles from my waggon, and had disposed of them to the *kaffirs*, and had afterwards treated them and been treated in return with brandy bought from me, and not only this, but at the very time that we were searching for Pete gold had been brought to Jan Steen by a *kaffir* of his own, to be changed into silver, the money being brought from and returned to Pete.

I must here remark that there is a law in the Transvaal which says that no intoxicating drink may be sold to a *kaffir*, without permission from his master, either written or verbal, under a heavy penalty. The law is broken every minute of the day in Pretoria, under the very nose of the *landrost*, but *landrosts* in the country parts are more particular. Jan Steen, however, had given me leave to sell as much brandy to his *kaffirs* as they liked to buy. The Boers were very angry—most virtuously indignant—they talked, until it was time to go to bed, over the necessity of making an example of the *kraal kaffirs*; they said if such villainy as that were to be allowed to go on, they might go so far as to rise against their masters and murder them.

De Clerc with flashing eyes, and Jan Steen with glittering ones, uttered all sorts of vague threats of the terrible reckoning they were going to have with those *kraal kaffirs*; and De Clerc said he would sleep with his rifle by his side close to the waggon to protect me from them, but he did not do it. In the meantime, Pete was committed for trial before the Landrost of Nilstrom. I may here mention that I found out on taking stock that I had lost about 50*l*. worth of different sorts of goods.

As the trial of Pete could not come on for a few days I was obliged to postpone my departure. This was inconvenient. Rain had not fallen, but it was evidently imminent. There was a long stretch of turf-country to be crossed—country which is frightful to pull through, except after a long continuance of dry weather. The waggon was very heavy, and so full that it would be impossible for me to get any shelter by creeping inside in case of rain. Added to this the weather was intensely hot, and I felt the fever beginning to creep over me. Under these circumstances I determined to buy from De Plessis a very good new waggon with a tent on it, to make two spans of the old span and of those oxen I had recently bought, and to divide the load.

On the day of the trial I rode over to Nilstrom early in the morning. Nilstrom, the capital of Waterberg, consisted then of four rather tumble-down buildings. One was the prison, another the *landrost's* office, a third his dwelling-house, and the fourth the church. The imaginary town is situated in the ugliest part of Waterberg that I have seen, and in a particularly unhealthy locality. The *landrost*, an educated German gentleman, must, in my estimation, be a person of very decided character, not to have (at some unguarded moment) committed suicide. Pete would not confess, and, on account of his contumacy, was sentenced to twenty-five lashes as well as six months' imprisonment with hard labour.

As he got out of the crazy old prison before many days, and disappeared, his punishment was not a particularly severe one; and as his trial had nothing remarkable about it, except that the ordinary unpleasantness of a little police-court was aggravated by the odour attached to black people, I may here conclude the history of Pete by mentioning that when I asked Jan Steen and De Clerc what they were going to do about the *kraal kaffirs*, they said that they thought I would prosecute them, but that if they did, they were afraid the *kaffirs* might murder them. The next day I started. Some of the oxen I had bought had strayed, and were missing. But the people said they would send them after me to my first outspan, and I could get on well without them till I got into the turf. The next morning, however, they had not arrived; so, before the sun was up, I started back to fetch them. I had breakfast with the De Plessis, and the oxen having been found, Willem De Plessis, De Clerc's young son, and I started for the waggon, driving them in front of us. It was now very hot, with a hot wind blowing; and in the evening, as I was sitting by the waggon, I remarked a fever sore coming on my hand, and I knew I was in for it.

We trekked that night, and I felt very ill. Little Hendrick had to act forelooper, and so I rode Dandy and led Eclipse. I did some trade along the road, but pushed on as quickly as I could, fearing that the rain would catch me before I got through the turf. It was very hot, and there was very little water to be got, some of the springs were quite dried up. The fever came on strong, and I was soon all covered with fever-sores, which made it very painful to ride, particularly as I had a led horse. But at last we were through the turf and through the Pinaar's river. As I crossed it the river was barely up to the horses' knees in the deepest part, and was a mere little rivulet running between very high banks; but the sky was heavy with clouds, the sun sometimes scorching, sometimes hidden, and there was a gusty wind.

I off-saddled near to a Boer's house, and threw myself down on the grass quite exhausted. I had been wondering whether I should be able to keep up until I had passed this river, for an hour or more; it was done now. Presently the waggons came over, the oxen looking very much knocked up. They had had nothing to drink for nearly twenty-four hours. By the time that they and the horses had to be tied up for the night, the first drops of the storm were beginning to fall. I saw the horses well blanketed and with their hoods on, then got into the tent-waggon myself. That night the rain came down in floods, and the next morning when I emerged from the waggon I saw an enormous lake stretching far and wide, with the tops of trees showing like little islands here and there with the current swirling round them. The waters were out over miles and miles of country along the little rivulet of the day before.

For the next few days it rained off and on, and I was laid up with fever. I used to crawl out of the waggon occasionally, but it would have been impossible for me to ride. The Boers, whose home was close by, were not very nice specimens, but were civil enough. At last the weather and I were sufficiently improved for a move to be made, and two days after, late in the evening, I rode into Pretoria, though still burning and shivering with, fever. The weather was still uncertain, and that very day I had had to ride through the rain, owing to there being no one but myself to mind the horses. I passed my Irish acquaintance's house as I rode in, and he gave me some wine, for which I am still grateful to him, and told me that the Basuto war had broken out, and that grain of all sorts was commanding a high price; so my speculation of trading grain turned out a success so far.

CHAPTER 29

Before I left Pretoria on this expedition Mrs. Felman had told me that I might have the use of the stable, and of a very tiny room partitioned off from it by a half-high wall, for my own occupation. This had two advantages—it saved me expense, and allowed of my being near the horses and the oxen and waggons. During my tenure of this room I repeatedly pressed her to receive payment for it, and for the stable, as well as for my food (for I was always invited to join the family at meal-times), but she persistently refused.

To the Felmans, therefore, I betook myself on this evening, and was greeted heartily. Going out to see to the oxen in the dark, I tumbled against Mr. Egerton. He still lived in my mansion by the swamp, but soon after this he left it, and went off with the volunteers to Basutoland. I had meant, after selling my loads, to return with the waggons for the grain I had left behind, but the fever had me in its grip now. I would never lie by completely, but the weakness and the intense pain from the dreadful sores quite prostrated me. I hired a groom (a half-caste Hottentot) called "Soldat," and sent the waggons back, with a few goods to trade with the Boers and *kaffirs*, under the charge of Hendrick, and a son of Swartboy's, called "Boy," whom I had engaged as driver to the new waggon at Jan Steen's farm. He had been brought up amongst the Boers there, and they gave him an excellent character. I was very averse to trusting these men alone, but under the circumstances I did not know anything better to do, considering the high character I had received of Hendrick, a character confirmed to me by various Boers.

Jimmy was in Pretoria now. He had left the Higginses' store, and had got employment as clerk to a surveyor. So soon as I felt a little better, although still far from well, I determined to go and put my new farm a little in order. So I bought an old half-tent waggon cheap, and a span of salted oxen. I had a long time to wait before I could get the oxen, and then there was a difficulty about getting a driver for most of the drivers were off with the volunteers to Basutoland.

There was beginning to be a feeling of insecurity in Pretoria. There was nothing to be seen, but people felt that the air was electric. I was pretty sure that the Boers would fight, after a certain conversation I had with De Clerc at his farm. On this occasion he had been talking with me about political affairs, asking me if I thought the Boers would be supported by any of the European powers or by America; and he suddenly said, "But in any case we shall fight;" then after a moment's pause continued, "I will tell you our plans. I don't count you as an enemy. This is what you will hear. Some man will refuse to pay his taxes; then your government will seize property to the amount of what is due; and then we shall rise; and we shall take that property out of the hands of the authorities, and if they interfere with us we shall fight; but until then we have done with talking."

"I should be sorry if you did what you say," I replied. "We have not many troops in the country now; but for you to go to war with the English nation is like a little child going to fight a man."

He assented to this, but in the conversation that ensued he told me that the Boers were not afraid of our cannon.

"We don't fight as you do," he said. "What is the use of cannon against men who scurry round singly on horseback, and who shoot at you from behind stones and trees without your seeing them? We shall not meet your troops in the open *ur-feldt*, don't you believe it; we shall go into Natal to meet you."

On my return to Pretoria I was still so impressed by De Clerc's words and manner, that I considered whether it might not be the right thing to do, to tell what I had heard and who I had heard it from, to Sir Owen Lanyon. But I determined not to do so, as I had not stopped De Clerc when he said he did not count me as an enemy, and had not cautioned him that I would not undertake to observe secrecy in respect to what he was about to tell me. Just before I started for Jackallsfontein the news came from Potchefstrom that a Boer had refused to pay his taxes, that his waggon had been seized in consequence, and that the Boers had taken violent possession of it in defiance of the law. Then I felt quite sure of my affair. The De Clerc programme was going to be attempted.

My waggon was ready packed; I had got my new driver and leader, and had kept them under my eye all the morning to take care that they did not get drunk. I saw the oxen brought up to span in, and then, having to transact a little business before starting, I told the driver that he was to meet me in a quarter of an hour at a particular store, and cantered off. My business was with the tenant of my house, a matter which I should have transacted in five minutes, but by the time I was at his door a tremendous and sudden storm had burst over the town, and it was half an hour before I could get away.

As I rode into the market-square I saw the waggon rounding a corner into it, the oxen all mixed up together, the driver drunk and swearing at them, the leader drunk and running about in front of them, entangling them more hopelessly every minute. They were turning another corner by the time I was alongside of them; the waggon was on the point of being upset. "Pull out the fore oxen—straight out!" I am afraid I shouted in a very unladylike manner, to the horror of some Pretorians who were spectators. The leader answered with a drunken laugh. There was no time to be lost. I gave him a sharp cut with my riding-whip, and he sprang forward pulling the oxen out. But it was no good, the two fellows were too hopelessly drunk to be fit for anything.

I got the waggon on to an open space and outspanned, left Soldat and his *kaffir* wife, "Clara," whose services I had engaged, in charge, took the oxen to the Felmans' *kraal*, then looked up Jimmy, and asked him to oblige me by sleeping at the waggon for that night, which he did. The next day the driver and forelooper were sober, but the man, although he was said to be able to drive, could not, and broke the *disselboom* before we were out of the village. I then dismissed him; and had to get the *disselboom* mended, and also to get a new driver. After considerable trouble I got one fairly recommended, but when I took him to the waggon I found the forelooper had run away. However, I managed to get another forelooper, and early the next morning we started. Hardly had we got on the camp-common when the leader threw up the tow, and leaving the waggon, sat down on the grass. I rode up and asked him why he did so.

"I am going no farther," he said.

"Indeed," said I, "you forget that you engaged to go to the farm with me."

The end of it was that I put Eclipse at him, and having made him stand up, hunted him, although he tried doubling, up to the head of the team, and then rode alongside with my whip raised. So we got out of the village. I never saw anything so bad as that man's driving. It was a wonder that the waggon was not upset and the oxen hurt. We did seven miles in five hours, and then stuck hopelessly in what is called the "seven-mile *spruit*," close to what is called the Red House—a place which has a tragic interest attached to it now.

The *spruit* was an absurd place to stick in, but the oxen were bullied by the bad driving, and had been too long in the yoke. I outspanned them, and off-loaded. Shortly after the guns and military train that were being sent to Potchefstrom came over the hill and down to the *spruit*, and crossed, the men looking at my waggon in disgust, for it was a good deal in their way. To the credit of the men be it said that only one swore at it, and he was reproved by a comrade, who remarked that probably I was more annoyed by its sticking than they were. They pitched their camp close by, and as soon as the oxen were rested I inspanned and tried to drag the waggon out. But my wretched driver only got the oxen more hopelessly entangled than ever, and at last I had to ask the Boer on whose farm we were to pull it out, which he very kindly did. I saw the things loaded up, and then told the driver to saddle the horses and take his blanket, as I was going to ride back to Pretoria. The sun had set, but there was a beautiful moon, and I got into Pretoria in good time.

The next morning I discharged the driver and engaged a new one; and in the meantime Jimmy turned up, and told me that his employer had discharged him, having no farther need of his services, and that he was unable to obtain any other employment, as everything was very slack in Pretoria. Under these circumstances I proposed to him to come with me, to which he gladly assented. So in the evening we started; Jimmy and I riding, and the new driver, a half-caste named Andreas, walking, and carrying his own and Jimmy's bundles. We were only on the outskirts of the village when we saw that a great storm was imminent, and turned back to the Felmans' house just in time to escape it, fortunately, for it was very severe. The next morning we started again, and when we arrived at the waggon, found Soldat, Clara, and the dogs anxiously expecting us; and here I must beg to introduce a third dog to my readers. He was a sort of sheep-dog, black and white, called "Nero," a most inappropriate name, for a milder dog never existed, although he was a very good hunting dog. I had bought him, and a splendid half-bred mastiff, Prince, for waggon dogs. Prince had gone with the waggons, but Nero gave the boys the slip, and ran back to me.

There had been heavy rain at the Red House as well as at Pretoria, and the *spruit* was very much swollen. The worst was that the weather looked very threatening. I inspanned after lunch, and started. This time the oxen pulled much better, and it was evident that, although not a good driver, Andreas was much superior to his two predecessors.

We had only got a few miles, however, and were on a bleak hillside, when the storm I had seen approaching for some time, burst upon us. It was something terrific. There was no making head against it. I had the oxen outspanned, blanketed the horses, and sheltered them as well as I could in the lee of the waggon. The flashes of lightning and the roar of thunder were almost continuous, the rain poured down in torrents, and the wind howled and raved until I thought the waggon would have been blown over. I was afraid that the horses would get alarmed, and stood by them until the fury of the storm abated, which was not for some hours. The rain was still falling heavily, and it was quite dark, when, at last, drenched through in spite of my mackintosh, I crept into the waggon along with Clara, whilst Jimmy made his bed (such as it was) under it, in the wet.

When I woke next morning the rain was still falling, nor did it cease till midday, when it cleared up. The waggon had sunk very deep in the soft ground, which was slippery for the oxen's feet, and after various efforts to pull it out, I was obliged to make up my mind to off-load partially again. The evening was very fine, and I trusted to being able to load up in the morning after pulling the waggon out. The whole ground was so wet and swampy that I determined to let the horses and oxen remain loose during the night; the moon was bright, and from time to time I inspected them. The morning dawned beautifully, but hardly had the first rays of the sun become visible, when I saw a heavy bank of clouds, which threatened hail, sweeping rapidly up from the horizon. I ordered all haste to be made to get whatever had been off-loaded up on the waggon, but before everything was ready the storm burst—such a storm, almost worse than the previous one, although the thunder and lightning was less severe.

Fortunately there was but little hail, for about this time there were hail-storms in other districts, which would have cut the tent of the waggon into shreds, and killed or maimed the animals and us. The rain poured down the whole day. Clara at last managed to make a sort of little tent with a tarpaulin and some sheets of iron roofing I had with me, and got some coffee made, which Jimmy and I, crouching in the waggon-tent together, were very thankful for; and she also managed to make some very bad griddle-cakes, but the only wonder was that she was able to make them at all. Night came on, and it was still raining and blowing—it was useless to attempt to tie up the animals, the waggon was standing in a swamp, so they had to take their chance. Jimmy and I slept in the waggon, the tent of which had begun to leak, and little Roughy and Moustache begged so to come in also, that I let the poor little brutes have their desire. When the morning dawned it was still raining, the horses were in sight, but the oxen were gone, and so was the leader. I sent Andreas on foot and Soldat on Dandy to look for them, and while they were away, seeing two government waggons going to Potchefstrom with strong spans of oxen, I asked the conductor to pull my waggon out, which he obligingly did.

It rained on and off the whole day, and in the evening the two boys returned, having seen nothing of the oxen. Soldat reported that the *spruit* was at flood. I determined to go to look for the oxen the next day myself, as I very much suspected that they had trekked off to the farm they had been feeding on shortly before I bought them. This is a favourite pastime of oxen. Unfortunately I did not know where this farm was, and hence I knew it would be necessary first to go to Pretoria to see the man I had bought the animals from, and inquire the way to it. The next morning was Sunday, and the weather was beautiful. Jimmy and I saddled up early, and taking Nero with us, started for Pretoria.

We got in there about nine o'clock, and having found the gentleman I wanted, and got the direction to the farm, and a note to its proprietor, we rode to the Felmans' to give the horses a rest and try to get a little breakfast for ourselves. On our way I met a *kaffir* who had just come in from Waterberg, and he gave me a letter written by "Boy," who had learned to write at the Mission station. It was a very funny production, but Mrs. Felman and I managed to decipher it, and it corroborated what I had previously heard from a Boer, *viz.*, that Hendrick was doing a good trade, and that the oxen were well.

We were, as usual, hospitably entertained at the Felmans', who had pressed me to come to them whenever I should be in Pretoria, and had told me that I might always consider the little room next the stable as my own, although I had given up the mansion by the swamp after Mr. Egerton left Pretoria, Mrs. Felman having taken charge of all things which I had not loaded up on the waggon to go to the farm. These articles which she took charge of, were goods for trading, which I did not care to take there until I had got the place into some order. It was very hot when Jiminy and I started once more. The road was rather pretty, and for a time was sufficiently good for us to be able to push along pretty quickly.

At last we came to a very steep decline, and after following the road in its windings between the hills, we saw a thick line of brush-wood marking the course of the river we had to cross, and at the same time heard the rush of the water, telling of its being in flood. The *spruit* we had crossed in the morning was part of this river that was before us; where we had forded it, we had not found it very deep, but it was evident that it was considerably deeper here. When we rode down to the ford, it looked very ugly. There was a farmhouse on the opposite side, and presently a small boy made his appearance, and looked across at us. I hailed this boy, and inquired if the ford was passable; his answer was, "Come across."

It was not altogether a satisfactory answer, because he might be a truculent young Boer, anxious to drown the enemies of the liberties of his nation; but as no other answer was to be got from him, I put Eclipse at the stream. Eclipse did not like the look of it at all, sniffed and snorted, and even, when he got into the full current, wanted to turn back; however, we got through with a good wetting, Jimmy followed, and poor Nero swam through after a struggle, for the current was very strong. Arrived on the bank, I said to the boy that I had a letter for Mr. P———, and felt much gratified by hearing that Mr. P———'s farm was some way down the stream on the side I had just left, so we had to ford back again!

A short canter took us to Mr. P———'s house, where we were very kindly received. Mr. P——— is an English Africander, I believe. Mrs. P——— gave us some coffee, which was very acceptable after our wetting, but Mr. P——— could tell us nothing about the oxen, except that that morning, looking with his field-glass for some oxen he had lost, he had seen, on a hill-side far away, a number of oxen which he had not recognized as his or as any belonging to his neighbours. The hill was in the direction of my waggon, so I thought this sounded hopeful. Mr. P——— told us that a number of his sheep had been killed by the late storms, and that several of his oxen were missing.

We mounted once more, and fording the river again at the same spot, took our way towards the hill Mr. P——— had pointed out to us, when suddenly Jimmy exclaimed that he was sure that he could see the oxen grazing in a valley at some distance. I could not make them out; but he was so confident that we altered our course, and presently coming to a farm, we asked the Boer who owned it, if he had seen any strange oxen, and he told us that he had seen fourteen strange oxen that morning with their heads towards the spot Jimmy had indicated. Thus encouraged we pushed on, and soon came in sight of our friends peaceably grazing.

It is an odd thing that oxen who play truant know quite well when they are found out. They are wonderfully sly about sneaking away; if they mean to run away in the daytime, they do not do so ostentatiously. They will graze quietly until they think they have lulled suspicion, and then walk off more quickly than any one not accustomed to their ways would think it possible for them to do. If they mean to run away at night, they set about it very softly, so as not to wake any one, but whenever they go, their expression upon being found out is the same. They do not, like the Elfin page, "*fall to the ground*," oxen being of a less emotional and demonstrative nature than elfins, but if there be any expression in an eye, they most unmistakably mutter to themselves, "found, found, found," and having so muttered, they visibly, to the least imaginative observer, turn round, "form," to use a military expression, and move off in front of their captor.

In the case of my oxen, there was one daring spirit of the name of "Blauberg," who had always been mutinous. He now maintained his character by perpetually trying to run away, tossing his head, and flicking his tuftless tail—for, like many of his brethren, he had lost a portion of that appendage during the illness consequent upon inoculation with "lung-sickness." We had to take the oxen over the *veldt* to the waggon, which was not an easy operation, for we did not know the country, there was no road, and our only guides were the slopes of the hills. Added to this the night was coming on quickly, and the moon did not rise until late. Blauberg's antics were, therefore, very inconvenient, and caused feelings the reverse of charitable towards that erring ox to arise in Jimmy's breast and my own. At last, some time after it was dark, Jimmy caught sight of our camp-fire, much to my delight, and after we got the oxen tied up, and the horses blanketed and fed, we sat down to the dinner Clara had been keeping warm for us. She had, by my orders, bought a sheep from a neighbouring farmer during my absence.

We started the next morning; but to make a long story short, we had a miserable trek. The weather was very bad; the road was very bad in places; the drift or ford of the Yokeskey River, which we had to pass, was in such a state, that I had to hire a span of oxen from a neighbouring Boer to put on to my span, and then, with three drivers, the oxen had a difficult job to pull the waggon out. I do not think that this Boer would have hired me his oxen had it not been for the persuasions of his good-natured wife. His name was "Durks." He had a good reason for not wanting to hire them, for they, and all the young cattle, were being used for tramping out the corn, rain was threatening, and it is no joke for rain to come on while the corn is on the tramping-floor. Of course, the fact of rain being imminent made it very desirable for me to get across the river, and kind, fat Mrs. Durks saw this.

The rain did come on heavily shortly after I outspanned, but the weather cleared after an hour or so, and we trekked again; to add trouble to trouble Jimmy was taken ill, and had to go in the waggon; so that I had to ride Dandy and to lead Eclipse, as well as drive the two loose oxen (for I had yokes for twelve oxen only with the waggon I was using). That evening we outspanned by the farm of an English Africander, of the name of Williams. He was from home, but his wife was very kind, giving us nice bread, milk, and eggs, which were all very acceptable, the more so as one required a little inner consolation to withstand the rain and wind which, coming on shortly after we outspanned, continued nearly all night. I here met a man who had just come from Waterberg, and who told me that the storms there had been something terrific. I afterwards saw in a paper the intelligence that "the public buildings at Nilstrom had been blown down by the hurricane!"

We at last reached Jackallsfontein in a storm, and found, alas! that the cottage had shared the fate of the "public buildings at Nilstrom." It had been blown down!

Chapter 30

There is not much to describe in Jackallsfontein in the way of scenery; no comparison between it and Grünfontein could be instituted. Jackallsfontein is undeniably ugly; it lies on a gentle slope of what, in England, we should call the "Downs" of the Wittwatersrandt. The few trees around it have all been planted, and not only around Jackallsfontein itself, but in all the country for miles round. But to counterbalance this, the material advantages of Jackallsfontein over Grünfontein are manifold.

At Jackallsfontein horses can be safely bred; they can be let run summer and winter without fear; sheep, too, thrive well, not being plagued with the ailments or by the ticks which render their lives a burden to themselves and to their proprietors, on the slopes of the Magaliesberg, and in a great part of the Transvaal. No herbs poisonous to cattle or sheep grow near Jackallsfontein, and that is a point greatly in favour of any farm in the Transvaal, where poisonous herbs are very common. Although I took great care of my sheep at Grünfontein, I had lost several through their being allowed to stray into pasture which was poisonous; and not far from my property there (although at too great a distance to endanger my oxen) a farmer had in one day lost sixty head of cattle through the carelessness of his herd, who had let the animals in his charge stray on to unhealthy grazing.

Added to the above-mentioned advantages, the quality of the soil at Jackallsfontein is excellent, the water good, and the site very favourable for opening a general Boer store. *kaffir* labour there is none, but Boer labour can be easily obtained from adjoining small farms, whose owners are glad for younger members of their family to earn something to assist in the general housekeeping.

My house being uninhabitable, I was obliged to engage a room in the house of some Boers whose farm adjoins mine. The name of these people is De Plessis, but they are no relations of Willem De Plessis. Their house consisted of three rooms and kitchen, and one of these rooms, separated from the family sleeping-room by a half-wall, they made over to me. It was not a very eligible apartment, having no window, and the door being composed of dilapidated reeds—however, it was better than nothing. I pitched my tent as a room for Jimmy, the servants had the waggon, and the horses were accommodated at night in a deserted house at a little distance, which once had been a dwelling of some pretensions, having several rooms, and bearing traces on the walls of the sitting-room of having been tastefully painted. There was yet another cottage quite close to the one in which I lodged, tenanted by members of the same family as mine hosts, and numberless small farms were dotted about the environs. The owner of the deserted house I have mentioned was an English Africander, who, I was told, was bankrupt, and the property was held by his creditors.

I cannot give a very lucid account of my hosts and their neighbours, they were all so mixed up, owing to the curiosity my appearance excited having a stimulating effect on the custom amongst Boers of running backwards and forwards between one anothers' houses. There was a very large number of dirty little children of all ages, and a sprinkling of dirty but helpful boys—boys who could drive a plough, or hold it, as well as their fathers; there was an entanglement of slatternly women with loud voices, who have left shadowy pictures on my mind, as bearing the more or less depressed expression common to the Boeress. With a life of dull toil stretching from childhood to the grave, it is no wonder that it should be so; and yet, those who have known the peasantry of other lands, must feel the question arise in their minds, "Why should the Boer peasant-woman look depressed, when the South Italian peasant-woman (for instance) does not?"

I think the answer to the question is, "Look at the men." It is not want of education, or rather of book-learning, that makes a life of toil dull, and the men and women who live such lives generation after generation incarnations of dullness. It is but in the latest generation that a gleam from the sun of knowledge has fallen on the peasantry of South Italy, yet who would have ever called them "dull?" who would have discovered that their women wore a general air of depression? The women of a race will not look depressed if the men be not "dull;" and *vice versa*, if the women look depressed the men must be "dull."

Although the Boers are in many ways cunning, any one who has any knowledge of them will corroborate the statement, that the vast majority of them are dull, and that the vast majority of Boeresses bear a stamp of depression, although in the elder women this stamp is somewhat effaced by a tendency to fat, which on first sight gives an appearance of jollity. I do not mean to say that I have not seen cheerful women amongst the Boers, but they are rare exceptions.

Besides the children, lads, and women, there was a group of big, rough-handed, grimy-looking, rough-voiced men, the only individual member of which I can distinctly remember was "Lo," a fine stalwart fellow, with kindly blue eyes, and whom I distinguished sufficiently from the general relationship to know that he was the son of mine host, and that he was unmarried.

These people were very kind in their way, but very annoying at the same time. They were willing to help at settling my room, so as to make it inhabitable, and willing also to help with the ploughing and sowing that had to be done; but they invaded me incessantly. To be certain of privacy, I had, from early dawn until the family retired to rest, to tie the reed door to with a piece of string, and then an enterprising youngster or an inquisitive female was as likely as not to push the reeds aside and peep in. Of course as there was no window the door had usually to be left open to afford light, and then the whole troop disported themselves from morning till night. If I did not talk to them, or even if I was engaged in writing, it did not matter; they would talk amongst themselves, and the children would scramble about at their mothers' feet, and the men would smoke, whilst all would spit on the ground in a manner trying to weak nerves.

They, as indeed all the Boers I have met, treated me to a certain extent differently from the way in which they treat most people. They never called me by any familiar name, although they were all very friendly. Perhaps they had some vague perception that if they had attempted to do so I should have stopped them; whatever the reason may be, although playful conversation amongst the Boers is frequently what we should consider both coarse and impertinent, I had only twice any occasion to check any acquaintance of mine. This point being attained, I felt that it would be unwise to try to put limits, marked out by my sense of the proprieties, upon conduct which these people considered as a proof of their friendly feeling, and which besides afforded to them a source of innocent amusement.

I felt this to be the more imperative owing to the dislike existing between the Boers and the English; a feeling which in so thinly populated a country as the Transvaal, each individual settler could either augment or diminish; for it is wonderful how trifling information respecting individuals spreads in the Transvaal. I may mention an instance of this in illustration.

In the month of April I had telegraphed from Pretoria to my banker's in London to ask how my balance with them stood. In the following September old Mrs. Nell in Waterberg asked me why I was trading when I had so much money in the bank! Neither is this a solitary instance of private matters, connected with an unknown individual, being subjects of common conversation amongst people who perhaps never saw him or could be supposed to take any interest in him. Certainly, so far as my experience goes, a Boer loves gossip as well as any man or woman in existence.

Lo De Plessis and Jimmy soon became quite chums, and I was glad to hear the latter improving in speaking the dialect of the country every day. In the meantime I rode to see various neighbours, and everywhere met with a kindly welcome, and heard a wish expressed that I should open a store at Jackallsfontein. The men were anxious to know all I knew of what was being done at Potchefstrom, and as to the general attitude of the English Government, while all professed an utter ignorance of occurrences either at Potchefstrom or elsewhere. I had no news to communicate, but I felt certain that they had; and their reticence only confirmed my opinion that the programme indicated by De Clerc was in progress.

The weather continued very stormy, and it was with anything but pleasure that I looked forward to having to ride back to Pretoria. Still it was evident that I should have to return thither, for my waggons from Waterberg were nearly due, and, of course, I had to be in Pretoria to meet them; so, after waiting as long as I could at the farm, I made a start.

The morning was so stormy that I could not saddle up until the day was far advanced, and hence I did not get into Pretoria until about ten o'clock at night. I rode to the Felmans as usual, but they had gone to rest, and I was only able to get into my little room, and put the horses into the stable. To my sorrow I found that the forage I had put by for them before leaving Pretoria had been used, so my poor animals, as well as their mistress and the boy, had to go supperless. I had taken Andreas with me instead of Soldat, as I did not wish to leave Clara on the farm without her husband. Andreas the next day went "on the spree," and never turned up again, so that I had to look after the horses myself.

In the meantime the tenant I had had in my house left Pretoria; and as, owing to the unsettled state of affairs, it was a bad time to let a house, I determined to prepare it for my own occupation, at least temporarily, although, with a view to the possibility of an outbreak, I determined only to put the most necessary things into it. The garden had been much neglected, and I employed two *kaffirs* to set it in order.

Day after day passed, and my waggons did not come in, and in the meanwhile alarming rumours were on the increase. The very morning that I left Jackallsfontein, a Boer had ridden over from a neighbouring farm with news that Paul Krüger and Pretorius had sent a message to the effect that every man who could, ought, in the name of God, to attend the now famous meeting at Perdekraal, which was to be held forthwith. Great excitement had been caused—the messenger had bargained for a saddle from me, whereon to ride to the meeting. Lo De Plessis and all the other men were going; they had pressed upon me the desirability of loading up my incoming waggons with various articles of consumption, and bringing them to the *Beeinkommste*, assuring me that they would guarantee a good trade to me. This plan I had revolved much in my mind. I had no doubt that it would be a good speculation, but I finally abandoned it, as I thought it would be hardly an honourable position for me to accept.

It will, I daresay, be remembered that the meeting of the final *Beeinkommste* had been fixed for the 8th of January, and was suddenly abandoned, much to the surprise of many of the Boers themselves, including my neighbour at Jackallsfontein; hence my plans, as well as those of a good many others, were considerably disconcerted.

One morning I had walked from the Felmans' early, to see whether the *kaffirs* were at work in my garden, when I was told by an acquaintance that Robert Higgins and most of my old friends from the Magaliesberg had come into Pretoria, having been warned by the Boers that if they remained on their farms their lives would not be safe. I thought this was but one of the many false reports flying about Pretoria, but resolved to go to the house of old Mr. Higgins and inquire. On my way there I met Robert Higgins himself, who confirmed the report. That day and the following one the whole of the village was greatly agitated, and there was a great demand for waggons amongst people who thought that their lives, in case of an outbreak, would be safer out of Pretoria than in it.

I determined to seize the opportunity of selling my old waggon, and the oxen I had lately bought, at a good price; and, saddling the horses, I started for the farm, riding one and leading the other. Andreas having levanted, and there being no boy to be got at the moment, I had no choice but to do this, for volunteers were being raised in Pretoria, and horse-stealing was so rife, that had I left Dandy behind me I should probably never have seen him again.

As owing to the torrents of rain which were continually falling, the Yokeskey river was likely to be at flood, I did not much relish the idea of crossing it with a led horse. I had hardly got to the outskirts of the village, however, when I saw a storm approaching, and turned back only just in time; and the next day I was fortunate enough to get a boy to ride Dandy, and to act subsequently as leader to the waggon, which I intended Soldat to drive, an office which Jimmy would otherwise have had to perform. It was on Monday, the 13th of December, that at seven o'clock in the morning I started for Jackallsfontein.

The morning was fresh after the rain, and I pushed on pretty quickly, taking a shorter road to the farm than I had taken with the waggon, and hopeful of escaping rain, although very heavy masses of cloud were lowering round the horizon. I was already near the Yokeskey river, and the rain appeared not far off, when I met a Boer on horseback. We both drew rein, and he asked me where I was going; I told him to my farm.

"Then," said he, "you will have to swim the river, there is no passing it otherwise."

He then asked me if I meant to stay at the farm or return to Pretoria. I told him that I was going to bring up my waggon to sell, with, I hoped, a light load of farm produce.

"Look at the clouds!" said the Boer; "the river is impassable now, and if it rains, as I think there is no doubt it will, it will be still deeper by the time you get your waggon back to it."

It struck me that what he said was true; so, much disgusted, I turned my horse and we rode alongside of each other for a short time. My companion asked me if I had heard any news of the deliberation of the *Beeinkommste* at Perdekraal (Perdekraal was within a ride of my farm). I told him that no one in Pretoria had any news about it. He then asked me whether it was true that no Boers were allowed to enter Pretoria, saying that such was the current report; and this I was able to contradict. Shortly after he bade me goodbye, and cantered off across the *veldt* in one direction, whilst I held on, likewise across the *veldt*, towards Pretoria.

My way lay past a large farmhouse, belonging to a well-known man amongst the Boers called Guillaume Pretorius. As I was passing he came out, and I stopped and saluted him. He asked where I was going, and I told him how I had turned back from going to my farm.

"If you mean to get into Pretoria, then," said he, "you had better push on: the *Beeinkommste* is broken up, and the commando rides today to Pretoria."

"Does it?" said I; "then I am in luck; I should like to see it."

The old fellow looked at me with an odd expression—I think he did not quite know what to make of my speech. He had never seen me before, although I knew about him, but with that habit of hospitality which has become a second nature to a Boer, he said, "Will you not off-saddle? although perhaps you had better push on if your horses are not tired."

At this moment we both caught sight of the Potchefstrom post-cart approaching the house, which was a post-station, and a minute after I recognized Mr. Cooper, the attorney, as one of the passengers in it. Our *rencontre* was a mutual surprise, and as he shook hands I noticed that his feet were bare, the result of the cart having been upset, one of the mules having been nearly drowned, and the passengers having to scramble and shift to set things straight in fording the river. Mr. Cooper introduced me to his fellow-passenger, the Attorney-General De Wett; and, hopeful now of hearing some authentic news from Potchefstrom, I dismounted, off-saddled, and went into the house with the others, while the fresh horses or mules for the post-cart were being brought up and harnessed. Seated in a large and rather comfortable sitting-room at the back of the house, the three men talked of the present and coming events, and I listened.

Mr. De Wett told us that the commando was not to ride into Pretoria until Thursday, and then only in case no compromise had been arrived at. He said that the *Beeinkommste* had appointed all necessary officers, both civil and military, and had despatched a messenger to Pretoria that very day to tell the administrator that if the government offices were not delivered over to the republic on Thursday, they would be taken by force, and that on Thursday the heads of the new government would ride into Pretoria with the commando to take possession. Mr. De Wett assured Pretorius that he had seen the Boer leaders, and that he was certain that by a little tact things might still be arranged.

It struck me that it was very little use to think of compromises when things had come to such a pass, but I held my peace, and listened, whilst Pretorius expressed himself to the effect that the Boers would accept of no compromise so far as the complete restoration of their independence was concerned. This Pretorius struck me as being a good old fellow, rough enough, but yet a superior man to the ordinary Boer. All this time we had been sipping coffee brought to us by Mrs. Pretorius, who must have been good-looking in her time, and been looked at by two or three pretty little girls, in much neater trim than the generality of Boer maidens.

The post-cart being now inspanned, Mr. Cooper and Mr, De Wett started; I waited, for I was anxious to hear what Pretorius would say when they were gone, as I observed that he spoke with reticence before them, and I thought he might perhaps speak more freely when I was his only English listener, I talked first about my farm, which he knew, and was interested in, then a neighbour came in, and the conversation drifted back again to politics, while we removed into another more homely sitting-room, and, upon hearing that I had had no breakfast before leaving Pretoria, Mrs. Pretorius brought me some Boer biscuits and more coffee.

It has always been my opinion that although the English Government were perfectly justified in annexing the Transvaal, the manner in which it was annexed was not only an unjustifiable blunder but an unjust act. My reasons for thinking that the annexation in itself was justifiable, are based on general principles, which it would be a hopeless task to attempt to explain to any Boer I ever met; but my reasons for thinking that the manner of annexation was altogether wrong are completely within the grasp of every one of them. In any expression of opinion to them, they inevitably missed my allusion to the general principles, which were unintelligible to them, and only remarked that I coincided with them in thinking that they had been very badly treated.

All the Boers I knew spoke before me with great frankness, and when (in order to prevent the idea that I sided with them from obtaining) I said that in case of war I should, in spite of what I had expressed, side with the English,, they accepted that as simply an inevitable consequence of my not being able to change my nationality, and it would have been a useless task to attempt to explain to them that under given circumstances I should feel myself bound to side against my own nation; but that in the Transvaal case I did not feel myself so bound. I confess I often felt seriously annoyed and depressed by this state of things in my intercourse with the Boers, so much so, that in the case of De Clerc, Willem De Plessis, Pretorius, as also of Barend Englesberg, all men superior to the common run of Boers, I should have attempted what I yet knew was impossible, namely, to explain my opinion thoroughly to them, but for my still imperfect knowledge of Boer language. That language is unfit in itself for the expression of abstract thought, because formed by people who never think abstractly; and this deterred me from the effort whenever I felt impelled towards it, and in after-reflection I always admitted that it was well that I had been restrained from so doing.

The party assembled in Pretorius's house talked, as usual, freely before me; and I heard it confidently asserted that if the public offices were not given up on the appointed day an attack would be made on Pretoria, and that even the presence of women and children would not deter the Boers from fighting from street to street until they had occupied the whole town. The innocent blood shed would be on the head of the English Government. As to all English on outstanding farms, Pretorius, his friend, and his wife (who took an animated part in the conversation), seemed to think that those who remained strictly neutral would be left unharmed, or even protected in case of necessity. Having heard all I needed, I changed my mind as to returning to Pretoria. Rain or no rain, it was evident that I must give Jimmy a choice whether he would remain on the farm or run into Pretoria before it was too late, for I felt sure that an outbreak was imminent; so, saddling-up once more, I turned towards the Yokeskey River.

I did not, however, take the way I had retraced, but struck off across the *veldt* for Durks' Drift. It was a long way out of the direct path, but this plan offered two advantages, first, that I should possibly find the drift so that I could get across without swimming, which, considering that I had never swum a horse across a river, and that I knew that Eclipse was rather shy of deep water, was, the wetting apart, a matter well worth considering; the other, that I should, by fording the drift, be able to judge whether it would be worth while to attempt to bring the waggon to Pretoria or not. At Durks' farm the Yokeskey River winds, so that one has to ford it twice in a few hundred yards, but at neither place was the water higher than the flap of the saddle, and I pushed on quickly to Mrs. Williams's, where I off-saddled, and met with a kind and hospitable welcome. I did not stop long, however, but after the horses had had some forage and a roll, saddled once more, and started for Jackallsfontein.

Just as I got on the highest part of the *randt*, the wind and rain came whirling up, but it was only the tail of a storm which went roaring away over the hills to one side, while another storm was pouring its fury on the distant hills at the other; and by the time Eclipse was picking his way down the stony slope above the De Plessis' cottage, all that remained of the rain was a watery sort of haze, gradually dissipating under the rays of the moon, which did not allow the party assembled outside the house, to see me until I was close to it. Then I was welcomed with a cordiality which would have made a stranger suppose that I had known, not only Jimmy, but the Boers, for years, while little Roughy, after executing some antics highly creditable to such a soft little mass of hair as he was, discharged a volley of little barks, and rushed at Moustache, who had offended him by espying and welcoming me first, and bit his long ears until they were forcibly separated, Nero, the while, wagging his short tail and giving little bounds indicative of satisfaction.

What a chattering; what an anxious asking and answering of questions; what a retailing of my news to each member of the small community—who, hearing of my arrival, hastened to the cottage—took place that night by the light of the moon! My last evening in the yet unmade home, before all the plans that I had carefully thought over, and toiled hard to realise, were to be swept away into a past as remote as if years lay between it and today!

At last, after I had retired to the interior of the cottage, and had eaten my supper, surrounded at first by the whole family, but with a gradually diminishing company, as sleepiness caused first one and then another to drop off to their beds, until Lo De Plessis bade me goodnight, I was alone with Jimmy. Then for the first time I confessed to him that I was anxious, and told him all that I had heard with regard to the treatment the Boers had it in their minds to bestow upon the English; told him not only what Pretorius had said, but what a farmer, whose cottage I had passed between Pretorius's farm and Durks' Drift, had said. This farmer's name was Joubert. He had called to me as I was riding past his cottage, and I had ridden up to the *stoop*, where he and some members of his family were congregated. A big, bony, black-haired man was Joubert; with a stubbly beard, high jawbones, and eager eyes.

"Where are you from?" he cried, as I drew rein.

"From Pretoria."

"What is the news?"

I told him.

"Yes, yes," he exclaimed, "that is well. Will your government give up the public offices, think you? "

"I am in no position to know what are the intentions of the government," I answered; "but I do not think it likely they will."

He drew his breath, and said, in a savagely suppressed manner,—

"Then the streets of Pretoria shall run with blood like water on Thursday."

He asked me eagerly what I thought of the action of the government; asked if I were going back to Pretoria; called Heaven to witness that the blood spilt would cry vengeance on us; his eyes glittering, his whole frame absolutely quivering with passion. He had laid his hand on my horse's neck as he spoke; there was a look in his eyes unlike anything I had ever seen before—a bloodthirsty look that made me involuntarily shiver.

"Then you don't think they will give us the country back?" he cried again. "Then we will fight; we will drive you from the country; not one of your nation shall remain alive; your blood shall run as water on Thursday; we will kill all—all of you! Where are your troops? sent away to fight against the enemies that are attacking you—the Russians—the Irish—the Americans."

"No, no," said I, "now there you are mistaken."

The blood rushed to his head, suffusing his very eyes until they looked red.

"Now I know you lie," he cried, his voice shaking with passion. "There is your path—begone!"

"Not like this," said I, not moving. "I am not the government. I wish the Boers no harm, and although I am English and you a Boer, there is no reason for our quarrelling personally. Give me your hand before I go;" and I held out mine. Joubert looked—hesitated—then out came the rough paw; and he bade me a civil goodbye.

All this I told Jimmy; and told him he must choose for himself whether he would remain on the farm or return to Pretoria with me. He chose the former alternative; and after a sleepless night, I called up Soldat and the *kaffir* at four in the morning to span in. I had packed up some things I required to take with me, but the waggon could not have got across the Yokeskey River with even a light load on it. The Boers before leaving me in the evening had promised that, in the event of hostilities breaking out, and of my being detained in Pretoria, they would protect Jimmy, and had also promised to give him his food until I returned, for Clara was going with me as well as Soldat.

The early dawn was just breaking when the waggon started, and I, mounted on Dandy, and with Eclipse by my side, bade Jimmy, who was holding Roughy in his arms, goodbye. They both looked so forlorn as he stood there in the cold, faint light. "It is not too late to change your mind yet," said I; "you have only to say the word." But he preferred remaining, and indeed I thought myself it was safer for him where he was than in Pretoria. The words I had heard that morning, when some movement I made had wakened the sleepers in the next room, were still in my ears.

"She is getting ready to inspan," said a sleepy female voice. "Well, she will never come back."

"Ah," remarked another equally sleepy female voice; "and if she don't, then who will pay us for the little Englishman's food?"

We forded the Yokeskey in a torrent of rain, the current running strong and deep, and outspanned at Durks' farm. Nero and Moustache had' broken loose, and followed me. Nero was nearly washed away, and little Moustache was only saved by being caught by his neck as he was sinking—the leader himself could hardly keep his legs. Mrs. Durks was friendly, her husband civil. He advised me, if my waggons had come in, to come out of Pretoria with them on Thursday as early as I could. He said even if I met the commando that I, as a woman working for herself, should be let pass, with the waggons and oxen, if I explained that I was going to my farm; but that if I remained in Pretoria I should hold my life in my hand. They gave me some milk and bread; and shortly after I inspanned, and that night I outspanned about three miles from the Red House, by a spring of water.

The moon was at its full, and I inspanned before dawn, and came into Pretoria as the clock was pointing to seven in the morning—to find, alas! that the whole village was in a panic, and that not only were most places of business shut, but that the auction I had counted upon for selling my waggon was postponed, owing to the unsettled state of things. My Waterberg waggons were not in!

I left the waggon at the auctioneer's for private sale; but I saw that, as I had failed in selling it on Wednesday, it would, in all probability, be too late to sell it at all; for, after Thursday, people were afraid to leave the village. In the meantime I took possession of my house, and sent for a carpenter to make shutters for the windows, in order to bring thither with safety the goods I had left in Mrs. Felman's care. I had only a rough shake-down for a bed, a chair or two, and a rough table, for, in the unsettled state of things and in the absence of my waggons, I did not care to go to any expense; indeed, could not have done so without incurring debt.

The dreaded Thursday came and passed quietly. I had gone to bed, when, at about eleven o'clock, I heard a tap at my window, and the voice of my next neighbour calling me. I got up and opened the door.

"I hope I did not frighten you," he began, in the usual formula, "but I have just had news that the Boers are coming in tonight;" and he told his story.

His great point was that the band-master's wife, whom he knew, and whom he had been to visit, was sitting up, expecting the signal to be given to go into camp for protection, and that she had told him that the colonel's wife was doing the same. He said that the Boers were coming over the hill singly or in small parties, to avoid detection, and were to form at a given spot and attack the town; that all sorts of preparations were being secretly made, and that the signal for going into camp was to be a bugle call.

I thought the whole story sounded odd, particularly the bugle call as a signal.

"It is odd that no notice has been given publicly of the likelihood of an attack, and of the signal to seek protection in camp," said I.

"That is because there are so many traitors about," was the answer.

My neighbour was deeply impressed evidently, and I thought it best to take some precautions; so I waked Soldat and Clara, told Clara to put a few things together for herself and for me, in case of our having to run for it, and then dressing myself, I started to walk down the village to old Mrs. Parker's cottage, for I knew that she was likely to be alone, her sons being in the country, and I thought I might be able to be of use to her in case of a sudden alarm. I told Soldat that, as soon as the bugle sounded, he was to saddle the horses and bring them, down sharp to her cottage, after leaving Clara with my neighbour's family to be taken into camp with them. My oxen were all *kraaled* in Mr. Felman's *kraal*, so nothing could be done about them.

It was a beautiful moonlight night, by no means a favourable night for a surprise, and I knew it to be against the usual tactics of Boers to attack at night at all; and as I stepped out I felt pretty sure that there was some mistake. As I passed my neighbour's cottage I saw lights inside, and through the open door I was aware of some commotion.

I had not gone far when I saw two orderlies with a saddled horse at the door of a cottage. I thought I might as well inquire of them if they knew of any report as to the Boer attack. They said that they had heard of nothing, but that in another minute Captain C—— would be coming out, and that he would be able to tell me. I waited accordingly. There was no special report as to an attack, only the possibility of such an event caused a certain anxiety. The officer was just on his way to visit the outposts, and seemed much amused at the idea that a bugle call had been suggested as an improvement on the three cannon shots always fired as a signal of danger, whereupon I went back and to bed.

The next day I heard that Mrs. Parker's sons had come in. The village was in a state of suppressed panic; but as I had a good deal to do in the matter of setting my garden in order, I went out but little the next day or Saturday, when at last my waggons came in late in the evening. They brought bad news. A good deal of the corn I had left at Makapan's-poort had been damaged by the floods of rain that had fallen there. Hendrick had traded grain and cattle, but on coming to the Pinaars River had found it impossible to cross it with heavily loaded waggons, or with loose cattle. He had therefore waited for it to run down, until he had been told by the Boers that if he did not get the waggons into Pretoria by Saturday, they would seize them and the oxen. He had then left the cattle and part of the loads behind with some *kaffirs*, and had swum the oxen through, the loads getting partly wet. It was a comfort that the oxen were in splendid condition, but a terrible disappointment otherwise.

The next day, Sunday, I spent writing, when, towards evening, Hendrick, who had been "on the spree," as is the custom with drivers in general when they come off a long trek, rushed up to me in a state of wild excitement. The Boers were coming in—the market square was being fortified—rifles were being given out—we should all be massacred that night—the danger for the half-castes and *kaffirs* serving in Pretoria was even greater than for the English—they must all have rifles, &c., &c. He quite took my breath away, but then I saw he had been drinking, although he was not absolutely drunk.

I ordered Eclipse to be saddled, and rode into the village, taking Hendrick with me on foot. My house lies at the outskirts, near to the camp; but I was soon close to the market-square. Then I saw that Hendrick had not exaggerated. Crowds of *kaffirs*, superintended by an engineer officer, were hastily throwing up earthworks round the church in the centre, whilst a mass of frantically excited white men

469

and lads of all ranks, was rushing after and crushing round a cart laden with rifles, that was being driven through it to the place appointed for distributing them.

It was with difficulty that I made my way through, and learned from an acquaintance that no rifles were to be given to the coloured population, till all the white population had been provided. The rifles in the cart were not nearly sufficient for those who crowded round it, so it was not worth while staying. I turned into the square, and approaching the little group of officers, waited till the one in command was at liberty. I then asked him whether it was true that an attack was expected that night. He said that there was reason to believe that such would be the case; and I then inquired what provision had been made for the protection of the horses and oxen belonging to people in the town.

"Where are you going for refuge?" he asked, disregarding my question.

"I was not asking about protection for myself, but for my oxen and horses," I answered.

"But what ward are you in?" he asked.

I said I did not know, but that my house was near the camp common.

"Well, then, you had better go to the convent," he said.

"I shall remain at my own house," I answered. "What I want to know is, whether any place of comparative safety has been appointed for the oxen in the town. I have three valuable spans; I don't want to lose them."

"Oh!" he exclaimed, "have you any waggons? "

Yes—three."

"I am greatly in want of waggons for barricading," he went on eagerly. "The best thing you can do is to bring them up here to me."

"But the oxen?" I remarked.

"I think," he answered, "the best plan for them would just be to let them loose in the square."

"Between the barricades and the earthworks?" I said, "just let them go loose?"

"Yes," was the reply.

I thanked him very politely, and rode off, thinking to myself how singularly beneficial to all parties it would be to have thirty-eight oxen, maddened with fear, rushing about a small square that was being desperately defended; unless, indeed, one looked upon the arrangement from a Boer point of view.

When the waggons were mentioned I had glanced in the direction of my old waggon, which I had left at the auctioneer's. It was gone; and the next day I discovered it in the barricade of one of the streets approaching the market-square, from whence, of course, I was not allowed to remove it

Having been unable to get any information from the engineer officer, I cantered quickly towards the camp to try to find Colonel Gildea, for it seemed almost impossible to me that some plan for protecting the large numbers of oxen and horses belonging to people in the village had not been devised, considering that in case of a siege of even a few days' length, such a provision was of the greatest public importance.

On my way across the common I met Mr; Hudson, the Colonial Secretary, hurrying down to the village on foot, behind a hand-cart drawn by *kaffirs*, and full of rifles. He told me that Colonel Gildea was not in camp; he did not know where he was, but as to the oxen, he said there was no place set apart for them; that he thought the best thing I could do was to let them run about the town loose that night. As this idea seemed inadmissible to me, I asked him whether, in case of an attack, the fire from the guns at the camp was likely to be directed so as to injure my house, which I pointed out to him. He said he thought it was in a safe position; so I determined to keep my oxen with me.

I had, since the arrival of my waggons, brought my other oxen from the Felmans' *kraal*, and let all the spans feed together; so now I had them all tied to the yokes inside the *erf*, barricaded the entrance to it with the two waggons, made my boys sleep close to the stable and the oxen, and determined to sit up myself.

The streets, by the time I was returning from the common to my house, were full of people wending their way to the various places of refuge; men with rifles on their shoulders, going off on patrol; women and girls carrying hastily-made-up bundles, mattresses, and infants, and dragging little children after them. There was no attack, but the morning brought the news of the massacre of the 94th; and the panic and excitement increased.

I managed that day to get old muzzle-loading rifles for my boys from the Ordnance Department; and, as I was riding back from camp, I saw a commissariat officer superintending the moving of stores into camp, in preparation for the siege which was now undoubtedly imminent.

There was evidently a great deficiency of waggons to convey all the stores, and yet haste was imperative, for the news that the Boers were close by was expected at any moment. All coloured men seen in the streets were being seized; horses, waggons, and oxen also. Now I had been revolving in my mind whether or not I would save my property by a trick. My waggons I did not think of moving, but my oxen were all grazing far out of the village. I had only to mount little Hendrick on Dandy, and with him as my companion ride out to them, drive them through a *poort* at some little distance, and not much under observation, and get them away to my farm. I knew pretty surely that what Durks and other Boers had told me was true—there was but little danger of the Boers robbing me, unless in some case of necessity; and should I meet the commando, I had little doubt that by speaking fair I could induce the commander to let me pass, even if I could not wheedle him out of a safe-conduct, which I deemed it very probable I should be able to manage.

It was a temptation to do this, not only on account of my own pecuniary advantage, but because I am very fond of my animals; and I thought it likely that they would get hard usage in government employ; but on the other hand it seemed, and seems to me, that when matters have been brought to the war-test in any country in which one happens to be residing, one is bound in honour to side distinctly with either one or the other of the combatants. On general principles I believed, and believe, that a vindication of British authority in the Transvaal would benefit, or rather would have benefitted the majority of its inhabitants; and hence I determined not to ask favours from the Boers, but to do all that lay in my small sphere of action to help the side that I felt was the one I ought to wish to win. I therefore, of my own accord, offered my waggons and oxen to the officer in question. He gladly accepted the offer, telling me that he should like to have the waggons and spans in an hour's time; and I sent out for my poor oxen, and by the given time had delivered them and their drivers and foreloopers over to the government.

I did not know that such would be the case at the time, but by doing so I gained several advantages which, had I not come forward in this manner, I should have missed. And as I am on the subject of my animals, I may as well say that I succeeded in saving my horses from being seized for mounting the so-called volunteers, by offering them to the government for a special service—which service, as matters turned out, was never required of them.

Everything was now confusion. The streets were full of waggons, *kaffirs*, half-castes, and white people, intermingled here and there with officers, orderlies, or volunteers on horseback. In every house the women were busy packing up, unless they were stupefied with fear, as they were in some cases. Arrests were being made every now and then on charges of conspiracy with the enemy, which were in some cases I know of made very lightly, although the suspicion may have been strong. Numbers of farmers from the immediate vicinity of Pretoria had come in with their families for protection, and swelled the already thick ranks of the emigrant population. I rode to the Felmans, and found them in a state of distraction. I had meant to speak about my goods, but it was impossible to obtain a hearing.

On Tuesday the order circulated that all the inhabitants were to go into camp, and we were also told that all those who adhered to the loyal cause should receive full compensation for any loss they might receive from so doing. I hastened to the Commissariat Yard, to see if I could get Major W——, who was in command, to let me have back my large tent-waggon. He was not there, but as I was riding away I heard a horse's gallop behind me, and turning saw him. He said he had seen me, and guessed what I wanted, so had followed me, and we cantered to where the waggons were working, and he gave me the order I required. The oxen were to be sent to him again the next day.

Once more I loaded up, not leaving anything in the house, and just as the oxen were inspanned, we heard the report of a cannon. Oh! the terror of those boys of mine! The Boers were upon us! We should not be in time to get into camp! All the roads to the camp were crammed with ox-waggons being hurried along, with mule-waggons dashing along, with people on foot, women, little children, some carrying a bundle, some a mattress, or a chair, some pulling a hand-cart piled up with articles hastily snatched from their dwellings; and all this in mud, and with the thunder growling overhead. Suddenly a rattling peal came through the *poort* near the camp, and a cloud of thick rain driven by the wind came sweeping towards us from it.

"The Boers! look at the smoke of the firing!" cried the boys.

But soon a torrent of rain showed them their mistake. Through this pelting shower I, and the rest of the Pretorian wanderers, made our way to headquarters, and were there told what? —That there had been a mistake as to our going into camp that day, that the camp was not ready to receive us, that we must go back and return the next day.

So all the poor women and little children, who had toiled up through the mud and wet, had to toil back again to the homes they had dismantled. It was a sad procession to look at. That evening, I, as having but little to move, a horse to ride, and last, not least, no little children, wet, cold, and tired, to console and feel anxious about, was probably the happiest person in Pretoria.

The next day we all fairly went into camp and prepared for the siege.

Chapter 31

Anyone who has paid me the compliment of reading this story of my adventures will, perhaps, remember that in the earlier chapters I mentioned that I was writing in the besieged camp of Pretoria; and, indeed, the principal part of my book was written there, partly with a view of recording facts which might prove interesting, and possibly instructive, to a few, and partly to while away the time. I am finishing the story when the war, of which the siege formed a small episode, is a thing of the past a past which, if I do not mistake, will have an important influence on numbers to whom the Transvaal is, and will remain, utterly unknown, except as a small part of Africa, which gave rise to a peculiar exhibition of political incapacity on the part of those who sway the British nation at the present time, and have swayed it for some time past. Our colonial policy is not a thing of to-day, nor are the ideas which have had their outcome in a convention—which, if it has not pleased, has certainly astonished everybody—ideas of sudden growth.

Before attempting to describe the life we led in camp, I must try and describe the camp itself. Although I talk of *the* camp, there were in reality three camps on the hill above Pretoria, exclusive of the camps formed in the convent, and in the prison within the village, of which I knew little. On the hill there was the military camp, which, although composed in great part of civilians, was called military, partly, I fancy, because most of the able-bodied men attached to families quartered in it were either members of the mounted volunteers, or in what was called the Reserve Force, and principally because it was circumscribed by the military lines. At a short distance from this, there was what was called the civil camp, the able-bodied men in which belonged to no corps, but had to do picket-duty; and at some distance from it, higher up on the hill, was a camp inhabited by coloured people.

Just below the military camp was the great *kraal* where the cows and slaughter cattle were kept at night, and a little above it was the so-called government *kraal*, made of waggons impressed by the government, or belonging to them, in which the government oxen, and all the impressed trek oxen but mine, and one span belonging to my old acquaintance, Mr. Brown, of Rustemberg, were kept. I may here mention that Mr. Brown had come on business to Pretoria, where his waggon and oxen had been impressed, and he himself stopped, whilst poor Mrs. Brown was left in Rustemberg. His oxen and mine were the only spans that had their own drivers and foreloopers, and hence they were kept separate from the others, and were always tied to the yokes of the waggons they served with, instead of being *kraaled*, which was a great advantage.

The native camp was composed of tents pitched round an old hut or two, and from its position it certainly struck me very forcibly that it was very possible for continual communication to be kept up between it and the insurgents. It is an absolute fact that their leaders knew most of our movements, and as it certainly was impossible for any doubt to exist that, if so inclined, a *kaffir* could any night have slipped in and out of the camp without being observed by the outposts, I have very little doubt that such communication took place.

The civil camp was composed of waggons with awnings, or side-tents made to them with buck-sails or other canvas; of tents, and of a few little canvas houses, although these last were only erected a week or so after the siege commenced. Some of these had boards put down for the floors, and were in some cases divided into rooms.

The military camp consisted of all these elements, and besides of the ordinary soldier's bungalows (long, low, stone buildings), and of other so-called bungalows, made of wooden framework with canvas drawn over it. All of these bungalows were given up to accommodating the women and children who could not be accommodated with tents, or who had no waggons of their own in the military camp; and the beds in them were almost touching each other. Every night the women and children of the civil camp had to come up to one or other of these bungalows to sleep, so as for them to be within the military lines in case of attack; and wretched work, indeed, it was for the poor things on wet evenings and mornings.

The first evening that the order came out, it happened to rain, and to continue raining all night. At the last moment it was found that there was not sufficient accommodation for all of them. Some, after standing in the wet, were obliged to paddle back through the running water to the civil camp, others got into tents not yet properly protected by trenches from the rain, and I saw them in the damp morning shivering with cold, their bedding, which they had had to bring with them, soaked through, and the floor of the tent one big puddle.

On the whole, however, I think, considering all things, the camp was well managed as far as the comfort and health of its inmates were concerned. With a number of people all crammed together in a confined space, discomfort is, of course, unavoidable; and the discomfort naturally tends to cause irritation between the members of the community. I had my own waggon in the military camp, and made a comfortable side-tent to it, and had besides the advantage of having my waggon at the end of a line of waggons facing a main road through the camp, so that I was not subject to the same annoyances as most of my neighbours.

A most miserable sight was that camp, early on a rainy morning, when I would be coming back from the lines where the horses were picketed, with my waterproof over me, and the water running, very likely, over my boots. Women of various ranks emerging from their tents, or from their waggons, slipping in the mud, or plashing into the water so soon as they stepped on the ground; making their coffee, or preparing the breakfast over the little fire some shivering *kaffir* was trying to blow into a blaze, while a little child, perhaps, held on to them and cried, or bewailed itself from within the tent. In many cases numbers of people were stowed away in one waggon, and both in these waggons and in the bungalows ablutions had to be very much restricted, and many people both looked and were very dirty.

Against this picture I may set that of a fine evening, after the band had ceased playing. Then all the various habitations were alight, and one caught glimpses of illuminated interiors, with dashes of bright colour in them, arranged in long *vistas*. The camp-fires burnt cheerily, and one heard nothing but merry voices and laughter from the groups of coloured people assembled round them and from the promenaders, whilst here and there a gay party would be assembled, and one would hear snatches of song—and even, in one bungalow, the sound of a piano.

Of course there was an unlimited amount of scandal and gossip of all sorts, and of course there was also an unlimited amount of squabbling, more or less serious, varying from the quarrel between Mrs. A—— and Mrs. B——, which raged femininely and furiously, but nevertheless privately, to the noisy vociferation between another pair of ladies, which woke the neighbours from their slumbers for some fifty yards around the scene of warfare. Besides these quarrels there were, of course, occasional rows between the inhabitants of the bungalow where the less aristocratic members of society were accommodated, which took the form of unparliamentary language, and which, when human patience (in the shape of the sentry on guard) could endure it no longer, had to be suppressed by the master of the ward.

These ward-masters had a hard time of it, I fear. They were civilians, appointed over different blocks of the camp, to see that the orders issued from headquarters were observed, and to be general referees on disputed matters. The smoke grievance, which was perpetually recurring, must have caused many of these persecuted mortals to become prematurely grey. It was a general conviction of the camp-mind that the owner of a fire could prevent the smoke from the said fire drifting into his neighbours' nostrils. This peculiar mental epidemic was not peculiar to females. Many a time an indignant head of the family would exclaim, appealing to his particular ward-master, "It is outrageous. I cannot allow the ladies of my family to be inconvenienced in this manner."

And then, if the bewildered official shrugged his shoulders in despair, an appeal would be made to the camp-quartermaster. This office was held by a youthful officer, who, I think, had a quiet enjoyment of a joke—a young officer who, although he never in my presence did wear them, always impressed me with the idea that he wore pale kid gloves—a young officer who never appeared to be in a hurry, although he worked hard, and who (as I learnt from many a conversation) had a singularly exasperating effect upon minds excited by the influences of camp-life. I remember seeing this young gentleman seized upon in his tent by an infuriated neighbour of mine, and carried off to decide a smoke dispute between her and an equally impassioned neighbour of hers.

"The smoke of that lady's fire absolutely suffocates us," cried the one.

"I declare I can't endure *her* smoke any longer," retorted the accused. "You really must do something to alter this state of things, Mr. H——."

But it was not only on the subject of smoke that the camp-quartermaster was assailed. Once, when he was speaking to someone just in front of my tent, a well-dressed woman rushed at him, exclaiming,

"Mr. H——, I want some soap. Where can I get it?"

I must give credit to the ward-masters for keeping their wards very fairly clean. There was one ward in particular which was particularly nicely kept, but of which the ward-master was of course particularly obnoxious.

Then there was the light grievance. At first all lights had to be out at nine, but the hour was advanced to ten. Of course there were refractory spirits who would not put out their lights, if only to show their free and independent spirit.

"Put it out now, ma'am," I have heard the soldier who went the rounds say. "You can light it again after I'm gone."

But then sometimes the ward-master or the quartermaster was inconveniently active, and one was caught, as I was once, and had my candle ordered out, interrupting me in a species of hunt attended with much anxiety in camp, *viz.*, the flea-hunt! If the camp was not a paradise for man and beasts, it certainly was for fleas and flies. Not but that there were many human beings who enjoyed the camp thoroughly. I have heard more than one girl and child aver it would be "nice" to have it over again. There were lots of flirting and lots of playing to be had. Every day was a holiday to the children, who swarmed to the gates of the camp to see the volunteers, the soldiers, and the cannon go out, as if they were going on parade—who swarmed there too, I am sorry to say, in a state of half-amused, half -frightened excitement, to see the wounded men and horses come in. They became wonderfully knowing did those children.

"Hark to the boom of the gun," I said to a little girl, as we were watching the engagement at Henning Pretorius's camp; "do you see the smoke?"

"That is not firing," replied the little wretch, quite confidently. "That is dynamite. They must have got to the *laager*, and be blowing it up."

One great event every day was the getting the rations at the booth appointed for the purpose in each ward. It was a frightfully tedious affair, and a most grotesque picture did it offer. Old and young—men and women—*kaffirs* with the name of their employer written on a piece of paper, either in their hands or fastened on to them, some carrying baskets, some dishes, cups, all sorts of things; all crowding round the unfortunate men who had to serve out the rations. There was plenty of grumbling, and also plenty of joking. One old farmer of the name of Cockcroft, who had been in the camp at Durban when the

Boers besieged it, had a standing joke with me when anyone grumbled about the meat being bad or the rations being small.

"They'll be glad to come to dine with us presently," he would say, chuckling. "I'm glad you've got that leather fore-tow. It'll make good soup yet."

He remembered eating soup made of the same ingredient, just before relief came to that gallant little band in Natal.

Mr. Cockcroft was a very fine old fellow, and very touching it was to see him leading his blind wife. They had lately bought a fine farm not far from Pretoria. They had worked hard and had got on well, and had invested their earnings in it. Their son was in the volunteers—a hard-working young farmer. When we were listening to the firing from Swartkopjee, two officers rode up to where he was standing near to me.

"Heavy firing, Mr. Cockcroft," said one of them, "I'm afraid there won't be much of your house left; they must be just close to it."

"Let it go," cried the old man, with kindling eyes; "if only it gives some shelter first to our poor fellows."

"Ah!" exclaimed one of the officers, "that's the right sort of spirit, Mr. Cockcroft."

Yet this gallant old farmer is now a ruined man.

As time went on, little concerts, bazaars, and theatrical entertainments were got up in camp—open-air performances of course—and there was a little camp newspaper. The band of the 21st played every evening, except, indeed, for some while after the disastrous fight at the Red House, for then there were many dangerously wounded, and it was thought that the noise would disturb them. There were invitations to dinner also occasionally, and on one occasion there was a grand birthday festival given by a certain old gentleman, who, on rising to make his speech returning thanks, remarked, "Little did I think this night sixty-two years ago, when I was born, that I should live to see," &c., &c., thereby, of course, bringing down the house.

My time was taken up in a routine, of which the following is the outline. I got up at dawn, and went to see the horses fed, and then walked to the government *kraal*, to see how the oxen were. Early coffee. Went to fetch the rations (for by going myself, instead of sending a boy, I got better rations); then breakfast; afterwards rode down to the village and let the horses graze, while I generally lay on the grass and either worked or did nothing, except when I would take pen and paper with me, and write some of this history. Home to dinner at about five; looked to the horses being settled for the night, inspected the oxen; then paid visits.

There was a great gathering of people from all parts in the camp. Mrs. Parker and Mrs. Farquason had waggons not far from mine; so had the young farmer and his wife on whose farm I had been outspanned before I went to the *bush-veldt*. The Robert Higginses had a waggon and a little house in the civil camp, which was shared by old Mr. Higgins and his family. Next to them was old Mr. Sturton, with his wife and his unmarried children. Alice Higgins had been married before the war, and had been at Potchefstrom, but had escaped thence to the Cape Colony. John Higgins and his family had gone also, but James had been stopped, and was a sort of prisoner at Fahl-plas.

Arthur and William Sturton, and also Mr. King, had been seized by the Boers on their way into Pretoria, and carried back to their farms. I may here say that when, at the end of the war, we learnt what had been happening to them, we were relieved to find that they had been well treated; but in the meantime the anxiety about them was very great, although after two months of suspense a *kaffir* managed to get through to them and then back to us, and brought us word that they were well; brought us word also, alas! that every head of cattle, every sheep, all ripe crops, all fruit, had been swept from both Surprise and Moy-plas, whilst in the case of the latter, every article of furniture had been seized, and the whole place laid desolate.

Robert Higgins and old Mr. Sturton were both obnoxious to the Boers. Half of my sheep, too, were reported as being gone. My old friends Sam and Dick had been impressed by government, and poor Sam lost his life at the fight at the Red House. Wellington was impressed also, as indeed all the horses in Pretoria but mine were. He was always ridden by whoever was in command of the Pretoria Carabineers; and, strange to say, Captain D'Arcy was wounded severely, and Captain Sanctuary mortally, whilst riding him, whilst he was only slightly grazed.

The weather was very stormy, and children and delicate people suffered severely. Many a coffin was taken down in a cart to the little graveyard with a few mourners walking after it; a few flowers plucked from some deserted garden strewn on it. Poor, inglorious martyrs, sacrificed for nothing! The number of deaths was at last so great that there was difficulty in obtaining planks for the coffins, and those earthworks in which wood had been used as a support, had to be demolished to supply what was necessary, the earthworks, being replaced by brick walls. I never thought the village of Pretoria so pretty as I did when riding through its deserted streets, in which the grass grew knee-high, until cut for hay for the horses in camp, whilst the neglected gardens bloomed in glorious luxuriance.

The Felmans' *erf* was now beautiful to behold, the thick luscious green herbage covering up all signs of former disorder and dirt. The stores were all closed, the streets almost deserted. Sometimes I came across the government horses and mules, sent out to graze under guard; and sometimes a few dropping shots would be heard, and they would be hastily collected and brought near to camp for fear of some sudden raid. On the hills around, the cattle were pastured under the surveillance of a guard, and they too were often to be seen hurrying home for fear of capture. Sometimes a storekeeper would obtain permission to leave the camp (all men had to obtain passes), and would half open his store for a few hours; then the place would be thronged by people, mostly women.

By order of the government, mule-waggons plied between the camp and the village three times a day. I never tried them, having my horses; but I heard that those who drove in them suffered excruciating torture, owing to their being springless. Sometimes Mrs. Parker used to visit her pretty cottage (it looked so sad to see it deserted), and then she used to ask me to a picnic there. Once when I was at my own *erf*, and the horses grazing quietly near me, I was a spectator of a small engagement quite close to the village. A party had been sent out as an escort to a mowing-machine. The Boers made a raid, reinforcements were sent out to our men, but the Boers had the best of it. They captured the mowing-machine!

There was great demoralisation among all the coloured people in camp. Very stringent orders had been issued against any violence being used to them, and the upshot of this was that they became very insolent, and that their masters and mistresses were afraid of punishing them. I openly punished a leader of mine more than once for neglecting my oxen, and was not interfered with, and I must say that my servants were better than most in camp; but I everywhere heard complaints, and saw myself that some very bad influence was at work among the coloured people. The drunkenness among them was very great, and this while civilians, not volunteers, could not obtain wine or spirits unless they got a special order from the provost marshal on a particular store, or an order from the doctor.

Of course it was supposed to be the rule that no liquor at all was sold to coloured people, unless they presented a written order from their employers, and the requisite order from the provost marshal as well; but the rule was openly and constantly disregarded, whilst the storekeepers were obliged to be very strict with white people. For instance, I once wanted some Pontac wine, so I went to the provost marshal and asked for an order. He asked me what wine I wanted, what number of bottles I wanted, and at what store I was going to buy the wine. I told him, and he wrote out the order, and I went to the store; then it turned out that at this particular store there was no Pontac, so my order was of no use. In the meantime my groom often got enough liquor to get drunk upon. The fact about the coloured population was, I believe, this. The authorities were afraid of them, and winked at their sins. The immense number of them in camp helped the general demoralization, and there were doubtless many messages sent backwards and forwards between the Boers and their secret friends in camp, by means of these people.

One day my driver "boy" told me that a friend of his had come in from Waterberg, and had brought word that Mapeela had broken out and had driven off numbers of the Boers' cattle, had also put all the women and children of the Boers in that part of the country into a sort of *laager*, and had provided for them, saying, that he would show his respect for the English by treating them well; but had dragged a man, whom he had found hiding among them, outside the *laager*, and killed him then and there. It seemed odd to me to think of this self-same Mapeela sitting by my waggon in his smart dress a short time previously. I heard afterwards that the Boers in part of Waterberg had cruelly ill-used unoffending *kaffirs* during the war, and this I learnt from the Landrost of Nilstrom, who came into Pretoria after the war was over. He told me he had seen them seize a *kaffir*, tie him up, and give him fifty lashes on his bare back for no fault.

On Thursday, the 6th of January, the first sortie from the camp took place. This was the occasion when the fighting occurred near Mr. Cockcroft's farm. The troops and volunteers went out long before dawn: we heard the firing early in the morning. This was our one successful engagement. In the afternoon the wounded and the prisoners were brought in. We had four killed. The prisoners were all Waterberg men, but I was glad to learn that none of my old acquaintances were among them. Their leader, who was severely wounded, and a prisoner, caused a good deal of, not very creditable, nonsense, as it seemed to me, to be talked in camp.

I believe it is true that he had allowed his men to fire under a flag of truce, still I think it would have been better, had there been no talk as to the desirability of curing him of his wounds in order to hang him afterwards. This was, of course, purely unofficial talk, but it was argued that as, according to the proclamation of the government these men were rebels, and as he, as chief, had allowed the white flag to be violated, it was evident that he must be hung, and I regret to say many who spoke thus seemed to hope he might be so treated. Now began the piteous sight of women, watching with pale, anxious faces, to catch the last glimpse of their dear ones, as they rode out in either the Pretoria Carabineers, or Nourse's Horse; hastening from point to point to see the last of their re treating figures, gazing with aching eyes and hearts at the little column until it was lost to sight, and then going back with pinched faces to their waggons and tents, to wait to hear the first gun, and so to wear away the day until the first few rode in to tell the fortune of the warfare.

I used to admire those women! There was no ostentatious anxiety or grief, but you would see their poor trembling lips, and nervously clasped hands, and eyes strained bravely to try to keep back their tears, as they hastened to where they could get tidings of those who might perhaps be destined never to return, or to return only to die. On Friday the funerals of those who had lost their lives cast a gloom over all, still we had been successful, and that was something. Two of Mrs. Parker's sons were in the Pretoria Carabineers as officers, and one was slightly injured in this engagement. Mrs. Farquason's husband was also an officer in this corps.

This was the only success we had. There were other small sorties without any engagement taking place, between the 6th and the 16th of January, when an attack was made on Henning Pretorius's camp, situated on the *randt* within view of our camp. An attempt was made to distract the attention of the Boers by exploding dynamite in an opposite direction, and the ruse partially succeeded; but after some heavy firing, which was watched with intense interest from our camp, we were obliged to retreat. While almost all our available men were absent, there was a sudden alarm that a body of Boers were advancing to attack the camp from the side opposite to Henning Pretorius's position. A shot or two from our guns caused them, however, to retire. On the return of our men we heard that two wounded men had been left in the hands of the Boers, and great dissatisfaction was expressed by the volunteers as to the management of the whole affair. The next day a *kaffir* brought a flag of truce from the Boer camp, to say that we ought to send an ambulance for these two wounded men. This *kaffir* said that Henning Pretorius was severely wounded, and that about thirty Boers had been killed.

With regard to the dissatisfaction of the volunteers, I may say that it increased as time went on, and that, so far as I know, the regular troops were dissatisfied also; and I think, from what I heard and observed, they had reason on their side. The volunteers said that they were sent on far in front of the guns and troops, riding in file, and were never properly supported, besides being often employed in work unsuited to their capacities; for that it was useless to try to take a lager with irregular or regular cavalry. The troops complained that they were shown off to disadvantage, being kept back from being engaged, and not receiving orders as to what they were to do. This particularly applies to the disastrous sortie on Saturday, the 12th of February.

Early in the morning of that day I heard sounds among the horses, indicating that there was going to be a move, and presently I heard the tramp and clank of the horses being harnessed to the guns; then that of the volunteers riding past my tent to headquarters. I got up and looked out. There they went—tramp, tramp, through the dark; and, as I looked at them, I felt one of those presentiments of evil, which may or may not be true, but which nevertheless affect one painfully at times. This was a large sortie, and was supposed to be a very secret one; but all the time the Boers knew all that we were planning. Colonel Gildea was in command. Captain Sanctuary, mounted on Wellington, rode at the head of the Pretoria Carabineers for the last time. I give my account of the action from what I was told by a volunteer officer who was present, and I have had corroboration of what I say from others. The Boers were quite prepared for us. Colonel Gildea was wounded early in the action; the second in command lost his head. The volunteers, pushed on in front as usual, were exposed to a galling fire from the Boers, whilst the troops and guns remained aloof, and took no part in the engagement.

Captain Sanctuary was shot through the leg, and Mr. Mackenzie Walker took command. His men were wavering; the only orders he could get from the officer who had taken Colonel Gildea's place was an exclamation,—

"Oh! what a —— mess we are in!" and then "Retire."

But Mr. Walker rallied his men to keep the Boers in check, and to try to save the ambulance, behind which the doctors were dressing Captain Sanctuary's wound. He pointed out to the commanding officer, that if they retired the ambulance would be taken; it was of no use, so, on his own responsibility, Mr. Walker formed his men, and tried to rescue the ambulance.

As he passed some infantry, he exclaimed, "Good God! why don't you fire?"

"We have no orders, sir," answered one of the men.

Captain Sanctuary's wound was not yet dressed; the troops were retiring; the Boers cutting the volunteers off from the main body.

"Better put him in," cried Walker, "and let us try to save him and the rest;" for there were other wounded.

No, the doctor thought he would finish the dressing first; and in despair Mr. Walker had to retire and leave the ambulance, the wounded, and the doctors. One of the Boers levelled his rifle at a man in attendance on it.

"For shame," cried the latter; "do you fire on the hospital?"

But fire he did, and killed the man; another shot at the ambulance wounded a man already wounded, who lay in it. In the meantime the volunteers, having protected the retreat of the troops, retreated themselves. They found a mule-waggon deserted on the road by the troops who had been in it. One of the mules was killed; the men had jumped off and fled, so the volunteers cut the dead mule loose, and one of them drove the waggon into camp, or it, too, would have fallen a prey.

When the news of this defeat came into camp, great was the grief and dismay. The greatest sufferer was an old Boer lady; her only son was the man wounded a second time while in the ambulance, and left a prisoner among his enemies; his father, a Boer from the old colony and a faithful English subject, was very obnoxious to the Transvaal Boers. The name of the wounded man was Desiderius (commonly called Deesy) Erasmus. He was one of a large family—the youngest, and the only boy, and was the darling of his sisters, and the very apple of his father and mother's eye. A fine, young fellow, broad shouldered and strong, but a mere boy in years and in innocence. His father had gone to Colonel Gildea when Deesy had joined the corps, and had so besought him in the name of the boy's mother and his own, to place him in the reserve, that the colonel had at last consented; but the young fellow held firm.

"No, father," he said; "I have never disobeyed you or caused my mother grief before, but now I must do so; this is a matter of honour; not even for your sakes can I let myself be called a coward."

Nothing would move him, and so he rode out after Captain Sanctuary on that dark morning; now he was a prisoner, and doubly wounded, in the hands of his enemies. His mother and one of his sisters (the wife of Major Ferreira, who had gone to the Basuto war) went to Sir Owen Lanyon, and prayed to be sent to the Boer camp under a flag of truce to see him, and the administrator granted their petition, and placed a mule-waggon at their disposal. It was the act of a kind-hearted gentleman, but surely hardly an advisable act, particularly when the enemy had been openly styled rebels.

When the ladies arrived at the Boer outposts and told what they had come for, the message was sent up to headquarters, and presently some of the chief men came to them, and laughed at the idea of allowing them to see the boy; but the mother and sister would take no refusal; they wept and prayed, and besought these men, by all they held dear, to let them see their darling, and at last they prevailed. They were taken to where he lay, and all night long they nursed him in a tent, the Boer commander coming in occasionally, and asking if he could assist them in any way. Outside in camp, all was joy and festivity over their victory, and the captured ambulance.

In the morning the ladies returned to Pretoria, bringing a message, that if we wished for the prisoners to be given up, we must release the prisoners we had taken at our first engagement, and must agree to send back the ambulance to the Boers, after it had conveyed the wounded to our camp. And so it was.

The next day the prisoners were brought in, the Boers sending a slaughtered sheep along with them, which (I was told by one bred amongst them) was a covert insult; and all the Boer prisoners were released. One of them, going to Lydenburg, was fallen upon by *kaffirs*, and torn in pieces. There were many wounded, most of them were severely wounded. Captain Sanctuary's leg was despaired of, and Deesy Erasmus' life, besides that of others. He had received a wound (which grazed the stomach) through the body, besides one in his leg. At first he seemed to rally, but it was a false hope, and in a few days he passed away, conscious and calm to the last—nay, almost cheerful, although he knew he was dying.

One of his comrades, a Mr. Simpson, died the day before, an artilleryman had died before him, and Captain Sanctuary, after his leg being amputated, lingered to the 7th of March, and then followed his companions in arms. There was a profound feeling of sorrow through all the inhabitants of the camp on the day when the body of this kindly and gallant officer was borne, with military honours, to the little graveyard in the valley.

In the meantime we had had news of the reinforcements that were coming to relieve us, and we were counting the days until we should see Sir George Colley ride through Bobian-poort at the head of a victorious column. Some said one day, some said another, would be the likely one for the welcome sight to greet our eyes, but none doubted that we should see him.

On the fifteenth (Tuesday) we saw about twenty waggons, under escort, defile through a *poort* to the east of the camp, and crossing the valley, outspan on the opposite ridge, while a Boer, bearing a flag of truce, rode towards us. Colonel Gildea, who had only just risen from his bed, rode out to meet him in company with other officers. They brought back letters for the administrator, and a Dutch newspaper, printed in the Free State; and the rumour that our troops had been defeated, and that Sir George Colley was killed, flew from mouth to mouth. But many would not, could not, believe it, and I was one of these. It seemed too dreadful, too incredible, to believe, until official confirmation came. Alas! it came too soon. We were now put on half-rations, but still there was enough to eat.

There was an armistice now, and it was very dreary. I used to wonder how the administrator and some others could have the heart to play polo of an evening. The true state of affairs was not known generally, and all sorts of rumours were continually flying about; still, there was enough known to cause a great feeling of depression, though no one expected what followed.[1]

On the evening of Monday, the 28th of March, I was sitting in Mrs. Parker's waggon talking to her, when a girl rushed up, and told us hurriedly that three officers had just ridden in from Newcastle; that there had been a great battle, in which Sir Evelyn Wood had completely defeated the Boers, and that he and some of the Boer leaders would be in Pretoria the next day to discuss the terms of peace. Oh! I shall never forget that moment! To leap from the waggon and hasten to headquarters was but the work of an instant. Crowds were pouring towards the same goal. It was quite dark.

---

1. It was commonly reported that Sir George Colley's reason for pushing on, without waiting for reinforcements of cavalry, was that he believed the people in Pretoria to be starving; had, in fact, said to his officers that he knew he was about to make a desperate effort, but that when women and children were starving, men must not hold back.

Arrived in the square, we all waited breathlessly for the news to be proclaimed. The officers who had ridden in were with Colonel Gildea, the administrator, and Colonel Bellairs. We waited and waited, but no sign was given, and then I heard whispers that there had been no victory, that peace had been concluded on the terms dictated by the Boers, that the country was to be given back! It seemed incredible; but a chill struck through all those assembled, and they dispersed gradually and silently, to wait until the morning should bring them some distinct official information. How well I remember that morning! I woke early, as usual, but with a dull, listless feeling of impending misfortune. I had then no reason to believe that personally I should be a very heavy sufferer.

It was not for myself that I felt the bitter ache at my heart, it was for the honour of England, a thousand times worse than any pain caused by personal loss: the one I could retrieve by courage and steadiness, but it made me feel almost mad to think that I was powerless to move so much as a feather's weight to retrieve the other. I went as usual to see to the horses, and as I stroked their sleek necks I thought with a keen pain, almost amounting to agony, how glad, how really thankful *I* was that I had been able to win a reprieve for my pets from having been uselessly, and therefore cruelly sacrificed, while many a mother was being ground to the very dust by the crushing torment of knowing that her boy, whose life she had told herself in the midst of her woe was lost in upholding a cause she cherished, had in reality been sent forth, recklessly, wantonly, to swell the ranks of death. For what? For the *dishonour* of that cause.

A volunteer, an Englishman, one who had no stake whatever in the Transvaal, but who, happening to be in Pretoria, had joined Sanctuary's corps, spoke to me as I stood there. "So it has come to this," he said; "we have been fighting for nothing! The country is given back."

"It can't be true," I cried, although, after the dead silence at headquarters the previous night, I knew in my heart it was, "I won't believe it till I see it in general orders."

"It is there now," he answered; "young S—— has just seen it; he is almost mad. He was a rich man in his own belief yesterday; today he is little better than a beggar."

Yes, it was quite true. I went to see the oxen. I was luckier than most. By hard work and incessant watching them, so that I got for them every nibble of grass that was to be got while they were not working, by buying the stalks of mealies out of private gardens for them at an enormous price, by covering them with rugs if they seemed ill, I had brought most of them through, when other oxen working for government were dying in numbers! I was the luckiest person in camp, and I felt almost as if I were selfish as I walked through the lines of tents and waggons on my way back, thinking of the ruin that had fallen on almost all in them. I went to the Higginses' little shanty. They knew they were ruined. They tried to take it bravely, did take it bravely, but you saw that the knowledge struck home. They had staked all, on their faith in English trustworthiness.

They had believed implicitly in the repeated asseverations of the government that the Transvaal should remain British territory; they had broken utterly with the Boers, they had lost all their oxen and cows, all their sheep, all their crops, all but two of their horses, and they were destined henceforth to be subject to the men whom we, by our promises, had tempted them to turn from friendly neighbours into enemies. The Sturtons were close to them in their waggon and tent. It was the same with them, only worse. Their very house had been despoiled, and they were old—very old. But it is useless to particularize. Wherever you turned in that little camp you saw faces, heard voices that told you of ruin; sometimes the thought of *it* was patiently borne, but the thought of the disgrace, which seemed to have been thrust on them, roused the anger of these men and women.

"Look at those fellows," cried one old tradesman as two officers rode past; "look at them with their well-groomed horses and their dandy airs! It's all they're good for to look pretty. *We* wouldn't have disgraced ourselves."

"You'd better take off your coats," cried another, as he passed some other officers; "you're only carrying about the badge of your disgrace."

Even the *kaffirs* jeered at us. In the midst of all this, a large body of Boers were seen riding close past the camp. I was walking through the volunteers' lines as they did so. The excitement was great. Some cried out to muster and charge them, not to submit to the insult that was being thrust on them; some swore; others cried out that they cared for nothing now, but would go and get dead drunk. This excitement had hardly subsided when Henning Pretorius, Joubert (I think), and Hendrick Schumann rode up to headquarters, on their shaggy nags, then rode through the camp to greet old acquaintances. How proud those men must have felt that day, when the handsomely dressed gentlemen in military attire had to acknowledge them (whom they had termed, and unjustly termed, "rebels") their virtual conquerors.

It was of no use trying to hide the fact under the cloak of generosity; the Boers knew in their hearts that we should not have attempted to fight if there had been any generosity in the matter, and so did we all, and we both knew also, that we had found them a harder nut to crack than we expected, and that the government at home had considered the game not worth playing out. I knew Hendrick Schumann, but I could not, and would not greet him then; but I saw him meet his only sister and kiss her, and that was a pleasant sight even to my eyes. But it was not pleasant to see men who had truckled to the English, now truckling to them—and that I also saw.

The next morning, I determined to take my waggon out, and return to my house. The whole camp was breaking up. I rode through the streets of the village early in the morning. Groups of Boers were riding about, looking proud and contented, a little insolent, perhaps, but that was not to be wondered at. Numbers of Boer waggons laden with produce had come in to the market. I saw Hendrick Schumann standing by his waggon in the midst of a knot of Boers, so I went up and spoke to him.

"I am sorry for the peace," I said, "it is a disgrace to my country; but so far as my feelings towards you are concerned, I heartily congratulate you; you have fought well and have got your reward."

He took my hand. "What you say is true," he said, "and I thank you;" and his friends gave a united grunt.

The village now became a scene of disorder. The canteens opened, the whole population, black and white crowded into them, and things got worse instead of better the next day. For some reason, the coloured men who had been impressed by government were not immediately paid off. They wanted to get away to their families, but they had to wait, and in the meantime, having nothing else to do, they drank. The streets were full of howling, reeling wretches. All order seemed gone. Horses were stolen in the most daring manner. If one, with a saddle and bridle, were left for a moment, whilst his owner turned his back, as likely as not he would be seized and carried off in broad daylight.

Mr. Higgins, after getting back Wellington safe, nearly lost him thus; and would have lost him entirely, if, leaping on a horse without a saddle, that stood close by, he had not pursued and caught the robber. Others, less fortunate, lost their horses altogether. Numbers of families had to be sent to their desolated homes with government oxen—having lost all their own. Many would not go, knowing that, without oxen to plough their land, it was of no use going to their farms. Men met me who told me that they had seen whole teams or individuals of a team of their own oxen, marked with their brand, in Boer waggons, bringing produce to the market, but they could not claim them; one man even showed me the oxen he spoke of. I met men who seemed crushed by the disaster at every turn.

Mr. N——, the trader I had met at Andreas Mayepee's, with his young Boer wife, almost wept as he said, "It has been cruel to us cruel! If the country was to be given back after all the solemn oaths that it should for ever remain English, why go to war? Why force us who *must* live amongst the Boers to declare openly against them, or be disloyal? It is not only that we are ruined, it is our domestic happiness that has been destroyed. I am but one amongst numbers who have thrown up the ties of relationship, of old friendship, only to be cast off like an encumbrance. Numbers like me have turned love into hatred, have closed doors upon themselves which were ever open to them before." And what he said is true. Heavily as the destruction entailed by the peace has fallen on us English in the Transvaal, the real sufferer is the loyal Africander, and the loyal Boer.

"Our policy has robbed them not only of their property, but of their home, of even their country; and they, unlike us English, cannot face the thought of leaving the land they have been bred in, to cross the sea and carve out a home for themselves elsewhere, but, if they mean to gain a livelihood for themselves and their children, must bend their necks to the taunts which will be lavished by the Boers on those, who, having fought for and been discarded by the English, are now dependent on them. But the one person I dreaded seeing in Pretoria was Mrs. Erasmus. She had been a fine-looking old lady before Deesy died. Now she was bent, shrivelled with grief. I often saw her, but it was ever the same sad wail that I heard, and what could I, or anyone, say in answer to it? Oh! if only he had died for any purpose! Oh! I clung to the thought that I had given him for his country's sake! But he was sacrificed—murdered! Why should they have sent my boy to be killed for nothing?" His father wandered about silent, the decrepitude of grief stealing over him visibly.

Only once he spoke to me of his son's loss, when asking me to let my waggon and oxen take a simple tombstone to his grave. "I could bear it," he said; "but his mother; oh! his mother!" and he turned away.

Chapter 32

In this my concluding chapter I trust my readers will excuse me if I enter into some details as to the manner in which the war and its results affected me personally. The narrative will hardly be entertaining, but, as hundreds have been ruined in a very similar manner, it will afford an illustration of how the process has been carried out in the Transvaal generally.

Not long ago an officer who sat opposite to me at breakfast in an hotel, speaking of the ruin that had befallen numbers in that part of the world, asked me whether I had suffered severely, and on my reply in the affirmative, asked whether the Boers had looted largely? I told him that they had in some few cases, but that in my case, and in the case of the majority of the sufferers, ruin was not the result of being robbed; and he then stated that he could not conceive how this could be the case.

If anyone who reads my story is of the same way of thinking, perhaps the end of it may throw a little light on the question.

The animals impressed by government were all valued some time after they were impressed, and had been working hard, while their food was stinted; they had in consequence become thin. Even in the state they were in, the valuation fell very much under the real value of the animals in a number of cases; for this reason, no allowance was made in favour of salted animals. I cannot blame the government for this, for, as there is no absolutely distinctive mark left by lung-sickness, red water, or horse disease, to have attempted any such valuation would have been impossible.

In the case of lung-sickness, it is true, the tail of inoculated animals is often distorted or lost; but then animals who have the disease naturally do not suffer in this way; and in the case of the other two diseases, although people who study such matters can make a pretty good guess from the general appearance of the animal whether it is salted or not, still it is but a guess at best. Yet the fact of an ox or horse being salted produces a very large effect on its price, and real value. My oxen were known salted oxen, but they were valued as unsalted, and they were but a few amongst a great number of others similarly valued. The consequence of this was that most people, including myself, refused the valuation. It is true that I should under no circumstances have sold my oxen to government, for the government animals are very cruelly treated, and I am afraid there is no remedy in the matter; but in this I am an exception.

When the peace was declared, I, and others, applied to have our animals returned to us, and there was considerable delay in the matter of the oxen. We also applied for hire of them and the waggons. We were told that the government did not intend to adhere to English law in the matter, but to Roman Dutch law—the old law of the Transvaal; and that the question whether by it we were entitled to payment had been referred to the attorney-general for his decision. That decision was not given for almost three weeks after the declaration of peace. In my case, and no doubt in others, this was productive of evil; for my already thin oxen had to be kept in Pretoria until, the decision being given, I could leave the village. I wanted to take loads to Natal, and the winter was coming on apace, while owing to there being hardly any grass to be had near Pretoria the poor beasts were getting thinner daily.

If the government had given over the country to the Boers at once without reserve, the results of the peace would have fallen less heavily on us; but as it was, all of us knew that the Boers would never consent to any partition of the Transvaal. The Boers themselves said so openly, but, in the face of the terms of the Convention, everyone believed that England meant to retain a portion of it, and this we all knew meant a renewal of war, and an alliance between the Free-State and the Transvaal. This knowledge determined numbers, at great personal loss, to leave the Transvaal, if only for a time. My belief in this eventuality made me determine to risk taking my poor oxen to Natal with loads, rather than take them to Mr. Higgins's farm for the winter; my own farm would have been too cold for them in their impoverished state .

The belief that war was imminent was prevalent amongst the military as well as civilians, and was increased by its being known that the forts round Pretoria were being strengthened. The Boers, too, spoke of the great probability of war; and indeed what official intelligence we received breathed the same thought. All work was at a standstill in

Pretoria. All those who could were leaving the town. Owing to the uncertainty with regard to the settlement of the country all credit was at an end, and people were obliged to realize at a great loss in order to meet current expenses. Numbers of waggon-loads of goods had been stopped on the road. The loads that were coming up to me had been stopped and warehoused at Newcastle. I had to pay for their warehousing, and now they were coming up, at heavy rates, to be thrown on my hands, when there would be no market for them, and I should only have the choice of selling them for a quarter of their value, or warehousing them. The only things which were saleable in Pretoria, at a fair price, were horses and fat oxen, and of the latter the Boers brought in numbers; the value of everything else was wonderfully depreciated.

The auctions were crowded with articles for sale, but there were no buyers, for there was no money. I saw a cart which would have been cheap at thirty-five pounds sold for five; a handsome silver-mounted biscuit-box (it was real silver) sold for less than ten shillings; a very nice house with a large well-stocked garden, put up without reserve, and not a single bid made for it. There was absolutely no money in Pretoria. The shops were offering goods for cost price, to get rid of them without loss, for loads which had been stopped on the road during the war were now coming up to them, and the market was diminishing daily. The whole village was in a fearful state of demoralisation, and it was hard to keep one's boys in hand at all. I have had to go personally to force a boy away from a canteen, and as a rule they were all either half or quite drunk. Thieving too was going on to a great extent in the village, for, once outside it, the thief could defy the law, so that the temptation to rob and bolt was very great.

The Felmans' house had been, I heard, broken into during the siege; I wanted Mrs. Felman to go there with me then, and see whether any of my things had been taken, but she always made some excuse, and refused to let me have the key of the house to look. I had told her husband that if I was not allowed to investigate the matter in my own interest then, so as to be able to make an affidavit as to my loss and ask for compensation, I should be obliged to hold him responsible. At the end of the siege it turned out that all my property was gone, but it was of no use holding him responsible, for he was bankrupt.

Mr. Higgins had gone to Surprise, to see how things were there. He brought me back word that all my lambs were gone—dead or stolen; that seventy of my sheep, including all my wethers and my best

495

ewes, were stolen, some of them having been taken after peace was proclaimed, and that my ram was also gone,—poor Hans, too; and he said that the remaining ewes were in a pitiable condition from neglect. All his sheep were gone, so I asked him if he would care to buy mine cheap. He answered that he had no money. Mr. Sturton had lost his sheep, but he too had no money to buy any, and, indeed, was living in Pretoria in his waggon, unable to leave, for it would have been useless for him to go, without oxen, to his desolated farm.

It appeared that the Nell family had been rejoicing greatly over the discomfiture of the Higginses and had been purloining freely. So much for gratitude!

Added to this, a notice had been sent to Mr. Higgins from the neighbouring Boers, telling him that all his standing crops, and indeed everything he had, was confiscated to the Boer Government, and that he was held responsible for nothing being wanting until the sittings of the Conference should come to an end, when he would be communicated with. I saw the letter stating this myself. Mr. Higgins returned to Pretoria, and reported the matter to the administrator for the time, Colonel Bellairs. Hendrick Schumann heard of it, and declared, on the part of the Boer Government, that such a letter was utterly unauthorized; also that the seizure of my sheep was an act of violence not authorized by the Boer leaders; but in the meantime Mr. Higgins and I were the sufferers.

I sent a waggon to Jackallsfontein, to bring Jimmy up, and was delighted to find that he had been kindly treated, and that two oxen which I had left on the farm had been kept safe. Little Roughy, too, came up flourishing, but nothing remained of all the crops I had sown. Of course his host made a good penny out of his board, &c., but I was in no humour to haggle—only too glad to see him safe and sound.

Lo De Plessis came up to pay me a visit, and try to borrow some money, in which he failed; and the way he asked for different articles—sweets and snuff, &c.—to be bought as presents for him was very amusing. Jimmy and I gratified him in this. I knew of one case where a woman had been turned off her own farm by the Boers, under pain of being hung, and had had to walk forty miles into Pretoria, and I felt very grateful that Jimmy had been spared.

I was getting anxious about the answer from the attorney-general. It was very bad for the oxen to remain in Pretoria, the grass being all eaten off; and every day the boys were going from bad to worse; besides, there were no means of making any money, for all work was at a standstill. Rumours of a fresh outbreak of war were rife, and as the Boers all vowed that they would not yield up any of their country, while it was stated distinctly by government that this was one of the conditions of peace, it seemed likely that the rumours were true.

Every day also brought accounts of the dissatisfaction of the *kaffirs*, and threats of a general rising against the Boers, if the Transvaal were given back to them. People did not know what to do, and numbers were leaving every day for Natal. I determined to do the same, and agreed to take loads down there. It was the only way of making money; but the danger was, that the oxen, already overworked, would not stand the journey in the winter. Every day now was of importance, so as to get over the Drachensberg before the great cold set in—and still the attorney-general sent no answer.

My oxen were already drooping from bad feeding, and I even lost one of them, a favourite of mine; Hendrick, too, was taking to very bad courses, and I had more than once discovered him in theft, but I contented myself with speaking to him, for it was almost impossible to get drivers, and I did not want to lose him. One evening, after a very hard day's work, I felt ill; I had been on my feet, packing up, so as to be ready to start at a moment's notice, when the decision about the hire of the oxen should be given, and had been in the saddle, too, looking after the oxen that were feeding at some distance, and after the boys, who were all drunk except little Hendrick. The next morning I had hardly got up when I was obliged to lie down again, and from that day I was unable to leave my bed for three weeks!

The news of the decision came two days after. It was what I expected. No one was to receive a penny for the use of their oxen and waggons. The government decided to act on the old Boer law, and by it no hire is allowed in time of war! I believe that it was in consideration of my having given up my oxen and waggons voluntarily, that I was allowed seventy-five pounds as compensation for deterioration in the value of the oxen and waggons. I was told by other sufferers that no such compensation was allowed to them. It was a terrible blow to those who had counted on being paid, and to me the delay in giving me the answer was fatal.

During my illness of course everything went to the bad, and at last I heard that Hendrick was stealing my oxen. I was getting better; had just been moved on to the sofa-chair, and was fortunately more capable of acting than I had been. I had him and the oxen caught, and so escaped this loss; but Hendrick bolted. Weak as I was, I saddled up, and pursued him as far as Derde-poort, taking my revolver with me, but he had the start of me on horseback, and I had to turn back. As it was, I was shaking in the saddle as I rode into the village. I managed after some delay to obtain two drivers ("Boy" and my other driver had left me to go home), neither of them good; and, although still ill, I started, taking Jimmy with me, and discharging Soldat and Clara. My goods had not yet arrived, but I could wait no longer, for the season was too far advanced as it was.

It was a terrible trek. I rode by the side of the oxen myself to see that they were tenderly treated, and not over-driven. I saw them blanketed every night before lying down, and often I have got up of a cold night from where I slept close to them, to see that they were covered. I watched them as if they were children rather than oxen, but all was vain, one by one they drooped, and lay down and died. The weather was very cold. Some I left behind in charge of farmers, but I knew they were doomed. They came to know me so well that I could not only work with them, myself, but they would come up to me as I sat by the camp-fire, would rub their noses on my shoulder, or take mealies out of my hand, and it was real grief to me to see them wasting away. If it had not been for this, I should often have enjoyed the picture round the camp-fire of a moonlight night before they were tied up, for the horses top would come and stand with their noses close to my shoulder, and often would try to take a piece of bread out of my hand as I was eating.

It was an unlucky trek throughout. Poor little Roughy was bitten by a snake, and handsome Prince shot through the heart by a Boer. At last my spans were so decimated, that at Harrismith they fairly gave in. I had to arrange for the loads to be brought on for me, and at first determined to try to take the oxen loose over the Drachensberg and try to get them on to a warm farm, while I, for a time, once more tried my fortune as a governess, in, if possible, the employment of the owner of the farm, so as to be able to watch over them; but the one day that I had to remain at Harrismith before starting with them showed me my error. It would have been cruelty to have exposed them to the long, toilsome ascent of the *Berg*, where numbers of them would have lain down in the cold never to rise again, whilst I had an offer of selling them to a man who had sheds to shelter them in, and plenty of good forage to give them.

So I sold all but two of them at a third of what I paid for them, and left all of them together with a gentleman who buys half-dying oxen as a speculation, having the means of caring for them, and having a fancy for looking after them. The last thing I saw of them was comforting to a certain extent. They were all busy eating loose forage which was thrown to them with a lavish hand, and seemed to be enjoying themselves, although one of them (one of the two I left as boarders) left his forage to come over to me when he caught sight of me, and put his great wet nose against me in sign of friendship.

The depression of trade in the Transvaal was making itself felt even at Natal. Firms there were offering goods as cheap as you could buy them in some cases in England, and this applies to Harrismith as well. Large stocks of articles had been sent over to firms for transmission to the Transvaal, and were now left on their hands. Crowds of emigrants were coming down from the Transvaal, and the market was overstocked with people wanting employment. There were no good prices being offered for anything except fat oxen, and garden or dairy produce, which latter, strange to say, always commands a high price in South Africa; and instead of being able to sell my waggons well, as I had hoped, I could get no more than about half value for them. The depression was so great that the auctioneers often refused to sell rather than let articles go so much below their real value, as they would have done by accepting the highest bid.

I think what I have told will show those who read it, how ruin has come to numbers owing to the war and the subsequent Convention, without being due to any looting on the part of the Boers. The compensation offered by the government, even if it be paid, which is doubtful, will come tardily, and only *direct* losses are to be admitted. As a fact, most of the people who have been ruined, have been ruined by indirect losses, and this without counting the loss entailed by the depreciation in value of landed property, which is such that properties which would have fetched a high price before the war are now unsaleable. It would be impossible so far as I see, for any government to contemplate compensation for indirect losses, but it is hard that a government can sign away that which numbers have toiled hard to earn; and yet this is what has been done in the matter of the Transvaal.

All that I have to add is, that I took Jimmy with me to Natal, where he got a fairly good situation; and that Eclipse and Dandy, and little Moustache, are well, and still belong to me. Herewith I make my bow, and end my story.

LEONAUR

ALSO FROM LEONAUR
AVAILABLE IN SOFTCOVER OR HARDCOVER WITH DUST JACKET

A DIARY FROM DIXIE *by Mary Boykin Chesnut*—A Lady's Account of the Confederacy During the American Civil War

FOLLOWING THE DRUM *by Teresa Griffin Vielé*—A U. S. Infantry Officer's Wife on the Texas frontier in the Early 1850's

FOLLOWING THE GUIDON *by Elizabeth B. Custer*—The Experiences of General Custer's Wife with the U. S. 7th Cavalry.

LADIES OF LUCKNOW *by G. Harris & Adelaide Case*—The Experiences of Two British Women During the Indian Mutiny 1857. A Lady's Diary of the Siege of Lucknow by G. Harris, Day by Day at Lucknow by Adelaide Case

MARIE-LOUISE AND THE INVASION OF 1814 *by Imbert de Saint-Amand*—The Empress and the Fall of the First Empire

SAPPER DOROTHY *by Dorothy Lawrence*—The only English Woman Soldier in the Royal Engineers 51st Division, 79th Tunnelling Co. during the First World War

ARMY LETTERS FROM AN OFFICER'S WIFE 1871-1888 *by Frances M. A. Roe*—Experiences On the Western Frontier With the United States Army

NAPOLEON'S LETTERS TO JOSEPHINE *by Henry Foljambe Hall*—Correspondence of War, Politics, Family and Love 1796-1814

MEMOIRS OF SARAH DUCHESS OF MARLBOROUGH, AND OF THE COURT OF QUEEN ANNE VOLUME 1 by A. T. Thomson

MEMOIRS OF SARAH DUCHESS OF MARLBOROUGH, AND OF THE COURT OF QUEEN ANNE VOLUME 2 by A. T. Thomson

MARY PORTER GAMEWELL AND THE SIEGE OF PEKING *by A. H. Tuttle*—An American Lady's Experiences of the Boxer Uprising, China 1900

VANISHING ARIZONA *by Martha Summerhayes*—A young wife of an officer of the U.S. 8th Infantry in Apacheria during the 1870's

THE RIFLEMAN'S WIFE *by Mrs. Fitz Maurice*—*The Experiences of an Officer's Wife and Chronicles of the Old 95th During the Napoleonic Wars*

THE OATMAN GIRLS *by Royal B. Stratton*—The Capture & Captivity of Two Young American Women in the 1850's by the Apache Indians

LEONAUR

ALSO FROM LEONAUR
AVAILABLE IN SOFTCOVER OR HARDCOVER WITH DUST JACKET

THE WOMAN IN BATTLE *by Loreta Janeta Velazquez*—Soldier, Spy and Secret Service Agent for the Confederacy During the American Civil War.

BOOTS AND SADDLES *by Elizabeth B. Custer*—The experiences of General Custer's Wife on the Western Plains.

FANNIE BEERS' CIVIL WAR *by Fannie A. Beers*—A Confederate Lady's Experiences of Nursing During the Campaigns & Battles of the American Civil War.

LADY SALE'S AFGHANISTAN *by Florentia Sale*—An Indomitable Victorian Lady's Account of the Retreat from Kabul During the First Afghan War.

THE TWO WARS OF MRS DUBERLY *by Frances Isabella Duberly*—An Intrepid Victorian Lady's Experience of the Crimea and Indian Mutiny.

THE REBELLIOUS DUCHESS *by Paul F. S. Dermoncourt*—The Adventures of the Duchess of Berri and Her Attempt to Overthrow French Monarchy.

LADIES OF WATERLOO *by Charlotte A. Eaton, Magdalene de Lancey & Juana Smith*—The Experiences of Three Women During the Campaign of 1815: Waterloo Days by Charlotte A. Eaton, A Week at Waterloo by Magdalene de Lancey & Juana's Story by Juana Smith.

NURSE AND SPY IN THE UNION ARMY *by Sarah Emma Evelyn Edmonds*—During the American Civil War

WIFE NO. 19 *by Ann Eliza Young*—The Life & Ordeals of a Mormon Woman During the 19th Century

DIARY OF A NURSE IN SOUTH AFRICA *by Alice Bron*—With the Dutch-Belgian Red Cross During the Boer War

MARIE ANTOINETTE AND THE DOWNFALL OF ROYALTY *by Imbert de Saint-Amand*—The Queen of France and the French Revolution

THE MEMSAHIB & THE MUTINY *by R. M. Coopland*—An English lady's ordeals in Gwalior and Agra duringthe Indian Mutiny 1857

MY CAPTIVITY AMONG THE SIOUX INDIANS *by Fanny Kelly*—The ordeal of a pioneer woman crossing the Western Plains in 1864

WITH MAXIMILIAN IN MEXICO *by Sara Yorke Stevenson*—A Lady's experience of the French Adventure